AUTUMN OF OUR DISCONTENT

"Curatola's richly researched and fascinating study maps the confluence of the Soviet atomic bomb, the rise of Communist China, and the internecine Air Force–Navy squabbles in fall 1949. This Clausewitzian 'paradoxical trinity' cast the die for the development of NSC 68 and an unprecedented shift in American national defense policy."

—Frank A. Blazich Jr., military history curator, Smithsonian National Museum of American History

"Curatola weaves an exciting and powerful narrative that brings a new perspective to a key turning point in American history. This reexamination of how U.S. defense strategy dramatically changed in the early Cold War is extremely relevant to present-day defense and foreign policy debates."

—Michael W. Hankins, curator, Smithsonian National Air and Space Museum, and author of *Flying Camelot: The F-15, the F-16, and the Weaponization of Fighter Pilot Nostalgia*

"We tend to look back at seminal history with a belief that the course of events was as obvious to those who lived them as they are to those who read about them in hindsight. In reality, nothing could be further from the truth; it is of this misnomer that John Curatola most directly dispossesses us. For what may seem obvious to those who lived through the end of the Cold War was far from a settled question in the critical year of 1949. With the Cold War just getting underway in the autumn of 1949, the events of that period have often become lost, forgotten, or taken for granted. It is against this backdrop that Curatola demonstrates the anything-but-settled questions over what the Cold War would be, how it would be fought, and who would win. The author's excellent research combined with insightful analysis leave little doubt as to the fact that the fall of 1949 was a turning point in the course of the Cold War."

—Trevor Albertson, author of *Winning Armageddon: Curtis LeMay and Strategic Air Command, 1948–1957*

AUTUMN OF OUR DISCONTENT

FALL 1949 AND THE CRISES IN AMERICAN NATIONAL SECURITY

JOHN M. CURATOLA

Naval Institute Press
Annapolis, Maryland

This book has been brought to publication with the generous assistance of Edward S. and Joyce I. Miller.

Naval Institute Press
291 Wood Road
Annapolis, MD 21402

Library of Congress Cataloging-in-Publication Data

Names: Curatola, John M., [date]- author.
Title: Autumn of our discontent : fall 1949 and the crises in American national security / John M. Curatola.
Description: Annapolis, Maryland : Naval Institute Press, [2022] | Includes bibliographical references and index.
Identifiers: LCCN 2021061120 (print) | LCCN 2021061121 (ebook) | ISBN 9781682476208 (hardcover) | ISBN 9781682476215 (ebook)
Subjects: LCSH: National security—United States—History—20th century. | Cold War. | Nineteen forty-nine, A.D. | United States—Foreign relations—1945-1953. | United States—Politics and government—1945-1953. | United States—Military policy—History—20th century. | BISAC: HISTORY / Military / Wars & Conflicts (Other)
Classification: LCC E813 .C87 2022 (print) | LCC E813 (ebook) | DDC 355/.033073—dc23/eng/20220201
LC record available at https://lccn.loc.gov/2021061120
LC ebook record available at https://lccn.loc.gov/2021061121

♾ Print editions meet the requirements of ANSI/NISO z39.48-1992 (Permanence of Paper).
Printed in the United States of America.

30 29 28 27 26 25 24 23 22 9 8 7 6 5 4 3 2 1
First printing

For Clara Jane, who endured, persisted, and loved.

Contents

Acknowledgments

This book is the result of four years of research and writing. Much of the text reflects the brutal, yet exceptional, editing skills of Dr. Janet Valentine. She spent many hours correcting my prose and syntax while surrounded by four cats clamoring for her attention. Her keen eye was an invaluable asset, making this a much better work and contribution to the field of history. Additionally, Drs. Rick Herrera and Tony Carlson were constant sources of encouragement, trusted colleagues, and fellow travelers. They helped me pursue a higher standard of scholarship, and I value their friendship and camaraderie. The archivists at the Truman and Hoover Presidential Libraries, the U.S. Naval History and Heritage Command, and the Library of Congress's Manuscripts Division were key in helping me locate the relevant documents. Furthermore the leadership of the U.S. Army School of Advanced Military Studies at Fort Leavenworth, Kansas, provided the time and resources for this endeavor. This is especially true of Dr. Scott Gorman and Ms. Candy Hamm, who were supportive at every turn to make this book a reality. I could not have written this work without their help. Finally, my gratitude to Adam Kane, who, despite a trying first year as the Naval Institute Press director, helped shepherd this work to publication.

INTRODUCTION

First Lieutenant Robert Johnson and the airmen assigned to crew 5A were having a frustrating day. Serving in the U.S. Air Force's 375th Weather Reconnaissance Squadron (WRS) on 30 August 1949, the men were scheduled to fly out of Yokota Air Base, Japan, just outside of Tokyo, to their home station of Eielson Air Force Base, Alaska. As they started the engines on their WB-29 aircraft, a modified version of the four-engine B-29 Superfortress bomber, one of the four R-3350 power plants sputtered, coughed, and quit before takeoff.[1] Determined to fulfill their mission, the crew took command of an "alert" standby aircraft. Simultaneously, a typhoon, common during this time of year around Japan, was bearing down on Yokota. With winds increasing and skies darkening, the crew hoped to beat the bad weather. While Lieutenant Johnson and his crew got airborne before the storm hit the airbase, their bad luck continued.

About an hour into their flight, while over the island of Honshu, the number-three engine, adjacent to the copilot's side, began spewing smoke. The rhythm and hum of the engine was interrupted by the disturbing vibration of mechanical failure. Instruments for the power plant fell out of their normal operating ranges, with fire-warning lights aglow.[2] With this dire emergency, Johnson immediately called for engine shutdown. Both he and the flight engineer immediately initiated emergency procedures and engaged the engine's fire-extinguisher system. With these actions the crew hoped to avoid having the flames burn through the firewall and into the wing, where they could ignite the fuel cells. The only thing they could do now was hope the fire had not spread.

Fortunately for the crew, the emergency procedures worked and the flames extinguished. But with only three fully operating engines, the plane was still in danger. If it lost another engine, the WB-29 would be unable to maintain level flight. Under the circumstances, Johnson could not risk the long, dangerous journey over the northern Pacific Ocean. While bailing out from or ditching an aircraft was dangerous enough, doing so over those waters meant almost certain death, with hypothermia setting in after only a few minutes. Additionally, given the large expanse of the northern Pacific combined with the fickle nature of the region's weather, the crewmen would have very little chance of being rescued. Lastly, given the political situation of the emerging Cold War, making an emergency landing somewhere in the nearby Soviet Union was definitely not an option.

With the three other heavily laden engines now operating at full tilt, and Johnson seeking a return to Yokota, his frustration mounted as the typhoon moved in over Yokota. Hoping for landing assistance, he radioed Ground Control Approach to receive specific landing instructions from an air-traffic controller on the ground. Looking at a radar screen and knowing exactly where the WB-29 was in relation to the runway, the controller would help guide the pilot to a specified point at which the runway would appear once the plane descended below the clouds. Yet adding to the pilot's string of bad luck that day, the base's radar failed, rendering it useless to both the controller and the pilot.[3] Johnson had to make a quick decision.

Weighing his options, Johnson diverted the Superfortress to Misawa Air Force Base, some 350 miles away on the northern tip of Honshu. Carrying almost a full load of fuel and a full crew compliment, and unable to dump hazardous fuel to adjust the plane's weight because of civilian populations below, he made for Misawa. Eventually, Johnson landed the plane safely, but the crew had little to show for their efforts and were emotionally spent by the day's events. What made matters worse was the condition of the WB-29. After having one engine catch fire and the other three operating at maximum power for over an hour, the aircraft required replacement of all four R-3350s.[4]

On 1 September Johnson and his men were joined at Misawa by another WB-29 crew, flying aircraft number 44-62214, from Eielson.[5] Two days later Johnson and his crew flew the aircraft on a flight home lasting thirteen hours and thirty-six minutes.[6] Cruising at an altitude of around 18,000 feet, their trip was far from ordinary. Working under the Air Force Office of Atomic Testing (AFOAT), the lieutenant's mission, and that of the 375th WRS, was ostensibly to conduct global weather flights.[7] But what the men of the squadron, including those in crew 5A, were actually doing was monitoring the airspace over the northern Pacific for evidence of Soviet atomic activity.

Knowing that the Soviets would eventually break the American atomic monopoly, the U.S. Atomic Energy Commission (AEC) pushed for the development of a long-range atomic-detection capability to monitor Russian progress. As early as 1947 Lewis Strauss, a founding member of the AEC, single-handedly initiated the effort to establish such a capability.[8] A nuclear-blast cloud rises into the atmosphere to some 20,000–60,000 feet, with radioactive particles carried away by the winds aloft. As a result the particles are not only spread to adjacent areas but also travel globally. During World War II, this phenomenon was discovered following the Manhattan Project's Trinity test on 16 July 1945. Personnel at the U.S. Naval Academy in Annapolis, Maryland, noted a significant increase in ambient atmospheric radiation with their Geiger-Müller counters as the Trinity particles traveled eastward.[9]

Interestingly, J. Robert Oppenheimer, head physicist at the Los Alamos Scientific Laboratory (LASL), scoffed at the idea of long-range detection, believing that radioactive material from an atomic explosion would dissipate to an undetectable level soon afterward. Erroneously, he thought atomic detection from long distances was an impossibility.[10] Yet not unlike the rainfall readings at Annapolis in 1945, American scientists also found airborne radioactive material from the spring 1948 Sandstone atomic tests in the Pacific halfway around the world.[11] As a result, the newly independent U.S. Air Force (USAF), seeded by funds from the AEC, in March 1948 started looking for Soviet radioactive fallout.[12]

Global meteorological patterns blow air masses over the Russian expanse eastwardly and eventually over the Pacific Ocean. If an atomic event occurred within the Soviet Union, evidence would ultimately manifest over the Pacific due to natural weather patterns. Lieutenant Johnson and the rest of the 375th WRS conducted surveillance flights from Guam, Bermuda, and the North Pole, sniffing this large expanse for Soviet fallout. Codenamed "Loon Charlie" routes, these sorties covered huge areas and required seven long-range flights every forty-eight hours.[13] Appearing as Air Weather Service (AWS) aircraft, crews measured atmospheric pressure, winds aloft, frontal boundaries, temperatures, and other meteorological data.[14] But they also sought evidence of Russian atomic activity.

Loon Charlie routes required aircraft specially equipped with a collection box attached to the exterior fuselage. These boxes, referred to by the crews as "bug catchers," were specifically designed to take in and trap airborne radioactive material. Within the device was a special nine-by-twenty-two-inch cloth paper that collected airborne particles.[15] After the plane landed, exposed filters were collected and analyzed for evidence of fissionable or other radioactive material.[16] By 1949 the AWS had fifty-five filter-equipped aircraft, with approximately 1,300 personnel supporting the effort.[17]

After the Sandstone test, scientists determined that filter papers yielding radiation totals of 100 counts per minute (cpm) was the minimum standard for evidence of an atomic event. This standard was in place when crews started flying Loon Charlie missions in April 1949. But based on experience gained during these early missions, the 100-cpm threshold was lowered to 50 cpm in early August.[18] Cutting the threshold number for evidence of radioactivity in half had unfortunate consequences. After the reduction, 111 false positives registered that were not the result of deliberate Soviet atomic activity but of various natural causes.[19]

After landing at Eielson, Johnson's crew turned in their filter paper. Initial analysis of the samples showed radioactivity measuring at 85 cpm—well above the newly established minimum. This initial sample had been exposed for three hours at 18,000 feet, while a companion paper showed an even higher reading of 153 cpm.[20] This increase was first detected by a local field lab in Alaska, but such a measurement required further verification.[21] Although the data was preliminary, the written report of this 112th alert announced the development of the anxiously anticipated Soviet atomic bomb.

Verification of the initial findings became a priority within AFOAT. Samples were flown to a new company in California called Tracerlab, which tested for radioactive materials. By 7 September Tracerlab reported that it found the fission isotopes barium and cerium and later discovered evidence of molybdenum.[22] By 10 September Tracerlab had finished its analysis and estimated the material was from an explosion between 26 and 29 August that resulted from a plutonium-based fissionable event. Piqued by these new findings and eager to validate a possible Soviet atomic blast, the USAF scheduled additional WB-29 flights. These were intended to find further evidence of radioactive material and determine if what Johnson found was the beginning, middle, or end of an atomic cloud floating eastward. While initial filter papers were being analyzed, on 5 September another Loon Charlie flight operating east of Japan toward Guam returned samples from an altitude of 10,000 feet that contained 1,000 cpm—some twenty times above the established threshold. Because of the initial findings, between 3 and 16 September, AFOAT ordered ninety-two special weather-sampling flights from Guam to the North Pole and from California to the British Isles. To ensure accurate sampling, filter papers were changed every hour instead of the standard three-hour interval. AWS aircraft collected more than 500 radioactive samples, 167 of which registered 1,000 cpm or more.[23]

Ground-based collection methods also validated the airborne findings. Earlier that year rainwater-collection points were established by the Naval Research Laboratory at Kodiak, Alaska; Washington, D.C.; Honolulu, Hawaii, and in the Philippines. From 9 to 20 September, rainwater at Kodiak produced "extremely hot samples from the fall out [and] yielded tens of thousands of counts per minute of the major fission produced isotopes." Washington samples also yielded similar results, as the laboratory reported an "unprecedented rise [in radiation] on 9 September . . . as the result of fission activity . . . [with] physical identification of fission products such as Ruthenium, Barium, and Iodine."[24]

By 8 September filter samples tracked the debris cloud leaving North America and heading for the British Isles. Two days later Pres. Harry Truman gave permission to notify the United Kingdom of the initial American findings. As a result the British also began monitoring their surrounding airspace for evidence of radioactive activity. Conducting their own series of meteorological flights, codenamed "Nocturnal" and "Bismuth," crews covered the areas south of the British Isles to Gibraltar and to the north past Scotland. Their samples verified the American findings.[25]

Tracerlab estimated that the time of detonation was 29 August at 0000 Greenwich mean time.[26] Further examination placed the explosion in south central Asia between the 35th and 170th meridians of east longitude. Acoustic records pinpointed a twenty-kiloton event at Semipalatinsk in remote Kazakhstan.[27] On 19 September Air Force Chief of Staff Gen. Hoyt Vandenberg convened an advisory committee of prominent scientists and veterans of the wartime Manhattan Project, including Oppenheimer, Vannevar Bush, Robert Bacher, and W. S. Parons. These men reviewed the data collected and the preliminary conclusions. The next day the advisory committee submitted its report: "After careful consideration of the facts presented by your technical staff, we unanimously agree with their conclusions as presented."[28] With the explosion of what the Americans referred to as "Joe-1"(also codenamed "Vermont"), there were no longer any lingering questions about the end of the U.S. atomic monopoly. As summer officially turned to fall with the autumnal equinox on 23 September, Truman announced, "We have evidence that within recent weeks an atomic explosion occurred in the USSR."[29] Although informed about the atomic blast days earlier, the president delayed his public statement due to other events. On 19 September the British pound was devalued by 30 percent, making global markets jittery and investors nervous. Additionally, with the pound's devaluation, domestic unrest from ongoing coal and steel strikes were a national concern. Given the weight of the discovery and the financial anxieties at the time, Truman thought it best to delay his announcement a few days.[30] Regardless, when the information became public, Sen. Arthur Vandenberg summed up the Joe-1 discovery succinctly: "This is now a different world."[31]

What made the discovery such a surprise was that only a month earlier, on 1 July 1949, American intelligence experts estimated that the Soviets were still years away from developing an atomic capability.[32] Given the biblical scale of destruction the USSR had suffered during World War II, building an atomic program from the ashes of the global conflict appeared far beyond Soviet capability. While fully understanding that the atomic monopoly was going to be limited in duration, the Joint Nuclear Energy Intelligence Committee that very summer had predicted that the Russians, in the best case, might be able to produce an atomic bomb by "mid-1950, and [that] the most probable date was mid-1953."[33] All were wrong.

While it exacerbated increasing Cold War tensions, Joe-1 signaled much more. Not only did the explosion mean the USSR had now entered the exclusive "atomic club," altering the balance of power in the postwar world, but it also marked the beginning of a tumultuous period for American national security. Following the Soviet blast, a host of events followed in quick succession that forced the United States to reconsider its overall national security policy, military posture, and role in the global environment. Joe-1 was the first of a series of occasions during the autumn of 1949 that changed the nature of the American military tradition. The intersection of these events occurred in such a rapid, and in some cases concurrent, fashion that the whole of their effect was greater than the sum of their parts. They served as impetus for a comprehensive review of U.S. military strategy and its overall objectives, resulting in a more assertive national security policy.

Following these events, in the spring of 1950 the newly appointed director of the Policy Planning Staff (PPS) at the U.S. State Department (DoS), Paul Nitze, drafted "US Objectives and Programs for National Security," National Security Council (NSC) Memo 68. Nitze recalled years later: "In the fall of 1949, [when] the Chinese communists consolidated their position on the mainland [of Asia and] the Russians exploded their first atomic bomb. . . . it appeared that a national security program costing some $50 billion per annum for a number of years, as opposed to the 13½ billion limit on defense expenditures was urgently required. This immediately raised a host of problems."[34] While the accepted narrative for this period pins the development of NSC 68 squarely on the explosion of Joe-1 and potential nuclear parity, this approach overlooks other salient actions. The world generally met the news of the Soviet success with little excitement, as it was expected that the USSR would someday become an atomic power.[35] But Joe-1 was merely a starting point. The jarring successive, and sometimes simultaneous, events were the catalyst and cause for the change in American national defense policy.

After World War II, the United States followed the tradition established after the American Revolution by reducing the size of its military machine. Americans generally rejected the idea of a large standing military for a number of reasons, as it could be a threat to civilian institutions, it was expensive, it increased the potential of global entanglements, and the nation was largely secured geographically. In this vein the fiscal year (FY) 1948 defense-budget authorization just exceeded $10 billion and was expected to remain at that level for the next few years. President Truman's primary postwar objectives focused on reducing defense spending, establishing a balanced federal budget, and transitioning to a peacetime economy. Toward this end, his administration planned to provide the military with enough funding "only for the minimum requirements."[36]

Considering themselves shortchanged in budgetary considerations, the military services needed to reevaluate their fiscal strategies. In June 1948 the first secretary of defense, James Forrestal, was trying to determine what the National Military Establishment (NME—forerunner of the Department of Defense) should forward as its budget for FY 1950. In determining what the military services should request in their respective submissions, Forrestal sought help from the DoS and their team of policy planners. In this effort he looked for guidance regarding larger questions of national defense: What should the NME budget reflect? What were the national security goals and objectives of the United States? Should the budget reflect a wartime footing as specified in the most current war plan? Should the military plan for something less? What were the larger national goals that required NME support?[37]

Five months later, on 23 November 1948, Forrestal got his answer—not necessarily the one he wanted. Officially titled "US Objectives with Regard to the USSR to Counter Soviet Threats to US Security" (NSC Memo 20/4), the document reflected the growing concern over Soviet actions and echoed the sentiment expressed by American Chief of Mission in Moscow George Kennan in his "Long Telegram" and the published "Mr. X" article in the academic journal *Foreign Affairs*. In these documents Kennan explained that the Soviet Union was inherently expansionist but rife with internal contradictions. For him, American foreign policy should focus on "containing" the Soviet Union and its influence until it eventually collapsed. This policy was eventually adopted and referred to as "containment." NSC 20/4 argued that "communist ideology and Soviet behavior clearly demonstrate that the ultimate objective of the leaders of the USSR is the domination of the world."[38] Additionally it claimed that Russia was "building up as rapidly as possible the war potential of the Soviet orbit," with "communists thinking that a future conflict was inevitable."[39] Furthermore, the DoS believed that the Red Army was capable of conquering Europe and much of the Middle East while simultaneously seizing important locations in East Asia.[40]

NSC 20/4 also speculated that by 1955 the Soviets might be able to conduct biological or atomic strategic air attacks against the United States. While the document outlined expansionistic Soviet intent, the DoS did not envision a deliberate war breaking out between the two powers. NSC 20/4 was based upon the premise that the Soviets were yet to develop atomic weapons and that the American monopoly would remain intact. Yet it did warn that conflict might come about due to miscalculation, misunderstanding, or "failure of either side to estimate accuracy of how far the other side could be pushed."[41]

In response to the potential threat, NSC 20/4 suggested that the United States needed to prepare itself by providing a long-term deterrent stance against possible Soviet aggression. Additionally, the document stated that the country "should endeavor by successful military and other operations to create conditions which would permit satisfactory accomplishment of U.S. objectives without a predetermined requirement for unconditional surrender."[42] While the language of NSC 20/4 painted a dark military picture, it failed to spur increased NME defense appropriations under Truman's budgetary constraints.[43] The memo made no reference to or suggestion of an increase in defense expenditures and seemed to fall in line with Truman's overall guidance as he was "preparing, not for war, but for peace."[44] In fact, it argued that the NME should not expect an increase in its budget and actually warned against excessive defense expenditures that would undercut U.S. fiscal solvency.[45]

Toward this end, DoS planners thought that America's economic power took priority over defensive armaments. Moreover, they felt secure in the U.S. nuclear monopoly. Joe-1 was thus an important event for the drafting of NSC

68, but it certainly was not the only one.[46] As the summer of 1949 passed into fall and leaves changed into their autumn colors, Americans began to see the world as a less secure place, with Communism as an increasingly nefarious agent. In fact a December 1949 Gallup Poll asked a group of Americans, "Was Russia trying to rule the world or just protect herself?" Seventy percent of respondents believed that Soviet actions were indeed offensive in motivation. Similarly, by February 1950 almost 40 percent of Americans polled thought that the United States was losing the Cold War.[47]

That same month Americans were split on whether or not the nation would find itself in another war in the next five years, and by May, 63 percent of Americans polled believed that national defense spending needed to be increased.[48] NSC 68 addressed many of those concerns. The document spurred an increase in defense expenditures from a paltry $14 billion in FY 1950 to $48 billion in FY 1951. Furthermore, the defense budget remained at that level for the remainder of the Truman administration and broke the president from his frugal spending habits. But more importantly, NSC 68 permanently changed the American military tradition by setting the conditions for building and maintaining a large standing army during a time of relative peace.

The germination of NSC 68 and the change in American popular sentiment occurred in the fall of 1949. On 1 October, only days after Truman's announcement regarding the Soviet detonation, Mao Tse-tung officially announced the establishment of the People's Republic of China (PRC), yet another major Communist power. While Mao's announcement was a formality, given his Red Army's progress in China during and after World War II, it combined with the recently published *China White Paper* stoked American fears over Communism's encroachment and increasing global influence. What was left of the Kuomintang Army remained on the Asian mainland, but Mao's announcement presaged the Nationalists' ultimate defeat and signaled yet another loss for democracy. Despite having Western assistance and modern weapons, the Nationalist forces were thoroughly defeated by Mao's Red Army. While this had been a long time in coming, the formal establishment of the PRC came within a week of Truman's announcement of Joe-1.

The Communist victory in China had been forecasted as early as 1946, when Gen. George C. Marshall and many others within the DoS observed glaring problems with Chiang Kai-shek's Kuomintang and its ability to either govern or conduct military operations. Truman tried to explain "the loss of China" by publishing the *China White Paper* in early August 1949. But this failed in its objective of mollifying Americans who believed the Truman administration was to blame for letting China fall into the hands of the "Reds." The *White Paper* also served as additional evidence for those infatuated with the idea of Communist infiltration of the federal government.

Already anxious over the growth of Soviet influence in Europe, Americans focused upon the security of democracy in the face of "red expansion" and the idea of global, monolithic Communism. In early September 1949, even before Truman's and Mao's respective announcements, a group of Americans were asked what they thought were the most important problems facing the country. The largest response, comprising 16 percent of respondents, claimed it was preventing war; 11 percent believed it was various foreign-policy issues (Russia, China, feeding Europe, and others); and 7 percent saw the rise of Communism as the gravest issue.[49]

In addition to international events, some domestic actions served as the catalyst to national security concerns. One of these dealt directly with the manner in which the United States would conduct the next war. After the creation of the NME in 1947 by act of Congress, the Departments of the Army, Navy, and Air Force were engaged in their own kind of war regarding roles and missions. While military expenditures in the United States for 1945 constituted an all-time high of 43 percent of the gross domestic product, this number was reduced to a mere 8 percent by 1948.[50] Given the smaller appropriations for the NME following the war, the individual services fought for every dollar in their respective budgets by arguing over roles, missions, responsibilities, and associated requirements. Chief among these was a continued rivalry between the Navy and the newly created USAF. Underlying arguments over unification also underscored this tension, as the two services found themselves embroiled in a fierce, bruising, and very public disagreement that would ruin careers, aggravate existing interservice rivalries, and reverberate in the arena of national defense for years.

Even before World War II the U.S. Navy and the U.S. Army Air Corps (USAAC) were at cross-purposes. The extended range and capabilities of new USAAC airframes like the B-17 threatened to overtake traditional Navy missions of coastal defense and fleet interception. USAAC publicity stunts, such as the interception of the Italian luxury liner *Rex* in 1938, goodwill flights to South America, and Billy Mitchell's sinking of the decrepit German battleship *Ostfriesland* in 1921, were seen as potential threats to the Navy's missions and its fleet. These competing interests during the lean years of the Great Depression, when defense dollars were scarce, pitted the two services against each other as they argued over responsibilities. These disputes even led to the Navy trying to impose limits on USAAC land-based aircraft patrolling over coastal areas.[51] After the war, and with the advent of the atomic bomb, this rivalry was renewed.

Atomic weapons and intercontinental bombers meant aviation was taking a primary place in military planning. While the results of the combined bomber offensive in Europe and the firebombing of Japanese cities were equivocal as reported by the U.S. Strategic Bombing Survey (USSBS), the atomic events over Hiroshima and Nagasaki seemed to have changed the military calculus wholesale. Wars in the future were envisioned as air-centric endeavors, with the other services in merely supporting roles. Illustrating this assertion was a very pointed presentation before a group of naval officers by Air Force general Frank Armstrong:

> You gentlemen had better understand the [Army] Air Force . . . is no longer going to be a subordinate outfit. It was the predominate force during the war and it is going to be a predominate force . . . whether you like it or not, and we don't care whether you like it or not, the [Army] Air Force is going to run the show. . . . You [Navy types] are not going to have anything but a bunch of carrie[r]s which are ineffective anyway, and they will probably be sunk in the first battle.[52]

Many military planners started to look at the efficacy of strategic bombardment in the postwar era, as did the public. Even as early as 1942, Americans began to view airpower as a defense priority over the other services by a wide margin.[53] This trend continued after the war, as illustrated by a February 1949 Gallup poll that found most Americans willing to pay more taxes for the USAF than for any other service.[54] George Gallup further added, "Airpower became a major 'love' of the American people, even before military experts were willing to admit the importance of it[s] role in warfare."[55]

In the spring of 1949, Secretary of Defense Louis Johnson canceled construction of the aircraft carrier USS *United States* without consulting Secretary of the Navy John L. Sullivan or Chief of Naval Operations Adm. Louis Denfeld. This decision was a catalyst for what became known as the "Revolt of the Admirals," as senior navy officers railed against the secretary of defense, his airpower-centric views of defense, and the administration's fiscally conservative policies. Not only were naval officers upset with Johnson and the shortchanging of naval aviation, but the "revolt" was also aimed at the USAF, as the Navy called into question the premise, morality, and efficacy of strategic bombardment as embodied by the Strategic Air Command.[56] A forged letter, claims of impropriety, and political favoritism on the part of Secretary Johnson, Secretary of the Air Force Stuart Symington, and individuals at Consolidated-Vultee Corporation came to the surface in May 1949. These charges lead to a congressional investigation, pitting the two services against each other in a very public discourse. Starting in August and ending in October, scores of officers gave testimonies that made for high political drama.

Also, the civilian-run Atomic Energy Commission (AEC) was struggling. Established as a result of the McMahon Act of 1946, the new organization formally began work on 1 January 1947. The AEC inherited the nation's atomic enterprise from the wartime Manhattan Engineering District (MED). Seeing the need for civilian oversight of atomic materials and production, the AEC took ownership of the personnel and facilities built under the structure of the district. But the new organization suffered from a number of postwar maladies, including a scientific "brain drain," as physicists and researchers returned to civilian academia. After the war, LASL experienced a loss of purpose and lack of direction, with outdated and worn-out infrastructure. Additionally, the AEC had a tense relationship with the NME since the civilian organization gained sole custody of atomic materials and associated components. In its new role the civilian commission jealously guarded its new responsibilities for storage of the fissionable materials and atomic-material production from military encroachment.

Tensions became so bad that a member of the AEC's Military Liaison Committee (MLC) quipped, "The members of the AEC thought all military officers were damn fools, and the officers thought all AEC people were damn crooks."[57] Exacerbating this problem, the commission kept information about the number of atomic weapons available and their expected yields and effects a secret. The civilians at the AEC refused to share results and associated data from the 1948 Sandstone series of tests with members of the NME. As a result, military personnel were unable to develop a strategic bombing effort in support of envisioned war plans with the latest information available. Established war plans Pincher, Halfmoon, and Offtackle called for dozens, and eventually hundreds of bombs, during the immediate postwar period. But unknown to the NME, the United States possessed no complete weapons in its stockpile and had the disassembled components for only a handful. In fact the president was not apprised of the size of the postwar American stockpile until April 1947. Even worse, during the same briefing Truman learned that there was an insufficient number of people capable of assembling the components into usable weapons. When the president realized the actual condition of the stockpile and the inability to build the bombs, the head of the AEC, David Lilienthal, reported that he looked "grim and grey, [and] the lines in his face visibly deepened."[58]

Although the AEC and NME were also at odds over custody and transfer procedures of bombs and their associated components, many in the armed services saw the need to increase the production of fissionable materials for atomic weapons. After the war the United States had only obligated one-fortieth of its already meager defense budget on atomic weapons.[59] With a small budget, limited number of munitions, and an ever-growing demand for more bombs given the approved war plans, a decision from the chief executive was required to expand production. On 8 April 1949 Truman approved a recommendation by the NME and the AEC to review the production of fissionable materials and atomic weapons. Later that year, on 26 July, the president advised the DoS, NME, and AEC that this decision would be placed before the NSC for deliberation.[60] Given his concerns over a fiscally sound budget balanced against national security, he had to make a decision. On 10 October, a few weeks after the Joe-1 explosion, a special committee of the NSC submitted its recommendation regarding the atomic-weapons expansion and awaited the president's assessment.

While the proposed increase of fissionable materials awaited Truman's judgment, an equally important decision regarding nuclear technology was also on the table during the autumn of 1949. In the course of the previous war, physicists at LASL focused the bulk of their research on developing fission as the basis for an atomic bomb. While the Little Boy and Fat Man weapons were based upon these principles, which created kilotons worth of explosive force, men like physicist Edward Teller thought that the concept of atomic fusion could create possibly even larger explosive yields. With wartime expediency a concern, the process of atomic fission remained the priority, and the potential of nuclear fusion became a lesser concern. Regardless, Teller and a small group of physicists at LASL worked on the idea of combining two or more atomic nuclei to create a much more powerful blast. The idea of fusion was a complex problem, remaining largely an academic challenge attracting some scientific activity.

By early 1949 prominent mathematicians and physicists laid some of the theoretical groundwork for fusion but still remained far away from making it a reality. The shock of the Soviet atomic success served as a catalyst to action. Teller and other like-minded individuals thought that if the Soviets successfully develop atomic weapons years ahead of intelligence estimates, they might do the same with fusion, producing thermonuclear weapons before the United States. Since these weapons could yield megatons worth of explosive energy thousands of times more powerful than the kilotons produced by fission, the USSR could conceivably hold a military advantage over the United States if it developed such weapons first.

In late September, after Truman's public announcement of the Russian bomb, the congressional Joint Committee on Atomic Energy (JCAE) met with members of the AEC and discussed the issue of increasing the size of the American nuclear stockpile. In addition to the increase, they also addressed the possibility of starting an "all out" hydrogen-bomb effort to counter the possibility of a Soviet thermonuclear device. On 13 October the JCAE reported to Congress that "Russia's ownership of the bomb, years ahead of the anticipated date, [was] a monumental challenge to American boldness, initiative, and effort." The next day the JCAE met with select members of the Department of Defense (DoD), including Gen. Omar Bradley and General Vandenberg, who advocated a "stepped up hydrogen program."[61] AEC Commissioner Strauss also strongly supported this "quantum jump" in weapons technology.[62]

Before October 1949 Truman had never heard of the idea of thermonuclear weapons, but now it had become a topic of serious political discussion.[63] Throughout the next four months, an alphabet soup of organizations all debated the efficacy, feasibility, morality, and necessity for such a weapon. Should the United States risk time, effort, and money on this speculative scientific endeavor? Would concern over the weapon's moral implications preclude its development? If such a bomb was indeed possible, what value did it have militarily? Was the deterrent value alone worth the cost? This debate was superimposed upon the other existing issues of this period, adding to the concerns of Americans during the autumn of 1949. As winter approached, it was increasingly clear that the United States needed a wholesale review of its national security policies.

Coming off his stunning victory over Thomas Dewey in November 1948, Truman was optimistic about his next term and felt politically emboldened. But in the summer of 1949, fear over Communist encroachment worldwide and a possible Communist infiltration of the federal government began to sweep the nation. Even Cardinal Francis Spellman, archbishop of New York, claimed the United States was in danger of a Communist takeover. The president tried to reassure the country by arguing that Americans should study their history, and after all this "hysteria [has] finally died down, and things straighten out, . . . [they will see that the] country [in the past] didn't go hell and it isn't now."[64] Despite the president's assurances, plenty of concern remained over national security.

American fear over the Soviet Union and its designs prompted Sen. Arthur Vandenberg to ask in the congressional chambers, "What is Russia up to? We ask it in Manchuria. . . . We ask it in eastern Europe. . . . We ask it in the Dardanelles. . . . We ask it in the Baltic and Balkans. . . . We ask it sometimes even in connection with events in our United States. What is Russia up to now?"[65] On Christmas Day 1949, *New York Times* columnist Arthur Krock wrote that Russia gained greater importance to the United States as the century progressed. As a result, the USSR now held greater influence over American consciousness and collective thought. He argued that every "governmental policy, act, and thought of Washington is based on that nation [Russia] and people" and claimed "any socio-economic or military development in Asia, Europe, Latin America or even Africa is instantly examined for its relation to the Cold War."[66] The increasingly important position that the USSR held in the American mind also fed the universal fear of most in the United States regarding Communism and its supposed infiltration into contemporary society. Fear of Communist encroachment had been a theme in American society since the end of World War I but had now taken on new importance following World War II.

This fear sank deep into the American psyche and was evident as early as 1933, when even the president of the Muncie, Indiana, Rotary Club submitted that every American was living in "a red fog," and he went on to claim, "We are getting pretty close to Communism right now in Washington."[67] Starting with the Overman Committee in 1919 and then in various other forms before the establishment of the Dies Committee in 1938 and the formation of the House Un-American Activities Committee (HUAC), fear over Communist activity remained a staple of the American twentieth-century political and social landscape. McCarthyism and the fear of Communist infiltration within the ranks of the federal government came about as a partial result of Mao's victory in China. Senior U.S. officials claimed Communist sympathizers within the DoS had undermined the best interests of the country during the Chinese Civil War.

On 9 February 1950, four months after Mao's declaration of the PRC, Sen. Joe McCarthy started his crusade against suspected Communists. Building upon the speculation generated by men like Maj. Gen. Patrick Hurley and members of the China Lobby, anti-Communist sentiment reached a fever pitch. This sentiment also manifested in other ways, such as loyalty oaths for federal employment starting in 1948, suspicion of left-leaning educators in colleges and universities, and Executive Order 9835, establishing the Employee Loyalty Program, all with the specter of atomic war as the backdrop.[68] In a poll taken in November 1949, 70 percent of those asked believed the USSR was trying to build itself up to rule the world.[69] By May 1950, 56 percent of

Americans surveyed thought that either war, Communism, or the atomic bomb was the most important problem facing the country.[70]

Throughout the postwar period and into the 1950s, the issues regarding the apparent appeasement of the USSR served as rhetorical fodder for domestic arguments and political positioning between the Republican and Democratic Parties. Charges of being "soft on Communism" served largely partisan ends in the domestic arena, as both parties used it to sway voters, discredit each other, and gain political leverage. The "sin" of Yalta dogged the Democratic Party, as that 1945 arrangement made by an ailing Franklin Roosevelt gave the Soviets access to Manchuria, left Poland an orphaned country, and ceded Eastern Europe to the Russian sphere of influence. Truman was left defending the decisions after they were portrayed as having "sold out" to the Communists. But Republican presidential nominee Thomas Dewey balked at such a tarring strategy during his 1948 campaign. Despite being encouraged to challenge Truman on this issue, Dewey considered the strategy beneath him and quipped that he was not "going around looking under beds."[71] In his loss during the presidential race, he finally admitted that "the [Russian] bear got us," meaning that he was not sufficiently critical of Truman's policies regarding the Soviets and their reach into Eastern Europe.[72] But Dewey's fellow Republicans would not make the same mistake. To one GOP loyalist: "Party labels don't mean anything anymore. . . . [You] are on the American's [side] or [with] the communist and socialists."[73]

In this same vein political leaders argued that the high standard of living for the American way of life proved the superiority of capitalism over Communism. The contemporary zeitgeist in America wove economic prosperity with patriotic overtones and connected consumerism and conventional family values as part of a safeguard against Communism.[74] The Christian-based nuclear family combined with capitalism was seen as a bulwark against godless Communism and the proletarian abyss. The ideological lines between the United States and the USSR had been clearly drawn. Hanson Baldwin, military editor for the *New York Times*, argued in 1947, "the United States and Russia are face to face in a struggle for the world, a conflict short of war, but a conflict none-the-less."[75]

With this backdrop and these events, America was indeed due for a significant policy change. The PPS and the DoS were already considering a reappraisal of U.S. international strategy as events continued to unfold. Decades later Nitze reminisced that the Soviet A-bomb, Mao's victory in China, and the question over thermonuclear technology were the impetus for his authored policy review.[76] But other domestic issues were equally on the table during this fraught period. All of this had profound significance to the development of NSC 68. The confluence of these respective actions, given the anti-Communist sentiment, the mandates of the federal government, the various agendas, and the concerns of the NME in the autumn of 1949, serve as an illustration of what nineteenth-century Prussian military theorist Karl von Clausewitz coined the "paradoxical trinity."[77]

The intersection of American popular sentiment regarding international Communism and the Cold War, the military's concern over grand military strategy given the global security concerns, and the advent of thermonuclear weapons had a significant effect on U.S. policies. The confluence of these elements were all factors in the development of NSC 68 in the late winter of 1950. The intersection of these components in the autumn of 1949 was key in the germination of a more assertive national security policy. This book addresses how these varied events served as the catalyst for NSC 68, with much of its genesis occurring over the period of one season.

—1—
SUMMER

At 0650 on 29 August 1949, the first Soviet nuclear device sat in a test tower about one hundred feet above the rain-soaked, barren, windy steppes of Kazakhstan.[1] Located sixty miles northwest of the remote town of Semipalatinsk, sitting atop the tower was an implosion-based atomic device much like the American bomb tested four years earlier. At its heart was a plutonium sphere surrounded by a layer of explosives. The bomb, referred to as "the article," was set for detonation at 0700.[2] Miles away in a two-room control bunker, an automatic timer began the countdown sequence, the tension among the watching physicists and engineers increasing with each passing second.[3]

Those assembled in the bunker that late summer morning anxiously awaited the results of the test for more than just scientific reasons. Having worked on the large and expensive project for years, the team of highly skilled scientists had much more at stake than just their professional reputations. Among those who crowded the control room was the infamous Lavrentiy Beria, head of the People's Commissariat for Internal Affairs (Narodnyi Komissariat Vnutrennikh Del), better known by its Russian acronym NKVD. As head of both state security and the Soviet atomic effort, Beria was more than just Josef Stalin's henchman. He was also a hard-nosed, efficient administrator able to navigate government bureaucracy—albeit at times using draconian methods. Beria had deservedly earned his deadly reputation. As a close subordinate to Stalin, he wielded great power and was able to leverage this relationship toward his own personal and professional ends.[4] As head of the Soviet atomic program, Beria used his skill and ruthlessness to remove any administrative roadblocks to this highest of Stalin's priorities. Beria was effective in obtaining the men, materials, and resources necessary for an atomic program.

Given the bomb's importance to Beria and, more importantly, to Stalin, the scientific leaders of the Soviet project literally had their lives on the line with this test. If the device failed to detonate, punishment would have been doled out commensurate with one's responsibility to the endeavor. In deciding who was to be rewarded in the event of success or punished for a failure, Beria purportedly adopted a simple, yet ruthless, rubric. In case of a failure, key leaders were to be shot. If a success, these same individuals were to be named Heroes of Socialist Labor.[5] Had the device been a disappointment, those of lesser responsibility would have received long prison terms in the infamous gulag system. With the success of an atomic detonation, however, those same individuals would receive the Order of Lenin. The list continued with lesser punishments or rewards, depending upon one's level of responsibility.[6] A veteran of the Soviet effort understood the power of the NKVD chief and the personal stakes involved: "Beria was a terrifying man, vile. We all knew this. Our very lives depended on him."[7]

Fortunately for the Soviet scientists, as well as their families, at 0700 a flash of bright light "more brilliant than the sun" signaled success of the bomb they dubbed "First Lightning."[8] In nanoseconds the explosion reached fifty feet in diameter, with the temperature rising as high as 540,000° Fahrenheit.[9] In the following seconds the fireball continued to rise as the blast wave traveled outward at supersonic speed, kicking up dust and debris that engulfed the surrounding area. After the blast wave hit the fortified control center, and with the characteristic mushroom-shaped cloud rising above the steppes, Beria embraced the two key leaders of the project, Igor Kurchatov and Yuli Khariton, in his exuberance kissing both of them on the forehead.[10] Both Kurchatov and Khariton played key roles in the atomic endeavor and no doubt would have suffered accordingly. With the results of the explosion still rising into the air, Beria intimidatingly told them, "It would have been a great misfortune if this had not worked out successfully."[11] The sense of relief was overwhelming, with one scientist saying he had not felt such joy since Victory Day in 1945.[12] While there were consequences for failure, there were certainly inducements for success other than just medals and titles. Some team members were given ZIS-110 or Podedas cars, dachas, and free education for their children, with their wives permitted free travel anywhere in the Soviet Union.[13]

Flush with success, Beria immediately phoned Stalin to inform him of the test result. When finally connected with the generalissimo, who was awakened from his morning slumber in Moscow, Beria reported, "Everything went all right." Much to his chagrin and disappointment, the dictator replied dryly, "I know already."[14] Stalin either wanted to humble his NKVD chief and downplay the event or had other sources of information onsite. Assuming that Stalin had been tipped off by the subordinate who had put the call through, Beria angrily pounded his fist into the suspect officer's chest and said, "You have put a spoke in my wheel, traitor! I'll grind you to a pulp!"[15] Despite Beria's anger and personal disappointment, the Russians had achieved a major Cold War victory. As the autumn of 1949 began, the Soviet Union effectively ended the U.S. atomic monopoly, marking the start of an anxious season in America.

Regardless of the dire consequences of failure for the scientists involved, it would be a mistake to state that the scientists working on Joe-1 were influenced purely by threats of death or promises of their own aggrandizement. Those involved in this project worked in much the same patriotic fervor and spirit as their American counterparts had during the war. While peace was at hand in the summer of 1945, the development of American atomic weapons was seen as a threat to Russian security and its international aims.[16] Soviet scientists believed they needed to provide their country with a corresponding capability to ensure lasting peace and deter capitalist encroachment.[17] Given the Soviets' weaker position as a result of the U.S. atomic monopoly, one scientist argued, "In this situation one can come to only one conclusion," build a bomb to protect the motherland.[18] Reflecting this same sentiment years later, the father of the Soviet hydrogen bomb, Andrei Sakharov wrote, "In 1948, no one asked whether or not I wanted to take part in such work. I had no real choice in the matter, but the concentration, total absorption, and energy that I brought to the task were my own. . . . Our initial zeal however, was inspired more by emotion than intellect."[19]

"It Seems That We Muffed It"

For Stalin, the recent war was the result of capitalism and its inherent failures. Thus he fully expected another conflict in the future that would require his nation to be armed commensurately. From a Russian perspective, American airpower and strategic bombing were significant threats to the USSR, with the U.S. Air Force (USAF) capable of potentially penetrating Soviet airspace at will.[20] Scientists thought that negating the American monopoly was as patriotic an effort as the defeat of the Nazi invasion. The members of the Soviet effort, much like their counterparts in the United States, had no moral qualms about the weapon they were developing. The patriotic tone created a breakneck work ethic, as one scientist described: "We worked without heed for ourselves, huge enthusiasm, mobilizing all our spiritual and physical strength. The working day for senior researchers lasted from twelve to fourteen hours. . . . There were practically no days off, nor was there any leave; permission to travel on business was granted comparatively rarely."[21] While fully aware that the program was supported by gulag labor, this was largely disregarded in comparison to the larger threat the Soviet Union faced.[22]

In addition to testing the bomb itself and fully recognizing its military nature, the Soviets also wanted to measure blast effects on various objects. To that end, the team built wooden buildings, brick houses, bridges, and other structures approximately 3,000–4,000 feet from the test tower. Additionally, at various distances from the bomb, scientists also positioned railroad locomotives, aircraft (one in a takeoff configuration and another in a turn), artillery pieces, tanks, and a running power plant. Workers even dug a subway tunnel some 50–100 feet deep. To further test the effects of the atomic blast and radiation, live animals such as pigs, rats, mice, and camels were secured in the adjacent areas.[23] According to reports, the blast easily upended the armored vehicles and obliterated the structures. The test tower itself was completely vaporized, with only a large crater to show where it once stood.[24] The device was the sole Soviet nuclear munition, but the atomic playing field was now level vis-à-vis the United States. While the explosion was by itself a threat to U.S. security, and even though the USSR had no actual weapons in their arsenal, the CIA estimated that the Soviet atomic stock by the end of the year might be as high as ten assembled bombs.[25] A CIA memorandum to the Combined Chiefs of Staff planners estimated that the Soviet stockpile would grow by approximately twenty-five "Nagasaki-type" (plutonium) bombs every year up to 1953.[26]

Understanding the military threat that atomic weapons posed, many Soviet scientists thought of themselves as soldiers in a "scientific war" with the United States.[27] Supporting this notion was the program's research head, Kurchatov, who often signed his correspondence "soldier Kurchatov," while his colleagues sometimes referred to him as "the General."[28] During the Great Patriotic War against the German Wehrmacht, Kurchatov grew what became his emblematic beard as a symbol of Russian patriotism. He was motivated by a popular Russian war ditty that included the line "there will be time to shave after Fritz is beaten."[29] Even after the German defeat, Kurchatov retained his distinctive facial hair and was often referred to by others in the program as simply "the beard."[30] As early as 1942 the thirty-nine-year-old physicist was tasked to review an intercepted copy of the British MAUD Report, which served as a stimulus for the American atomic effort.[31] Kurchatov, a diligent and hardworking scientist who had been working at Leningrad's Physico-Technincal Institute's Physics Department, was selected to lead the Russian program.[32] He was an excellent pick, chosen over more prominent Russian scientists. His management, technical acumen, leadership, and skill were key components in the Soviet push for atomic parity.

As the mushroom cloud rose near Semipalatinsk, prevailing winds carried Joe-1's radioactive fallout eastwardly, some of which was eventually collected by the "bug catcher" on 1st Lieutenant Johnson's WB-29. While realizing that the Soviets would eventually acquire atomic weapons, most intelligence experts were surprised by the September 1949 evidence. Secretary of Defense Forrestal reflected American confidence regarding the length of the U.S. monopoly, writing in his diary, "The Russians cannot possibly have the industrial competence to produce the atomic bomb now and it will be 5 or even 10 years before they could count on manufacture of it in quantity. . . . [T]hey have notebook know how, but not the industrial complex to translate that abstract knowledge into concrete weapons."[33] When the samples from the WB-29 were validated, experts in the American intelligence field were left wondering how they were so wrong regarding Soviet atomic capabilities.

Just a year earlier, in July 1948, a CIA memorandum for the president reported that Soviet leadership was "seriously disturbed by the[ir] lack of progress" regarding atomic technology.[34] This same tone was evident in a USAF report published as late as 1 July 1949, only weeks before the Joe-1 detonation. It corroborated the CIA estimate on the lack of Soviet progress and claimed that the first Russian atomic bomb could not be completed before mid-1951.[35] According to the report, whenever the Russians finally cracked the code on atomic weapons, it would still be years before they could employ the capability militarily.[36] This erroneous estimate was generally accepted by the American defense establishment. But that does not mean everyone was lulled into a sense of security about a Soviet weapon. As early as June 1947, in testimony before the Senate, the first USAF chief of staff, Gen. Carl A. Spaatz, warned, "There is a current dangerous theory which says Russia will need ten to fifteen years to lick her wounds, refurbish her economy, and gird her loins. . . . Russia is now an arsenal and absolutely all energy [is] directed to building up the military."[37] Unknown to the Americans, in the early morning of 25 December 1946, Kurchatov's atomic pile (built with uranium-graphite layers) became functional as its control rods were slowly removed.[38] While still short of uranium and plutonium, the Soviets now had a working reactor.

Spaatz went on to testify that the Soviets might develop atomic weapons as early as 1948 but correctly anticipated that it might come only a year later. Despite the general's testimony and speculation regarding Russian efforts, most security experts still expected that a Soviet atomic weapon was still some years away.

After the Spaatz testimony, the most pressing question was how long the Soviets had operated an atomic program. Because no one in the West knew the answer, it was harder to figure out just when the USSR would truly be an atomic threat. But after the Joe-1 success, in a meeting of the JCAE, Sen. Eugene Millikin (R-CO) asked CIA head Adm. Roscoe Hillenkoetter: "It seems that we muffed it at least [by] a year and maybe longer.; . . . how did we muff it and what is wrong with our [intelligence-gathering] system?"[39] There were many answers to this question.

Clouding the U.S. intelligence perspective was the fact that the Soviet bomb project was, not unlike the Manhattan Project, a secretive, compartmentalized program. Only a few members of the effort clearly understood the full intent of the undertaking. Even at the project's headquarters at Arzama-16, a closed city about 280 miles southeast of Moscow, not everyone understood that they were working on atomic weapons.[40] Arzama-16 was the counterpart to the American LASL and home of the newly designated KB-11 (konstruktorskoe biuro-11) design bureau; some jokingly referred to it as "Los Arzamas."[41] Adding to the secretive nature of the effort, many scientists wrote their notes in code, with no secretaries or administrative assistants, to ensure security. Furthermore, the Soviet Union had always been a closed society with little flow of information outside official channels.[42] In this vein much of the atomic effort's infrastructure, factories, and important plants were far from public view, with the required large-scale labor force for the endeavor provided by gulags flush with prisoners of war (POWs), criminals, or other enemies of the state.

Additionally, during the immediate postwar period, the West had very little intelligence on what was happening within the Soviet Union. While the United States and its allies were electronically monitoring the USSR and getting information about its activities near the borders, what occurred within the country's vast interior largely remained a mystery. With the USSR spanning eleven time zones and comprising a land mass of some 8.5 million square miles, getting timely and accurate assessments on events deep in Soviet territory was difficult if not altogether impossible. During the postwar years, much of the intelligence available to American analysts was obtained through Project Wringer. This was an oral-interview program that interrogated some 300,000 former POWs who were once held in the USSR during the war. These people had been used as slave laborers in factories, kolkhozes (collective farms), and other heavy industry. Interrogators asked them to describe what they had seen and where they had seen it as they toiled in support of the Soviet state during the war years.[43] While their accounts provided some information, in the postwar period such information was certainly dated. Were those factories still standing? Had they been moved? Were they repurposed? Were they even functioning now? With no way to verify this information, intelligence analysts could only speculate.

Although the military services and the CIA published estimates on Soviet atomic weapons progress, CIA Director Hillenkoetter identified shortfalls in

American intelligence gathering. In a spring 1949 memo, he wrote that U.S. estimates of Soviet atomic progress were dependent upon the very limited information available. Hillenkoetter stated further that the CIA needed to have a better understanding of the events preceding a potential Soviet detonation and to improve its estimates on bomb production thereafter. He finished the memo by stating that the military services and the CIA were already committed on other projects and that the FY 1950 budget had not included additional funding for expansion of atomic-intelligence activities.[44]

The limited intelligence regarding the Soviets was addressed after the discovery of Joe-1. On 17 October 1949 the JCAE met with the CIA director to discuss the intelligence shortfalls. During the session one member of the committee quipped, "I get no comfort out of anything that the Admiral [Hillenkoetter] has said to us. We have not had an organization adequate to know what is going on [in the USSR] in the past and he gives me no assurances that we are going to have one in the future."[45] With a lack of definitive and timely information, the closed nature of Soviet society, and the program's secretive and compartmentalized organization, it should not be surprising that the Joe-1 detonation came as a surprise to the West.

Ironically, the Americans themselves helped the Soviets in their efforts. Following the atomic strikes over Japan, on 12 August 1945 the U.S. government published an official accounting of the Manhattan Engineering District (MED) and its work to the public. Titled *Atomic Energy for Military Purposes*, it was commonly referred to as the Smyth Report after its author, Princeton physicist Henry D. Smyth. A surprising bestseller, the Smyth Report was also published in foreign languages and eventually made its way to the USSR, where it was read thoroughly by Soviet scientists. A carefully crafted document, painstakingly devoid of classified information, it addressed many issues regarding the MED and included theories directly relevant to the program. It articulated the various problems addressed, solutions developed, and the order in which they were solved.[46] While the document was expunged of the most sensitive information, it was still very useful to Soviet physicists looking to replicate the American success. The Smyth Report provided a good general outline and roadmap for the direction their efforts should take.[47] One of the key pieces of information it provided to the Russians was the use of gaseous diffusion as the best way to secure isotope separation.[48] While there were three ways available for the enrichment of uranium—gaseous diffusion, electromagnetic, and thermal—each required constructing infrastructure that was both difficult and costly.[49] Focusing on gaseous diffusion as the Americans had allowed the Russians to forgo the expense and trouble of building all three kinds of plants.

But the Smyth Report was not the only source of Soviet information regarding American developments. While clearly benefiting from the published report, the Russians had already infiltrated the Allied atomic efforts.[50] In June 1942 one of Beria's deputies transmitted a coded message that directed Soviet agents in the United States, Germany, and Great Britain to obtain information on "the theoretical and practical aspects of the atomic bomb projects, on the design of the atomic, nuclear fuel components, the trigger mechanism, [and] various methods of uranium isotope fission."[51] At that time Vyacheslav Molotov, a protégé of Stalin, was in charge of the atomic effort, and he shared with Kurchatov the intelligence gathered by these agents. In the spring of 1943, Kurchatov spent a number of days reviewing the fruits of Soviet espionage and came away with a new perspective regarding the problems he faced.[52] Throughout the war years the Soviets benefited from a stream of atomic secrets pilfered from the West. As Kurchatov reviewed this material, stolen Allied ideas were already helping point out the specific direction for the Russian atomic effort.[53]

Yet using stolen information from the Manhattan Project was a secret even to members of the Soviet effort.[54] Most of Kurchatov's subordinates were completely unaware of the acquisition of these American technical plans. After the success of Joe-1, many Soviet scientists steadfastly refuted any notion of outside influence. While ignorant of Kurchatov's access to stolen technical data, they were also ignorant of his direct involvement in the espionage effort. As an academic, Kurchatov knew of important scientific establishments in the United States and helped aim Soviet agents there toward labs working with plutonium or addressing atomic energy.[55]

Despite Kurchatov's receipt of stolen information and the deliberate espionage effort of the NKVD, to many Soviet scientists Joe-1 was a wholly Russian design.[56] Although using stolen ideas, they still had to check, measure, validate, and confirm a myriad of details to ensure the correctness of the information. Having to work through these various technical and difficult issues would lead anyone to believe that their work was original. Validating the purloined information was a monumental task and required a dedicated, concerted effort. Even those who were aware of the espionage were still concerned that the technology obtained might be American disinformation and an attempt to throw the Soviets off track.[57]

Russian scientists were looking into fission before the war and followed the international discourse in scholarly venues. Interestingly, by 1942 Soviet scientist Georgi Flerov and other Russian physicists noticed that any dialogue on fission was now largely missing from international professional journals and that associated works on the topic were no longer being published.[58] The absence of such a discourse spoke volumes to the young physicist, hinting that the Americans and the British had gone underground with their research. Flerov surmised that it meant a secret Anglo-American atomic collaboration.[59] He wrote letters to members of the Soviet government, including Stalin, to help stimulate an effort for Mother Russia. Flerov's actions, combined with a flow of other materials regarding growing Anglo-American atomic research, spurred the State Defense Committee (Gosudarstvennyj Komitet Oborony; GKO) in the spring of 1943 to formally establish a Soviet program, with Kurchatov as its leader.[60] With the German offensive threatening the Soviet state, the USSR was in no position to actually construct an equivalent of the MED. But during the war, members of its existing smaller-scale program did at least begin addressing the technical and theoretical problems.[61]

What the Americans did not know at the time of the Joe-1 explosion was that the USSR had already benefited from the work done at LASL years earlier. In fact, by the autumn of 1945, the Soviets had a general description of the Fat Man design courtesy of Klaus Fuchs, David Greenglass, and their associates.[62] In September 1949, after the Soviet success, the Truman administration downplayed the potential role of espionage. The official response regarding Joe-1 was: "There is no reason to believe that this development is the result of anything that was stolen or copied from us. Nearly four years ago the President pointed out that . . . the essential theoretical knowledge upon which the discovery is based is already widely known."[63] Despite this measured and prudent response, a discovery in the Venona Project helped spur the FBI's investigation into Fuchs. In September 1949 references to classified atomic information connected Fuchs to the Russians. Subsequent investigations unearthed the physicist's Communist sympathies. Throughout the autumn American agents pieced together his espionage activity but were still not in a position to draw any definitive conclusions. A British subject, Fuchs returned to the United Kingdom in December 1949; FBI officials notified their counterparts in London about their suspicions.[64] British authorities followed up on the American tip in January 1950. Fuchs confessed to spying and was arraigned on 3 February. Upon his arrest, it became obvious to the Americans that they had to admit that Soviet espionage efforts were probably ongoing since 1943.[65]

Fuchs worked at the very heart of the Manhattan Project, and his actions were a key element in the eventual Soviet success. During the war, much of the work at LASL was directed at the development of the implosion-design atomic device. This was the basis for the Fat Man bomb and later served as the model for Joe-1. While initially sent to the United States to work on the problem of gaseous diffusion for uranium enrichment, Fuchs was eventually transferred to LASL. After arriving in New Mexico in August 1944, he was subsequently assigned to the T-1 Implosion Dynamics Division, where he had access to much of the larger MED organization and was at the very center of the atomic effort.[66] Simultaneously, David Greenglass, a machinist working on the toughest aspects of the implosion design, also spied for the Soviets. He assisted casting of the Baratol and Composition B explosives used in the implosion blast onto the weapon's plutonium core. Fuchs' wide-ranging security authorization within the MED placed him in a unique position to understand and comprehend all the components of the American implosion design. His and Greenglass' intimate knowledge of the lenses and implosion actions made their information especially useful for the Soviets and helped corroborate other data.[67]

Fuchs was born in 1911 in Russelsheim, Germany, near Darmstadt, to a leftist-leaning father. As a student at the University of Leipzig, he joined the Socialist Party of Germany and later the Communist Party during the Weimar years.[68] He escaped Hitler's Germany for the United Kingdom in 1933. In Great Britain he continued his studies in physics, receiving his doctorate at the University of Bristol in 1937 with a dissertation titled "The Cohesive Forces of Copper and the Elastic Constants of Monovalent Metals."[69] But because of his country of origin, in June 1940 Fuchs was arrested as a suspect enemy alien and deported to Quebec, Canada.[70]

By December he was cleared and made his way back to the United Kingdom. A fellow German émigré and scientist, Rudolf Peierls, was already involved in the British atomic effort and subsequently hired Fuchs to work on unclassified, yet relevant, atomic equations. Moving in with Peierls and drawing a salary, the young physicist eventually became part of the British atomic effort, known by the codename "Tube Alloys."[71] From this initial work Fuchs eventually assisted in drafting the now famous MAUD Report.[72] In his work with the report, Fuchs helped determine calculations regarding the amount of uranium needed to create a fissionable event. Not only did MAUD energize U.S. atomic efforts but, when it was passed to the Soviets, the report also emboldened Russian research in this area and simultaneously confirmed their suspicions of a British-American collaboration.[73]

Despite Fuchs' Communist past, during the war the British were more interested in having competent, intelligent scientists than wholly politically acceptable academics. Given the experience of the Depression, many Europeans had flirted with the idea of Communism, and such leftist political activity was not unusual. Furthermore, after Hitler invaded the USSR, Fuchs' Communist affiliations were less of a concern than the defeat of Nazism, especially since both the Russians and the British now shared that common enemy. Sympathetic to the Soviets and believing that a nuclear monopoly would be a threat to world peace, while also hoping to prevent such a weapon from being used, Fuchs provided the Soviet Union with secret materials as early as 1942.[74] Some estimate that his information saved the Russians one to two years' efforts in research and development.[75] He contacted the Soviet embassy as early as December 1941 and met with a Russian agent six times before leaving for the United States.[76] When caught and interviewed, Fuchs confessed that he felt "no hesitation in giving [Moscow] all the information I had."[77] Indicative of his high-minded, if not misplaced, ideals regarding atomic parity, Fuchs was supposedly appalled at the idea of being offered money for his espionage efforts.[78]

Quiet and unassuming, Fuchs was both bright and industrious. He faded into the background, given the intellectual power of the LASL leaders, and worked long hours. Keeping to himself and looking ever the outsider, Fuchs was dubbed by one LASL physicist "poverino," the pitiful one.[79] According to T-1 Division head Hans Bethe, he was "one of the most valuable men in my division. One of the best theoretical physicists we had, . . . if he was a spy, then he played his role beautifully."[80] After the espionage became known, J. Robert Oppenheimer, then head of LASL, quipped, "If Fuchs had been infinitely compartmentalized, what was inside his [T-1] compartment [alone] would have done the damage."[81] Bethe elaborated on this: "He's the only one who mattered [of all the atomic spies]. Greenglass himself was quite unimportant. He was a terrible dope. But he [Greenglass] simplified the working of our explosive system for the Russians. Fuchs did much more than that. He told the Russians exactly how to assemble the bomb; how to use implosion; how the explosive and nuclear material was arranged; how to calculate the yield of the bomb and the neutron diffusion."[82] Fuchs had a very good memory and could easily recall important technical details, and his position at the heart of the American effort was key to its success.[83] Working on the gaseous-diffusion process to refine uranium at Oak Ridge, Tennessee, in 1943, he was eventually sent to LASL in August 1944. Once in New Mexico and involved in the T-1 Division, he became intimately familiar with the implosion design of Fat Man, using plutonium as a way to spark a fissionable event.[84] But his recall abilities cut both ways.

In June 1945, before the Trinity explosion in New Mexico, Fuchs provided the Soviets a detailed description of the components and function of the American design.[85] Meeting his contact, Harry Gold, in Santa Fe, Fuchs provided the general sketch along with a description for the implosion/plutonium design. The information also included various descriptions of the components required and their composition. With corroborating information received from Greenglass, by October 1945 Beria had in his hands a fairly detailed report about the weapon's general description, active materials, and the layers of explosives and lenses.[86]

During this same period, Soviet scientists developed a better, more efficient atomic-bomb design based upon the work of V. N. Nekrutkin. Their design weighed half as much as its American counterpart, providing twice the yield and having a smaller diameter.[87] The idea of a Soviet design was championed by prominent physicist Peter Kapitza, who was the first Russian to suggest weaponization of the technology. While this was in the offing, the American weapon was a proven, workable design. The risk of the unproven Soviet design was too great given the larger imperative. As a result, Kurchatov directed that the project remain on its American-inspired path.[88] The Soviet design was later tested and validated, but the greater concern in 1949 was gaining access to the "atomic club" in the shortest time possible with the least risk.

Early on, Kurchatov and his program were plagued by what they referred to as the "uranium problem," meaning that they never had enough of the isotope on hand. While having access to the espionage materials coming from Fuchs and others, he learned of the value of plutonium for a fissionable event and saw this as a new direction.[89] As a result of this news, Kurchatov specifically requested that the NKVD send its agents and resources to those locations in America where plutonium research was potentially being conducted.[90] This was a significant hurdle to the atomic effort. The Americans believed that most of the available uranium deposits were in the hands of democratic countries and that this would delay any Soviet weapons development. Before and during the war, the Americans and the British had done their best to secure world uranium supplies to keep them out of the hands of the Germans. Following the war, the Americans launched a deliberate program, called "ALSOS," to scour Europe and obtain German uranium stocks to prevent them and other atomic materials from falling into the hands of the advancing Russians.[91] A fairly successful endeavor, the ALSOS mission removed ninety metric tons of sodium urinate, twenty grams of pure radium, and existing uranium supplies from various locations in Germany.[92]

Furthermore, the United States and the United Kingdom did their utmost to prevent uranium ore from being purchased by other countries, thus securing it for themselves. As a result of these efforts, the head of the MED, Maj. Gen. Leslie Groves, believed that the British and Americans had secured 97 percent of the world's known uranium output, although he later admitted he did not know what the Russians had within their own territorial control.[93] Considered an expert on the topic and convinced of his own success in securing stockpiles worldwide, Groves further claimed it would take the Soviets ten years to obtain the uranium needed for such an effort.[94] A Russian informer supported this assertion, stating "the biggest drawback to making a Soviet atom bomb is the terrific lack of pure uranium which is available to the Soviet Union."[95] Given Groves' position as a leading expert, his statements added to the U.S. sense of security regarding its atomic monopoly. But years later he admitted that he underestimated the amount of uranium available in the Soviet-controlled areas of Germany and Czechoslovakia.[96]

Immediately after the war the Soviets secured one hundred tons of uranium ore from the Auer Company in eastern Germany.[97] While this was a good start, Kurchatov needed much more to fully supply his effort. The Soviets set about securing fissionable ores and processing them for use in their weapon. Unbeknown to the West, the Erzgebirge region of eastern Germany was rich with uranium ore; when the USSR discovered the deposits in 1946, it initiated a large mining effort.[98] Because these sites had been inactive for years, a massive labor pool was required to reopen the mines and extract the ore. The Soviets pressed tens of thousands of German nationals into work gangs at locations in Aue, Schneeberg, Oberschlema (known today as Bad Schlema), and Johanngeorgenstadt.[99]

Working in unhealthy and horrendous conditions, Germans of all classes were forced into the mines. Workers suffered from a lack of housing that forced them to sleep in shifts; many slept on the ground without blankets. Hygiene was a constant problem, as was rape, all combined with a lack of protective work clothes, proper gear, and medical supplies to add to their misery.[100] Additionally, the long-term effects from exposure to the dangerous ore and the toxic dust created by the dry-drilling methods used were never considered by the Russian overseers or the German laborers.[101]

In addition to these sites, the Soviets also secured uranium mines in Joachimsthal, Czechoslovakia, that contained some of the richest deposits in the world.[102] Conditions at this location were equally appalling, and German prisoners and petty criminals were forced to work in similarly unhealthy conditions. With poor food and shelter available, the toll on workers was equally deadly. A worker-prisoner at the Czech mine described his daily rations as "four slices of bread and [a] few mushy vegetables, . . . and three times a week came watery soup which was lukewarm water added to dry vegetables."[103] Worker safety was never a concern, and the laborers were also subject to the effects of radiological emissions suffered by their counterparts in the German mines. While the eastern mines would eventually transition over to the use of "volunteer labor," in Germany alone it was estimated that some 20,000 people died from the labor itself or from radiation-induced diseases.[104] Highlighting the risks, one laborer who escaped to the West claimed, "The Russians have opened a uranium mine. . . . Aue is like a prison camp. . . . [T]o work there for half a year means death."[105]

American intelligence analysts failed to appreciate the dedication and resources the USSR put into their atomic research, given the devastation of World War II. The atomic program was one of Stalin's highest priorities in the postwar years, and he allocated considerable material and financial support to it. Prior to 1945, the exigency of the war precluded a large atomic effort because conventional military applications were the main concern. A diversion of resources and time during the war on a scale required for a speculative atomic device was not worth the risk given the dire situation along the eastern front. Even if the Soviets had all the theoretical knowledge required to construct a bomb, the ability to mine and refine uranium, along with the associated infrastructure, was a bridge too far during the war. Only the Americans, with their industrial base intact, fully mobilized, and supplied with plenty of labor, had that luxury.

While the Russians celebrated their hard-won victory over the Nazis in the summer of 1945, the atomic explosions over Hiroshima and Nagasaki were scarcely mentioned within the Soviet Union.[106] But many in the USSR, especially those in positions of power, thought the American monopoly and the advent of atomic warfare made the sacrifice to defeat the Germans a waste.[107] This new technology, combined with the advent of strategic bombardment, appeared to make all previous forms of warfare obsolete. As a result, with the return of peace, the reorientation of production assets, and the success of American atomic efforts, Soviet leaders made atomic research a priority. Kurchatov and Khariton had plenty of support from the Communist Party, which suspected that the Americans now looked to dictate their will globally.[108]

In February 1946 at the Bolshoi Theater, Stalin argued that the war had occurred "as the inevitable result of the development of world economic and political forces on the basis of modern monopoly capitalism."[109] Because capitalist states still existed and the experience of military offensives into Russia over the past two centuries, Stalin and his comrades expected more of the same. The nation needed to prepare militarily. The CIA estimated that between 1948 and 1949, USSR defense expenditures rose from $12.5 billion to $16.5 billion. While this difference of only $4 billion seems reasonable, it represents a significant increase in Soviet gross national income—a difference of 23.2 to 28.9 percent.[110] From a Russian perspective, three major invasions in the past two centuries were a harbinger for what would come in the future.

On 26 January 1946 Stalin had given Kurchatov and other leaders of the atomic effort his full backing, telling them "it was not worth engaging in small-scale work, but necessary to conduct work broadly, with [a] Russian scope," meaning on a large and massive scale.[111] In keeping with his larger intent to overtake and outstrip the Americans, Stalin further instructed Kurchatov, "If a child doesn't cry, the mother doesn't know what it needs. Ask for whatever you like. You won't be refused."[112] This was in keeping with the dictator's larger grand strategy to "overtake and outstrip" the Americans and gain atomic equilibrium.[113] One of the symbols of this objective was the development of an atomic weapon to show the world that the USSR was undeniably a global power—militarily, technologically, and industrially.[114]

Immediately after the war, analysis estimated that the Soviet Union had lost 25 million individuals, with a similar number left homeless by the conflict. Additionally, it had lost approximately 25 percent of its prewar industrial fixed capital and 40 percent of its agricultural capacity.[115] Recovery would require years, with the Russians themselves predicting as many as ten years for the USSR to recuperate from the war. In the immediate postwar years, the average Soviet family was able to buy one leather shoe, a pair of socks, and a quarter pair of underwear each year. Food was also scarce, with roughly 1.5 million people succumbing to malnutrition or associated illness.[116] Additionally, a crushing famine in the Ukraine, resulting from a drought and the lasting effects of the war, did not help the Soviet state in its recovery efforts. Dealing with this and other issues, American intelligence believed, would be the focus for the Soviet economy in the immediate postwar years.[117]

Unlike the assistance received by Western Europe through the Marshall Plan starting in 1948, the Soviet Union refused such aid. The wartime Lend-Lease program, which was a key component in keeping the Soviets in the war against the Germans, was quickly terminated after the Allied victory.[118] While Russia was initially open to the idea of accepting U.S. aid, the idea was discarded as Stalin refrained from becoming dependent upon the West.[119] With the Allied victory over the Axis states complete, East-West relations rapidly began to chill. Preexisting mutual suspicions between Communism and capitalism meant the Soviets were on their own. The shotgun marriage between the United States and the Soviet Union was dissolved.

While certain regions of the USSR, like the Urals and Siberia, experienced an increase in total production, other areas suffered appreciably. The industrial output of the Ukraine and Belorussia were only one-fifth and one-quarter, respectively, of their prewar outputs.[120] Despite the emergency ramp-up of wartime production while engaged in the conflict, many of the USSR's heavy industries still experienced an appreciable drop in production figures during the war years.[121] But the Soviets had to return to a prewar or wartime industrial mode while adjusting to the new geopolitical situation and rebuilding their domestic infrastructure.[122]

In addition to industrial mobilization during and after the war, Stalin also placed emphasis on scientific research and development. As previously noted, technical research during the war was limited, even on the atomic bomb. Yet efforts to develop Soviet technical capabilities were not completely stagnant. Looking forward technologically, some scientists were exempted from military service to continue their work.[123] During the war, the USSR established centers of scientific research at various locations, continuing these efforts after the conflict ended. The atomic program was part of this.

For Soviet leaders, looking to bring their country abreast of the rest of the world technologically, the atomic program provided further impetus for scientific activities. In support of scientific research, the USSR's budget for the Fourth Five-Year Plan appropriated 5 billion rubles (approximately $1 billion) for scientific research, a 240 percent increase from the previous plan.[124] The economic program also looked to repair much of the damage done to the nation's scientific infrastructure and laboratories, among other things constructing approximately fifty major buildings for the Soviet Academy of Sciences alone.[125] Under this push for increased technological applications, the atomic effort flourished. The CIA estimated that the Soviets had between 300,000 and 460,000 people supporting the atomic endeavor. Most were in mining the all-important uranium ore, with the remainder engaged in construction, production, or research.[126]

Looking to leverage potential German atomic technology, the Soviets also had an interest in seizing German atomic materials and focused on capturing prominent scientists involved in Nazi research. While the possibility of a German atomic bomb served as the impetus for the MED, it became clear after the war that Hitler's effort fell far short of creating a weapon.[127] Members of the MED found that the Germans never got beyond the laboratory stage and determined that what had been done was more an effort for power generation than for weapons development.[128] The Nazi program was largely fractured, with few resources to draw from given the amount of infrastructure required for such an undertaking. But according to one German scientist, Nikolaus Riehl, the biggest problem was that a priority for atomic research in the Third Reich never materialized from the national leadership: "I believe strongly that the relative laxity in the pursuit of the program rests primarily on the primitive level of intellectual understanding of Hitler and his advisors. They had perhaps a good comprehension of rockets that roared with a great deal of noise, . . . but they had no real understanding of the unfamiliar, abstract concepts associated with the release of energy through nuclear fission."[129] Still, the Soviets made a concerted attempt to obtain the German scientists involved in Hitler's atomic program. Those captured were sent to Moscow but did not provide the boost in help the Russians expected.[130] Given the lack of real progress in the Nazi atomic endeavor, the scientists were only marginally helpful, mainly with uranium enrichment and other supporting issues rather than with bomb development. The Soviets shipped related refining equipment from the Auer plant in Germany to Russia. With the information provided by the Smyth Report and other espionage efforts, by the summer of 1946 the captured Germans began enriching uranium for their Soviet overseers.

During the war, Kurchatov became dissatisfied with the management and oversight of the atomic program provided by Molotov. In order to keep the program moving, Stalin replaced Molotov with Beria in 1945.[131] After the war, and given the importance Stalin placed on the project, the entire endeavor needed to grow exponentially. Officials began to recruit talent, establish sites for various labs and installations, determine the required resources for both facilities and research, and develop the necessary scientific strategies.[132] Beria was a key player in establishing these priorities and can be credited with the speed of the Soviet atomic response.[133]

Despite the condition of its postwar infrastructure, the USSR successfully constructed an atomic industry. Fortunately for the physicists and engineers working on the expansive project, Beria had millions of slave laborers, referred to as "camp dust," in his gulags.[134] The NKVD, by virtue of these prisoners, was one of the largest construction and labor sources in the entire country, possessing 23 percent of the country's nonagricultural labor force. Its generals were among the most influential agents regarding the state's labor-intensive projects.[135] As a result, the atomic program always had the workers to clear sites, build camps, establish research facilities, and mine materials. Seventy thousand laborers were used to build just one large-scale reactor facility at Cheliabinsk-40.[136] The use of gulag labor meant not only that overhead costs to house, feed, and care for workers could remain low but also that the effort could remain out of view of the general public.

In addition to heading the NKVD, Beria was also a member of the five-man State Defense Committee and conveniently responsible for decisions regarding economic and military production. The latter organization also oversaw the structure of the Soviet armed forces.[137] In these positions he was able to direct, divert, and prioritize national labor and material resources as he saw fit. Given the priorities established by Stalin and the national priority to reach and surpass the West in terms of production and technology, Beria had motivation, labor, and resources to assign the assets required for the atomic endeavor.

While notoriously sadistic and cruel, Beria was also intelligent, efficient, and a highly persuasive administrator who could accomplish difficult tasks.[138] Arriving in Moscow in 1938, he quickly ingratiated himself to Stalin and was able to manipulate the leader's opinion of rivals and other government officials.[139] According to one member of the atomic effort, "Scientists who met him could not fail to recognize his intelligence, willpower, and purposefulness." But his authority over everyone was ever present, as one Russian physicists recalled: "One gesture of Beria was sufficient to make any of us disappear."[140] Yet in him they found "a first class administrator who could carry a job through to completion."[141] Although ruthless, Beria could also be courteous and tactful, with an ability to simplify complex issues effectively.[142]

Because he was inherently distrustful of intellectuals and academics, Beria often had disputes with physicists in the atomic program. After the first Soviet reactor became operational on 25 December 1946, he was called in to witness its function. When the neutron counters clicked away indicating a fissionable event, an unimpressed Beria asked, "Is that all? . . . Nothing more?" Since he could not actually see the event or go into the reactor room himself, his suspicions of academics made him skeptical about what the physicists experienced.[143] Yet Beria respected their technical knowledge. According to an NKVD subordinate, "Beria had the reputation of a good boss, who went to a great deal of trouble to look after the welfare of his staff. As a result of his forcefulness and drive we NKVD personnel had the best of what there was."[144] He visited every location associated with atomic production and was fully cognizant of the program's progress. During these visits the NKVD chief instilled "both fear and enthusiasm" in those associated with the effort.[145] When overseeing the building of Europe's first plutonium plant near the remote town of Kyshtym near the Ural Mountains, Beria held individuals personally responsible for missing deadlines, enacting consequences for failure.[146] He gave each manager a pool of labor and security personnel to manage. For incentive, each manager could establish allotments for housing, food, or other supplies at their discretion as a way to ensure meeting production goals or construction target dates.[147] Human costs were not considered in the development of these sites, and the management of the various construction programs was carried out with callous efficiency.

While the Soviet Union and Stalin put great emphasis on the development of atomic weapons, they also had the luxury of knowing that such technology was indeed feasible. The American success had already proved that. In order to catch up, the Soviets needed only to copy their U.S. rivals. Although espionage helped develop and design Joe-1, what was also important for the Russian effort was what they did *not* have to make or develop themselves as a result of the American model. Kurchatov and his colleagues did not have to go through the trouble of experimentation with facilities like the Y-12 electromagnetic isotope-separation plant or the inefficient S-50 thermal-diffusion plant, both located at the Clinton Engineering Works in Oak Ridge. While the Soviet effort was a large endeavor with its own gaseous-diffusion plant at Kefirstadt and a plutonium extraction and generation facility in Kyshtym, a full comparison of it to the MED is not necessarily accurate—the Russians had a road map to follow, they were not blazing the trail.

In the development of the American atomic bombs, 978 independent businesses or contractors were involved in an effort that cost U.S. taxpayers $2,163,393,503. (Of particular note, the Y-12 and K-25 plants themselves constituted half the cost of MED, together totaling $1,157,420,190.)[148] Although they initially had a shortage of uranium, the Soviets needed only to focus on the method for creating plutonium and on following the plans provided by Fuchs and other spies. This allowed an efficiency that was not available to the Americans because the scientists at LASL experimented, developed, and designed different atomic technologies simultaneously. Little Boy, a failed Thin Man design, and Fat Man research were all occurring under the auspices of the MED at an enormous cost in manpower, material, and resources. With U.S. plans in hand, the Russians avoided many scientific dead ends.

With the development of Soviet atomic capability, the architect of America's containment policy, George Kennan, was chagrined as he saw the nation "drifting toward a morbid preoccupation with the fact that the Russians conceivably could drop atomic bombs on this country, regardless of the question as to whether it would be profitable or otherwise to do so."[149] This fear drove much of the nation's security concerns for decades. As a result, and much to the mortification of U.S. military planners, the Russians quickly negated the American monopoly and effectively changed the geopolitical status quo. While the Americans firmly believed that the Soviets would enter the nuclear club eventually, their early arrival served as a starting point for a review of national security policy. But the explosion of Joe-1 was followed by many other events in the autumn of 1949.

Old Rivalries in a New Era

As the Soviets were preparing their first atomic device for testing in Central Asia, disturbing events were unfolding in the United States. Long in coming, they occurred at first within the walls of the Pentagon but were exacerbated in 1949 as they spilled over into the chambers of Congress and eventually into the public forum, coming to a head by early fall. The issues at hand would affect the relationship of the military services, the entirety of the National Military Establishment (NME), and in some cases the careers of select military officers directly involved. They served as a lightning rod for arguments, accusations, and recriminations involving national defense strategy and the way the United States envisioned conducting future conflict.

With the National Security Act of 1947, the old established War and Navy Departments were significantly reorganized, breaking old paradigms. Looking to unify the services for better coordination and efficiency, the 1947 legislation provided a way to integrate policies and procedures for three newly established military departments while providing authoritative and unified direction under civilian control.[150] It reorganized the Department of the Navy (which included the Marine Corps), created the Department of the Air Force (placing the new service component on equal footing with the others), and renamed the old War Department as the Department of the Army. Each service department now had a civilian secretary to oversee the respective uniformed service chiefs. Furthermore, the newly created post of secretary of defense oversaw all of the individual service secretaries. Initially, the service secretaries were cabinet positions along with their boss. The early act organized all the military branches under the larger header of the NME.

But in 1949 Congress passed the National Security Act amendments, which made a number of modifications. The most visible change was creating the Department of Defense (DoD) from the old NME, further corralling all the services under the new executive department. But the legislation was more than cosmetic. Approved by Congress on 2 August, the changes saw the service secretaries lose their cabinet-level status as well as their seats on the National Security Council (NSC). Subsequently, they were placed directly under the authority of the secretary of defense, who, as a result of the reorganization, was now directly responsible to the president and given much greater influence in national security matters. Furthermore, the later legislation also created the position of chairman of the Joint Chiefs of Staff (JCS) in an effort to quell dissention among the service chiefs. While the reorganization outlined sounded simple enough, there were plenty of problems associated with this new structure. Furthermore, not all the services viewed unification as progress—especially the Navy.

After World War I the nation demobilized, with the respective services shrinking appreciably. As the 1920s became the 1930s and with the Depression gripping the country, defense dollars became scarce. The military services were in a struggle for funding, causing a review of their roles and missions. Furthermore, with America in an isolationist mood and loath to engage overseas, many wondered why bother spending large amounts of money on armaments. Strapped for cash, Congress asked policymakers where they could find the "best bang for the buck." Furthermore, with the limited dollars available and given the isolationist tone in the country, many wondered which service was best suited for defending the United States against enemy fleets or invasion. Both the U.S. Army Air Corps (USAAC) and the U.S. Navy claimed they were the most qualified to fulfill this largely defensive role.

Before World War II the USAAC was perceived as intruding into the Navy's missions as bigger, faster, and higher-performance aircraft were capable of crossing vast distances to strike enemy forces, an ability previously belonging exclusively to the Navy.[151] During the nineteenth and early twentieth centuries, American fleets circumnavigated the globe, engaged enemies, enforced policies, conducted show-of-force operations, opened trade with foreign nations, and served as a symbol of national power. But with the advent of military aviation, air-minded officers began making statements that drew the ire of their naval counterparts. As early as 1920, proponents of airpower argued before the House Appropriations Committee that aviation in the future would be the first line of defense for the nation against an invading enemy fleet. While this statement obviously encroached on traditional Navy missions, Army aviators argued further that air attacks against surface vessels would be so devastating to any naval flotilla that "it was only a question of a very short time before a navy will get under the water [meaning submarines] and stay there."[152] Statements such as these clearly drew the anger of the maritime service.

As early as 1931 the USAAC was assigned the mission of coastal defense and conducting maritime reconnaissance. While appearing to cede a traditionally Navy mission, the Chief of Naval Operations (CNO), Adm. W. Y. Pratt, agreed to the USAAC role. By allowing the Air Corps a defensive mission, he hoped that the Navy's carrier aviation might evolve with a more offensive role to play. Yet many in the Navy saw this not as an opportunity for carrier aviation, but as a power grab by the Army looking to assume authority over all land-based naval air stations.[153] Throughout the 1930s the issue continued to simmer. In an effort to help delineate service responsibilities, during discussions at the Federal Aviation Commission in 1934, representatives of the Navy argued, "The Army should develop and build those types of airplanes required by the Army to fulfill its land operations. The Navy should develop and build those types of airplanes required by the Navy in its operations over the sea or for operation from fleet air bases or naval stations. The Army should have paramount interest over the land and the Navy over the sea. Neither service should build or operate planes intended to duplicate the functions of the other."[154] Meant to establish service parameters, the actual execution of such an idea was clearly problematic, given the development of aviation technology and capability. Many types of aircraft could have met both services' needs. This same issue was raised again during World War II. Because aircraft production in the United States was finite, who had priority, the Navy or the USAAC? During the war, the Procurement Assignment Board was established to wrestle with this very question.[155]

But with Billy Mitchell's bombing and sinking of the *Ostfriesland* and increasingly bold statements regarding airpower coming from the Air Corps Tactical School in the 1930s, lines were being drawn. In the 1937 joint Army-Navy maneuvers off the Pacific coast, B-17s easily located and "attacked" USS *Utah* using their new Norden visual bombsights, hitting the vessel with practice bombs filled with water.[156] Later in 1938 Army aircrews intercepted the Italian liner *Rex*, validating airpower's utility in coastal-defense missions. In this environment the USAAC and the Navy became increasingly more suspicious of each other's motives. Navy protestations resulted in a

War Department verbal directive that Army flights were now limited to only a one-hundred-mile zone from the nation's shorelines.[157] Ironically, this restriction was not applicable to land-based naval aircraft capable of exceeding such distances.

Airpower seemed a much cheaper solution than the Navy's fleet of large and expensive warships. While naval aviation was coming to the fore during the interwar years, in 1935 the USAAC unveiled its new B-17 bomber, with a range of up to 2,000 miles and a speed of 230 miles per hour (mph). Simultaneously, the Air Corps Tactical School formally framed the idea of strategic precision bombing, with the B-17 as its centerpiece.[158] The potential for war in the late 1930s spurred increased defense spending, with the services growing exponentially in both size and capability. In 1938 President Roosevelt submitted a Navy expansion proposal to Congress, and in November he issued instructions claiming that air forces—not ground or naval forces—would influence Axis actions in future conflict and called for an increase in the USAAC to 20,000 planes.[159] On 24 August 1939, days before the German invasion of Poland, the War Department rescinded the one-hundred-mile limitation on USAAC aircraft, allowing them to operate within the range of their capability.[160]

During the war, the combat record of naval aviators and pilots of the U.S. Army Air Forces (USAAF, as the USAAC was renamed in 1941) reflected great credit upon their respective services. Both appeared to have proved their worth in the recent conflict, with the Army Air Forces conducting land-based air operations in both theaters while the Navy smashed the Imperial Japanese Navy's offensive fleet almost single-handedly. Naval aviation doctrines of the interwar years were validated in the Pacific, as carrier aviation controlled sea lines of communication and effectively struck land targets. As a result of these and other engagements, the battleship began to wane in influence as aircraft carriers became the primary platform for power projection. While the battleship still had a place in a naval campaign during the war, the basic organization of naval flotillas was now centered on the flattop, with all other ships in support. Many in the Navy hoped to build even bigger carriers, with naval leadership dominated by aviators commanding fleets of aircraft capable of delivering atomic ordnance. Some naval officers thought these new ships might be more capable of effectively delivering atomic bombs than the emerging USAF.[161]

Results of the USAAF's strategic precision-bombing campaign were hardly definitive. In hopes of validating the strategic bombing effort, in 1944 Secretary of War Henry Stimson recommended that Roosevelt authorize an in-depth study of the effectiveness and efficacy of the air campaign.[162] The president's order initiated the U.S. Strategic Bombing Survey (USSBS), an exhaustive and expansive study of the bombing effort by many notable authorities and others. But the conclusions were largely equivocal, with many in the USAAF taking issue with the published results. Its basic conclusion was that strategic bombing was "a" factor in the Allied victory but not "the" definitive reason. The executive summary of the USSBS stated, "The role of air power cannot be considered separately . . . from the roles of ground and naval forces nor from the broad plans and strategy from which the campaign was conducted."[163] The head of the Army Analysis Division replied with a strongly worded rebuttal of the USSBS findings, arguing that the report "lacked focus strength, and impact to make it a compelling instrument" of measurement.[164] Regardless whether one agreed with the USAAF's arguments regarding the results of the strategic bombing campaigns over Europe and Japan or accepted the lukewarm response of the USSBS, a new method of warfare was now in the offing.

With the introduction of atomic warfare in the Pacific theater, strategic bombing received a significant boost from the associated technology of splitting the atom. Now a single aircraft with a single bomb could have devastating strategic results in a matter of minutes. If this was what future war would look like, what role were the other services to play in the next conflict? For the Air Force, now independent of the Army, this meant that it was now the leading service. For the Navy, atomic bombing was also possible through the use of naval aviation and the aircraft carrier. With both air fleets hoping to establish relevancy in the postwar world, a lingering question for the NME was how to balance roles, missions, and prioritization within a parsimonious budget.

Returning the nation to a peacetime economy was clearly a major aim of the Truman administration's postwar efforts. A strong American economy itself was seen as a bulwark against Communist international expansion in the postwar period. As the only major war participant with its full infrastructure intact, the United States found itself in a dominating economic position. Yet this did not necessarily mean the country could be profligate with its spending. In his 1947 State of the Union address, Truman argued, "National security does not consist of an army, navy, and an air force. . . . It depends upon a sound economy of prices and wages, on prosperous agriculture, on satisfied and productive workers, [and] on competitive private enterprise free from monopolistic repression."[165] Military expenditures thus took a back seat to other elements of the national budget, as consumerism and capitalism were viewed as the best antidotes to Communism generally. As a result of the recent victory over the Axis powers and in accordance with national tradition, the military services were again reduced in size and capability. More importantly, the nation was apparently secure because of its atomic monopoly.

Given Truman's budget priorities and the preexisting animosities between the Air Force and Navy, the idea of unifying the military services under a single organization served to put gas on smoldering embers still existing from interwar arguments. With the Air Force emerging as an independent service out from under the Army, would it again press for the expansion of its roles and missions at the expense of the Navy—especially with limited defense funds? Would land-based aviation supplant its naval counterpart? There had already been a precedent for this just a few years earlier in the United Kingdom.

During the interwar years the British also looked to reduce defense expenditures as a wave of antimilitary sentiment swept over the United Kingdom following World War I. Looking to cut costs and increase efficiency, London established an Air Ministry and enacted a "Dual Control" policy. In the Dual Control structure, the Air Ministry oversaw both the Royal Air Force (RAF) and the Royal Navy's Fleet Air Arm. With the ministry staffed largely with RAF personnel, and with the growing idea of strategic bombardment being a cheaper and more efficient way to conduct war, British naval aviation languished.

After the war, and with unification on the horizon, U.S. naval aviators were concerned that carriers and their associated air wings might languish as had their U.K. counterparts years earlier. If the air domain was the primary responsibility of the USAF, then it might be concluded that most aviation missions and assets—including those of the Navy and the Marine Corps—should fall under the purview of the new service. The idea of an American "Dual Control" equivalent was actually proposed at one point, validating the fear of those wearing Navy wings and gold braid. Secretary of the Army Kenneth C. Moore suggested in October 1948 that naval aviation be absorbed into the USAF as an organizational efficiency.[166] Although these proceedings were secret, word got out nonetheless. Moore's suggestion resulted in a flurry of discussion, accusations, and further entrenchment of service parochialism.

In response to this idea, Deputy CNO Vice Adm. Arthur Radford and Assistant Secretary of the Navy John Nicholas Brown countered that the USAF itself was not capable of accomplishing its primary mission with its current fleet of aircraft. The testimony given to the Federal Aviation Commission displeased Secretary of Defense Forrestal, who immediately issued guidance that the services were free to defend their own mission but were not to attack the competency of another service. When the Navy made additional accusations on 31 October, Forrestal directed the services to adjudicate their differences within his office, not in public. Furthermore, on 8 November he required all public speeches and presentations that criticized a sister service to be reviewed by his office first and that officers and civilian administrators exercise "great caution" when being questioned by outside organizations.[167] Regardless, in what has been referred to as the "Battle of the Mimeograph Machines," the Air Force and the Navy continued their information wars.[168]

Truman was not oblivious to the interservice feuding. Suspicious of flag-grade officers and the military in general, he believed that they wasted large sums of money while noting that "naval officers were engaged in propagandizing and lobbying" and likewise observed that the USAF "had no discipline."[169] The president thought the Navy's budget requests were especially extravagant and that CNO Louis Denfeld was one of the "worst offenders."[170] While Truman articulated no specific animosity toward any individual service, some noticed that the pictures depicting sailing ships and naval scenes in the White House had been replaced with prints of early generation airplanes from the dawn of flight.[171]

During Roosevelt's tenure, the Navy enjoyed a special status with the chief executive. A one-time undersecretary of the navy during World War I and designated as an honorary Marine, Roosevelt advocated naval development and approved many fiscal expenditures during his administration. The Navy also enjoyed a special status among those on Capitol Hill, with some in power claiming, "There are two governments in Washington, the Government of the United States and the United States Navy."[172] When President Roosevelt died in office, the Navy lost its most powerful advocate. While no longer having "most favored service" status within the White House, this did not mean the Navy was at a distinct disadvantage. Nevertheless, losing the special favor of the chief executive may have been, in the eyes of the Navy, more detrimental than ever having enjoyed it at all.

Despite Forrestal's attempt to stop the feuding, the Air Force–Navy quarrel continued in the open. In late 1948 *Reader's Digest*, a popular monthly periodical, ran a series of four articles that were critical of naval aviation and decidedly pro-USAF in tone. While *Reader's Digest* was not a government-sponsored entity, the articles were written by professional writer William Bradford Huie, a former sailor who eventually became an airpower advocate. During the war he published a book titled *The Fight for Air Power*, which argued for unification while criticizing the Navy's obstructionist views on the matter.[173] The first article appeared in December, with the other three published the following spring. It was widely concluded that Huie could not have written the articles without deliberate USAF help.[174] So pro-USAF was his message that Huie's works became required reading at the Air War College.[175] His claims were refuted in a very pointed manner in the halls of Congress in April 1949 by a Navy friendly representative, James Van Zant (R-PA). Van Zant argued, "Huie's articles not only evade the truth, they employ deliberate falsehoods to bolster a preconceived notion."[176] Internecine fights continued into 1949, coming to a head that autumn.

One of the significant events regarding roles and missions of the services was the Key West Conference, held in March 1948. Chaired by Secretary Forrestal and attended by the various service chiefs, this meeting was intended to hammer out the roles and missions of each military service. While attendees also discussed the role the Joint Chiefs of Staff would play in the NME, the larger issue was figuring out "which" services required "what" capabilities. This would go a long way in determining military requirements, responsibilities, force structure, and most importantly budget requests. One of the larger issues addressed was the ongoing Navy–Air Force feud. In the deliberations the USAF claimed responsibility for air warfare, especially strategic bombing. While the claim seemed reasonable enough, the Navy argued that that mission did not preclude the sea service from building the aviation capability required to maintain sea lines of communication. Yet a key provision of the conference was the establishment of collateral roles and missions, whereby one service could provide support to another in the execution of their primary mission. One of the key outcomes of the conference was a memorandum of record that seemed to address the Air Force–Navy dispute. In the memo the USAF denied any intent to "deny the Navy of its carriers."[177] For its part the Navy refuted the idea of building its own strategic air capability that would duplicate those of the USAF.[178] Nevertheless, the declaration was still open to interpretation.

One of the key individuals in the interservice fight was CNO Denfeld. After serving as commander in chief of the Pacific Fleet, Denfeld was surprised at the contentious nature of the unification process. Broaching the issue with his new boss Forrestal, the defense secretary replied, "Louis did you ever hear of the dollar. . . . Everybody is trying to get the largest chunk of the military dollar that Congress appropriates."[179] Ironically, as Truman looked to balance the federal budget and reduce military expenditures, the services looked for ways to purchase new and more expensive equipment.[180]

Connected to the issue of military budgets were arguments over roles and missions. The FY 1950 requests had yet to be finalized, and the services sought to stake out their requirements. In preparation for the NME budget submission, plans regarding the FY 1950 allocation started in July 1948, when Forrestal directed the services to submit their initial fiscal recommendations.[181] Preliminary guidance given to him by the president was not promising. The day before the secretary gave his guidance to the JCS, Truman reportedly said that "he was preparing, not for war, but for peace . . . and was basing his military strategy on the assumption that there would be no war."[182] Given the administration's concern for a strong peacetime economy and minimizing defense expenditures, Bureau of the Budget Director Frank Pace Jr. recommended that the NME budget ceiling be placed at $13.5 billion, with the three departments each given roughly an equal share.[183]

Unfortunately, the aggregate estimates from the three departments ballooned to $30 billion.[184] While Truman had held firm in earlier budget battles, the fight for FY 1950 was different. Up until this time each service looked upon itself as its own entity with little regard for joint operations.[185] Anticipating the JCS inability to reconcile the budget disparities, Forrestal established his own panel, staffed by officers of his own choosing, to review the submissions.[186] But in response Forrestal's effort, the JCS set up its own panel, known as the Budget Advisory Committee, in August 1948 and staffed it with representatives from the three services.

Even with the drop in expenditures for defense after the war, the cost for armaments remained a significant figure. Military planners were constantly having to consider the rising costs of maintaining current capabilities with Truman's plans of reducing overall defense expenditures. The military also used the standpoint of "an ounce of prevention is worth a pound of cure" by arguing that a solid, credible military deterrent was far cheaper than another large-scale war. In their thought process, if the United States looked weak militarily, it might entice the Soviets to attack, resulting in another costly conflict.

The emerging vision of a future war was based upon an air-centric application, with atomic weapons serving as the knockout blow to any potential enemy. Long-range strategic bombers were going to circumnavigate the globe, penetrate enemy air defenses, fly deep into an adversary's territory, and smash its infrastructure and war-making capabilities. In this scenario a single bomber could carry the war to the very heart of the enemy, with atomic weapons providing a quick victory. While wars of the future might take less time to decide, they would also be more destructive and impose higher casualty rates. As early as late 1945, Air Force leaders envisioned that the United States would not have the time to build military capability as had happened in the previous conflict.[187] For them, the nation needed a USAF "in being" and ready to strike. With this vision, the newly created service saw itself as preeminent, with the other services taking secondary roles. In remarks made in a 1948 radio address, Lt. Gen. Curtis E. LeMay, commanding general of the Strategic Air Command (SAC), declared, "Strategic bombardment is the most powerful weapon in the world today. It has rendered obsolete old geographical barriers which formerly determined the defense of a country."[188] But the Navy, still confident from its victories in the Pacific over the Imperial Japanese Navy fleet that carrier-based aviation was also able to navigate the globe, saw itself has having a role to play in the new air-centric atomic warfare. Some even went so far as to state that the Navy could lead the strategic atomic campaign, with the Air Force serving a defensive role.[189]

The USAF's main argument was that naval aviation did not possess aircraft with sufficient range to reach manufacturing regions deep inside Russia. Naval aircraft launching from ships were usually limited in size and weight. As a result, these warplanes were often single-engine designs with a smaller fuel capacity than their land-based counterparts. In testimony given before members of Congress, General Vandenberg pointed out that the bulk of Soviet industry, and subsequently USAF targets, lay well within the Russian land mass in the immense Moscow-Gorki-Ural region.[190] While reaching the Soviet Union could be accomplished relatively easily via polar routes, getting to targets deep inside the country required significant range. Such endurance could not be achieved by current naval aircraft.

As a demonstration of the USAF's ability to fly extended distances, in February 1949 a standard B-50 bomber nicknamed "Lucky Lady II" made a nonstop around-the-world flight using the emerging capability of in-flight refueling.[191] The flight covered 23,452 miles in ninety-four hours, refueling four times, with the plane carrying a normal load of .50-caliber machine guns (minus ammunition) and a bomb bay loaded with extra fuel tanks as a safety measure.[192] The extra fuel tanks could easily have been swapped for a bomb load of equal weight, with aerial refueling conducted as required. As a result, the USAF demonstrated that it had global range.

Moreover, during the Pacific War, the Navy's priceless aircraft carriers were usually steaming far from enemy shores in order to minimize their exposure to land-based attack. In the next war, even if the Navy was willing to send these most prized assets close to an enemy's shoreline, they would risk attack from land-based aircraft or short-range vessels utilizing emerging technologies. The development of antiship missiles and other radar-guided munitions could make the aircraft carrier even more vulnerable than it had been during the war. Even if the warships steamed closer to shore, USAF planners argued that naval attack aircraft lacked sufficient range to reach the Russian heartland.

In a briefing to the Senate in 1947, USAF Chief of Staff Spaatz graphically depicted the short legs of carrier aviation, pointing out that the best naval airpower could do was merely penetrate the littoral regions of the Soviet Union by a few hundred miles. In order to emphasize his point, he displayed maps showing the range fan of B-36s launching from various points on the globe compared to that of naval aircraft. The differences between the range fans were stark.

Conversely, there were some in the Navy who wanted naval aviation's role to continue growing. In a December 1947 memo to Deputy CNO Radford, Rear Adm. Dan Gallery observed, "The time is right now for the Navy to start an aggressive campaign aimed at proving that the Navy can deliver the atom bomb more effectively than the Air Force can."[193] This reversing of the strategic air offensive was problematic, given the sensitive nature of the unification issue. When the memo was made public, the USAF howled, and the CNO and the Secretary of the Navy publically apologized.[194]

But a year later, and just a month after the Key West Conference, CNO Denfeld suggested to Secretary Forrestal that the written agreement include a supplement that stated, "The Navy shall be prepared to participate in the overall air effort, . . . and the capabilities of naval aviation will be utilized to the maximum in the air offensive against vital strategic targets."[195] With this proposed inclusion, the CNO was trying to make some headway into strategic bombing. This was seen as a ploy to undercut the USAF and what it saw as its primary postwar mission. Upon hearing the suggestion, both Chief of Staff Spaatz and Secretary Symington rejected the idea outright, viewing it as a surreptitious effort to encroach on the strategic bombardment mission. As a result, the suggestion was largely ignored. Later that same year on Navy Day, 27 October, a number of public speeches by naval leadership continued to challenge the USAF claim. In Grosse Isle, Michigan, one admiral proclaimed to his audience, "To reach the heart of any continent in the world, the Navy can get more airpower over a target 6,000 miles away than you can get any other way."[196]

The icon of the USAF strategic fleet was the B-29 Superfortress. Classified a "Very Heavy Bomber," it was first proposed in 1940 and, once operational, was capable of flying from bases on Tinian in the Mariana Islands to Japan, a round trip of around three thousand miles. The design was a leap in aviation technology, and it required a significant part of the American aviation industry to develop and build the new bomber. Initially suffering from a number of design problems, the Superfortress did not fly its first mission until the summer of 1944. B-29s were infamously used to firebomb Tokyo in March 1945, before specially designed versions, called Silverplates, were used to drop the atomic bombs on Hiroshima and Nagasaki. By the end of the war, the airframe itself became symbolic of America's military might. In the postwar years the B-29 and an upgraded version, designated the B-50, were the mainstays of the strategic bombing fleet.

But even during the war, the Air Force was planning for a larger and more capable aircraft than the B-29. If the United States had to conduct strategic flights from North America, the B-29 was too limited in range. Planning for what would become the B-36 Peacemaker strategic bomber came as early as 1941. Specifications called for an aircraft with a range of 10,000 miles (with a combat radius of 4,000 miles) and a 72,000-pound payload capacity.[197] The B-36 became the symbol of the ascendency of the USAF immediately following the war and would serve as the lightning rod for interservice rivalry. Eventually designed with six rearward-mounted propeller engines, two jet engines on each wingtip, a wingspan of 230 feet, a crew of thirteen airmen, and a loaded weight of 260,000 pounds, the B-36 was referred to as a "Jesus Christ airplane" due to its incredible size.[198] The mockup for the bomber was inspected in July 1942, with the production model taking to the air in December 1947. The first B-36A was delivered to an operational squadron in the spring of 1948.

While the B-36 was an impressive aircraft in terms of size and potential range, it was more of an evolutionary step in bomber development than a revolutionary one. With the advent of jet engines and the development of swept wings, propeller-driven, straight-wing aircraft like the B-36 would soon be obsolete. Technologies developed during the war created a plethora of aviation advances and designs that increased aircraft ranges, payloads, and speeds. As a result the B-36 was largely looked upon as an interim solution and not the "ultimate" in bomber design.

Like most new aircraft, the B-36 suffered from a number of design maladies that took years to fully correct. Initially unimpressed with the aircraft, the first commander of SAC, Gen. George Kenney expressed his misgivings about the B-36 to Chief of Staff Spaatz. Kenney recommended that the entire program be reviewed, questioned the aircraft's performance in terms of range and speed, and claimed it was vulnerable to enemy fire because it lacked self-sealing fuel tanks.[199] Installing self-sealing tanks would add to the aircraft's already heavy weight and further decrease its performance.[200] Moreover, in order to outrun enemy fighters, the B-36 would need to burn more fuel, thus decreasing its range further. The counterargument for the bomber was that subsequent models might make up for these initial performance deficiencies. But with the development of jet engines and better aerodynamic designs, many questioned the survivability of the B-36 given the Soviet's new jet fighter.

The Russian MiG-15 was equipped with a Soviet copy of the British Rolls-Royce Nene jet engine. With swept wings, a service altitude of 50,000 feet, and capable of speeds approaching 700 mph, the MiG-15 was a formidable aircraft for any large bomber trying to penetrate Russian airspace. The design was a true leap in Soviet aviation technology. The jet fighter paired with an effective air-defense radar network might then make the B-36 an easy target to defeat. Despite concerns, the USAF continued with the development of the B-36 for now, with faster, more capable bombers planned for the future. While later models addressed many of the early performance issues, including having new engines and additional jet power plants installed, many viewed the bomber as a "white elephant." One naval officer referred to its expense and vulnerability by calling it the "3 billion dollar blunder."[201]

Initial operations with the B-36 were less than stellar. Of the forty aircraft delivered, only about a half dozen were ever considered combat ready.[202] A shortage of spare parts forced ground crews to cannibalize parts from one aircraft to make others airworthy. This shortage became a concern for the second SAC commander. Lieutenant General LeMay in May 1949 phoned Lt. Gen. Benjamin Chidlaw, deputy commanding general of the Air Material Command in Dayton, Ohio, to address an administrative matter. When Chidlaw pressed him about the "B-36 versus fighter war," LeMay replied that he was more concerned about the "B-36 versus spare parts war." He then mentioned that he was thinking about telling Chief of Staff Spaatz that the Consolidated-Vultee Aircraft Corporation (Convair), manufacturer of the B-36, should "not turn out any more 36s until the ones they already had can be supported with spare parts."[203] Despite the internal gripes with it, the bomber eventually gained support within the USAF.

Given the emphasis on strategic bombing, the B-36 was viewed as an imperative for the USAF. Regardless of the service's budget, it became the priority over other airframes, much to the chagrin of other USAF communities. Given the paltry budget, in the winter of 1948–49 a board of senior USAF officers determined how to reprioritize and allocate the service's budget.[204] To make allowances for the bomber, thirty RB-49s were cut, with a savings of $103.5 million.[205] This was made because the B-36 was considered a more capable airframe than the B-49. With this reallocation of money, the USAF proposed to purchase thirty-nine additional B-36s and modify ninety-four others.[206]

Outside the DoD, others raised questions about the B-36 and its role in national security. Budget Director Pace expressed concerns about the expenditure of such large amounts of money for the new aircraft. He worried that future capital investment in both the bomber and in the AEC might create a "straightjacket" approach to national security. In his estimation a strategic bomber force might become the default answer to any national security exigency, writing, "If the initial defensive strategy is based on plans for the mass atomic bombing of 70 Soviet targets, the president may be effectively committed in advance of an emergency. . . . [T]his strategy calls for atomic attack at the outset of war, the very timing of the situation would put the president in a most awkward position if he desired to alter the strategy in the midst of the intense pressures of the hour."[207] Pace suggested that Truman reevaluate the B-36 as the default response to a national security emergency. For many outside the Air Force, including those at the Navy, this seemed like a good idea.

The USAF saw the Navy's carrier-launched air fleet, with smaller, less capable airframes, as ancillary to the larger strategic effort. In 1946 the Navy had only just started to develop an airframe capable of carrying a 10,000-pound atomic bomb from a sea-based platform. Seeing a role for naval aviation in the atomic offensive, the Navy's Bureau of Aeronautics began planning for a carrier aircraft that could deliver such a weapon.[208] The Navy's AJ-1 Savage was designed as a medium bomber capable of carrying a 10,000-pound load. While not initially designed as an atomic platform, the Savage was modified to carry an atomic payload approximately eight hundred miles.[209] Early designs had the AJ-1 weighing 30,000 pounds fully loaded and able to operate off the Navy's largest *Midway*-class carriers. But the design soon ballooned to 45,000 pounds, then to 100,000 pounds, which would require an entirely new kind of aircraft carrier (and accompanying support vessels). By the early fall of 1947, the Navy accelerated the AJ-1 program, with the flight of the first production model taking place in May 1949.[210]

But like the B-36, the AJ-1 also suffered from a number of design flaws. Initial models of the Savage lacked the intended bombing and navigations system, thus it relied on older, less capable ones for years. The airframe also suffered from faults in its hydraulic, fuel, and flight-control systems in addition to power-plant problems. As a result the plane's safety record was awful, with numerous crashes and lost aircrews. Subsequent redesigns never fully solved these problems, and it remained a hexed aircraft. Eventually, flight crews began calling the Savage "Pride's Folly," after the head of the Bureau of Aeronautics, Rear Adm. Alfred M. Pride, who had first championed the design.[211]

Simultaneously, the Navy was looking to another airframe to carry atomic ordnance. It tested the land-based P2V Neptune long-range maritime-patrol aircraft as a carrier-launched atomic bomber. In March 1949 a modified P2V (designated P2V-3C) was craned aboard USS *Coral Sea* fully loaded. The Navy fitted the aircraft, which weighed some 74,000 pounds, with eight rocket-assisted take-off packets providing additional thrust to the plane's engines. Using all nine hundred feet of the carrier's flight deck, and with its starboard wingtip missing the carrier's superstructure by only ten feet, the Neptune cleared the ship and successfully took to the air.[212] Once airborne, it was considered too heavy to land back on the ship.[213] The crew flew from a location off the Virginia coast to Muroc, California, and dropped a simulated atomic weapon. Afterward, the aircraft returned to the East Coast, landing at Patuxent River Naval Air Station, Maryland. While a success, the Neptune was hardly a true sea-based atomic-weapon delivery platform. If the Navy was going to leverage the P2V-3C, a carrier would need to be moored in port, have the modified Neptune craned aboard, then steam to the launch point—hardly a stealthy or expeditious application of atomic force.[214]

While the P2V had significant range for a sea-based platform (some 4,800 nautical miles), its airspeed was slowed appreciably by carrying such a heavy payload. The Neptune flew a little over 300 mph with its two R-3350 piston engines. But the P2V-3C, like the B-36, could have been easy prey for any swift, jet-powered MiGs trolling for incoming aircraft and guided by air-defense radar.[215] The P2V was also too heavy for the arresting gear that slowed landing aircraft on a carrier and was therefore unable to return to its launch ship. As a result its crew had two options upon returning from an atomic attack: land at a friendly airfield within range of the aircraft's flight characteristics or ditch in the ocean—hopefully alongside a U.S. recovery vessel to save both crew and aircraft. While the Navy built eleven versions of the P2V-3C variant, it was not really a viable solution for operational use. More importantly, the Neptune could only carry the MK I uranium-based Little Boy bomb because the girth of the MK III Fat Man precluded it fitting into the plane's bomb bay.[216] Unknown to the Navy at this time, the AEC had no MK I bombs available, with none in production. Yet with this clumsy and poorly coordinated arrangement in place, the Navy could at least claim it had an atomic-delivery capability.[217]

Given the eight hundred-mile range of the AJ-1 and the shortcomings of the P2V-3C, naval aviation would be at a disadvantage in trying to reach the all-important Russian industrial centers.[218] This same argument was echoed by the chair of the House Appropriations Committee, Rep. Clarence Cannon (D-MO), who argued, "The Air Force is now considered our first line of American defense and will get the lion's share of military airpower funds.... Why should we waste vast sums of money on naval planes? ... Let us spend it for long-range land based bombers."[219] Furthermore, in a classified briefing in 1947, the USAF argued that aircraft carriers and other surface vessels in the postwar environment were now more vulnerable to air attacks, especially from newly developed radio- or radar-guided weapons.[220] Two years later, with cost cutting as a primary concern within the defense establishment, the USAF appeared to be winning its argument against naval aviation. In June 1949

Secretary of Defense Louis Johnson announced that the number of *Essex*-class carriers was to be cut from eight to four, with the smaller *Saipan*-class carriers cut from ten to eight. In addition to the reduction in carrier numbers, the associated air wings were also to shrink, from fourteen to six, with Marine Corps squadrons reduced almost by half.[221] Yet from a Navy perspective, the problems with the B-36 and its performance were a significant issue. Relying on only one application for American defense was part of the concern.

For the Navy, attacking the Soviet Union required a wider effort that included various strikes from numerous locations. Its bombing aperture was much larger, with aircraft operating from multiple forward bases on the periphery of the Soviet Union instead of the single polar route embraced by the USAF. Furthermore, attacking vital enemy production capability as proposed by the Air Force would yield no immediate results, according to the Navy. Through the use of mobile airfields (carriers) in concert with fixed bases in Europe, naval air could strike distribution nodes and supporting networks that would have an immediate and devastating effect upon the enemy's combat power and operational reach. Although bombing production centers and factories was effective for a long-term campaign, the Navy expected an enemy to have up to a six-month stockpile of supplies and equipment. Thus, the concept of strategic bombing was tantamount to a siege mentality that was counterproductive to offensive operations. For naval aviators, B-36s flying from fixed airbases violated the military principles of mobility, flexibility, and surprise. Smaller platforms launched from various locations simultaneously would tax enemy air defenses and have a more immediate effect on capability than a strategic campaign.[222]

With these competing mindsets, the Navy–Air Force rivalry was again clearly in play in the postwar environment. Indicative of the animosity between the two services, when LeMay addressed students at the Air Command and Staff College at Maxwell Air Force Base in September 1949, a student asked him why the nation should rely on strategic bombers when fast naval carriers could do the same job using moving bases. Pausing a moment, the lieutenant general condescendingly replied, "If you don't know [by now], its too late [for you]."[223]

USS *United States*

As the situation between the Air Force and Navy festered for years, the relationship started becoming fully malignant in the spring of 1949 after Louis Johnson replaced James Forrestal as secretary of defense. The recent fight between these branches now focused upon two material solutions with each service considered imperative—the Air Force's B-36 and the Navy's supercarrier USS *United States* (CVA 58). Both of these material solutions were foundational components of their respective services future. Much like the interwar years, the lines between service responsibilities and missions were again becoming unclear.

As early as October 1945, the Navy looked to build a bigger, more capable aircraft carrier that could handle larger and heavier airplanes.[224] Unceremoniously titled Project A, the new ship would have a flush deck, meaning it would not have the superstructure island seen on the starboard side of conventional U.S. carriers. While monies for the ship had yet to be fully appropriated, the Navy began the design process in 1947 and expected to obtain funding for the vessel in Fiscal Year 1949.[225]

The new design was without a doubt a marked improvement from the previous *Essex*- and *Midway*-class carriers. The envisioned ship could launch an aircraft (like the AJ-1 Savage) weighing as much as 100,000 pounds—twice as much as its predecessors. CVA 58 would also weigh appreciably more, displacing some 65,000 tons compared to a *Midway*-class carriers' 45,000 tons.[226] To support flight operations for larger and heavier aircraft, the new design was roughly twenty feet wider abeam and well over one hundred feet longer than previous carriers. In addition to flight-support operations, CVA 58 would also incorporate a number of improvements in ship survivability, crew quality of life, and damage-control features.

Conversely, the USAF was not only looking at procurement of the B-36 but also lobbying to increase its number of active groups from fifty-five to seventy. Underpinning its argument were two committees that echoed much the same sentiment about the future of airpower. In 1947 Truman established the Air Policy Commission, headed by Philadelphia lawyer Thomas K. Finletter. What eventually became known as the Finletter Commission explored the role of both military and civilian aviation in hopes of identifying the "greatest possible benefit from aviation."[227] In the end, the commission recommended that the USAF expand to seventy air groups, with part of that expansion accommodating seven hundred heavy bombers.[228] Similarly, Congress established its own panel to review airpower requirements in the future. Called the Hinshaw-Brewster Committee, it also supported expansion to seventy groups. To USAF leaders, the seventy-group structure merely represented the minimal needs for the service, and anything less was considered a step back in both readiness and capability. By April 1949, with help from Rep. Carl Vinson (D-GA), a previous proponent of naval aviation, the USAF received approval from the House Appropriations Committee for its seventy-group structure while lawmakers reduced the budgets for both the Navy and the Army.[229] The decision was to the consternation of the other services and Secretary Forrestal, who had a quarrelsome relationship with Air Force Secretary Symington.[230] But the battle over the Pentagon's budget was far from over.

With the passage of the initial National Security Act, Forrestal became the first secretary of defense on 17 September 1947. The irony of his new appointment was that, as the former Secretary of the Navy, he had overseen the service that was the biggest opponent to unification. But Forrestal's biggest challenge was his rapport with his boss. As time passed, his relationship with Truman eroded, and the secretary eventually lost the chief executive's trust. While he enjoyed a solid reputation in the Roosevelt administration as Secretary of the Navy, Forrestal was never within Truman's inner circle, and his loyalty to the president remained suspect.[231] This lack of confidence in him was further exacerbated by the rumor that Forrestal politically flirted with Republican presidential challenger Thomas Dewey. During the 1948 election cycle, rumors circulated that he lobbied Dewey to stay on as defense secretary if the Republican candidate won.[232]

Months before his formal resignation in 28 March 1949, most people concluded that Forrestal's days were numbered.[233] The continuing squabbling between the Air Force and the Navy and other issues related to national defense were a challenge for Forrestal's leadership abilities.[234] The first defense secretary led by consensus rather than authority.[235] He preferred to value teamwork over decree, harmony over hostility. Given the interservice fights during this time, his management style failed to address the ill will resulting from unification. Often viewed as weak and ineffectual, Forrestal, Truman concluded, suffered from indecisiveness and appeared unable to make decisions independently. The president grew tired of his constant requests for guidance. During the Berlin Crisis in 1948, Truman wrote of this frustration in his diary, "Jim [Forrestal] wants to hedge—he always does."[236] In one instance Forrestal sought the president's opinion about a problem only to have him reply, "That's your responsibility."[237] Further evidence of Truman's displeasure with Forrestal's decision-making skills was a conversation he had with his naval aide, Rear Adm. Robert L. Dennison. When the chief executive queried Dennison as to who the secretary of defense was, the aide replied, "Jim Forrestal." To this Truman responded, "You're wrong! I'm the Secretary of Defense. . . . Jim calls me several times a day asking me to make a decision on matters that are completely within his competence, but passes them to me."[238]

The chief issues for Truman were the large defense budget and Forrestal's apparent inability to corral the military services, which in his opinion consistently "bulldozed" Forrestal.[239] In addition to a deteriorating reputation, Forrestal's mental health also declined, as he became increasingly paranoid and indecisive in the final months of his tenure. Fearing enemies all around him and convinced that he was under constant surveillance from various dubious organizations, he was truly mentally ill. This was also reflected in his physical appearance, as General of the Army Dwight Eisenhower remarked: "Jim is looking badly. He gives his mind no recess, and he works hours that would kill a horse."[240] Others, like AEC Commissioner Lewis Strauss, described the secretary's appearance as "haggard."[241] Scarcely a month after his resignation, a gaunt and sallow Forrestal was admitted to Bethesda Naval Hospital on an inpatient status for depression. Despite apparent progress in his emotional and mental state, Forrestal's illness got the better of him. He jumped to his death from the sixteenth floor of the hospital in the early morning hours of 22 May 1949.[242]

Months before Forrestal's resignation, Louis Johnson was already making plans to insert himself into the Truman administration. A lawyer from West Virginia with a large physical frame to match his oversized ego, Johnson was a key player in Truman's 1948 election campaign. Ambitious and energetic, he started his political career while in his mid-twenties and won a seat in the state legislature in 1916. He interrupted his political career to serve in the Army during World War I.[243] After participating in the Saint Mihiel and Meuse-Argonne Campaigns, Johnson continued his political endeavors. But at the end of his term in the state legislature, he decided not to run again for elected office. He returned to practicing law while remaining politically active and helping establish the American Legion.

He secured a position as the assistant secretary of war in the Roosevelt administration, serving from 1937 to 1940. But his relationship with his superior, Secretary of War Harry Woodring, was fraught with conflict and disagreement.[244] With Woodring an isolationist and Johnson an interventionist, the two clashed over the need to increase defense procurement and allocation—especially for aircraft.[245] Brig. Gen. George C. Marshall, then acting Army chief of staff, had to deal with this internecine squabbling, later calling it "the most miserable experience of my life."[246] In November 1938, under direction from President Roosevelt, Johnson asked the USAAC to develop a detailed plan for an expansion to 10,000 planes in as little as two years.[247] While the American aviation industry was not yet ready for such an increase in production, Johnson was keen to see the nation's airpower grow as war clouds loomed. When Woodring submitted a heated letter of resignation to the president over the dubious legal status of arms shipments to Great Britain before America's entry into World War II, Johnson stood poised to succeed him. But to everyone's surprise, and much to Johnson's chagrin, Roosevelt named Henry Stimson as secretary of war.

Additionally, Johnson suffered a further political blow when passed over for Henry Wallace as Roosevelt's running mate at the 1940 Democratic National Convention. Disappointed and frustrated, the West Virginian left Washington and, for a short period of time, served as liaison to the Indian government for American Lend-Lease.[248] After the war he was on the board of directors for a number of major companies, including Consolidated-Vultee. But Johnson eventually worked his way back to Washington as a major fundraiser in Truman's 1948 campaign. With the president's growing dissatisfaction with Forrestal, Johnson's reward for his political patronage was appointment as the next secretary of defense.

Assuming his duties on 28 March 1949, Johnson looked to make his mark. Where Forrestal was a consensus builder, Johnson was a pugilist, using force, intimidation, and bullying on those who stood in his way. One news outlet described Johnson as a "tornado that walks like a man, . . . kicking anything that gets in his way," while an official Army history commented on his "relentless drive and tireless energy."[249] Fully supporting Truman's limited military budget and getting the respective services under control, the new secretary wasted little time enacting his agenda. According to one observer, "Johnson viewed the military establishment and [the] Navy in particular as his personal and deadly enemy." Because of this, Johnson worked to eliminate much of the Navy's air arm while subsuming the Marines under the Army.[250]

Perhaps what drove Johnson more than anything else was his own political ambition to one day win the White House. As Woodring, his old boss at the War Department, commented, "Many men are overambitious, Louis is overambitious. It is sort of like being oversexed."[251] If he could establish himself as a Washington insider, he would be in a good position for a presidential run. *New York Times* military-affairs correspondent Hanson Baldwin loathed Johnson and saw his appointment as a disaster due to these political ambitions. According to Baldwin, "everything Johnson did was approached from a political point of view."[252] With this motivation, the secretary would not necessarily do what was right for national defense but only what was right for Louis Johnson. Although he agreed with the president's desire to cut military spending, many saw him as a poor choice. One administration member argued, "He's made two enemies for every dollar he's saved."[253] This ambition did not go unnoticed by Truman, who believed as early as August 1949 that his new defense secretary intended to be a presidential candidate in 1952. Truman later commented, "Louis began to show an inordinate egotistical desire to run the whole government."[254]

One of the first issues Johnson attacked was the USS *United States*. Wanting to appear both decisive and energetic, he saw the Navy program as a suitable target. Given his perceived mandate for cost cutting, Johnson sought to strike the $43 million for the supercarrier's construction.[255] In addition to his frugality, Johnson was also pro-USAF. His earlier tenure as assistant secretary of war displayed this tendency. With his rash personality and driving political ambition, Johnson was not prone to deep reflective thinking, extensive study, or weighing numerous complex variables.[256] With interservice rivalry growing, the secretary remarked that he might need to "knock some heads together."[257] For him, action was more important than reflection, and time was of the essence.

Little less than a year earlier, in June 1948, the Navy had secured congressional approval for CVA 58, and the service agreed to stop modifying other vessels in future budget allocations in order to procure the new carrier. The allocation of funds in the FY 1949 budget for the ship was approved by the budget director, the secretary of defense, the president, and the House and Senate Armed Services Committees.[258] Laying of the keel for the new ship was scheduled for 15 April 1949, only a few weeks after Johnson assumed his new responsibilities. Skeptical of the program anyway, the new secretary was afraid that if the supercarrier was canceled or further allocations of funds were disapproved, any construction on the ship would be a waste of time and money. Johnson had a meeting with Navy Secretary Sullivan on 18 April regarding various service-related matters, but the topic of the new carrier was never broached.[259] The next day Sullivan forwarded a letter to him requesting a meeting to discuss CVA 58. Johnson agreed and promised to make no decisions prior to the meeting with Sullivan. But such a meeting never took place.[260]

At the earlier JCS meeting in Key West, Florida, in March 1948, the topic of the flush-deck supercarrier was brought to the table. Forrestal presented CVA 58 as something of a fait accompli.[261] Yet funding and appropriations for the vessel and its accompanying air fleet were still pending congressional approval.[262] For the USAF, the new carrier was a mere duplication of its own strategic-bombardment mission. If the Air Force was America's "big stick" in terms of future military application, why did the Navy need to have a similar capability? Given the defense budget, many thought this was clearly a waste of money—not to mention an encroachment on USAF mission sets. On 15 April 1949 Johnson sent a letter to Eisenhower (who was a principal military advisor to the president for military matters) and to each member of the JCS asking for their opinions regarding the supercarrier.[263] Days later the three service chiefs forwarded their positions. The responses were entirely expected given the fiscal situation.

Obviously, CNO Denfeld was the chief proponent of the vessel. He argued that naval aviation had obtained an "undisputed offensive capability" and that the ship was "necessary for the progressive improvement of naval capabilities." For the Navy, the design and size of USS *United States* was necessary

- to operate the heavier aircraft required to attain higher performance, increased endurance, and carry the more complex armament and electronic equipment presently available;
- to operate large numbers of smaller aircraft, particularly fighters;
- to provide essential antiaircraft armament, radar and communications equipment in the ship itself;
- to carry fuel essential for prolonged operations of both ship and aircraft; and
- to provide the armor and compartmentation to withstand air or submarine attack.[264]

For Denfeld, the ship was never intended or designed to conduct "strategic" bombing. Furthermore, this was not intended as any part of the naval concept of war.[265]

But Army Chief of Staff Gen. Omar Bradley saw things differently. In his written response to the secretary of defense, Bradley argued that naval aviation had a sufficient number of aircraft carriers and that the new supercarrier would employ heavy long-range bombers that the USAF already had to perform this function. He argued further that buying the carrier would require the purchase of support vessels, aircraft, and other equipment that would preclude a balanced approach to national defense expenditures. Bradley went on to argue that the construction of USS *United States* or additional aircraft carriers was "militarily unsound."[266]

USAF Chief of Staff Vandenberg argued much the same as Bradley, claiming the Navy's carrier was inferior to the land-based capabilities of his newly independent service.[267] In a letter written earlier that year, he had rejected the idea of the new carrier for a number of reasons: The usefulness of the carriers bigger than the current designs had not yet been established; the same was true for larger aircraft operating from current carrier designs; and given the fiscal environment, the program could not be deemed essential for national defense.[268] In direct response to Johnson's query, Vandenberg argued that the role of the new carrier was already a mission conducted by the USAF and that the USSR, because it was not a naval power, did not require the maintenance of any sea lines of communication. He argued further that a seven-hundred-mile radius of action from current naval aircraft was sufficient to conduct the Navy's missions. Besides, according to Vandenberg, carrier aviation was only good as a temporary force until the USAF provided the sustained operations necessary against an enemy.[269]

Days later Vandenberg wrote to Secretary of Defense Johnson, noting that the JCS were, at that time, using a "red brick" method of determining requirements.[270] The term "red brick" referred to the basic materials needed to build a strong and stable house. Thus, "red brick" requirements were what Eisenhower had defined as "the absolute minimum unit or force essential to meet the requirements [for] the strategic [defensive] concept[s]."[271] In this regard Vandenberg "could not agree to any carrier of this type on a red brick basis."[272] This is not say that the USAF chief wanted to eradicate the carrier fleet, for he believed they were still required for maintaining sea lines of communication and antisubmarine operations. Yet he rejected the idea of a new carrier type specifically designed for bombardment operations.[273] Adding to the Navy's woes was Eisenhower's concurrence that the ship should be canceled.[274]

With this input from the various services, a desire to keep military expenditures down, and wanting to appear decisive and engaged in his new post, on 23 April Johnson canceled USS *United States*. Before issuing his decision he checked in with Representative Vinson and Sen. Millard Tydings (D-MD), the respective chairmen of the House and Senate Armed Services Committees, and then notified the president.[275] With only eight days passing since the ship's keel was laid, the cornerstone of what the Navy had thought was their new flagship and an important step in the advancement of naval aviation was canceled. Making matters worse for the Navy was the fact that Johnson had made his decision without first consulting CNO Denfeld or Navy Secretary Sullivan.[276] The defense secretary never allowed any redress from Navy leadership. While he earlier promised Sullivan a follow-up discussion on the carrier and a delay on any decision regarding the ship until after the two men had another consultation, Johnson had in fact lied.[277]

There was never a subsequent meeting with Sullivan or any other Navy representative before Johnson canceled CVA 58. His decision completely blindsided Navy leadership. Johnson failed to inform Sullivan in person; the Navy Secretary learned of the cancellation by phone call. An incredulous Denfeld received the news only forty-five minutes *after* he submitted his memo to Secretary Johnson regarding the ship.[278] For Denfeld and the rest of the naval aviation community, this act was the result of the USAF's desire to downplay the Navy and severely cut funding for the development of its air arm. Furthermore, those in the naval services also viewed it as part of a larger effort by the Air Force, in collusion with the Army, to finally minimize their ground counterpart and rival, the Marine Corps. With the loss of Marine aviation, the Corps could be reduced to little more than a garrison force with limited combat power.

Having heard about the cancellation over the phone, Sullivan returned to Washington in a rage. Despite a quickly scheduled meeting with Truman about the issue on 25 April, the president yielded his authority to Johnson.[279] As a result of Johnson's actions, the next day an infuriated Sullivan fired off a resignation letter as Secretary of the Navy to his immediate superior. (While undeniably a letter of protest, it may have lacked sufficient punch, as Sullivan had asked Truman earlier in March 1949 to leave office for personal reasons.) It specifically called out Johnson's failure to allow further discussion over CVA 58 and the surreptitious manner in which its cancellation was announced. The tone was clear, with Sullivan expressing his disgust, but it was written in the most diplomatic language possible. Sullivan pointed out that the defense secretary acted "drastically and arbitrarily."[280] He fired off a second letter, this one to the president, though it showed no animosity toward the chief executive and was a cordial submission. Sullivan only made a passing reference to the situation that had unfolded, writing Truman, "I regret the circumstances that prevent me from continuing in my present post."[281] In his farewell address Sullivan hinted publicly at his ire for Johnson when he told those assembled that he was leaving "a Navy that no *foreign* foe has ever defeated."[282]

While the Navy Secretary decided to make a statement with his resignation, as did Undersecretary W. John Kenney, CNO Denfeld decided to try and fight for the naval services.[283] Some thought that the admiral might exacerbate the effect of Sullivan's departure by following the path of his civilian superior.

While a CNO resignation might have sent another important message to the president and fired a proverbial "shot across the bow" to the rest of the NME (soon to be the DoD), Denfeld believed that the better course of action was to remain in his current post. He thought he could do the most good for the naval services by carrying on the fight over roles, missions, and especially the budget. Denfeld continued as CNO and was even approved for a second term in August. But his second term was cut very short—and rather abruptly.

With the departure of Sullivan, a new Navy Secretary was required. Through the grapevine, an Irish Catholic financer by the name of Francis Matthews came to the fore. A virtual unknown by the political operatives, Matthews was an active Democratic Party loyalist who had played a role in the last presidential campaign.[284] A committed Roman Catholic and member of the Knights of Columbus, he was appointed a papal chamberlain by Pius XII and offered a post in the Vatican if he ever desired.[285] Johnson had never met Matthews, but his religious faith had an appeal. As a Catholic, Matthews would be an ideal choice to replace Sullivan, who was of the same faith. If Johnson wanted to secure the White House in a future election, appointing a Catholic made political sense as it would appeal to those important voters in a 1952 presidential run.[286] While this was not necessarily an unusual method of picking a political appointee, what was curious was the nominee's distinct lack of experience for the job.

Matthews was a midwesterner from Omaha, Nebraska, whose background was in law and financing; the appointment would be his first federal job. During the war, he had worked with the United Service Organization but never served in any military capacity or with the naval services. Coming from Nebraska and lacking significant familiarity with ships, an ocean, or even a shoreline, he joked that his only naval experience was owning a rowboat at his summer home in Minnesota.[287] By admitting as much, he was derisively referred to as the "rowboat secretary."[288] While Matthews himself acknowledged a lack of experience for the job of Secretary of the Navy, he claimed to be a quick study. He argued further that his responsibilities would be largely administrative, leaving the military problems to the admirals.[289]

What made Matthews even more attractive as an appointee was that as a Washington outsider, he would easily fall in line with the dictates of the secretary of defense, his mandate for cutting the budget, and his drive for service unification at the expense of naval aviation. Unfamiliar with either the military or the Pentagon and indebted to Johnson and Truman for his appointment, Matthews was a safe bet. He was an earnest and honest man who had a sterling reputation in Nebraska. But naval officers were skeptical of his appointment and never warmed to the new secretary. According to future CNO Arleigh Burke, Matthews' relationship with naval leadership was problematic: "He isolated himself, and he opposed most everything naval officers did. He didn't trust anybody."[290] Others made similar observations, with one naval officer deftly crafting a mixed comparison: "Matthews was badly miscast—a Cinderella in Wonderland."[291]

The manner in which Johnson conducted the CVA 58 affair did not escape notice by Truman, congressional legislators, or the press. Although many criticized him for what they perceived as an overreach of authority by canceling a ship that had both congressional and presidential approval, Johnson was within his authority to make the decision. With his continued suspicion of the secretary's motives, Hanson Baldwin questioned his unilateral decision and feared that such choices based upon a single individual's judgment might prove detrimental in the future.[292] Other members of the press expressed similar sentiments, arguing that the decision was a "violation of the spirit of the Key West Agreement" and was "not unification but disintegration."[293] A month later, on 17 May, Rep. Henry Latham (R-NY) introduced into the *Congressional Record* an article from *American Aviation* titled "A New Maginot Line," by James Haggerty.[294] The piece included much the same argument the Navy had been making all along and called into question the efficacy of the B-36.

Furthermore, for the president, the defense secretary's dismissive attitude and ham-fisted action was inappropriate and disquieting in tone. What Johnson probably did not realize at the time was that Sullivan was highly regarded by Truman. After receiving his letter of resignation, the president claimed that he did not blame Sullivan for resigning.[295] Johnson's brusque and impolitic manner during this event left a bad impression with the chief executive, especially with the press questioning the secretary's decision and its possible effects in the national interest. While the sea services lost this particular battle, some in the

Navy were not willing to merely lay down at the feet of the defense secretary. A few were willing to resort to subterfuge and deceit.

The "Dirt Sheet"

With the Navy reeling over the loss of its aircraft carrier and its seemingly second-place status vis-à-vis the Air Force, the interservice rivalry remained tense. Unfortunately for the Navy, the situation would go from bad to worse. The vision of USAF strategic bombing was gaining strength as the budget for the B-36 grew. While the procurement process for an additional thirty-nine B-36s (thirty-two bombers and seven reconnaissance versions) had been in the works for months, on 8 April Truman approved allocation of an additional $172,994,000 for these airframes.[296] Also in June, as mentioned earlier, Secretary Johnson unveiled further cuts in the number of carriers and accompanying air wings.

Even before these issues came to the fore, as little as a year into the unification process, the Navy had already decided it needed an organization dedicated to monitoring all activities that might pose a problem to its missions. Given the existing service rivalries, in December 1948 CNO Denfeld appointed Captain Arleigh Burke, a decorated war veteran with an excellent reputation, to head what became known as OP-23, formally titled Organizational Research and Policy Division.[297] OP-23 was specifically designed to monitor the unification process, identify potential issues, and keep naval leadership abreast of developments.[298] Yet according to historian Walter Millis, the real purpose of OP-23 was to do battle with the USAF.[299] When finally on board, Burke met with CNO Denfeld about his posting, during which the Navy chief gave the captain a disconcerting five-minute briefing. Denfeld told Burke that all naval aviation and the Marine Corps were in danger from the establishment of the USAF and the advent of intercontinental bombing. Hearing this, Burke realized that the naval services were in "desperate trouble" if the USAF and the Joint Chiefs had their way.[300]

Given the distrust among the services, Burke was fully aware that OP-23 could be seen as a disreputable agent within the defense establishment. Eventually, to those outside of the Navy, it was seen as part of the unification problem, serving only the interests of the naval services at the expense of the others.

Hoping to maintain good standing, Burke went so far as to establish guidelines for operations in order to keep his office out of the internecine political fray.[301] Toward this end, he instructed his assigned personnel to act with "scrupulousness" and in a transparent manner.[302] In addition to monitoring legislative actions, OP-23 also became involved in compiling data and information regarding CVA 58, the merits of naval aviation, and the progress of the B-36. Regardless of Burke's intent, by the fall of 1949, OP-23's reputation, as well as the reputation of many of its members, would be permanently damaged.

Not only were Navy aviation roles and missions in serious jeopardy of being completely dismantled, but the current tone also led to a decline in sailor morale. As with many in the ranks, dark humor was—and remains—a way to deal with disappointment. Reeling from the number of budgetary and mission setbacks, a little ditty about Secretary Johnson's dislike of the naval services and the cancellation of CVA 58 came about, titled "O'Kay Louis Drop Your Gun":

All right Louis, drop our giant
We are sad, but not defiant
We can even be suppliant
All right Louis, drop our giant

Louis, save us our Marines—
Stick to the ribs like Navy beans
Take the last cent out of our jeans
But Louis, leave us our Marines

All right Louis, of renown
Don't pot-shot our heavenly crown—
Without our flyboys we'd drown
And freedom of the seas go down

All right Louis, drop your gun
Before we hit the setting sun
You're not fool'n anyone
Fights at sea must still be won.[303]

With such an outlook, members of the sea service took it upon themselves to fight against the rising popularity of strategic airpower at the expense of naval aviation and looked to force a larger dialogue on the matter. With a larger forum, they could possibly make a better argument in the chambers of Congress and in the eyes of the public than they had in the halls of the Pentagon.[304]

One of the men who endorsed the idea of forcing the issue to a larger forum was Cdr. Tom Davies, aide to Vice CNO Radford.[305] Davies was a noteworthy naval aviator who had flown a modified PV2 Neptune on a record-setting long-distance endurance flight in September 1946. Traveling from Perth, Australia, to Columbus, Ohio, he and his crew flew more than 11,000 miles in fifty-five hours in a plane subsequently christened "The Turtle."[306] In addition to his responsibilities to Radford, Davies was given additional duties as assistant head of OP-23 under Captain Burke. Davies, hoping to highlight naval aviation's plight, enlisted the support of Cedric Worth a Naval Reserve officer with a background in journalism and public affairs who worked as a special assistant to Undersecretary of the Navy for Air Dan Kimball.[307] Conveniently, Worth, a former Hollywood scriptwriter, was well known to members of the press interested in defense-related matters as an informed Pentagon insider.[308] To naval personnel, the cancellation of CVA 58 was the proverbial "straw that broke the camel's back." Perceiving the pro-USAF tone during the unification process, Davies and Worth colluded in mid-April, a few days before CVA 58 was cancelled, hoping to soon engage a larger forum regarding the future of naval aviation. In their frustration over the perceived slight to the Navy, and with suspicions about the B-36, they sought to collect all the information they could to call into question USAF. claims and procurement practices. Their intent was to release their findings to both Congress and the press.

Glenn L. Martin, chairman of the board for the Martin Aircraft Company, had a long history with military aviation. His company was best known for producing one of the finest medium bombers of World War II, the B-26 Marauder. The sleek twin-engine bomber was both powerful and heavily armed. With short stubby wings and high wing loading, the plane's landing and takeoff speeds were unusually fast. The Marauder gained a reputation as a hot, high-performance aircraft but with a dangerous disposition. As a result its early safety record was less than desirable, and pilots dubbed the

B-26 the "Baltimore Whore."[309] Along with designing and building other airframes for both the Navy and Air Force, the Martin Company assisted in the production of Boeing's B-29s during the war and was also responsible for pioneering many large seaplane designs for both military and commercial use.

While the Martin Company established a solid reputation building airplanes, its founder had a dubious character. A shrewd businessman with the ability to recognize talent, Martin had alienated himself from many in the USAAF due to his self-serving business practices and consistent complaining about unfair treatment by the federal government.[310] When the war started and lucrative contracts for aircraft were plentiful, he complained that he and his company were being ignored by the defense establishment for the larger, more profitable orders.[311] After the war, when defense funds became scarce, military aviation contracts were few but still potentially very profitable. Any one of these new aircraft contracts would be a financial boon to a firm lucky enough to secure one. Martin was not one of them.

Even before the end of the war, the USAAF was looking for the next generation of bomber aircraft. With the revolutionary German jet-powered ME-262 interceptors making their debut over Europe in April 1944, the USAAF looked to develop similar technological capabilities. In that same year, the USAAF issued a requirement for a new jet-bomber design that could fly at 500 mph, reach an altitude of 40,000 feet, and have a combat radius of 1,000 miles.[312] Officials called for a payload of four tons, but the design also had to accommodate a single weapon of eleven tons for 500 miles.[313] To meet this requirement, four designs were in the offing: North American's XB-45, Convair's XB-46, Boeing's XB-47, the Martin's XB-48.

North American was a favorite of the USAAF, having produced the best fighter of the war, the P-51 Mustang. Its engineers leaned forward with the service's request and by September 1946 rolled out the first B-45 Tornado.[314] While a conventional design with straight wings, the B-45 was the first major jet-bomber project developed for U.S. forces. But the Tornado was limited in both range and payload when compared to other potential designs. Being the first did, however, have its utility. The USAAF saw it as meeting its immediate requirement, though it was not the long-term design that the service was seeking.[315]

Convair's XB-46 was a sleek, beautiful design that looked more like a large fighter than a bomber.[316] While ascetically pleasing, the shape belied substantial problems. The aircraft was five times heavier than the B-45 but used the same power plants, making the design slower than other competitors and, given the configuration, also limited in range. Additionally the plane was prone to control problems, had a fuselage that was too small for planned equipment, and had a limited the payload.[317] As a result, the design was not feasible as an operational aircraft.

Martin's XB-48 was similar in design to its successful wartime straight-wing B-26 but was powered by six axial-flow J-35 engines affixed in two nacelles. The uniquely designed nacelles channeled air between the engines in hopes of improving airflow and of acting as a lifting body.[318] But in practice they created enormous amounts of drag. In addition the prototype was six tons overweight and fell short of the payload requirement. Furthermore, Martin Aircraft was also developing airframes for the Navy and commercial interests and was not fully committed to the XB-48 project.[319] USAF procurement officers noted this lack of focus.

Boeing's initial designs for the proposed bomber were rejected by the USAF, sending the company back to square one. While a temporary setback, this was more a blessing in disguise. Incorporating cutting-edge technologies, Boeing's new proposal, the XB-47, was a thing of beauty, with excellent aerodynamics, handling characteristics, and performance. Rolled out in December 1947, the XB-47 had a 35-degree swept wing with four engine pods hanging underneath housing six engines. Looking more like a big fighter than a bomber, the plane clearly surpassed its competitors in almost all aspects. By 1948 most USAF officers and Secretary Symington thought the new Boeing design had greater potential to fulfill the medium-bomber role.[320] Much to the other manufactures' chagrin, Boeing easily came out the winner.

Regardless of the superiority of the B-47 over its competitors, Martin again felt slighted by military procurement officers and took his case to those in power. He hoped his home state senator, Millard Tydings (D-MD), would intercede on his behalf and help influence Symington. Yet Martin's pleading yielded no results.[321] For Martin, things went from bad to worse, dealt another blow when his new 2-0-2 passenger aircraft was not adopted by the USAF for cargo hauling. For Martin, poor timing was a significant cause for this lack of success. In addition, with the war over, there were plenty of surplus C-47, C-48, and C-54 cargo aircraft available at a minimal price. This existing-airframe availability put a huge dent into civilian sales of the new airplane.[322]

Given his intent to address the perceived slight of naval aviation, Worth connected with a resentful Martin, who was still smarting from his recent USAF snubbing. On 13 April Worth, along with Commander Davies and Harold Mosier (Martin's representative in Washington), made the short trip to Martin Company's main plant, located nearby in Baltimore, Maryland.[323] There, Martin eagerly shared his concerns with the Navy representatives. Worth listened intently to his predicament and frustrations regarding bomber procurement. He eventually admitted that it was in the last ten minutes of his meeting with Martin when he decided to "prepare a compilation of facts, which I had collected from my own information trying to grasp why things were going as they were, . . . a compilation of that and the rumors."[324] In this effort Worth began collecting or recording every innuendo, piece of gossip, or item of hearsay he could find regarding recent USAF contracting practices.[325] For the Hollywood scriptwriter, substantiated and credible evidence was not required. In this compilation Worth deftly strung together a host of actions and combined them with conjecture and supposition. With these fabrications he wove an intricate tale of subterfuge.

Through this effort Worth created the infamous "anonymous document." This paper served to push the ongoing Air Force–Navy spat to the halls of Congress and into the public forum—which was what Worth had wanted. His creative-writing skills were put to use in crafting an extensive document levying various charges at USAF leadership and the Consolidated-Vultee Corporation (Convair). While the "anonymous document" was an attempt to bring the integration issue to the fore and push back against the marginalization of naval aviation, OP-23 head Burke remarked later, "The charges had some basis in fact, but were not provable, and some of them did not have basis in fact. It was a scurrilous letter. That was absolutely the wrong thing to do. It got the Navy into a lot of trouble. It got us [OP-23] into a lot of trouble."[326] While OP-23 was a source of some information for Worth's effort, the document itself was not an official Navy-sponsored endeavor, only his response to the Navy's dilemma. Yet for some in the service, the ends justified the means.

Written in a bullet-point format, Worth's document consisted of fifty-five relatively short statements largely centered around the chairman of the board for Atlas Corporation, Floyd Odlum, and Air Force Secretary Symington. Atlas was the larger parent company of smaller firms, including the maker of the B-36, Convair. The first few bullets laid out the background of the B-36 and the initial requirement for the aircraft. After that, it began to describe, in an opaque but accusatory tone, improprieties in the bomber's production and with Atlas' various subcontractors. Worth also called into question the survivability of the airplane in combat while disputing claims made about its actual performance. More importantly, he claimed the USAF continued to pursue the purchase of an "obsolete" bomber only because of Odlum's personal connection with military leadership.[327]

The "anonymous document" also claimed that Odlum was forced to make substantial contributions to Democratic Party coffers to support Truman's 1948 presidential campaign. Worth contended that a total of some $6.5 million was donated by Odlum and his associates at the insistence of Secretary Symington and the soon-to-be secretary of defense, Louis Johnson. Along this same line, the appearance of impropriety was hinted at by claims that Symington made frequent trips from Washington to Odlum's ranch in Indio, California, on a specific Lockheed Constellation aircraft. Worth's document stated that the logbook for aircraft number 2600 provided the frequent travel. But the charge that Symington and Odlum were conspiring was only insinuation. Worth stated that the logbook proving the relationship was so sensitive he could not gain access to it.[328] He otherwise offered almost no proof for any of his accusations but still sparked a good deal of speculation about Symington's relationship with Odlum. When directly asked about his influence in B-36 procurement as insinuated in the document, Symington firmly replied, "It's a lie."[329]

On an even larger scale, the document falsely claimed that Convair began trying to merge with other aviation companies, including both Northrop and Curtiss-Wright. This new aviation conglomerate could corner a larger part of the military aviation market. More importantly, according to the document, the conglomerate would require a new chief executive—rumored to be Stuart Symington—with the insinuation that the Air Force secretary, who would be in a unique position to profit from the endorsement of various contracts and projects once he left office, and after the FY 1950 budget was approved.[330] In the end, according to Worth, both Northrop and Curtiss-Wright refused the merger.

Furthermore, Worth falsely intimated that Northrop was given the unusual task to transfer production of its B-49 Flying Wing to Consolidated. When the company refused, the contract for the Flying Wing bomber was canceled altogether.[331] Similarly, Worth wrote that Curtiss-Wright then lost a contract to build the F-87 Blackhawk fighter for the USAF. The money allocated for the F-87, some $80 million, was then allegedly redirected largely to Convair for training aircraft. Additionally, the document claimed that the USAF canceled contracts for other aircraft, including North American's B-45 and F-93 aircraft, Northrop's reconnaissance version of the Flying Wing (RB-49), thirty of fifty-three Northrop C-125 cargo planes, and ten Kellett helicopters. By dropping these projects the USAF supposedly saved some $312 million, which was then redirected to the modification and building of additional B-36s.[332] While these contracts were canceled, their termination was based upon the USAF's failure to gain approval for the seventy-group structure it proposed, not specifically for the B-36 as the "anonymous document" insinuates.

Laying out these speculative charges, Worth also proffered the canard that Odlum was in the running as the next director of the National Security Resources Board. In this position he could also sponsor or steer other projects to friends or associates.[333] Given this position, Odlum would have to divest himself of his holdings in Convair. Yet with the potential contracts and mergers speculated in the document, Odlum would derive a substantial profit when he cashed out his holdings. As serious as all these accusations were, none were true.

Finishing his work of fiction by early April, Worth provided copies not only to Martin but also to members of Congress and to the press in an effort to create a widespread buzz about USAF malfeasance. A copy also was sent to Senator Tydings. But the most effective copy went to Rep. James Van Zant (R-PA) at the end of April.[334] Van Zant was a captain in the Naval Reserve and a member of the House Armed Service Committee. As a result, he was one of the few sea-service advocates in Congress. It was Van Zant who had railed against William Bradford Huie's pro-USAF *Reader's Digest* articles earlier that year that argued for the marginalization of naval aviation. With a copy of Worth's document in hand, Van Zant read them into the *Congressional Record*, calling for an investigation into what he referred to as "ugly, disturbing reports."[335] The representative wanted to know why the USAF still supported the procurement of the bomber "in spite of the fact that its flying men only a year ago were ready to abandon the Consolidated B-36 on the grounds that they were wholly unsatisfactory bombers."[336]

Van Zant failed in his first attempt to initiate an investigation because Carl Vinson, chairman of the committee, did not wish to exacerbate the existing service rivalries. But still hoping to call attention to Worth's charges, Van Zant had *Time* reporter Frank McNaughton pen an address for him that highlighted the charges in the "anonymous document." With this speech in hand, on 26 May Van Zant took his case directly to the House floor and submitted a resolution calling for a select committee to investigate the matter.[337] With prodding from Speaker of the House Sam Rayburn at the behest of Symington, Vinson finally gave in and sponsored House Resolution 234 appointing a committee to investigate the B-36.[338] On 9 June the Armed Services Committee approved a select committee to investigate the charges, with Vinson as the chair and Van Zant as the junior minority member. The panel was given eight specific tasks in its investigation:

1. Establish the truth of the charges made by Mr. Van Zant.
2 Locate and identify the source of the charges.
3. Examine the performance characteristics of the B-36 and determine if it is a satisfactory weapon.
4. Examine the roles and missions of the Air force and Navy and determine if the decision to cancel USS *United States* was sound.
5. Establish whether or not the Air Force is concentrating upon strategic bombardment to such an extent that it is injurious to tactical aviation and fighter techniques.
6. Consider the procedures used by the JCS regarding weapons development and the use of new munitions and systems by the various services.

7. Study the effects of strategic bombing to determine whether the nation is sound in following the concept to its present extent.
8. Consider all matters pertaining to the above that may be brought to light during the investigation.[339]

The first two items were the priority, with deliberations set for early August. A second series of deliberations was also scheduled for early October to address the remaining items.[340]

But as the scurrilous claims became public, Secretary Johnson, speaking at the National War College, professed his support for the Navy and for carrier aviation. In defense of his actions he claimed, "The cancellation of construction plans for a naval supercarrier has been twisted into a charge of persecution against the Navy." He stated further that he was convinced of the need for carrier aircraft and later that same day announced the modernization of two *Essex*-class carriers. This modification effort would provide the Navy with eight carriers capable of handling modern jet planes.[341] For advocates of naval aviation, however, this was too little, too late and hardly a worthy progression.

To those in the Pentagon and elsewhere who had a vested interest in national defense, it was obvious that this situation was more than just a few charges levied against individuals who were potentially abusing power for personal gain. The forthcoming hearings were a general indictment of strategic bombing. This investigation would play a part in determining not just the kind of military hardware the nation needed (ships versus planes) and its budgetary implications but also the very basis of American defense. While charges were aimed at specific individuals, there was more at stake than just personal reputations.

Seeing the potential threat, the USAF prepared extensively for the hearings and garnered the best minds it could to testify. Building a solid foundation and countering the specious charges, the service pulled out the legal stops. On 2 June the USAF brought in a reserve officer and Harvard law professor, Col. W. Barton Leach, to serve as "Director-Coordinator" for the defense.[342] Top priority was given to a careful, deliberate argument to exonerate the B-36 procurement process and rebut the personal attacks levied against Symington, Odlum, and others. During that summer, several high-ranking USAF officers and civilians were employed as investigators to research the charges. Given the importance of the matter to Symington, the members received carte-blanche authority. The group investigating the charges included Lt. Gen. Lauris Norstad, Maj. Gen. Kenneth Wolfe, and Maj. Gen. Fredrick Smith, with assistance from USAF general counsel Brackley Shaw and Undersecretary Arthur Barrow.[343]

As a result of the investigative team's combined efforts, the USAF produced a detailed account of the bomber's acquisition titled "History of B-36 Procurement."[344] This lengthy document addressed the bomber's development and laid out the nature of its mission, design, and intended employment. Written by four dedicated officers over the course of two months, the account was well researched.[345] Presented by Major General Smith, deputy director of programs for the USAF, it served as the foundation for the service's defense in the August hearings. Earlier that year, in April, Colonel Leach even developed a set of responses for senior officers and officials to use when asked about naval capabilities or questions about the USAF.[346] As a result, they came to the committee proceedings well prepared and ready to argue their case in a public forum. When Secretary Symington came to give his testimony, his personal copy of the "anonymous document" had a small handwritten annotation on the top of the first page, "dirt sheet."[347]

In May the Air Force received more bad news. This time, however, it was not a single-handed work of fiction but a studied analysis of the proposed atomic aerial offensive. In December 1948 at the direction of the JCS, a committee formed under USAF lieutenant general Hubert Harmon was tasked to evaluate the effectiveness of the current atomic offensive plan (codenamed "Trojan") in the event of war against the Soviet Union. In what became known as the Harmon Report, the panel's findings were a disappointment to proponents of strategic bombing. Submitted on 11 May 1949, the report repudiated much of the Air Force's claims while providing some support for the Navy's larger arguments.[348]

A controversial and closely held document, the Harmon Report contended that while Trojan's atomic air offensive would cripple the Soviet war machine, estimating a 30–40 percent reduction in Soviet industrial capacity, the degradation would not be permanent.[349] But the use of atomic weapons reportedly was "the only means of rapidly inflicting shock and serious damage to vital elements of the Soviet war making capacity."[350] Addressing an atomic blitz, the committee concluded, "the advantages of its early use would be transcending."[351]

The Harmon Report estimated that such an aerial assault would not affect a grand Soviet offensive into Western Europe and that the Red Army's combat power would only diminish because of a failure to resupply. Strategically, the U.S. aerial offensive would "produce certain psychological and retaliatory reactions detrimental to the achievement of allied war objectives and its destructive effects will complicate post-hostility problems."[352] Ultimately, the use of atomic weapons might prevent the successful achievement of American objectives. The most damning comment was the conclusion that "the planned attack on 70 Soviet cities would not per se, bring about the capitulation, destroy the roots of Communism, or critically weaken the power of Soviet leadership."[353] Moreover, the report surmised that such an attack might serve to further unify the Russian people and stiffen their resistance. The German Wehrmacht's experience in 1941–45 demonstrated that Russian determination was an abundant commodity.

The report tacitly endorsed the Navy position that hinted at a more wholesale approach to a war, leveraging all American air assets (Navy and Air Force) and avoiding the primacy of strategic airpower. Although a disappointment to advocates of airpower, the Harmon Report admitted that this remained the best option to counter the Soviets' extensive ground-combat power. Nevertheless, it undercut some of the USAF's, and Johnson's, positions. Forwarded to the defense secretary on 28 July, he never made the report available to Truman even as events unfolded that autumn.[354] Although the president was ignorant of the committee's findings, in April he was briefed on SAC's current war plan. USAF leaders assured the president of SAC's competency and capability despite what they had read in the Harmon Report. Unconvinced by this briefing, on 20 April Truman directed Johnson and the JCS to evaluate jointly the potential success of the plan and its expected results.[355]

Given the limited time available and the small staff of the Harmon Committee, the report on the Trojan plan was not considered definitive, with Air Force Chief of Staff Vandenberg asking that its conclusions be revised to avoid the pessimistic tone.[356] Army Chief of Staff Bradley thought that the report's many qualifications and unknowns made it "maddeningly ambiguous."[357] Vandenberg claimed it contained "unwarranted conclusions," but his was the dissenting opinion in the JCS.[358] Given the report's conclusions, USAF advocates wanted it suppressed and felt betrayed by Harmon.[359]

Yet while the Harmon effort was established at the behest of the JCS, earlier in December 1948 Secretary Forrestal established a permanent organization to conduct such analysis for the secretary of defense. He wanted "rigorous, unprejudiced, and independent analyses and evaluation of present and future weapons systems under probable future combat conditions."[360] That October, skeptical of USAF claims regarding bombing, Forrestal asked for an in-depth study of the service's ability to strike targets. In this effort he established what became known as the Weapons Systems Evaluation Group (WSEG). The organization quickly became a permanent fixture within the DoD until is disestablishment in 1976. During its twenty-eight-year history, the WSEG conducted just under three hundred individual assessments of land, sea, and air applications of force. While its studies were comprehensive, its findings were nonbinding and used only in an advisory capacity.[361] Initially led by Army lieutenant general John Hull, the organization spent the first half of 1949 acquiring staff, establishing structure, and developing operating procedures.[362] By early fall the WSEG began to evaluate the atomic offensive as described in the new Offtackle war plan.[363] Staffed with both military and civilians, the group's findings were scheduled for release in January 1950 and were anxiously awaited by those in uniform and those on Capitol Hill.

In early August, as the Harmon Report was beginning to circulate and the WSEG was finishing its ramp-up, anonymous Navy advocates fired another salvo in the interservice war. A new document surfaced that specifically called into question the efficacy of strategic bombing during World War II. While not directed at any specific individuals, the pamphlet *The Strategic Bombing Myth* was a crude and simplistic collection of graphics and quotes of cherry-picked data from the U.S. Strategic Bombing Survey (USSBS) and selected airpower advocates. Regardless of the controversy of the USSBS itself as a standalone document, *The Strategic Bombing Myth* took many findings and numbers in the survey out of context and painted a distorted picture of the entire effort.

While referencing quotes from airpower advocates like "Hap" Arnold and Claire Chennault as well as from the 1922 Washington Arms Talks, the pamphlet directly questioned strategic bombing's overall effectiveness. The document included headers such as "The So Called Strategic Bombing of Axis Europe" and "The Tragic Ploesti Story" and promoted the value of tactical bombing over strategic.[364] Smaller twin-engine aircraft like the B-25 and B-26 did yeoman service supporting Allied ground troops by clearing enemy defenses, severing lines of communications, and reducing enemy fortifications, but they were overshadowed by the heavy bombers laying waste to Axis cities. Tactical bombing was nearer to the capabilities inherent in naval aviation. With smaller airframes used directly against enemy defenses and units, naval aviation fell predominantly under the auspices of close air support and interdiction rather than strategic efforts. The author(s) of the pamphlet made a concerted effort to promote tactical applications over the USAF's more publicized, and preferred, strategic effort.

Fifteen hundred copies of *The Strategic Bombing Myth* were mailed in July to the press and government officials.[365] One copy found its way to the desk of the former chairman of the USSBS, Frank D'Olier. In a letter to Secretary Johnson on 23 August, he decried the pamphlet and specifically argued that the "document quotes the survey out of context, injects parenthetical expressions not in the original work; links together short quotations which establishes a train of thought not found in the original documents; alters a survey chart; omits qualifying phrases; and in general appears to me to paint a picture diametrically opposed to the findings of the survey."[366] To further his argument D'Olier argued, "In the public interest, these errors should be judged as such and should not be taken as guides in the making of our defense policies and programs."[367] His letter would be referenced later in October to counter the Navy's continued arguments.

Additionally, on a national level Rear Adm. Daniel Gallery, a naval aviator, published his own article in the 25 June issue of the popular periodical *The Saturday Evening Post*. Titled "An Admiral Talks Back to Airmen," it specifically calls out Huie's *Reader's Digest* articles and their partisan support of airpower.[368] Gallery, a serving officer, took a professional risk writing in a public forum in support of naval aviation in contrast to the prevailing view of Secretary Johnson. Having heard about the article beforehand, Johnson attempted to have its publication blocked, but to no avail.[369] Again referencing the USSBS, Gallery refuted the strategic bombing claim while explaining that amphibious assaults and ground actions were still required in both the European and Pacific theaters of the war. Concluding, he argued that the atomic blitz makes war look all too easy, kills civilian populations without necessarily damaging enemy forces or the regime that controls them, and gambles the nation's security on bombers while abandoning the Army and Navy in a war that "fail[s] to ensure the peace."[370] While the article itself was problematic for Johnson, what made it all the more embarrassing was that some of the information Gallery used came from OP-23.[371]

Shortly after Gallery's article was published, the Navy suffered yet another defeat at the hands of the Truman administration. While the arguments over roles and missions eventually boiled down to a fight over dollars and military budgets, on 1 July the president published his military budget for FY 1951. Budget Director Pace advised that the threat of a budget deficit necessitated a reduction in military spending. He assured Truman that "sizeable reductions are possible . . . without improperly reducing the Nation's relative readiness for an emergency."[372] Heeding this advice, the president set the defense budget at $13 billion—far less than what the services had wanted. Moreover, the Navy came out with the short end of the budgetary stick, receiving an allocation of $3.8 billion compared with the Air Force receiving $4.5 billion and the Army $4.1 billion.[373] CNO Denfeld argued that, at that level, the Navy would be unable to conduct offensive operations and that the carrier fleet would probably have to be reduced. On hearing this news, Captain Burke at OP-23 wrote to Vice Admiral Radford, "The outlook is now extremely black. . . . I think naval aviation will take a drastic beating."[374]

In preparing for the August hearings, responsibilities for the Navy argument eventually defaulted largely to those in OP-23. While the USAF made a deliberate, well-organized, and well-staffed effort to address the charges in the "anonymous document," the Navy's preparations were chaotic and fairly anemic.[375] On 20 June Undersecretary Kimball established a working group of four admirals and four captains to prepare the Navy's response. Its first product was a paper titled "Study of the Nature of a Future War." Initial versions of this paper were distinctively anti-USAF in tone, and the document was not well received by members of Navy leadership. The group continued their work and subsequently briefed their positions to the undersecretary on 22 July. At the conclusion of the session, an incensed Kimball found the submitted paper unsatisfactory and "too extreme," subsequently removing the group's de facto leader, Vice Adm. Charles "Cat" Brown.[376] With the dismissal of Brown, the remaining members of the working group slowly left the project as well, leaving Burke to carry on alone. As a result, through July and early August, OP-23 was solely responsible for the Navy's response.[377]

Based upon the mandate for the division's existence, the August hearings were not OP-23's sole concern, and other issues competed for attention. As a result, the Navy came to the proceedings less prepared than their Air Force counterparts. Without definitive guidance from flag-grade officers on how to proceed, OP-23 was left to do the work on its own discretion. In summarizing this lack of support from within elements of the Department of the Navy, historian Paul Hammond has argued, "In view of his [Burke's] background in dealing with the issues involved in the forthcoming investigation, it was understandable for him to take a prominent role. . . . But in effect, he was performing what should have been Denfeld's duty as CNO, acting as the chief spokesman for the Navy."[378] Despite the fictitious nature of the "anonymous document," Navy leadership failed to effectively deal with the festering situation. Poor preparation and staff work set the service up for a sorry showing in the upcoming hearings.

A Nonexistent Stockpile

As the Air Force and Navy prepared for public battle, another issue directly relevant to the argument at hand came to the fore. Fighting over roles, missions, and budgets during the summer of 1949, the touchstone issue for the two branches was their perceived place in the envisioned atomic air offensive. With both jockeying for position, one fundamental problem existed, a distinct lack of munitions. In the late 1940s, at the behest of the JCS, the Joint Staff developed a host of war plans, with names like Broiler, Halfmoon, and Offtackle, each of which at first called for using dozens, then hundreds, of atomic bombs against target sets in the USSR. With the passage of the Atomic

Energy Act of 1946, on 1 January 1947 the newly formed AEC took custody of all fissionable materials and components from the wartime MED. With this peacetime transfer of atomic custody from military to civilian hands, there were actually very few bombs available to support these emerging war plans. What most in the military planning teams and the JCS did not know was that, in reality, the American atomic threat was largely form over substance.[379]

Given the postwar military drawdown and the shift of emphasis to a peacetime economy, the small stockpile of munitions on hand was really just a collection of bomb components rather than a set of complete weapons ready for delivery. Immediately following the war, the MK III bomb design was the primary atomic munition available in the American arsenal. A complex weapon, each MK III required three days for a team of experts to assemble, including gluing certain components into place. Once assembled, a live weapon had a useful life of approximately one week; if not expended, it had to be completely deconstructed and rebuilt.[380] Largely a result of an expedient wartime scientific process, the MK III was hardly a refined or sublimely designed weapon. Each bomb was more like a science project—referred to once as a "Rube Goldberg affair"—with physicist Norris Bradbury commenting, "We had, to put it bluntly, lousy bombs."[381] Furthermore, even as late as 1946 most of the details and instructions about the atomic designs were largely notes or handwritten instructions left over from members of the wartime effort.[382] As a result, those who staffed the postwar atomic effort were left trying to piece together a highly complex and technical process from various scraps and memos left by members of the MED.

When the first chairman of the AEC, David Lilienthal, came to inspect the atomic storage facility in early 1947, he was surprised to find that America's nuclear arsenal was *literally* in pieces. Because an assembled bomb had a limited shelf life, he saw no completed weapons—just pieces and components. During his visit he realized, as did the AEC-nominated commissioners, that "the [atomic] defense did not exist. We did not have a stockpile."[383] Lilienthal recalled, "It was assumed we had a stockpile. We not only didn't have a pile, we didn't have a stock!"[384] This same sentiment was expressed by Dr. Robert Bacher, a member of the wartime MED and part of the Trinity experiment's assembly team. When he took inventory of the current supply in 1947, he was "deeply shocked to find how few atomic weapons we had at that time."[385]

Truman, too, was largely oblivious to the condition of the atomic arsenal, and it was not until April 1947 when he was finally briefed by AEC Chair Lilienthal on the status of the atomic magazine.[386] The JCS, who were ultimately responsible for developing the published war plans utilizing atomic bombs, were also ignorant of the situation. Based upon the production capabilities at the time, the AEC could only provide enough fissionable materials for one bomb every two months.[387] Production requirements for atomic munitions had remained unchanged since 1945, with the commission lacking the capacity to accelerate production substantially even if the JCS had submitted any requested change.[388] Later that year the Joint Chiefs established their first production goal for atomic weapons, expecting four hundred bombs in the stockpile by January 1951.[389] While Lilienthal's April 1947 briefing document leaves the space for the actual number available for assembly blank, historians speculate that the "stockpile" at that time had components for roughly a dozen weapons.[390] Regardless of what the number actually was, it was hardly sufficient to support existing war plans.[391] While the AEC was unable to maintain production in concert with the JCS's developing war plans, fault for the discrepancy lay with both camps: the military failed to communicate its growing requirements, and the civilian organization poorly articulated its capabilities.

For the AEC, bomb production remained slow for a number of reasons. The scientists associated with the wartime MED returned to their peacetime activities in academia after the war, resulting in a "brain drain" for the program. In addition, the reactors used to produce fissionable materials began to show wear due to use. These combined with a lack of direction and vision precluded an expanded effort.[392] In a session of the JCAE in July 1947, the joint committee's chairman, Sen. Brien McMahon (D-CT), noted that the Military Liaison Committee (MLC) had yet to forward any new production requirements because the Joint Chiefs had yet to forward any formal requests. Rear Adm. Ralph Ofstie of the Joint Chiefs of Staff's Evaluation Group echoed the sentiment by pinning fault on the JCS, testifying, "I think it is the responsibility of our group [the MLC] to continue to carry out the plans of the Joint Chiefs, and if they are not moving along as fast as they should, then it is a problem for the Joint Chiefs." When this issue came to light, McMahon merely responded, "That's got to be done."[393]

Despite the lethargy of production and the failure to identify new requirements, military planners continued to develop war plans that increasingly relied upon atomic ordnance. When pressed to submit what the military requirement was, the JCS demurred, claiming that they would have an answer in two weeks. Even after prodding by JCAE member Sen. Bourke Hickenlooper (R-IA), it took another three months for the military to respond.[394]

Nevertheless, when the JCS actually submitted a new requirement on 19 December 1947, the number requested was only a slight increase and based largely upon the production capacity of the AEC at that time. In their response the Joint Chiefs also stated the new requirement "will probably be satisfactory until such time as any possible enemy country possesses atomic weapons in quantity and an air force capable of launching a massive attack on the United States."[395] Chairman Lilienthal, who was not a proponent of increasing atomic munitions, concurred with this and stated the AEC could meet the requirement with its existing production facilities. He did, however, notify the JCS that starting in 1949, production levels would start to fall short.[396] Regardless, the military saw no need to raise requirements significantly, but the AEC did increase production, with enough components available for approximately fifty bombs.[397]

But in January 1949 the MLC expressed concern to the AEC regarding the number of weapons available, stating, "it is now evident that the currently established military requirement for scheduled bomb production should be increased substantially and extended."[398] This request was forwarded just as Forrestal established the WSEG and as the Harmon Committee began its analysis of the Trojan war plan. On 16 March the JCAE met with Maj. Gen. Ken Nichols of the MLC, who testified that the military was not getting "enough bombs nor . . . getting them fast enough."[399] Two months later, when the Harmon Report was released, JCS members were dismayed at the findings and immediately looked to increase the atomic stockpile in order to address the newly identified shortfalls.

On 26 May 1949 AEC Chair Lilienthal testified before the JCAE that production was at its highest level ever, with potentially greater amounts of fissionable material produced in the future. On that same day the MLC forwarded a request to the commission to increase production as a result of the disturbing Harmon Committee findings.[400] Yet this time the request for fissionable materials exceeded the current or planned production capacity by 15 percent.[401] In June the JCS echoed this sentiment and requested an acceleration of the atomic-energy program.[402] While maintaining a small military budget was a presidential concern, at this time the AEC budget was a separate line item from that of the DoD. The proposed figure for such a production expansion was estimated at $500 million.[403] Cognizant of Truman's fiscal conservatism, when Budget Director Pace was notified of the new requirement, he balked. On 28 June Pace suggested that any increase in spending for atomic weapons in the AEC should be offset by a reduction in DoD fiscal allocations.[404] Keeping true to the presidential mandate, he was no spendthrift but looked to Truman to authorize such an expenditure.

Lilienthal expressed concern that the military was basing its requirements merely on AEC production capabilities rather than on a deliberate, planned review of bomb requirements. In other words, the military was planning to use all the bombs available from the AEC instead of reviewing the number of targets and their relation to national objectives.[405] In a 23 July entry in his personal journal, Lilienthal expressed his dismay with military planners: "If we [the AEC] had not been a civilian agency—mark this well—there would have been no one who would have raised the questions I insisted be raised, . . . asking why and wherefore and what about our basic policy, what kind of war is this to be, what are we doing afterward, [and] is this to be piled on top of all the other defense expenditures?"[406]

In mid-July Senator McMahon wrote both Secretary Johnson and Chairman Lilienthal about his concern over the small number of bombs produced. He suggested that the number of weapons available might mean the difference between victory and defeat.[407] Unaware of the Harmon Report findings but supportive of an effort to clarify the issue at hand, on 26 July Truman contacted NSC Executive Secretary Rear Adm. Sidney Souers.[408] The president directed him to initiate a study group, comprising the secretaries of state and defense along with the AEC chairman, for a proposed increase in the acceleration of the AEC program.[409] Specifically, he wanted to know the adequacy of the present program, the soundness of such an increase, the effectiveness of its timing, the relative gain to national security, and its overall effect upon the budget.[410] Knowing full well about the fiscal implication of this decision, Truman was also aware that such an increase in expenditures might have an effect on the nation's foreign-policy objectives.[411] What no one knew at the time of this request was that, when the NSC submitted its final report in the beginning of October, the geopolitical situation differed significantly from when the president first issued his study directive.

The August Hearings

The B-36 had been a festering topic for months. As early as January 1949, Symington had complained, "I've been here for some years, and I think the hatchet job that is being done, and has been done on the B-36 is the best hatchet job that I have seen since I have been in town."[412] The committee investigating the program began its work on 9 August under guidance from Chairman Vinson. The initial part of the hearings evaluated the charges levied against the USAF, with a planned review on the larger issue of unification scheduled for October. During the first part of the hearings, the USAF delivered a well-prepared document titled "History of B-36 Procurement." Initiating this defense was Robert Lovett, who was assistant secretary for air during the war and one of the primary advocates for B-36 procurement. After explaining the initial wartime rationale behind the need for the bomber, Lovett was followed by Major General Smith, who read the report making the case for the B-36 based upon technical and strategic grounds. His testimony refuted the charge that procurement of the aircraft was for personal gain.[413] During the hearings, the USAF provided an earnest accounting, highlighting its own errors and irregularities in the bomber's procurement process. While the service certainly made mistakes, none were equal to or even close to the charges contained in the "anonymous document."[414]

Further, Smith stated that "there was [in the USAF] a constant reexamination of basic military concepts, chief among them the role of strategic bombing."[415] He also argued that, given the postwar environment and what he referred to as "the deterioration in the international political situation," the B-36 was required to operate along with the fleet of B-29s and B-50s. In addition, Smith pointed out that it was only an interim solution until the envisioned all-jet B-52 replaced it.[416] Finally, the B-36 was also required not just to deliver atomic ordnance but also to be the "work horse" during a strategic bombing campaign that would include conventional bombing operations.[417]

Regarding the numbers procured, Smith used previously published studies that recommended a seventy-group USAF.[418] Giving a detailed explanation of various B-36 program reviews, the USAF effectively refuted the allegations in the "anonymous document." Using previous studies as a guide, procurement of the B-36 was consistent with congressional studies and fiscal policies established by the president. Smith reported, "All in all, the Air Force felt that it had been given a clear cut mandate to plan for an orderly build up to a 70 group force."[419] The presentation was so effective in defending the program that the select committee's final report came out strongly not only in support of the B-36 but also in validating its mission profile.[420] This, of course, was the very opposite of what Worth or the Navy wanted.

Further supporting the B-36, the USAF then paraded a number of general officers familiar with the application of strategic bombing to endorse its procurement. Among them were George Kenney, the first commander of SAC, followed by his successor and SAC's current commander, Curtis LeMay. For two days both men testified as to the utility of the B-36 and to the efficacy of strategic bombing. Kenney was at first disappointed with the performance of the Peacemaker and suggested limiting its purchase. The committee discussed his complaints about the plane's engine problems, its apparent inability to attain a 10,000-mile range, and its requirement of a 10,000-foot runway for operation.[421] These comments were from 1946, but by June 1948, Kenney had changed his mind.[422] The general still questioned the B-36's vulnerability as it pertained to daylight operations in the face of enemy jet interceptors, but he now supported the bomber. He explained that this change of heart resulted from significant engineering modifications made in the last couple of years that improved the aircraft's performance.[423]

LeMay was equally, if not more, supportive of the bomber, arguing that it was the best airframe available for the mission assigned. While the current SAC commander was looking forward to validating air-to-air refueling concepts and the nascent B-47 design, he contended that the current fleet of B-36s were a significant part of the SAC bomber force until newer, more capable aircraft became available. Colonel Leach's procurement history clearly articulated that the B-36 was the "only weapon that would enable the US [to] launch . . . an [atomic] attack without having to acquire bases overseas."[424] While LeMay downplayed the fighter threat that Kenney feared, he hoped for even newer bombers for SAC. Addressing the vulnerability of the B-36 to enemy fighters, he stated, "there will come a time when a fighter can shoot down eighty percent of the B-36s, but by that time the B-36 will be obsolete."[425] He went on to argue that he was not worried so much about the bomber being shot down as he was "whether the proper number of B-36s in the proper tactical disposition can penetrate enemy defenses and destroy a target with acceptable losses to ourselves, and I believe the B-36 can do this job." Perhaps his most memorable argument for the B-36 was when LeMay was asked if he would assume responsibility as the chief advocate for the plane. To this he replied, "Yes I certainly would. . . . [I]f I am called upon to fight, I will order my crews out in those airplanes, and I expect to be in the first one myself."[426]

Following LeMay and Kenney, former Air Force chief of staff Spaatz, his successor General Vandenberg, and Secretaries Symington and Johnson all added their testimony in refuting allegations of impropriety. Furthermore, the committee found no favoritism by the USAF for Consolidated Aircraft or undue influence by Floyd Odlum regarding campaign contributions to Truman.[427] In fact, the committee found that Odlum contributed a mere $3,000, the same amount he had contributed to the Democratic Party for the past twenty years. When combined with Odlum's friends, the committee found that these men contributed in total only $28,000 and not the millions claimed in Worth's document.[428]

When Symington testified, he clearly bristled at the questions pertaining to the charges Worth made against him personally. Not only did the secretary outline in detail the acquisition decisions regarding the bomber but also he argued with Representative Van Zant and countered the accusations made against him.[429] In his testimony to the committee, Symington addressed seventeen specific charges made against him or the USAF. At the end of almost all of his responses, he finished with the same word, "untrue."[430] In his closing remarks Symington had more to say about the "anonymous document," arguing, "Back in what we think of as the evil days of flagrant political corruption, the circulation of scurrilous and anonymous attacks was common practice.

These dirt sheets of their time were prepared by pamphleteers whom a person in political life would hire for the sordid business of character assassination. . . . I for one thought this business died a century ago. I have never known a single incident like [it] in my lifetime—until this document got its circulation on Capitol Hill."[431] After his rebuttal, the *Washington Post* reported, "Mr. Symington met insults and innuendo with a combination of angry retort and studied indifference and the result was to throw his adversary on the defensive."[432]

After the Air Force testimony, Van Zant was now on the defensive. Symington's arguments with him were effective, as even Chairman Vinson chimed in, declaring, "Mr. Van Zant you have given voice to rumors," and noting the "funny coincidence" that the charges levied by the representative were similar to those in the "anonymous document."[433] With this exchange, the select committee adjourned for two weeks while its members traveled to California to make further inquiries at aircraft manufacturers in the Los Angeles area.

With these testimonies and the detailed "History of the B-36 Program," the charges levied in the "anonymous document" were systematically disproved and shown to be wildly inaccurate. As the case against the USAF began to crumble, Van Zant looked to save some face and credibility. He was able to deflect some of the attention he had brought to himself when the select committee reconvened later that month. Then the investigation began focusing on the origin of the "anonymous document," members demanded to know who authored the document. By this time USAF investigators had revealed Worth as the author of the charges.[434] At the beginning of the session on 24 August, Van Zant requested that Worth be subpoenaed and compelled to testify immediately.[435] Committee members assumed that Symington already knew who authored the document and immediately called him back to testify. But the Air Force secretary was not the only one aware of the author's identity. After testimony from General Bradley regarding unity of the services and just as Symington was preparing to testify again, Chairman Vinson inquired, "Is Mr. Worth in the Room?" After asking the question, a tall, well-dressed man rose and quietly walked to the witness chair. Once seated, he identified himself as Cedric R. Worth, special assistant to Assistant Secretary of the Navy for Air Kimball.[436]

After being seated and taking the oath, the whole story began to unravel. After Worth admitted that he had distributed the document to various parties, Vinson waved a copy of it, asking, "Where did you get this document from?"[437] In response, Worth replied plainly, "I wrote it."[438] During his testimony he also admitted not only writing the document on his own accord but also having done so without official direction from anyone in the Department of the Navy.[439] One account reported that Worth repented his actions with the "exaltation of a reformed sinner."[440] Regarding his intent and the result of his fictitious document, he admitted, "I will state to anybody that [what] I've done [did] the Navy no good."[441] He freely admitted there was no evidence of corruption in the B-36 program and that those implicated were not guilty of impropriety.[442] When asked about why he had written the document, Worth replied that he was "concerned" over defense policies that were "weakening" the nation.[443] When questioned as to where he got the information used in his work of fiction, he answered that he had gotten some information from Martin, Commander Davies, and a number of different places.[444] While Davies may have given him the information, whether or not it was done intentionally was never determined; many speculated Worth could not have crafted his accusations without a significant amount of assistance. As for Martin, he eventually testified that he provided information to Worth but was unaware of his intent.[445]

Following Worth's testimony and admission of guilt, Secretary Matthews suspended him, and the Navy began an investigation led by Adm. Thomas Kinkaid.[446] It uncovered very little—with Worth's admission, there was little to investigate. The hearings exonerated the Air Force and left the Navy to ponder its future under a cloud of suspicion. As a result of these findings, the select committee eventually reported, "It is the view of the committee that the long history of the B-36 discloses that the procurement of this aircraft was motivated solely by considerations of the problem of national defense and the policy laid down and the missions assigned by the Joint Chiefs of Staff." After the August hearings, the panel determined that there "[was] not one scintilla of evidence to support the charges, reports, rumors, and innuendoes which have been the subject of inquiry under item 1 of the agenda."[447] It went even further when, on 25 August, it concluded, "There has not been . . . one iota . . . of evidence offered thus far in these hearings that would support charges of fraud, collusion, influence or favoritism played any part whatsoever in the procurement of the B-36 bomber."[448]

Hoping to mend some fences with the Navy, Odlum wrote to Secretary Matthews. He reiterated a statement from his testimony: "Convair is in the business of designing and building airplanes for both the Air Force and Navy. It builds for them what they order and it strives to merit their continuing business."[449] Odlum was clearly making a play for future Navy aircraft contracts. In addition, the head of Atlas Corporation wrote to Secretary Johnson, "It is a terrible state of affairs when an anonymous poison pen communication can end in a parade of all the top men in defense before a public committee with the information broadcast about the world."[450] Symington also took the high road by writing to Secretary Johnson that he had "confidence . . . in the character and integrity of not only Secretary Matthews, but also of Undersecretary Kimball, Admiral Denfeld, . . . and all those fine officers of the Navy who have done and are doing so much to protect the security of the United States."[451]

Following the August hearings, Representative Van Zant was excoriated by some members of the press. One newspaper's editorial section proffered, "James E. Van Zant . . . has proven himself, in our opinion, unworthy of the congressional post he holds, of the Navy uniform he once wore, and the national command of the Veterans of Foreign Wars which he once held. . . . They [the USAF contingent testifying] proved him to be, in our opinion, a cowardly scandal mongerer who was ready to knife the national security of his own nation for personal aggrandizement and personal glorification to say nothing of falsely smearing the president of the United States."[452] Adding insult to injury, Hanson Baldwin, the *New York Times* military editor who was decisively pro-Navy, wrote that the first session of hearings were "an impressive Air Force vindication."[453]

This first round of select-committee hearings clearly had the Navy reeling. One person's actions had taken a toll on the entire naval service. Yet it still had an opportunity to plead its larger vision of national military strategy and to argue the merits of naval aviation. In lieu of the select committee's full mandate to address eight agenda items, the August session addressed only those accusations against USAF officials in charge of procuring the B-36.

Those questions clearly answered, the next round of hearings began on 5 October. The outstanding items addressed dealt with investigating the roles and missions of the two respective services, the apparent concentration on strategic bombardment, and a debate over its overall effectiveness. Because of the clear failure of the August session, the Navy arrived better prepared, with many flag officers effectively supporting their positions and the cause of naval aviation. Only a month later, the next discourse between the two services would culminate at the same time other significant issues were taking center stage.

As the Summer Ends

Throughout the summer of 1949, a number of issues unfolded that came to a head in the autumn months. The culmination of the Soviet atomic effort with the explosion of Joe-1 and the subsequent American response were key factors in the decisions made in upcoming seasons. With the Soviet explosion arose new questions and concerns. It exposed a weakness in the American intelligence effort and, more importantly, tipped the geopolitical balance of power, prompting a wholesale review of U.S. national security policy.

Furthermore, rivalries between the various services began anew because of the National Defense Act of 1947, which established the NME. As the NME grew and was renamed the DoD, arguments over unification, roles, missions, and budget created a hostile environment within the Pentagon. These existing rivalries and suspicions were highlighted with the procurement of the B-36 and the cancellation of USS *United States*. Additionally, President Truman's tough fiscal policies were the benchmark for an ambitious and arrogant secretary of defense hoping to establish himself in the Washington political scene. Furthermore, the perceived slight to the naval services at the hands of the USAF led to more infamous actions with the distribution of the "anonymous document" and the release of *The Strategic Bombing Myth*. While the summer was fraught with intrigue, as the seasons changed and autumn arrived, more was to come.

Events in Asia along with continued internal domestic pressures unfolded in the following months, leading to a season of tension, debate, argument, and discontent. Seismic shifts in the way America viewed itself and its military were soon to come. When the turmoil ended, the United States would endeavor to establish a new national security strategy that was fundamentally different from any that had preceded it. Furthermore, the country needed to decide if it should build the most lethal and technologically advanced weapon ever built. By the time the spring of 1950 arrived, the seeds for change in the American traditions of national security and limiting a standing military were already planted and would come to fruition shortly.

—2—
AUTUMN

On 1 October 1949 on the Tiananmen Square Gate, Mao Tse-tung formally announced the establishment of the People's Republic of China (PRC). He told the assembled masses, with his words broadcast throughout China, "the People's War of Liberation had been basically won, and the majority of the people in the country have been liberated."[1] With delegates from the Chinese People's Political Consultative Conference cheering, a forty-nine-piece band played Communist-inspired tunes in the background.[2] While certainly a significant event in world history, the rest of Mao's statement that day was little more than formality and hardly stirring. The salient event was the hoisting of the new Communist country's colors on the flagpole set in the crowded square. But on 21 September, two days before the start of autumn, at the First Plenary Session of the Chinese People's Political Consultative Conference, Mao was more eloquent:

> It is because we have defeated the reactionary Kuomintang government backed by US imperialism that this great unity of the whole people has been achieved. . . . In a little more than three years the heroic Chinese People's Liberation Army . . . crushed all the offensives launched by several million troops of the US supported Kuomintang government and turned to the counter-offensive and the offensive. . . . We have stood

> up. Our revolution has won the sympathy and acclaim of the people of all countries. We have friends all over the world. . . . Hail the victory of the People's War of Liberation and the people's revolution! Hail the founding of the People's Republic of China![3]

With this, Mao moved China beyond centuries of dynastic rule and united almost a quarter of humanity under one flag. In a struggle lasting decades, Mao achieved what was, even as the most cynical would have to admit, a stunning historical victory.

The establishment of yet another major Communist country was indeed a loss for the United States. As painful as Mao's proclamations were for the Western democracies, they came scarcely a week after Truman's surprise announcement of the Soviet atomic bomb. This one-two punch of significant Communist successes exacerbated their separate influences. Years later Department of State (DoS) strategist Paul Nitze clearly and plainly identified these two salient events as rationales for a new national security policy: "The origins of NSC 68 [came] after the Chinese Communists had consolidated their position on the mainland and the Soviet Union had tested their first nuclear device."[4] These two events occurred just as summer turned to fall—as the United States began its autumn of discontent.

Wars before the War

While Mao's success was a seismic shift in the global geopolitical balance, it was not a sudden or unforeseen surprise. His proclamation was a long time coming. Years before, Gen. George Marshall, Gen. Joseph Stilwell, and members of the DoS were continually dismayed with the leadership of the Kuomintang (KMT; the Nationalist Party of China). Graft, corruption, incompetence, and exploitation of the peasant masses were key elements of the KMT failure. While the Nationalists had an army in terms of material, it was at best a loose conglomeration of sometimes-willing commanders more than it was a cohesive military force. KMT leader Chiang Kai-shek was head of both the political and military branches in China, but his ability to exercise control was tenuous. Regarding the KMT army, Lt. Gen. Albert C. Wedemeyer observed, "Americans imagined that Chiang could simply give an order and it would be carried out. I realized that the Generalissimo, far from being a dictator, was in fact only the head of a loose coalition, and at times experienced great difficulty in securing the obedience to his commands."[5] Despite being equipped with modern weapons and Western advisors, the KMT army failed to defeat Mao's Red Army before the Japanese invasions of Manchuria and China proper. While a tenuous truce was called between the two sides during the Japanese occupation, they expected a resumption of internal hostilities once the common enemy was defeated. With the surrender of the Japanese in September 1945, the United States hoped to preclude the continuation of the civil war, but both the Chinese Communist Party (CCP) and the KMT were already positioned to renew their internal conflict.

During World War II, with Japanese forces occupying much of the Chinese coastal areas and Manchuria, President Roosevelt hoped to leverage Chinese help after the attack on Pearl Harbor. In this effort Chinese troops were seen as important allies to offset the Japanese offensive juggernaut. Even before December 1941 and as early as 1937, Roosevelt provided monetary support to China and eventually material aid from the United States under Lend-Lease.[6] This support became even more formalized and significant when the United States insisted that China be included as a signatory in the Declaration of Four Nations on General Security on 30 October 1943. This document recognized China's right to participate (with the other major powers) in the conduct of the war, in the organization for the postwar peace, and in helping establish the groundwork for the international environment following the conflict.[7] This was followed a month later by the Cairo Declaration, issued on 1 December, which called for the restoration of Chinese sovereignty, independence of the Korean peninsula, and a reiteration of the "unconditional surrender" mandate from the Casablanca Conference (14–24 January). In all of these actions the KMT served as the representative of the Chinese people to the United States and the world, with little official recognition of Mao and the CCP.

While many Chinese studied Marxist ideas in Europe, the first Communist groups started organizing in Peking in 1919 and formally established the CCP in 1921. With foreign aid coming from the USSR, the CCP joined with the KMT to form what became known as the United Front. This collaboration was beneficial to both parties as they sought to eliminate the existing feudalism of the northern warlords, unify the country under one government, and strengthen the collective power of a fractured nation.[8] In the summer of 1926, United Front forces headed out of Canton in what became known as the Northern Expedition. Under the command of Chiang, who was a stubborn and ruthless leader despite the limits of his authority, the combined armies swept aside the warlords of southeast China and taking the cities in the Yangtze River valley, thus beginning the unification process.[9] By autumn the combined army had routed the remaining Hunan warlords.

Despite these victories, a splintering of the KMT began. While Chiang made provisions for the Communists, many within his own group became suspicious of the "Red" elements and their Soviet supporters. With the military campaign dominated by KMT factions, the CCP focused on growing political movements in the rural areas and urban labor unions.[10] Yet as aid came from the Soviet Union and the international Comintern, many in the KMT feared growing Communist influence and believed that Chiang's position in the United Front was increasingly in peril.[11] Chiang walked a delicate balance between supporting his Communist partners on the left (and keeping the unification and nationalist ideals of Dr. Sun Yat-sen intact from earlier revolutionary movements) while satisfying the larger KMT membership on the right. Simultaneously, he also had to try to avoid being seen as too powerful or ambitious from all sides at this precarious time in Chinese history.

Due to growing suspicions over Communist influence, including personal animosities, on 12 April 1927 Chiang turned on the CCP. In what became known as the Shanghai Massacre, countless CCP members were killed or imprisoned by KMT forces. The numbers of those killed in Shanghai alone was estimated in the thousands, but the massacre was not restricted to the city alone. This purge took place in numerous KMT-held areas, with many thousands more arrested, killed, or simply "disappearing." Backed by bankers and other industrialists, Chiang had the tacit support of Western powers in his action while playing to the rightist elements of the KMT base.[12] But the deliberate purge of the CCP elements in the Unified Front put in motion the decades-long civil war that would climax in the autumn of 1949.

The United States rewarded Chiang's efforts by recognizing the KMT as the legitimate government of China on 25 July 1928.[13] Overcoming military and political obstacles, he established himself as not only a military leader but also a head of state. Yet Chiang and his KMT were in control of only a part of the country, as many areas were still occupied by warlords or by the CCP. Within those parts he controlled, Chiang instituted a myriad of reforms, ushering in what became called the "Nanking Decade" (1927–37).[14] During this time he modernized urban China, wanting the world to see his country as developing into a contemporary power.[15] The KMT standardized the monetary system, centralized tax collection, built new roads and inland waterways, established telephone facilities, allowed the greater introduction of Western ideals and fashions, and promoted a substantial growth in industry.[16] Although these urban advances were lauded by the larger global community, China remained primarily an agrarian economy.[17] Few of these improvements made their way into the countryside. As a result, the gap between the rural and urban populations grew. Chroniclers of the period have observed that a cultural divide existed in China between the Western-influenced, relatively wealthy cities and the more traditional, poor rural peasantry.[18]

While Chiang continued the vision of Sun to both unify and modernize China after the purge of the Communists, the CCP retreated into the rural areas. Mao and his followers established an encampment north of Hong Kong in Jiangxi Province. Working among the peasants in the countryside, the CCP licked its wounds. In a series of "annihilation campaigns" to rid rural areas of this Communist influence, Chiang continued his assaults against his former allies. In 1934 the KMT again sought to rout the CCP holdouts, this time enjoying a victory of sorts by driving the Communists from their bases. Conversely, Mao's followers succeeded in escaping the grip of the KMT by embarking on the famous "Long March." Enduring immense hardship, they eventually made their way to Shaanxi Province in northern China after marching some six thousand miles (equivalent to crossing the United States twice). Fighting the KMT, hunger, and the elements, the ragtag Chinese Red Army endured for over a year even as its numbers dwindled. Eventually stopping in Yennan, the CCP would eventually regroup, reorganize, and appoint Mao as its leader.

The Imperial Japanese Army (IJA) invaded China in September 1931 after staging an explosion along the South Manchurian Railway near the city of

Mukden. With the framing of Chinese dissidents as instigators, Japanese forces subverted the local civilian government and used the "attack" as the provocation for military action. Ignorant of the army's subterfuge, the Japanese people overwhelmingly supported the move. Establishing a puppet government, the Japanese placed the deposed Chinese emperor Henry Pu Yi as the head of the new state of Manchukuo. Ignoring protests from the larger global community and the League of Nations, Japan remained indifferent to world opinion.

After the Japanese annexation of Manchuria, in 1932 the CCP clearly identified Japan as an enemy of China. Even before the "Marco Polo Bridge Incident," the party called for a truce and a partnership with the KMT to rid their country of the Japanese.[19] While Chiang still focused on destroying the remaining warlords and the CCP, others within China called for a deliberate effort against the invaders. Looking for a respite from the KMT while trying to influence the peasant population, in August 1936 the CCP offered the Nationalists a renewed United Front to fight the Japanese incursion. As far as they were concerned, a second United Front was the "only proper way to save our great country today."[20] It took a de-facto kidnapping of Chiang on the part of two subordinate generals in December 1936 to force the generalissimo to change his military priorities, at least temporarily. Chiang agreed to a partnership with the CCP and refocused his efforts on defeating the Japanese. With this understanding, the CCP and KMT again entered into an informal partnership in a combined effort against the occupying forces.[21] In a 28 September 1937 speech announcing the joint effort against the Japanese, Chiang asserted, "China today has only one objective in its war effort."[22] While the United Front proclamation was political theater on the part of both sides, what was even more important is that the agreement gave validity to the CCP in the eyes of the Chinese people.

Regardless of the renewed CCP-KMT partnership, tension remained between the two parties despite the common foe. Command protocols and liaison were practically nonexistent, and any coordination between the two Chinese forces was tenuous at best. Suspicions remained on both sides, with incidents of KMT-CCP conflict occurring regularly up to 1941. CCP forces in the northwest were designated the Eighth Route Army and supposedly fell under KMT central control; in reality it operated independent of Nationalist command.[23] The situation soured even more in January 1941, when Chiang's troops destroyed the headquarters of the Chinese Red Army's New Fourth Army. As a result, whatever KMT and CCP cooperation that had existed effectively ended.

While supposedly focused on the Japanese, both the CCP and KMT armies avoided large-scale offensive action against the IJA. Both adopted a generally defensive strategy throughout the war.[24] Largely cut off from the rest of the world, material and supplies were limited, and those that did come from American Lend-Lease support landed only in the hands of the KMT. The absence of offensive action and tactical success was in part because the average Chinese soldier lacked proper training for the rigors of modern combat and was often pressed into service unprepared and ill equipped. While many soldiers were individually brave and determined to fight for their homeland, during the early years of the war, Chinese forces were largely no match for the better-equipped, commanded, and trained IJA.[25]

Despite the questionable quality of its troops or their lack of equipment, the KMT served as the face of Chinese resistance to both the Americans and the world at large. But Joseph Stilwell, Chiang's American chief of staff and commander of U.S. forces in Burma, was less than impressed. Along with many of the Americans assigned to China, Stilwell fumed about the generalissimo's lack of fighting spirit against their common foe.[26] Almost from the beginning of their relationship in 1942, Chiang thought little of Stilwell's tactical acumen, and the two men were constantly at odds. From Chiang's point of view, the Chinese, British, and American losses from early operations in Burma were the result of U.S. incompetence. With this as a starting point, the relationship went from bad to worse.[27] Despite their best efforts, the Americans were viewed as interlopers by their KMT counterparts, with cooperation being marginal.[28] While the Americans at one time thought they had an effective partnership with the KMT against the Japanese, they eventually became hostage to a government that gave only a semblance of cooperation. The relationship largely served KMT interests, as they garnered combat power from the United States for an eventual conflict with the CCP.

Much to their frustration, what many Americans in China came to understand was that both sides, the KMT and the CCP, husbanded their respective strengths. Despite the common Japanese foe, both were positioning themselves for the domestic conflict ahead. Reporting after his visit in January 1945, Rep. Mike Mansfield (D-MT) stated what most Americans in China had come to know: "It appears to me that both the Communists and the KMT are more interested in preserving their respective parties at this time and have been for the past two years than they are in carrying out the war against Japan."[29] Furthermore, the U.S.–China military relationship between Stilwell and Chiang remained acrimonious at best and regressed to personal insult, with the American referring to the generalissimo as "peanut" in both his own personal diary and to other members of the U.S. staff.[30] Even before Mansfield's visit, months early in September 1944, Stilwell wrote to Army Chief of Staff Marshall, telling the future U.S. representative to China,

> Chiang has no intention of making further efforts to prosecute the war. . . . [He] believes he can go on milking the United States for money and munitions by using the old gag about quitting if he is not supported. . . . I believe he will only continue his policy and delay, while grabbing for loans and post war aid, for the purpose of maintaining his present position, based upon one party government, a reactionary policy, or his suppression of democratic ideals with the active aid of his gestapo.[31]

Chiang harbored his combat power for use against the CPP while selfishly retaining his political and military power within the KMT. Despite the global exigency to defeat Japan, both Chiang and Mao knew a future conflict between themselves was in the offing, even if the generalissimo's American benefactors were naïve enough to think a compromise coalition government in China was possible.[32]

Both the Japanese and the KMT established most of their military and political strongholds in urban areas. Expanding CCP control in rural areas was a deliberate part of Chinese Red Army policy with a twofold purpose. Militarily, by expanding control into the countryside, the CCP denied use of a province or region to the Japanese. By holding these areas, it precluded IJA movement by rail, road, or river ways outside of established city limits. Avoiding operations beyond roads, IJA formations were subject to guerilla attack when confronted away from these lines of communication.[33] For millennia and well into the twentieth century, the Chinese demographic was overwhelmingly composed of rural peasants. While the KMT was strong in urban spaces, a key component of Maoist doctrine focused on developing support among the Chinese peasant masses who tilled fields, tended to livestock, and reaped nature's bounty. By focusing operations on this group, the CCP politically indoctrinated and influenced the nation's single largest demographic. Given the enormity of the indigenous rural population, this deliberate focus resulted in an exponential rise in party membership. As a result, the CCP grew its base of power during the war and harnessed it in the postwar civil conflict.

Indicative of this effectiveness, estimates place CCP membership in 1937 at a mere 40,000 people, which then grew some thirty times to 1.2 million by war's end.[34] The same was true for the Chinese Red Army, as its ranks ballooned over twenty times, from 50,000 soldiers at the time of the 1937 Marco Polo Incident to 1.2 million by 1945, with another 2.6 million troops in organized militias in an ever-increasing geographical area of control.[35] While still four times smaller than their rival Nationalist Army, the growth of the Red Army was still significant.[36] Equally important was the nature of KMT occupation. When the Nationalists occupied territory, they treated local peasants with brutality, imposed taxes, and appointed corrupt officials. The graft and inherent corruption of the KMT was not lost on either the Chinese or foreigners.[37] While many Westerners praised the work ethic and industriousness of the general population, many working in China found that corruption was an inherent part of the political, social, and economic landscape. Even money allocated for KMT troops themselves was siphoned off, finding its way usually into the bank accounts of individual officers and commanders.[38] In 1942 the United States made a $500 million Treasury loan to the government in Chungking. After an investigation by Secretary of the Treasury Henry Morgenthau, he surmised that as much as $300 million was sold on the black market or made its way to KMT officials, who then invested heavily in U.S. stocks.[39] The dichotomy between an accomplished and storied civilization compared with such a venal government and inability to establish an effective army left many Westerners dumbfounded.[40]

While the KMT army was still larger in size and better equipped, with World War II coming to an end, it now faced a renewed CCP with stronger grassroots support. The corrupt nature of the KMT and the manner in which it treated local populations only served to exacerbate the appeal of the CCP. Due to such practices, by the end of the Sino-Japanese War, it is estimated that the CCP governed some 20 percent of the Chinese population.[41] Building its ranks, membership, and territorial control during the war, the CCP and the Chinese Red Army established a firm hold among the rural populations that would pay future dividends.

War after the War

With the surrender of Japan, the Allies had to oversee one of the biggest postwar efforts, repatriating soldiers from all sides and the civilians displaced by the conflict. For the Japanese alone, this was a monumental task, as one in twenty Japanese citizens were located elsewhere in the Pacific or on the Asian mainland. Three million Japanese soldiers or civilians were in either Manchuria, Korea, or China proper.[42] Moreover, the power vacuum generated by the Japanese surrender and subsequent evacuation became a dangerous situation for the competing interests of the KMT, CCP, United States, and USSR. With all these disparate concerns following the war, China was a powder keg with a burning fuse.

A year before the official surrender came a change in American representation in China. The relationship between Stilwell and Chiang finally became intolerable. Differences in opinion and methodology regarding use of Chinese troops, strategy, and command came to a head in September 1944 during the Japanese "Ichi-Go" offensive. When pressed by the United States to install Stilwell as commander of all Chinese forces because of the ineffectiveness of Nationalist armies, the "peanut" bristled and pushed back on his American benefactors.[43] Loath to lose command of his armies, the generalissimo confided in the newly appointed U.S. ambassador, Maj. Gen. Patrick Hurley, that he planned to demand Stilwell's recall.[44] Still hoping to keep Chiang as an ally and looking to leverage KMT forces against the IJA, on 18 October Roosevelt acquiesced to his request. The president recalled Stilwell, replacing him with (then) Major General Wedemeyer.[45] Wedemeyer had a long track record of working strategic level issues with allies and, unlike his predecessor, initially saw Chiang in a different light. He treated the Chinese leader with greater deference and respect and often provided a rosier picture of him and the KMT than had Stilwell or other Americans in theater.[46] At this time Wedemeyer's optimistic depiction raised American hopes that the generalissimo could indeed be reasonable.

But the choice of Hurley as the new ambassador to China was far from perfect. Vain, arrogant, stubborn, and poorly prepared both diplomatically and intellectually for his new assignment, Hurley would do little to ameliorate the U.S. dilemma in China.[47] Coming from simple beginnings in Oklahoma, he fit the mold of an obnoxious rancher with steadfast opinions and outlandish behavior.[48] Always concerned about his personal appearance, Hurley was full of self-confidence and often careless in both words and deeds with his Chinese counterparts.[49] He was respected by neither side, with Mao referring to Hurley as "the clown" while the KMT called him "big wind."[50] Despite meetings with both the CCP and KMT, Hurley clearly sided with Chiang and the KMT. Both he and Roosevelt naïvely believed that providing aid to the Nationalists might enact a kind of political reform and transformation on their part.[51] Despite the concern over a potential civil war, Hurley idealistically hoped that some compromise was possible between the KMT and CCP that might result in a "free unified and democratic government."[52] Having simplistic, anti-intellectual views, he saw little contextual difference between the struggles in China and the domestic American landscape, with its political factions.[53]

Yet most U.S. officials in China came to realize that Mao and the CCP had more to offer the larger Chinese population than the KMT and their corrupt institutions. While the KMT was both harsh and cruel in its dealing with the masses, as U.S. military and DoS representatives came in contact with CCP forces, they found a rapport established between the peasantry and the Chinese Red Army. As CCP members enjoyed ever-increasing support from locals, U.S. representatives reported that this relationship was "a reality which we must consider in future planning." DoS officer Raymond Ludden made a journey deep into CCP-held territories. During his sojourns he observed, "The simple Communist program of decent treatment, fundamental civil rights, sufficient food, and sufficient clothing for the peasant has brought about a genuine unity between the 8th Route Army [CCP] and the people."[54] Ludden was not alone in this assessment. As time passed more Americans came to the conclusion that Chiang and the KMT were more interested in their own fortunes and were alienating those they were supposed to govern.[55] According to John Lacey, a U.S. naval officer in Beijing near the end of the war, "At that time under Mao's leadership the Chinese Communist forces unquestionably were well disciplined. Unlike Nationalist forces, the Chinese Communists would take over cities and towns, and instead of raping women and looting precious stores, they would take off their shirts and work the fields. It was a majestic example of how good propaganda can be a partner of diplomacy."[56] While the American in-country team was increasingly impressed with Communist gains, Hurley remained less enthusiastic and still threw his support behind Chiang.[57]

Adding to the attraction of the CCP for some Americans was a belief that Mao and the CCP were not truly Communists but just strong nationalists. As independence movements began to gain steam in the twentieth century, the rise of nationalism undermined existing occidental empires. But others not as liberally minded feared that Mao was the latest extension of growing global Communism.[58] While the Americans loathed the idea of Communism and its spread, many within the DoS warned that giving too much support to Chiang would only exacerbate his self-importance and push the CCP more to the Soviet sphere.[59]

Americans now found themselves in a complex diplomatic dilemma: How to help establish a friendly democratic government that included the increasingly popular CCP yet keep Communism at bay in the Far East and prevent its further extension? Concurrently, should the United States still provide aid and assistance to Chiang's Nationalists, who were tying down a large number of Japanese forces but were simultaneously the biggest obstacle to the envisioned (American) solution in China? The U.S. position was based upon the assumption that a strong yet conciliatory Nationalist regime could come to a compromise and form a coalition with the CCP. In this vision the United States idealistically wished for a Nationalist China that included sharing power with the Communists. Yet the chances of an agreement between factions that had been warring bitterly for years were slim.[60]

Following a visit by Hurley to the White House in March 1945, an ailing Roosevelt continued to support Chiang and the KMT. But a splintering of the

American perspective emerged earlier that year. For Hurley, an embarrassing message from the China chargé d'affaires staff (members of his own team in Chungking) reported the growing CCP influence. In the 26 February communication the chargé d'affaires staff identified Chiang's "lack of willingness to make any compromise" and that the generalissimo had "unrealistic optimism" regarding his standing with the Chinese masses.[61] Additionally, the communiqué argued that one of the major stumbling blocks to the entire problem in China was that "Chiang Kai-shek will not take any forward step which will mean loss of face, personal power, or prestige."[62] In the same message the in-country team further conveyed that American alienation of the CCP would increasingly help drive Mao and his supporters toward the Soviets.[63] Regardless of the chargé staff's subject-matter reports regarding the KMTs eroding support, Hurley continued to push for backing the Nationalists.[64]

Embarrassed with the report, it was obvious that Hurley was at odds with his own staff, who did not support his views. He returned to China both humiliated and infuriated. Their frank, expert opinions were not appreciated by the senior U.S. representative in China, especially while he was meeting with the president. What Hurley failed to recognize was that these experienced staffers were not pro-CCP by political leaning nor did they wish to see the expansion of its ideology. They were, however, justifiably cognizant of the CCP's growth, its integrity in dealing with the peasantry, and its standing as an attractive alternative to the KMT for the Chinese people. When contrasted against Nationalist corruption, mismanagement, and growing political failings, the chargé staff were merely realists, given the unfolding situation.[65]

After Hurley's return to China, many of the DoS officers who identified the CCP's popularity, having been there for years and understanding the nature of the Chinese, were soon reassigned. Despite their years of professional experience and astute observations about both the CCP and KMT, Hurley no longer welcomed their assistance. Exiling these seasoned staffers from China, he exacerbated problems within the CCP–U.S. relationship further when he imposed a ban on any American travel to the Communists' headquarters in Yennan.[66] Hurley attempted to facilitate negotiations between the two parties with some minor success. But during the latter half of 1945, and out of his depth in this international diplomatic realm, his attempt to mediate the struggle between the KMT and CCP ended in disappointment.[67] With his failure came frustration, and on 27 September Hurley abruptly resigned. Rather than show a true appreciation for the realities of the situation, he blamed his lack of success on professional diplomats in the DoS.[68] His resignation letter was a scathing indictment:

> The professional Foreign Service men sided with the Chinese Communists armed party and imperialist Bloc of nations whose policy it was to keep China divided against herself. Our professional diplomats continuously advised the Communists that my efforts in preventing the collapse of the National Government did not represent the policy of the United States. . . . I requested the relief of the career men who were opposing the American policy in the Chinese theater of war. . . . In such positions most of them have continued to side with the Communist armed party at times with the imperialist Bloc against American policy.[69]

In his letter Hurley clearly articulated his displeasure with the foreign-service officers who saw things differently and, in his opinion, worked against U.S. policy objectives.[70] These kinds of accusations and verbiage helped bolster the domestic critics of the Truman administration.[71] While they charged the president with being weak on Communism, what was more important domestically is that the China situation provided kindling for fervent anti-Communist "witch hunts" under McCarthyism, which would start in February 1950. This rhetoric also helped foment the domestic narrative in the United States over the "loss of China" in 1949 along with the creation of what became known as the "China Lobby."[72] But the more astute observer to the situation in China saw not the problems of U.S. policy as much as the numerous failings of Chiang and his inability to compromise, understand, or even realize his own shortcomings.[73]

Upon assuming the presidency, Truman had no illusions about China. He described Chiang's government as the "world's rottenest grafters and crooks" and equated any aid sent to the KMT as "pouring sand in a rat hole."[74] Conversely, the president also had no love of "commies" or the CCP.[75] Yet that did not mean he could avoid or ignore the events in the Far East, given the concern over emerging Soviet influence. Incensed upon hearing of the Hurley's resignation on the White House news ticker, Truman burst into his next cabinet meeting and yelled, "See what a son-of-a-bitch did to me!"[76] Given American interests in the region and the potential expansion of Soviet power in Asia, he came to the conclusion that decisive action was required.[77] Needing to shore up the U.S. position there, Truman called upon one of the most respected men in the nation, Gen. George C. Marshall.[78]

With the ink on his 17 November 1945 retirement paperwork barely dry and much to the chagrin on the general's wife, Katherine, days later Marshall was called on by the president to be his personal representative to China. Truman later wrote in his memoirs, "China appeared headed for trouble. . . . The only thing we could do was to exert whatever influence we might have to prevent civil war. The man for this job would have to possess unique qualifications and rare skill."[79] Marshall was indeed that man. In the president's mind, if Marshall could not fix the situation in China, no American could.

The CCP was well aware of U.S. transportation support for and the sale of excess equipment to KMT forces. For Mao, the United States was more a nefarious agent than a benevolent one. Concurrently, the KMT saw the inclusion of other political parties and evenhanded mediation as a deceitful ploy, with Chiang believing that military action was the only solution.[80] Since the KMT was more at the mercy of the United States in terms of support, the Nationalists grudgingly went along with the American plan. But Marshall's influence over the CCP to ensure their cooperation was significantly less as they relied on no American support.[81] While the United States did send some 50,000 Marines to help stabilize areas of northern China, this commitment was far less than what would be required to secure the whole country—had the United States attempted such an enormous task. But the American people, and especially Truman, were in no mood for a continued land war in Asia.

In his initial discussions with Wedemeyer, Marshall learned that neither side was interested in relinquishing power, and each looked only to aggrandize its current position.[82] Formal articulation of the American position came on 15 December in a statement by the president. In addition to ridding China of any Japanese influence and the evacuation of the occupying troops, Truman's official statement threw his support behind the KMT and proffered that autonomous armies, like those of the Communists, were a road block to national unity. He hoped that the KMT's forces and the Chinese Red Army might integrate into one unified Chinese National Army.[83] The Americans were still hoping for some kind of CCP-KMT power-sharing arrangement.[84]

Not everyone in the United States felt that way. Looking at the situation in China, many American businessmen, journalists, and right-wing activists formed a loose-knit, semiorganized group known as the China Lobby.[85] A key member and organizer, Alfred Kohlberg, railed against the Truman administration in a tone similar to Hurley's, claiming, "we had a policy-making group in the State Department which would have preferred a peaceful conquest of China by the Communists [as] evidenced by the presidents official statements of 15 December, 1945 . . . in which he called on Chiang Kai-shek to accept Communists in key posts in the government, while allowing retention of her own armies."[86] This was a bit of disinformation on Kohlberg's part, as the 15 December statement clearly states that a Communist army is "inconsistent with, and actually makes impossible, political unity in China."[87] Clearly this group of Americans saw any Communist inclusion as a retreat before a "Red" expansion with global aspirations.

One of the major developments affecting the China situation was the occupation of Manchuria by the Soviet Red Army. With the surrender of the Japanese and arrival of the Soviet Red Army, the CCP could easily move into the northern territories the IJA once held. Concurrently, with the help of U.S. transportation assets, the KMT was in a hurry to move its forces into these same regions in order to establish its claim in the postwar political land grab.[88]

Despite sharing political ideologies, the Soviets were less interested in the CCP and more concerned with their own territorial ambitions. At the Yalta Conference (4–11 February 1945), Stalin had pledged his support to the KMT despite his ideological kinship with the CCP.[89] Looking for more access to raw materials, ports, and rail lines in Manchuria, Chiang and Stalin signed the Sino-Soviet Treaty of Friendship on 14 August 1945, alienating the CCP and recognizing the KMT as the central government in China.[90] Despite what appeared a political betrayal, Soviet forces occupied northern China and kept the Nationalists out while allowing the CCP to effectively occupy the newly liberated areas of China.[91] For the KMT, the reoccupation of the northern areas was a priority, not just politically but also because it contained the heavy industries vital to China's future economy. Leveraging U.S. air and sealift capabilities, Nationalist forces were quickly flown to northern areas not yet occupied by the Soviets. While this support helped the KMT, more importantly, it was interpreted by the CCP as a warning that the United States could not be trusted as an impartial mediator.

The first attempt at mediation occurred on 7 January 1946. Marshall, KMT representative General Chang Chung, and Chou En-lai of the CCP met and formed what became known as the Committee of Three.[92] From this initial meeting, there was mistrust all around. The KMT remained suspicious of the CCP occupying lands in the north while seeing the USSR desiring territorial aggrandizement. The CCP was convinced that the KMT was bent on its destruction and believed they would not allow any Communist participation in a coalition government until the Chinese Red Army had been disestablished. Furthermore for the Communists, the Shanghai Massacre of 1927 provided precedent for their concerns, making them wary of dismantling their military capability until their legal political status was guaranteed.[93] Given the long history of the internal conflict, all sides had good reason to be suspicious.

Even with the uncertainties and animosities, days later a ceasefire was reached. Scheduled for 13 January 1946, it was accompanied with an agreement to form the Executive Headquarters in Peiping (Beijing) staffed by all concerned parties for continued dialogue. Most of the Chinese populace heralded the cessation of hostilities, though fully aware that the agreement was only worthwhile if its provisions where adhered to by the warring parties.[94] Marshall was convinced that the military and political situation could only be solved with additional economic reform in China and further aid from the United States.[95] Looking to capitalize on his recent, if illusory, success, the general returned to the United States in February to address Chinese economic concerns.

By the time Marshall returned to China on 18 April, the military situation had degraded, as heavy fighting occurred between CCP and KMT troops. According to the official U.S. government accounting, Marshall's frustration with the KMT and Chiang mounted as a result: "General Marshall characterized [KMT] acts as stupid actions of no benefit of the Nationalist Government, which not only served as ammunition to the Chinese Communists, but what was far more serious, stimulated their suspicions of government intentions."[96]

In order to influence Chiang, Marshall imposed an embargo of U.S. military aid to the KMT on 29 July.[97] In August Truman sent a carefully crafted message expressing his support for a peaceful resolution but blamed both sides' extremist elements for the continued tensions. The American position lost credibility with the CCP, however, when it agreed to give the Nationalist government nonmilitary war-surplus equipment. Communist propaganda saw this as yet again a deliberate U.S. effort to side with the KMT. While proposals for mediation and another cease-fire were made during the latter half of 1946, none of these efforts came to fruition, and military clashes only became more frequent.

Realizing the futility of the situation on 6 January 1947, Truman recalled the general. From the American perspective, it was obvious that the extremists on both sides had displaced the moderates and now held the reins. The idea of compromise and a coalition government held little promise. Despite his international reputation, Marshall's standing itself could not overcome the existing animosities and visceral distrust between the two sides.[98] In retrospect, his mission was doomed from the start as he appeared to have contradictory objectives, both sides seeing him as an agent for the other.[99] Indicative of his difficult position, in a letter to General of the Army Eisenhower months before his recall, Marshall complained, "My battle out here is never ending with both ends playing against the middle—which is me."[100] While his mission to China was a clear failure, it did not necessarily reflect on Marshall himself, as he was named secretary of state only weeks later, on 27 January 1947. Yet with the failure of the Marshall mission, U.S. interest in China did not evaporate or diminish. In fact, with the resignation of Hurley and the failure of Marshall, many on the American domestic scene began to sense that the nation was "losing China" to the Communists.

The China Lobby

Even after Marshall's failure to mediate the KMT-CCP rivalry in 1946, and in contrast to the U.S. foreign-service officers in China, many Americans still firmly stood behind the KMT and Chiang. For them, the generalissimo served as the best hope for a democratic nation to emerge from the complex mess of postwar China. The staunch anti-Communist "China Lobby" hoped to reverse KMT fortunes and see to the defeat of the CCP through continued U.S. aid. Yet this group overlooked the problems of the KMT and saw only the struggle against the extension of global monolithic Communism at the behest of the USSR. It was largely these individuals and their supporters who fomented the construct that China was "lost." In their view China was not necessarily lost because of Chiang's ineptitude and stubbornness or won by the CCP because of Mao's effective grassroots organization. Rather, it was lost because the United States failed in its support of the KMT. For this group, aid to China was just as important as Marshall Plan support was to Western Europe, and it linked the two regions geopolitically. As early as 1946 the group reasoned, "America's strategic frontier [lay] not on the Rhine or the Elbe or the Dardanelles. It [was] the borderline of the Soviet-American confrontation in Northern China."[101]

Hardly a hierarchical or formalized organization, the China Lobby was a loose association of individuals with diverse interests in Asia. Some were staunch supporters of Chiang, while others had more moneyed concerns.[102] One of the most visible members of the lobby was a private citizen named Alfred Kohlberg. Sometimes referred to as "Mr. China Lobby," Kohlberg was a New York City textile importer with a business focused on Asian goods.[103] After World War II he founded the China Policy Association and looked to promote a democratic China through support of the KMT. A fervent anti-Communist, he not only provided financial support to the association but also began publishing a magazine in October 1946 titled *Plain Talk*.[104]

Although never having a circulation over 12,000, *Plain Talk* endorsed right-wing politics and exacerbated anti-Communist sentiment.[105] Published to enlighten the American public about the dangerous and nefarious nature of global Communism's attack on Western civilization, *Plain Talk* featured articles from famous authors such as Margaret Mitchell, Ayn Rand, Victor Serge, and Bertrand Russell. The magazine warned that the KMT and Chiang were being undermined by Communist infiltrators in the U.S. government. In fact, about one-third of the content in the periodical focused on infiltration efforts by Communists toward American political and labor movements.[106]

Ironically, the term "China Lobby" was supposedly coined by Communist sympathizers to identify those forces working against their efforts.[107] Despite the name's etymology, the lobby held the opinion that the loss of China lay mostly within the DoS and the infiltration of Communists into the policymaking departments of the federal government.[108] With Hurley's departure and Marshall's recall, members of the China Lobby began to formulate this idea along with the betrayal of Chiang. As early as January 1949 Rep. Walter Judd (R-MN) argued that "left-wingers" were the root of the problem regarding China, echoing Hurley's earlier 1945 claims.[109] To members of the lobby, his resignation and indictment of the DoS was a clear warning of Communist infiltration.

Within Congress, representatives and senators solidly behind the KMT were referred to as the "China Bloc." To these elected officials the threat of Red China was not only a national security issue but also, pragmatically, a domestic political issue that might help strengthen their hand in the upcoming 1948 elections. The 1946 midterm elections saw the Eightieth Congress switch from Democratic to Republican control. The bloc's focus was not only to defeat Chinese Communism but also to gain the White House in order to continue the "Open Door" policy that promised lucrative trade deals for investors.[110] With the candidacy of Gov. Thomas Dewey in the 1948 presidential contest, the GOP was looking for issues to counter the Democrats and the Truman administration. Accusing Truman and the Democrats of being "soft on Communism" was at the vanguard of the Republican attack. In this vein the topic of China became a postwar partisan issue.[111]

In partial response to GOP political charges, the president announced the "Truman Doctrine" on 12 March, which provided $400 million in aid ostensibly to counter Communist encroachment in Greece and Turkey. Nine days later the president signed Executive Order 9835, which required a loyalty-security program for all federal employees. A little over a month later, in June, Truman proposed a draft of the Marshall Plan to assist Western Europe in its wartime-recovery efforts. While both a humanitarian and an economic program to reduce the suffering of Europeans, the plan was also an incentive to deter Communist incursions into the political landscape of recipient nations. By reinforcing capitalism in Western Europe, the Marshall Plan envisioned those countries recoiling from the temptations of international Communism.

Looking to undermine the Truman administration's anti-Communist credibility and gain political capital, congressional Republicans in the China Bloc argued that the same kind of support allocated for European nations should also be provided to China. Months after Mao's declaration, China Bloc member Judd argued, "We didn't say to the Greeks, Italians, and French . . . we'll help you if you take in Communists into your governments. . . . [We said] we'll help you if you keep them out."[112] Leveraging the administration's own policies as a basis for argument, Judd claimed that Communism was stopped in Europe. Subsequently, he argued that the denial of such aid to China and the requirement to include the CCP in any national government facilitated Communist encroachment, making a further connection that if China goes "Red," so too would Asia.[113]

On 27 March, during hearings on assistance to Greece and Turkey, Judd queried Undersecretary of State Dean Acheson "why aid wasn't being allocated to China as well." Acheson argued that China was not in the same precarious position as the Greek government and that Chiang's Nationalists were not on the verge of collapse. The undersecretary argued further that the war between the KMT and CCP had been going on for twenty years and that Chiang's forces were in no immediate danger of being defeated.[114] Acheson did not lie, but he did not exactly tell the truth. Reports out of China by this time were clear about the KMT's failures and the growing Communist gains and momentum. With the fall of KMT garrisons in northern China at this time, Acheson already knew more than he was telling.

Two months later Kohlberg claimed in *Plain Talk*, "The mysterious American policy in China, which made many a senator and congressman wonder why the Truman Doctrine of stemming Communism is not being applied in the Far East is largely the handiwork of the pro–Soviet Bloc headed by [DoS Director of Far East Affairs] John Carter Vincent."[115] While certainly an indictment of Vincent, he was no Communist. Yet as an observer of the CCP's operations in China, he saw the futility of continued KMT support. Regardless of the facts, Kohlberg's kind of claim only served to underpin the Communist-infiltration concerns that would become so prevalent later and added to the argument that China had indeed been "lost" by the Truman administration.

Whether Communist sympathizers were infiltrating the DoS or not, as 1947 passed and the CCP continued its march south, the collapse of the KMT on the mainland was coming to pass despite Undersecretary Acheson's claims. Given the success of the Chinese Red Army in 1947–48 and what was to occur in the autumn of 1949, Acheson's earlier words were indeed ironic. Furthermore, the embargo placed by Marshall in 1946 served to support the China Lobby's argument that the Truman administration was to blame for the fall of the KMT. Given the unfolding events, critics made the argument that the United States was ignoring the larger issues in Asia. They also simultaneously ignored the problems inherent in KMT leadership and its function.

In July 1948 Congress took up the issue of Communist espionage and included the events in China to underpin the larger argument of infiltration in the federal government. Furthermore, the House Un-American Activities Committee (HUAC) was gaining strength regarding suspicions of Communist influence and infiltration in Hollywood. While the committee had been around since the late 1930s, given the emerging threat and America's role in the postwar period, it found fertile ground for continued its existence. As a result, the domestic political scene was having a direct effect upon U.S. policies regarding China and support for the KMT.

Within Congress, members such as Charles Hallek (R-IN), Joseph Martin (R-MA), Robert Taft (R-OH), Owen Brewster (R-ME), Styles Bridges (R-NH), William Jenner (R-IN), and Ken Wherry (R-NE) were all pushing for continued support of Chiang regardless of his fundamental flaws, mistreatment of the masses, and rampant corruption. In fact, as late as July 1949, politician and diplomat Clare Boothe Luce, wife of *Time*, *Life*, and *Fortune* magazine publisher Henry Luce, wrote an article in *Plain Talk* defending the KMT against charges of corruption. In it she argued, "Corruption is most especially a product of war's tyrannies and tribulations. . . . [T]he smear word corruption had been trumpeted by the communists throughout America as the real reason we must not aid China. . . . Corruption is not the policy of the Kuomintang, . . . but mass murder–genocide is an official principle of communists."[116] While American observers in China were opposed to a further U.S. commitment and aid, men of the China Lobby and the China Bloc were either hopelessly optimistic about Chiang's chances of success, blind to the reality that existed, or looked to score points politically.

China Lobby members made trips to the country to assess the situation for themselves. When meeting members of the DoS in Nanking, they received briefings that usually challenged their pro-KMT notions. In one of the many trips made by Representative Judd, he asked DoS staffers, "What can we do? What can we do?" The country team replied with few useful suggestions given the situation, and according to one attendee, the session was described as altogether "gloomy." When Henry Luce went to see the situation firsthand, he too was chagrined by what he saw. Born in China, Luce was an influential member of the Republican Party, a strong proponent of the lobby, and an advocate of proselytizing Christianity in Asia. When hearing of the impending loss of the KMT, he told one foreign-service officer, "We [Christian missionaries] had made a lifetime commitment to the advancement of Christianity in China. . . . You're asking us to say that all our lives have been wasted; they have been futile. They've been lived for nothing."[117]

Despite these bleak accounts, those in the China Lobby continued to voice their political rhetoric. This fear of Communist encroachment was seen everywhere and added to the anxiety of the time. Yet while the lobby howled, members of the China Bloc shied away from calling for a full-scale military intervention by the United States. As a result Truman was stuck between the proverbial "rock and a hard place": either continue aid to a corrupt and inefficient government that would eventually lose to the Communists, all for the expedient of domestic political consumption, or deny such aid and face the wrath of the China Lobby and the upstart GOP.

In July 1947 Wedemeyer was sent back to China for yet another assessment. Earlier in 1946, during Marshall's mission, the lieutenant general was among those who saw the situation different from the former Army chief of staff. Having served for an extended period in China, Wedemeyer was considered an expert on the region, and his words held sway. In November 1946, two months before Marshall's recall, Wedemeyer addressed the National War College: "We learned that the Generalissimo and his associates will cooperate. They can and did improve the condition of their armies and people. They made rapid strides when they had the benefit of friendly and concrete American advice." Furthermore, he refuted the overall assessment that the KMT was wholly "totalitarian, corrupt, and oppressive," while the Communists, despite their claims, were not "democratic in either agrarian economy or political organization."[118] In Wedemeyer's opinion, Mao and his Red Army were pawns of the USSR, and their first interests lay with Stalin rather than their fellow Chinese.[119]

Yet following his 1947 trip to China, Wedemeyer changed his tune and turned 180 degrees from his previous assessment. In this later visit Wedemeyer, not surprisingly, found poor administration within the KMT, corruption, and lethargy.[120] Perhaps sensing the political winds changing and looking to maintain his own standing, in his submitted statement of 19 September, he reported, "The Communists have the tactical initiative in the overall military situation. . . . [C]ontinued deterioration of the situation may result in early establishment of Soviet satellite government in Manchuria and ultimately in the evolution of a Communist-dominated China. . . . Maladministration and corruption cause a loss of confidence in the [KMT] government. Until drastic political and economic reforms are undertaken United States aid cannot accomplish its purpose."[121] At the end of his findings, Wedemeyer recommended continued U.S. advisory and material support to the KMT despite their faults and dire situation.[122] Yet while he recommended continuing material aid, he also commented that the KMT needed to enact "drastic political and economic reforms," something Chiang had already proven loath to do.[123] For most in Washington, any more aid to the generalissimo would yield little benefit, and there was no support in the United States for a commitment of ground forces on the behalf of the KMT. Wedemeyer's discouraging report was suppressed by Truman since it might empower the growing China Bloc in their calls for increased aid to Chiang.[124] But Truman's actions would only exacerbate the tension between the two political parties in the fall of 1949.

Despite the military situation in China in 1947, the China Bloc did influence Truman's support for the KMT. Regardless of Marshall's imposed embargo on military materials to the Nationalists in July 1946, when the Marines withdrew from northern China, they were instructed to leave 6,500 tons of ammunition and other materials for the KMT.[125] Furthermore, in May after being in effect for ten months, Marshall's embargo was lifted, and 130 million rounds of 7.62-mm rifle ammunition was sold at a considerable discount. Then in October Congress allocated $22.7 million in economic aid and allowed an Army advisory group to help train KMT forces in Taiwan. Finally, in November, Maj. Gen. David Barr was ordered to head another advisory group but warned not to take any responsibility for Nationalist plans and operations.[126] In February 1948 Truman sent a message to Congress calling for additional support to China. Called the China Aid Act, the president proposed sending an additional $570 million of assistance for "essential imports" and "reconstruction projects."[127] With these actions, the Democrats could at least parry some of the Republican charges regarding the impending loss of KMT forces. Yet many within the China Lobby still pointed to Marshall's embargo as a reason for the KMT failure despite the hopelessness of the situation.[128]

By mid-September 1948 KMT troops numbered some 2.7 million. Yet by 1 February 1949, just after the Huai Hai fight, those numbers stood at only 1.5 million, with 500,000 being only service troops—a drop of 45 percent in a four-month period.[129] By the time Chinese Red Army forces finished the Huai Hai campaign, they were poised to cross the Yangtze River, capture Tientsin, and eventually take Peiping without a fight.[130] In April the Communists continued their offensives and crossed the Yangtze; within two weeks they had pushed south of the river by some 120 miles. Without opposition they moved west into the capital city of Nanking and then occupied Shanghai on 25 May.

As the picture became bleaker, Chiang left mainland China in December 1949, vowing to come back. Despite his defiant rhetoric, his evacuation led one DoS officer to remark, "Chiang squandered in four years greater military power than any ruler in the history of China . . . and was now reduced to the status of a refugee on a small island."[131] Others at the DoS observed the KMT was a fractured force unable to deal with its internal problems.[132] While Nationalist forces had modern weapons and training, Chiang's shortcomings resulted in their defeat. Unable to see his faults himself and correct them, Chiang was his own biggest liability. Mao, too, observed these KMT shortcomings, writing as early as 1936, "It [the KMT] opposed the agrarian revolution and therefore and has no support from the peasantry. Though it has a large army, the KMT cannot make its soldiers or lower ranking officers . . . risk their lives willingly. Its officers and men are politically divided, which reduces its fighting capacity."[133]

These events occurred as Truman was just beginning his second term.[134] Despite the president's electoral victory, he was not immune to continued attack by the China Bloc. As 1949 began Representative Judd again spoke as a member of the bloc: "The administration had been making every possible effort to help . . . the governments of western Europe resist further expansion of Communism and no real effort to help the Chinese government resist Communist expansion. . . . Since December 1945 our policy in Asia, in fact if not in words, had been one of abandonment of the Chinese government."[135] Others saw the "loss" as an intellectual shortcoming and an inability of those policymakers to see the true evils of Communism. In July 1949 an article in *Plain Talk* argued, "The tragic failure of our times has been the failure of many of America's so-called 'intellectuals' to grasp the economic, political and spiritual consequences of the Soviet ideology. This failure to grasp abstract ideas, and to make deductions from them, has made these American intellectuals unworthy. . . . [T]heir failure was the failure of a whole post war generation of intellectuals."[136]

While, like Truman, bloc members tried to avoid a large-scale military commitment in China, the lobby and bloc were still persistent in decrying the lack of uniformity by the Truman administration in the application of George Kennan's concept of "containment." With a focus on Europe, the hardcore Republicans found plenty to complain about in 1949 regarding China. As the military situation there worsened, so too would the criticism. In a meeting with House Republicans on 24 February regarding the deteriorating situation, newly appointed Secretary of State Acheson argued that the course of American policy in China would have to wait until "the dust and smoke of the Chinese civil war had settled."[137] By this time it was pretty obvious how this dust would settle.

Others also complained about the KMT's future on the Asia mainland, but there was little the United States could do. In correspondence to concerned constituents regarding the situation in China, Sen. Bourke B. Hickenlooper (R-IA) drafted a standard answer: "The China situation is a most difficult one. Despite the great volumes of money and materials we have poured into China, it appears now that the Nationalists Government is disintegrating. The menace of communism is well recognized, and the question of what further aid can be given under most careful consideration and study by appropriate authority here."[138]

The *China White Paper*

Considering the military circumstances in China in early 1949, most observers knew it was only a matter of time before the complete rout of the Nationalists on the mainland. In March 1949 Rep. John McCormack (D-MA) suggested a fact-finding commission be formed to inquire about the state of Asia and U.S. policies in China.[139] Truman replied negatively to the suggestion, adding, "we all know too well what the facts are."[140] Given both the situation in China and the American domestic political landscape, the Truman administration had to respond to the perceived "loss of China" to the public, the China Lobby, and those Republicans looking to score political points. To fully account, or possibly atone, for the events in China to the American people, Truman directed a full written account of U.S. actions during the civil war and the preceding events.[141] By revealing the nation's collective efforts given the anticipated Communist victory, the president and his allies hoped to clarify why a friend of America, however uncooperative, had fallen to the "Red Menace." More immediately, according to DoS official John Melby, one of the chief authors of the document, they "set forth to record, and set it straight, no matter who got hurt." The authors looked to make the most earnest and straightforward accounting of events. According to Melby, "it was not to be a propaganda job, presenting one side."[142] But he understood that there was a large political component to the work, confessing, "The purpose was to call off the dogs from the China Lobby, insofar as you can define it."[143]

Melby's work became known as the *China White Paper* and was a painstaking review of actions, letters, documents, reports, and personal observations relating to the Sino-American relationship from 1844 up to the spring of 1949. The job of compiling this vast amount of information was entrusted to only a handful of officers with recent experience in China. For five months they worked around the clock to collect, edit, and produce the volume, a monumental task.[144] The day before its official publication, Truman claimed that U.S. relations with China had "been subject to considerable misrepresentation, distortion, and misunderstanding." In directing such a document, he hoped to provide a "frank and factual record . . . to insure that our foreign policy toward China . . . shall be based on informed and intelligent public opinion."[145] When finally published on 5 August 1949, officially titled *United States Relations with China* (DoS Publication 3573), the document comprised over one thousand pages.

In a letter of transmittal at the beginning of the work, Secretary of State Acheson wrote, "This is a frank record of an extremely complicated and most unhappy period in the life of a great country to which the United States has long been attached by ties of closest friendship."[146] Yet in reading all of Acheson's transmittal, his opinion was clear: Chiang and the KMT failed to make the proper changes required both politically and militarily while rejecting advice offered by their American benefactors. Additionally, the CCP was able to capitalize on this intransigence and garner wide public support through promised reforms and propaganda. Acheson further came to the conclusion that only a huge amount of effort in time, money, and manpower could have "saved" China. But the enormous commitment of such resources was not worth the cost given the recent return to peace.

The overall message that the administration hoped to send was that the United States did all that it could to support Chiang and the KMT. Given the inflexibility, corruption, and stubbornness of the Nationalist regime, there was little else for America or Truman to do. In an introduction to a 1968 reprint of the *China White Paper*, Asian historian Lyman Van Slyke wrote, "If there was no possibility of withdrawing support from Chiang, there was no way of getting him to make changes he did not choose to make."[147] As a result the United States faced a Hobson's choice: pour in more money and possibly large amounts of manpower while getting involved in a land war in Asia and possibly provoking the USSR (after a major global conflict to back a corrupt and increasingly unpopular Nationalist regime) or provide what aid it could to the KMT and let the chips fall where they may.

Regardless of the "lose-lose" scenario Truman was facing, once published the *China White Paper* failed to mollify his enemies, political or otherwise. With the KMT army still in the field, detractors thought the document was prematurely "throwing in the towel." Prominent among them were the Joint Chiefs.[148] Unhappy with the military narrative, the JCS claimed that it made the CCP look blameless for the events and further argued that the Communists' skills in propaganda had distorted the accounting.[149]

Many read the contents and viewed them in the context to which they had already subscribed. Those in the China Lobby still blamed Marshall for his 1946 embargo and claimed that more military aid could have made a difference. Some criticized that the paper omitted documents that fully told the whole story. Representative Judd claimed that the omission of some sixteen key documents precluded a full accounting of U.S. policy.[150] He complained that the military-intelligence reports of 1944–45 were absent. Judd believed that had these reports been acted upon, the loss of China could have been avoided.[151] In this same vein Kohlberg of the China Lobby immediately attacked the document, claiming, "The real purpose of the White Paper seems, in spite of the omission of many important documents, to be to reveal to the Chancelleries of the world the story of American betrayal of the Republic of China."[152] Others claimed that it was a "brazen effort to falsify history," that when "fully understood" would show how Chinese Communists had "manipulated United States officials and America China policy so as to take control of China," and that it omitted more than it clarified.[153]

Critics of Truman argued that the paper illustrated five reasons for the "loss." First was that the United States betrayed China at Yalta by asking the USSR to participate in the war against Japan when that conflict was essentially already over.[154] This agreement gave the Soviets access to important parts of Manchuria, with pro-KMT periodicals calling this the "Sin of Yalta."[155] A second reason was that Marshall's mission and his mandate to create a CCP-KMT coalition government was not only a betrayal of Chiang but also validated Mao and caved in to the Communists' expansion.[156] Third was the claim that suppressing the Wedemeyer report of 1947 precluded effective aid being sent to China at a time when it might have made a difference.[157] The fourth reason was related to the third, specifically that had sufficient aid been rendered in a reasonable time frame, the KMT might have hung on to power. This reasoning disregarded the fact that by February 1949 the United States had distributed $123,950,685.71 under the China Aid Act of 1948. Fifth was that the Communists and their sympathizers within the DoS had an overwhelming effect on U.S. China policy.[158]

Perhaps this last charge was the most serious, with implications lasting years and having a devastating effect on the American diplomatic landscape. In one official's estimate Hurley's accusations against the DoS, combined with Senator McCarthy's Communist hunts of the 1950s, adversely affected the reputations of the foreign service for at least a generation.[159] Suspicion of the DoS continued for years. Indicative of this was a December 1950 letter from Kohlberg to Truman five months after North Korea's invasion of the South. In the open letter he asked the president, "Why have you for 5 years, and why do you still, reject the advice of General MacArthur on the Far East, preferring the advice of a State Department, which is on public record as having no policy and intending to prepare none until the dust settles?"[160] For these detractors and critics of the administration and the Democratic Party, it was easier to make claims of mismanagement and malfeasance than to truly analyze the situation.[161]

Now What?

With the mounting military defeats and with the CCP pushing south in late 1949, Chiang and his army withdrew to Taiwan in early December. While the China Lobby and the China Bloc were indeed eager to support the KMT, the Truman administration was less than enthusiastic. Shortly after Mao's declaration of the PRC in October, the National Security Council (NSC) revisited the U.S. position regarding possible military action in defense of Taiwan. On 6 October, in conjunction with the JCS, the NSC came to the conclusion that the island of Formosa lacked sufficient strategic value to justify U.S. military intervention. Months later, in January 1950, Truman announced that the United States would not provide military aid to KMT on the island, much to the disdain of the China Lobby. In essence, this announcement terminated the U.S. role in Chinese civil war. While a potential loss of Taiwan would indeed weaken the American position in the Far East, the United States still had strategic footholds in the Philippines, the Ryukyu Islands, and Japan proper.[162] Supporting this decision was a JCS estimate that $125 million worth of military equipment provided to the KMT was already stockpiled on Taiwan.

Furthermore, the NSC reported that Chiang stated privately that he could hold Taiwan for up to two years without any reinforcement.[163] Perhaps more telling was that the council feared further support would convince the KMT of unending U.S. support regardless of its mismanagement and corruption.[164] The report went on to argue that any reasonable course of action on the part of the United States needed to be met with "corrective action" on the part of the KMT.[165] Hence, the administration was unwilling to throw any more good money after bad, especially if the money would only end up in the pockets of KMT officials or wasted in ill-conceived military operations.

While this was the official position taken, Defense Secretary Johnson provided false hope to KMT representatives in Washington, D.C., claiming he would still call for military action. Johnson promised Madame Chiang and the Chinese ambassador, Wellington Koo, that he was prepared to support further military aid. As a result Acheson, who believed the defense of Taiwan was not in the U.S. national interests, was now at odds with the defense secretary. Despite Johnson's promises, Truman not only sided with Acheson but also instructed Johnson to make no further efforts in this issue.[166]

The issue at hand now was whether the United States should recognize Mao's government. However, while other countries were quick to do so, the United States withheld its formal approval (and did so for decades, until 1979). While some called for military action in the form of a blockade, the JCS and President Truman rejected the idea.[167] Although the idea of U.S. recognition seemed farfetched at the time, on the same day as the NSC estimate on Taiwan was published and the October B-36 hearings started, the DoS began a three-day roundtable discussion on the way forward for Sino-American relations. Attended by men such as Kennan, W. W. Butterworth, Bernard Brodie, and John B. Rockefeller, the discussion grappled with how to proceed with U.S. interests in the Far East. The answers to many of the questions were fairly pragmatic and hardly what the China Lobby or the China Bloc expected. Regarding American responsibility toward saving China from a totalitarian (CCP) regime, the consensus was "this is none of our business what kind of regime the Chinese people set for themselves, . . . a totalitarian regime [was] set up for the Chinese by Chinese." As to the question of U.S. recognition of the PRC and possible future trade relationships, the group suggested that the word "Communist" be eliminated from the discussion and replaced with "Chinese."[168] In this way it would appear more palatable to trade with an ethnicity rather than a political party or philosophy. Some even believed that fractures between the USSR and the PRC might result in Mao becoming a Marshal Tito (the neutral Communist ruler of Yugoslavia) in Asia.[169]

By the end of the session, the general conclusion was that political upheaval in China was due to internal strife and conditions and not necessarily the result of Communist infiltration or expansionist policies. The group argued that any external intervention on the part of the U.S. military was a waste of effort and would only exacerbate the Communist position. In this argument they made direct connection to the failed 1918 U.S. Polar Bear Expedition in Russia during that country's civil war.[170] In the course of discussions the members concluded that the new Communist regime came about from Chinese domestic problems, and no amount of intervention would change that fact. In their collective opinions these problems now belonged to the new regime. If the CCP did not fix the existing problems, then another revolution was in the offing.

Yet this pragmatism was not welcomed or accepted by the general public or by select members of Congress. With the nation on the very cusp of the McCarthy era, any recognition of Communist influence anywhere was a vice. Marshall's inability to reconcile the KMT and the CCP would continue to provide fodder for those staunch anti-Communists looking for any perceived appeasement.[171] As late as 1951, in a purely partisan attack on the general, Senator McCarthy penned a short book castigating Marshall and framing him as a Communist dupe. In his work of character assassination, McCarthy wrote, "If Marshall were merely stupid, the laws of probability would have dictated that at least some of his decisions would have served the country's interests."[172]

The "loss of China" helped underpin the unfortunate events of the McCarthy witch hunts of the early 1950s, when everyone was under suspicion. A catalyst to these persecutions was the events unfolding in Asia and the appearance of Communist infiltration in Washington. But for understanding the more complex issues involved in China, perhaps the best embodiment of this group's perspective regarding the KMT's failure was a tongue-in-cheek comment by a DoS official: "Let's not act like a child who got mad, kicked its block-built house all over the nursery floor and now howls if anyone else touches his blocks."[173]

Despite this rather pragmatic view of the world at this time, a few days later on 12 October, Acheson laid out three requirements for recognition of a new government: That it control the country it claimed; that it recognize all international treaties and agreements; and that it rule with the approval of those it claimed to represent.[174] While the CCP could indeed claim to have met the first and third requirements, the second was a significant issue. Earlier that year, the Central Committee of the CCP declared void all treaties and agreements drafted by the Nationalists, including any loans provided by foreign governments during their rule. This line of thought was also supported by Mao in 1949, when he refused to recognize the legal status of diplomats and took control of foreign assets, among other actions.[175] With this framework in place, the CCP was hardly worthy of recognition given Acheson's criteria.

Perhaps the situation at the time was best summed up by Truman in a letter to a friend, attorney Maury Maverick of San Antonio. Maverick, a Democrat who served in the House of Representatives from Texas, recommended as early as 1949 that the president recognize Communist China. Maverick knew full well the implications of this, as he had lost an election as mayor of San Antonio in 1941 after accusations of Communist affiliations. With the polarizing nature of the decision, Truman was not short of advice or suggestions. In his response to his friend's advice, the chief executive wrote, "There are so many crackpots who know all about what to do and who [in reality] really know nothing about what to do."[176] This seemed to sum up the entire situation.

Rebel with a Cause

After the August hearings the U.S. Air Force could breathe a sigh of relief. With the testimony given and Worth's confession, strategic-airpower advocates publically turned the tables. At the end of August DoD's Office of Public Information confirmed that the USAF had successfully defended itself in the court of public opinion. After reviewing media accounts regarding the B-36 investigation, it reported the service had made a "good case for itself" and that Secretary Symington was completely vindicated. Regarding the B-36 and its mission, the office determined Americans saw the new aircraft as a valid requirement and strategic bombing as an integral part of the U.S. military. Furthermore, the suspension of Worth was largely lauded by the press, with his claims against the B-36 considered "farcical."[177] By all accounts the USAF had rebuffed the accusations and cleared the names of those accused of inappropriate action.

Given the outcome of the August hearings, Representative Vinson considered canceling or at least delaying the scheduled October session.[178] Pushing the date back would allow time for Weapons Systems Evaluation Group (WSEG) to complete its evaluation of the atomic air offensive component of the Offtackle war plan. While the Harmon Report, published in May, provided insights into bombing effectiveness, its results were not wholly conclusive. Many officials, both civilian and military, were looking forward to the WSEG assessment. But this more detailed study would not begin until September, with its findings scheduled for release no sooner than January 1950, months after the October hearings.[179] Awaiting the WSEG report might provide Vinson with a convenient reason to force a delay, maybe an indefinite one. A postponement might also provide Secretary Matthews time to address specific Navy concerns directly with Defense Secretary Johnson before proceeding with further arguments before Congress.[180] Additionally, it might prevent further embarrassment for the Department of the Navy. But not everyone agreed with Matthews' thinking. In addition to speaking their minds in defense of their service, many naval officers rejected the idea of postponement, as further budgetary decisions might be made in the intervening months. If the current trend continued without them expressing their concerns, naval advocates feared additional funding cuts.

Regarding the August hearings, the Navy immediately held a court of inquiry, with Admiral Kinkaid as the presiding officer, to identify who else might be involved in creating the public embarrassment.[181] Over the course of a few weeks, Kinkaid's inquiry found no further information regarding the drafting of the "anonymous document." While a number of naval officers were questioned and gave sworn statements, they all testified that whatever support they provided was done with no knowledge of Worth's real intentions. According to those called before the panel, any material provided to him was thought to be fodder for other investigations or valid endeavors.[182] Even aircraft manufacturer Glenn Martin was called to testify. Martin intimated the same response as the naval officers. For his part, Worth again admitted his guilt in these proceedings and implicated no one else.[183]

Nevertheless, even with the August hearings behind them, Navy leadership found no respite with the coming of autumn. Regardless of the false accusations and innuendoes drafted by Worth, naval aviators still felt only resentment and frustration. In a private letter to CNO Denfeld, the military editor of the *New York Times*, Hanson Baldwin, warned that Worth "only represents what a great many of our naval aviators with the finest war records believe, and some of them are so bitter and violent on this whole issue that they are about ready to turn in their suits." For him and those of his ilk, what was happening to naval aviation was considered "Billy Mitchell in reverse."[184] Baldwin was sympathetic to the Navy's cause, and in other letters to the CNO, he echoed much of the sentiment expressed by the aviators. While Denfeld acknowledged the harm done to the service's reputation, he hoped the scheduled hearings would repair the damage.

Dismayed at the idea of a potential delay, some in the Navy wished to continue the public fight immediately. While Worth wrote his document to generate an open forum for the Navy, another naval aviation advocate, fearing that their side of the story was still being ignored, looked to push the plight of the U.S. carrier fleet to a larger venue. Yet this next effort to publicize the Navy's dilemma did not come from a civilian, but from a uniformed active-duty officer subject to military law.

Capt. John Crommelin was a decorated naval aviator who had served with distinction in the Pacific War. On board USS *Enterprise* for much of 1942–43, he was assigned as the ship's "air officer" (also known as the "air boss" in naval terminology), responsible for all aircraft operations on board the carrier. During the warship's participation in the intense battles of Guadalcanal, Santa Cruz Islands, and the Eastern Solomons, Crommelin's service as air boss was widely respected. His time on the "Big E" won him praise and admiration from both peers and superiors alike.[185] Following his duty on *Enterprise*, he became chief of staff for USS *Liscome Bay* and was on board when the escort carrier was sunk by a Japanese submarine off the Gilbert Islands on 23 November 1943. Below deck when the attack commenced, Crommelin made his way to the flight deck and jumped in the water, suffering severe burns in the process. Receiving the Purple Heart and recovering from his wounds, he returned to active duty in early 1944 and again served in combat. Known as "Bomb-Run John" for his aggressive nature, following the war Crommelin continued his sea duty and became commander of the training carrier USS *Saipan*.

Yet it was not his combat heroics or sea duty that made Crommelin notable, rather it was his belief that naval aviation was being short-changed at the behest of DoD leadership. Eventually stationed at the Pentagon and placed with the Joint Staff of the JCS in 1949, Crommelin was a tireless advocate for the Navy. Like many others, he saw his service under threat of becoming irrelevant, or at least offensively neutered. With the sting of the August hearings still fresh, adding salt to the Navy's wounds was an announcement by the Defense Management Committee on 8 September proposing a cut in its expenditures by some $353 million.[186] While Secretary Matthews believed that the reduction would be ameliorated at a later date, this latest blow was more proof to Crommelin and like-minded officers that the Navy was being sacrificed on the altar of unification. Adding to his frustration, the captain was scheduled to appear before Kincaid's board of inquiry. His appearance was later canceled.[187]

Crommelin decided to take matters into his own hands. Risking his professional career, he publically entered the fray. Taking the initiative, he independently called a press conference at his own home on 10 September, where he publically railed against DoD leadership on behalf of the Navy. At the core of his argument was the new joint structure, arguing that the recent budgetary action was designed to "gradually destroy the offensive potential of naval aviation by budgeting curtailments. The plan is now proceeding along this line."[188] He complained that the Navy was continuously shortchanged by unification starting in 1947, and in his frustration he "just can't stand it any longer."[189] Perhaps the captain's most memorable quip was when he declared that the Navy's offensive power was being "nibbled to death."[190]

Crommelin rejected the idea of the Joint Staff, moreover that of the JCS, as it was currently structured. For him, he saw the Air Force and the Army dominating both the military establishment and national strategy as a combined team.[191] From the naval perspective, this duo continued to reconcile their own differences while imposing their collective will on the sea service.[192] For the Navy this collective effort undermined progress and improvement regarding national security and led to an authoritarian environment that was "inflexible, unwieldly, and slow moving."[193] Simply put, the other two services could easily thwart any naval progress by a simple majority on the Joint Staff.

The captain declared that he had nothing to do with Worth's efforts but believed the author of the "anonymous document" had acted with "the highest motives of patriotism and selflessness."[194] During his press conference, Crommelin criticized the constant downsizing of the Navy and the current joint structure. He argued that military efficiency was "going to pieces" because the individual armed services were dominated by the general staff. More specifically he charged that the "Joint Chiefs of Staff [have] a land-locked concept of national defense."[195] This charge became even more pointed when Crommelin claimed that the chairman of the JCS, Gen. Omar Bradley, "was in a position to wield tremendous power and he too may have land locked philosophy. Such a condition is intolerable in the greatest democracy and the greatest maritime nation in all history."[196] Feeling personally invested, and in much the same spirit as Baldwin remarked in his letter to Denfeld, Crommelin declared that he was willing to resign his commission over this issue or even face a court-martial. He concluded his remarks by insinuating that James Forrestal's suicide was connected to the former secretary's erroneous support of unification.[197] While hardly a claim that could be substantiated, it raised some eyebrows.

Despite Crommelin's bold public pronouncements criticizing DoD leadership, a serious breach of the chain of command and grounds for a potential court-martial, naval officers quickly came to his defense. Those who agreed with his argument included Fleet Admiral William Halsey, who stated, "He [Crommelin] was trying to do something good for the country and . . . showed wonderful courage in jeopardizing his career. . . . [He] deserves the help and respect of all naval officers."[198] Another admiral went so far as to say, "Captain John Crommelin is one of the greatest naval aviators of all time [and] the American people should listen to him."[199] By supporting the notion penned by Baldwin to the CNO regarding the ire of naval aviators, Crommelin was flooded with messages and letters of support. Instantaneously the renegade officer attained folk-hero status within the aviator community for his sacrificial act. But this act would not be his last.

As far as DoD leadership was concerned, Crommelin was now a political lighting rod and a liability. Because of the captain's comments at his unsanctioned press conference, Navy Secretary Matthews believed Crommelin was no longer qualified to serve on the Joint Staff. Looking to avoid public scrutiny, Defense Secretary Johnson largely recused himself from the matter, leaving the Navy to deal with the renegade officer. The Navy Secretary left it to Undersecretary Dan Kimball to have Crommelin reassigned just five days later, on 15 September.[200] Since the captain was at one time seen as a promising candidate for flag rank, the usual procedure was for an officer with his potential to be assigned a billet requiring a rear admiral. Initially, Crommelin was ordered to fill such a post as director of naval aviation personnel.[201] But when Secretary Matthews heard of the assignment, he viewed it as a reward for Crommelin's act of insubordination, a sort of a pat on the back for thumbing his nose at DoD leadership.[202] He thus had the posting changed. Instead of serving in a billet *as* a rear admiral, Crommelin was assigned to serve *under* a rear admiral in the Air Warfare Division.[203]

Furthermore, the day before Crommelin's transfer and looking to avoid another public scandal, Matthews imposed a gag order on all naval personnel regarding the press. In his written instructions the Navy Secretary told his officers, "I believe a more appropriate and effective procedure would be to transmit [your views] to me through channels in accordance with Article 1245, Navy Regulations."[204] By issuing this lawful order, any officer violating this directive could be subject to punitive action by a court-martial. Yet for all the decorum sought by the Navy Secretary regarding the B-36 and the associated controversy, Crommelin was not finished with his singular assault on DoD leadership.

Just ten days after Crommelin's unofficial press conference, Vice Adm. Gerald Bogan, commander of the First Task Fleet in the western Pacific, penned a letter to Secretary Matthews expressing his concerns about the Navy's current situation. While not necessarily approving of Crommelin's actions, Bogan did provide tacit support to the captain's concerns. He argued that the morale of the Navy was at low ebb, the worst he had seen since being commissioned in 1916. Bogan more pointedly wrote that his generation of officers were "fearful that the country was being . . . sold a false bill of goods."[205] On the eve of the autumn season, 22 September, just one day before President Truman's public announcement regarding the Soviet atomic detonation, Adm.

Arthur Radford, commander in chief of the Pacific Fleet, endorsed Bogan's letter. In his endorsement letter Radford argued, "Rightly or wrongly the majority of officers in the Pacific Fleet concur with Captain Crommelin and the ideas expressed by Admiral Bogan."[206]

The letter was forwarded to the CNO, with Denfeld further endorsing the opinions expressed by Bogan. In his 28 September endorsement, Denfeld concurred with the sentiments of the chief of the Pacific Fleet and went on to use historical precedent to underscore the points being made by the subordinate commanders.[207] But the letter from Bogan and its two supporting endorsements were not intended for public consumption and quickly marked "Confidential." Public disclosure of such sentiment not only would be an embarrassment to Johnson and Matthews but also would cause further uproar regarding DoD's current policies. By endorsing Bogan's letter and then forwarding it, Denfeld was indeed arguing against the policies and decisions of both the defense secretary and the Navy Secretary. When Matthews learned of Denfeld's endorsement, he claimed he began losing faith in the CNO despite earlier recommending him for a second term.[208]

Days later, on 3 October, Secretary Matthews met with Representative Vinson and his legal counsel to discuss the value of the October hearings, scheduled to begin on the sixth. Given the embarrassment of the August session, Vinson and others looked to postpone this next round, but many in the Navy remained anxious to express their opinions sooner, not later.[209] With Matthews also looking for a postponement, he seemed to get support from Vinson during the course of the meeting. Yet the move toward postponement was about to become derailed by two concurrent actions of naval officers acting on their own recognizance.

Just how the October hearings came about depends upon which of two different accounts one accepts—or possibly a combination of both. The first claims that Admiral Radford jumped into the Vinson-Matthews discussion and significantly changed the tone. Reportedly arriving late to the meeting, Radford expressed the ideas espoused by his fellow aviators and convinced the Georgia Democrat for continued public discourse.[210] While Matthews hoped for a less public venue and hoped to work out any issues within DoD, Radford, in direct disagreement with the secretary, felt the time was right to publically state the Navy's case.[211] Eventually agreeing with the admiral's argument, Vinson decided to hold the scheduled session.[212] Leaving the representative's office, Matthews reportedly remained silent but seethed as a result of Radford's veiled act of insubordination.[213] The admiral's push for the hearings undercut the secretary's desire to avoid another public fiasco and highly visible confrontation. If Radford indeed conducted his own act of insubordination, he was not alone.

The second account, and one that is easily verified, credits Crommelin. Thinking the October hearings were in jeopardy, the captain again took the initiative and acted on his own. Unaware of Radford's actions, Crommelin walked over to the Associated Press, United Press, and the International News offices located in the National Press building. Once there he handed over a copy of Admiral Bogan's "Confidential" letter to various journalists.[214] While Crommelin was unaware of Radford's supposedly successful efforts in Vinson's office, he took matters into his own hands, hoping to force Congress into action by publicly unveiling Bogan's letter and the subsequent endorsements. By releasing the letter and publicizing the admirals' concerns, the captain hoped such information in the public sphere would ensure the scheduled October hearings. The document's release not only violated the Navy Secretary's earlier directive regarding public announcements but also potentially compromised classified information. Since the document was marked "Confidential," its release was a violation of operational security and a punishable offense.

The letter's publication poured gas on embers that looked to be slowly cooling after the August hearings. Regardless of its "Confidential" nature, Crommelin argued that its release was "necessary to the interests of national security."[215] The resulting headlines on 4 October were all he had hoped, with a *New York Times* front-page headline reading, "Navy Morale, Shot Pieces"; the *Washington Post* writing, "Top Admirals Criticize Pentagon"; and the *Baltimore Sun* reporting, "Naval Moral at Low Ebb."[216] Even if the account regarding Radford's actions in Vinson's office was a false narrative, scholars of this episode agree that the October hearings would have been postponed had Crommelin not acted.

As a result of one or both incidents, the hearings commenced as scheduled. But with this act of outward defiance, the captain once again found himself in hot water with Navy leadership. Called into Matthews' office to answer for his insubordinate actions, Crommelin reportedly told the secretary, "There's only one way to get loyalty, and that's to be lucky enough to inspire it." Dismissed from the secretary's office, the captain surprisingly came away with an optimistic attitude and described Matthews as "a good Joe; fine chap, trying to do a job under impossible circumstances."[217] Despite his positive feeling about the meeting, Crommelin was suspended from service for his insubordination and placed under house arrest, with charges compiled for a pending a court-martial.[218] Despite facing punitive action, for the captain this sacrifice was worthwhile, as on that same day the decision was made to proceed with the hearings.[219]

The "Revolt"

Regardless of whether Radford's actions singularly or in conjunction with Crommelin's forced the October resumption of the hearings, the stage was now set for another punishing round between the Air Force and the Navy. The second set of hearings began on 6 October and lasted for twelve days.[220] The two military services yet again expressed their views on national security and argued their respective roles and missions. But the October session took place in a new strategic context. With Mao's PRC proclamation days earlier and scarcely two weeks since Truman's announcement of Joe-1, international Communism had scored two major successes since the end of the August hearings. These two geopolitical events significantly tipped the scales.

Although many Americans may not have bothered concerning themselves with these events, they were indeed significant. With this new strategic context, many believed a reassessment of national security was in order. Paul Nitze, the soon-to-be head of the State Department's Policy Planning Staff (PPS), was just learning about the idea of a thermonuclear weapon and its potential implications. Established in 1947 at the behest of Marshall, the PPS's role was to develop long-range strategic thinking regarding the West and Moscow.[221] While new to the PPS, having arrived earlier that summer, Nitze was no stranger to strategic bombing, being a member of the USSBS and fully aware of airpower's potential for massive destruction. But the upcoming discussions would help Nitze formulate a new path for U.S. military strategy.

On 5 October, the day after the Crommelin-initiated headlines, Vinson set the stage for the hearings. He reminded members of the House subcommittee that Resolution 234, passed during the summer, had eight questions as part of its charter. While the August hearings addressed the first two, dealing largely with B-36 procurement and charges levied against USAF personnel, the October session addressed the remaining six. Vinson specifically spelled out the outstanding questions still needing to be covered:

1. Examine the performance characteristics of the B-36 and determine if it is a satisfactory weapon.
2. Examine the roles and missions of the Air Force and Navy and determine if the decision to cancel USS *United States* was sound.
3. Establish whether or not the Air Force is concentrating upon strategic bombardment to such an extent that it is injurious to tactical aviation and fighter techniques.
4. Consider the procedures used by the JCS regarding weapons development and the use of new munitions and systems by the various services.
5. Study the effectiveness of strategic bombing to determine whether the nation is sound in following this concept to its present extent.
6. Consider all other material pertinent to the above that may be developed during the course of the investigation.[222]

As to any matters involving the first two items of the resolution, Chairman Vinson declared that those issues were closed and the rest of the hearings would focus only on the remaining six. He went on to direct that the subcommittee would not tolerate any reprisal against the witnesses and planned to get to the bottom of the Navy's unrest and concerns.[223]

On 6 October, the same day the NSC was starting its deliberations regarding Taiwan, Secretary Matthews testified first. Before he spoke, though, he tried to have some witnesses heard in closed session for national security reasons. In the interests of transparency, Vinson rejected the proposal. Disappointed with Vinson's decision, Matthews made remarks that swiftly responded to the content of Bogan's published letter and refuted claims of the service's poor morale.[224] He went on further to chastise Crommelin's actions specifically and to state that he would hold various parties accountable.[225] Matthews characterized the captain's actions as faithless and insubordinate, pointing out that such instances were "rare in her [the Navy's] proud tradition."[226] When addressing the B-36 and the Air Force's mission compared to that of the Navy, the secretary largely equivocated. While testifying that the USAF was planning to create an unbalanced force for strategic bombing at the expense of tactical aviation, he claimed that any answers regarding the B-36's capabilities were premature and required further study (referring to the ongoing WSEG evaluation).[227]

When addressing the canceling of USS *United States*, the secretary's words failed to satisfy Navy officers. Matthews argued that canceling the new carrier was sound and did not necessarily stop the progress of naval aviation. Supporting Johnson's actions, Matthews mentioned that the Defense Secretary already had approved modernizing two existing *Essex*-class carriers, hinting that such action was certainly indicative of naval aviation advancement.[228] Perhaps the biggest disappointed to those in the Navy was Matthews' support for the existing JCS structure, arguing, "I think it is proper for the services to consider weapons of sister services. . . . [T]hat their determination is not necessarily the final one, I feel there is no reason for concern."[229]

The most interesting part of his testimony occurred during the question-and-answer portion. When queried about the silencing of naval officers talking publically, Secretary Matthews stated he did not know how a naval officer could be blocked in expressing his views to the public. The irony was not lost on those wearing the uniform. Matthews' remark was immediately met with jeers and laughs of disbelief from Navy personnel present, given the fact he had specifically ordered such silence.[230] Ironically, at the conclusion of the day's testimony, Matthews directed CNO Denfeld to prefer charges against Crommelin for his release of the Bogan letter in violation of the secretary's earlier order.

Following Matthews, the next day's testimony had a decidedly different and distinctively pointed tone. Admiral Radford, who not only endorsed the Bogan letter but also pushed for the October hearings, railed against the B-36 and the USAF vision of future warfare.[231] With a packed committee room,

Radford directly attacked the bomber and its role by specifically addressing one of the questions posed by the June resolution, "Was the bomber a satisfactory weapon?" For Radford the answer was a resounding no. In the admiral's argument he called the bomber an unproven platform, then went further to say the concept of an "atomic blitz" was an unproven application. He made the connection that the B-36 was indeed the symbol of the doctrine. Claiming that the USAF was promising a "cheap and easy victory," the admiral stated that such ideas were "not generally accepted as sound by military men."[232]

Using a naval analogy, Radford made comparisons between battleships and aircraft carriers. In this example he argued, "Are we as a nation to have 'bomber generals' fighting to preserve the obsolete heavy bomber—the battleship of the air? Like its surface counterpart, its day is largely past."[233] Adding to his argument, Radford referenced famed Air Force general Claire Chennault's recent criticism of the air service for drifting back to the same fallacious prewar doctrine of emphasizing unescorted bombers.[234] He further referred to the USAAF's bloody experiences over the skies of Europe during the early days of the combined-bomber offensive. This faulty assumption saw aircrews suffer up to a 10 percent overall loss rate and led to a short halt to strategic bombing operations during the autumn of 1943.

The concern over unescorted bombers was raised earlier in 1948 by Secretary Forrestal. The defense secretary called Secretary of the Air Force Symington to ask about the B-36's ability to operate without escort. Given the long range of the Peacemaker, fighters could not protect it deep in enemy territory. Symington claimed that the bomber could conduct its mission without escort and arranged to have Lieutenant General LeMay comment on the matter. Over dinner the next night, LeMay told Forrestal about a particularly dangerous mission during World War II. According to the SAC commander, "The [friendly] escort fighters didn't come up, so when the B-17s broke into the sun around 20,000 ft we had no fighter escort at all; and when we hit the Dutch coast, we ran into the whole German fighter air force. . . . [We lost a lot of bombers,] but we wiped the target off the face of the earth." When Forrestal asked him how he knew about this event, LeMay put down his trademark cigar and dryly replied, "I led the first group." To this Forrestal replied, "That's good enough for me." The overall message of the USAF was that bombers were more effective *if* they had escort but could still conduct their mission on their own. While escort was desirable, it was not necessarily a requirement to destroy important targets, albeit at great sacrifice.[235] This was certainly not something the USAF wanted to advertise, but given the exigency of war, the use of unescorted bombers was considered a calculated risk.

For Admiral Radford, the Air Force was too vested in strategic platforms and not enough in fighters and other tactical aircraft. He testified that USAF procurement placed major emphasis on the heavy bomber to the detriment of aircraft for ground support.[236] In his arguments against the B-36, Radford brought along seven experts to corroborate his claim and to address specific shortcomings in the design, performance, and capabilities of the bomber. These experts testified for three days, addressing technical shortfalls of the plane. The admiral also explained that earlier that year, on 23 January, was the first time he learned of an expansion of the B-36 program. Before then he assumed that the program was to be reduced. He testified that this was the first time Secretary Forrestal had also heard such news.[237] For Radford, this was evidence that the USAF was circumventing the normal budgetary processes and conducting a clandestine effort to purchase more bombers. In closing the admiral argued, "Our defense budget should not be used for unproven weapons.... American taxpayers cannot afford billion dollar blunders."[238]

Before yielding to his experts, Radford specifically addressed the cancellation of USS *United States*. Predictably, he disagreed with the decision and made the case regarding the efficacy of "mobile airpower in future war." For him and for many in the naval service, carriers were not designed to usurp the USAF's mission of atomic bombing but served as part of a combined effort in projecting combat power. The use of tactical airpower from naval platforms contributed to the overall effort by supporting operations ashore through close-air-support, reconnaissance, and air-superiority missions. These were conducted more than just in support of the Navy, as they assisted in the victory of Army and Marine units on the ground. He further elaborated, using the Pacific War as an example, that carriers served not just as an offensive platform but also as a defensive one.[239]

During Radford's question-and-answer session, the issue of Navy morale came up. Rep. Porter Hardy (D-VA) asked him if the men in the Navy had confidence in the secretaries of defense and Navy. Before Radford replied, Vinson chimed in, telling the admiral plainly, almost daringly, "put your cards on the table." Selecting his words carefully, Radford replied, "I feel the general impression in the Navy is that the decisions are being made in the highest offices of the Department of Defense without adequate information that can come only from the Navy." This response did not fully answer the question and resulted in further inquiry from Hardy. The representative asked the same question, only in a somewhat different manner by inquiring if there was "a lack of confidence or a wall [that] separates you from the secretary of Defense." To this question Radford simply replied, "I think so."[240]

During the proceedings Rep. George J. Bates (R-MA) asked about the FY 1950 budget and its implications on the Navy. Bates stated that in the planned allocation for naval aviation, the air arm would receive only forty new planes a month compared to the four hundred it had received before the attack on Pearl Harbor in 1941. After announcing these figures, the representative set up the admiral for an easy answer with a leading statement: "This seems to me to be a move to scuttle the air arm of the Navy." Happy to oblige the him, Radford replied simply, "It is."[241]

While Vinson thought that the October proceedings might be just a venting of steam for the naval services, the charges levied by Radford regarding the expenditure of funds for more B-36s were serious. When Secretary Johnson heard of the admiral's claims regarding the misuse of official funds for defense, he responded by sending Vinson a 26 January letter signed by Forrestal authorizing the expenditure. The letter was proof that the USAF was fully informing Congress about the additional B-36 purchases. In addition to countering Radford's claims, Johnson also requested he be invited to testify in the current proceedings and recommended that additional general officers be summoned. Vinson encouraged the additional testimony by welcoming "anyone else who will help us out."[242]

After his testimony Radford brought forth his crew of experts. With their testimonies, the admiral hoped to convince subcommittee members of the B-36's vulnerabilities and prove that it was an unsatisfactory weapon. Lt. Cdr. Ed Harrison, a radar engineer, testified that flying at its prescribed altitude of 40,000 feet, the B-36 would be easily visible to any air-defense radar network.[243]

Claiming that such radar "know-how" was widely available, he argued that any potential enemy would have such capability.[244] As a result the bomber would be easily detectible at that altitude by Soviet radar operators who then could simply direct air-defense interceptors to shoot down the plane.

In concert with this idea was testimony from Capt. Fredrick Trapnell, head of the Navy's Air Test Center at Patuxent River, Maryland. Trapnell testified that the B-36 could not fly into enemy territory undetected and attacking it at altitudes above 40,000 feet was relatively easy with modern radar.[245] He went on to state that tests had shown that aerial gunnery at that altitude proved effective; a pair of F2H Banshee fighters, currently in the Navy inventory, could easily down a B-36 with gunfire. With this thought in mind, the captain went on to say, "The enemy will have fighters as good as ours. The British [already] do. And the Russians have publically demonstrated numbers of very advanced [interceptor] designs."[246]

Cdr. William Martin, executive officer on the Navy's Fleet All-Weather Training Unit in the Pacific, echoed Trapnell's sentiments. He argued further that the B-36 would be equally vulnerable in daylight or nighttime operations. Martin stated that during the hours of darkness the moon shines for half of the month, with 40,000 feet usually being above most weather conditions.[247] Supporting his claim, the commander reported that the bomber's six propellers made it "the best possible radar target" and was visible by electronic-detection measures 250 miles away.[248] Abraham Hyatt, a civilian and chief of the Navy's Aviation Design Research Branch, stated that unless there is some engineering development that applies to bombers and not to fighters, losses for the intercontinental bombers "could well prove catastrophic."[249]

Other subject-matter experts also gave similar testimony. By the end of their presentations, they all made a convincing technical argument. Yet there was one claim made by an expert that caused many to scratch their heads. Cdr. Eugene Tatom, a naval ordnance officer, gave testimony regarding the efficacy of atomic weapons. He argued that regardless of all the power released by nuclear fission, atomic weapons still required precision placement. While these bombs were indeed powerful, they still had a prescribed blast radius and needed accurate placement to leverage their full effect. Tatom claimed that dropping such weapons from 40,000 feet precluded the kind of precision required. While there was validity to his argument, the commander overstated his case by saying, "You could stand in the open at the end of the north–south runway at Washington Airport, with no more protection than the clothes you now have on, and have an atom bomb explode at the other end of the runway without serious injury to you."[250] While certainly a dubious claim given the effects of the atomic blast alone, Vinson humorously replied to this statement: "I, personally, would rather be in Georgia."[251]

When Rear Adm. Ralph Ofstie, a liaison officer with the AEC, testified, he took the argument further. While Radford and his team of experts addressed the issue of strategic bombing largely from a technical and tactical military perspective, Ofstie addressed the concept from a moral perspective. For him, strategic bombing was problematic because of its humanitarian consequences. Ofstie's testimony was especially relevant as he, too, served as a member of the USSBS in the Pacific, evaluating the American aerial offensive against Japan. Furthermore, he was also part of the evaluation team during the Bikini Atoll atomic tests of 1946. With these bona fides, Ofstie had a clear understanding of the consequences of atomic bombardment. He testified, "We [the Navy] consider air warfare as practiced in that past and as proposed for the future is morally unsound and of limited effect; is morally wrong; and is decidedly harmful to the stability of the postwar world."[252] He went on to argue, much like Commander Tatom, that pinpoint accuracy from 40,000 feet was not possible with the B-36. Ofstie made the connection that such bombing would create massive casualties and be considered ruthless and barbaric, leading to a moral breakdown that had been the guiding force for American democracy.[253] With this, he claimed further that the United States would be creating "hunger, poverty, and disease that serves as the greatest promoters of Communism."[254] Toward what end would be the result of an atomic offensive? Was such a conflict politically, militarily, and socially feasible? Echoing the concerns of the earlier Harmon Report regarding the effects of atomic weapons, for the rear admiral, the answer to these questions was clearly no.

Following Ofstie, other Navy and Marine officers came to the defense of naval aviation and USS *United States*. A "who's who" of naval officers testified, including Adms. William Blandy and Ray Spruance, Fleet Adms. William

Halsey and Ernest J. King, and Pacific fighter-pilot hero Capt. John S. "Jimmie" Thach.[255] With his excellent reputation as an aviator and tactician, Thach reiterated the vulnerability of the B-36 to radar identification, location, and interception while arguing that night operations for the bomber offered no defensive advantage.[256] Interestingly, a month before Thach testified, Captain Burke of OP-23 asked the hero if he knew any USAF pilots who were not satisfied with the B-36, fighter pilots who were unsatisfied with the subordinate role given them in relation to the bombers, or any potential witnesses unhappy with the idea of strategic bombing.[257] Given Thach's singular testimony, it could be assumed that he found no USAF pilots that either agreed or were willing to risk their own career in the endeavor. When Burke later testified to the subcommittee, he defended the flush-deck carrier and refuted Secretary Matthews' earlier statement about the value of modifying two *Essex*-class carriers.[258] The captain claimed that the modernization effort would help but that upgrading existing platforms fell short of what was required for the future of naval aviation.

Fleet Adm. Chester W. Nimitz, a retired hero of the Pacific War, testified and was supportive of joint operations, although he was unsure of what the USAF's role would be in a future war. He questioned the mission of long-range, intercontinental, horizontal, high-altitude bombers as an efficient weapon of war. Nimitz argued that strategic bombing was not accurate enough and that the greatest damage would occur to civilians. Although the Fleet Admiral agreed with the possible deterrent effect of atomic weapons, he was unsure as to what degree the United States should depend upon them. Nimitz testified that they "*not* be considered as our main weapon of offense and that proportionate resources be set aside for other weapons."[259] This argument was also in line with the Harmon Report. It also stipulated that bombing alone would not necessarily bring about victory and would have severe secondary and tertiary effects during both the war and the envisioned peace.[260] For Nimitz, atomic consequences undercut the entire effort. In his statement he highlighted the utility of tactical weapons, especially aircraft, that reflected Navy capabilities and the ability to defeat a foe without depending solely on strategic bombing or fixed airfields. Illustrating this point, the Fleet Admiral stated that the successful amphibious assault of Okinawa could not have succeeded without carrier-based aviation and other naval support.[261] The difficult fight on the largest of the Ryukyu Islands depended heavily on naval fire-support shelling inland targets, with carrier assets providing close air support to Marine and Army units on the ground.

The most anticipated witness of the October hearings was Admiral Denfeld. Scheduled for the afternoon session on 13 October, Denfeld not only represented the Navy but also served at the pleasure of the Truman administration. Representing the service, he worked for President Truman, Secretary Johnson, and Secretary Matthews. His testimony carried exceptional weight, as he was reappointed CNO for a second term by Matthews just two months earlier in August. Everyone wondered if his testimony would be supportive of naval aviation and the Navy, or if he would fall in line under the mandates of his political bosses. His tenure as CNO was clearly on the line. Keeping his superiors guessing, Denfeld kept his cards close to his chest and gave little indication as to which way he would argue.[262] When queried as to the admiral's allegiances before the CNO's testimony session, Secretary Johnson purportedly squinted his eyes and replied, "Denfeld hasn't been disloyal—yet."[263]

Reportedly, the CNO was so tightlipped about his position that he was finally pressed by his wife about it while sitting at the breakfast table the morning he was scheduled to testify.[264] Supposedly, Vinson phoned Denfeld to advise the CNO to take a strong stand for naval aviation. To help make the strongest statement possible, he asked members of Radford's team to help draft his testimony.[265] The morning of his testimony, Denfeld had his staff start putting the finishing touches on his remarks. Since they were still making edits and changes at this late hour, no one outside his office had any idea what his testimony might reveal. As a result, hours before the CNO's appearance in front of the subcommittee, Johnson and Matthews remained in the dark as to their subordinate's position.[266]

Taking his seat in front of the panel that afternoon, Denfeld's opening words left little doubt as to his position. He started his forty-two-page testimony quite directly: "My name is Louis E. Denfeld. I am an Admiral in the United States Navy, and the Chief of Naval Operations. . . . I want to state forthwith that I fully support the conclusions presented to this Committee by the Naval and Marine officers who have preceded me."[267] Following his opening remarks, Denfeld testified as to the lack of cooperation and consideration given to the Navy. His service was not looking to destroy unification, he noted, but complained that it "has not been admitted to full partnership therein." The admiral went on to say that the testimonies heard by the subcommittee arose from an effort to diminish the Navy.[268] Avoiding a direct attack on the B-36 specifically, the CNO laid out the argument for the Navy's frustrations given the current fiscal environment, its perception regarding the lack of consideration given unification, and the furtive nature of the CVA 58's cancellation. Recognizing the evolution and importance of air warfare, he argued that it was a combined-arms effort that was important to national security and that airpower was not singularly the domain of the USAF.

Denfeld believed the capabilities of the Navy were deliberately curtailed, and perhaps his biggest frustration was the limits imposed upon it "without consultation and without understanding of the Navy's responsibilities in defense of the nation." He testified further that these limits were imposed arbitrarily. With this Denfeld was clearly taking a swipe at the civilian leadership at the Pentagon. He continued by expressing his concern over continued Navy reductions each year, noting that the "gravest" problem was lack of choice by the Navy in how to apply these reductions.[269]

In his conclusion Denfeld summarized his comments by laying out six tasks that Congress should address to safeguard national security:

1. Expedite the report of the WSEG in order to determine the military worth of the B-36.
2. Literally support the National Security Act and the Key West Agreement on roles and missions of the armed forces.
3. Support the principle that each service within budgetary limitations be permitted to design and develop its own weapons.
4. Provide the Navy adequate and appropriate representation in key positions within DoD.
5. Limit the scope of activities of the JCS to those specifically mentioned in the National Security Act.
6. In the present stage of unification, it must be recognized that the views of a particular service are entitled to predominate weight in the determination of the forces needed by that service to fulfill its missions.[270]

In both tone and temperament, the CNO clearly supported his fellow naval brethren and deliberately broke with his civilian superiors. With the conclusion of Denfeld's testimony, several naval officers rushed to shake his hand and congratulate him. Afterward, one member of the committee told the admiral, "I don't know what you had for lunch, but brother it was a correct diet. There will be a lot of starch added to the shirts of the Navy." Vinson also praised Denfeld, telling him he had "rendered a distinct service by putting your chips on the table."[271] Despite the celebratory mood, not everyone was as effusive with support and congratulations. Matthews, realizing he had been undercut by his own subordinate, stormed out the room red faced, with some claiming the Navy Secretary "went wild."[272] With no testimony scheduled for the next day, Denfeld met privately with Matthews back in the Pentagon. During the meeting the Navy Secretary angrily told the CNO he was "stunned" at his comments.[273] With this break from his civilian leadership, the CNO had put the proverbial "nail in his own [professional] coffin."

The very next day an incensed Matthews contacted former CNO Fleet Admiral Nimitz. Flying up to New York City and meeting Nimitz at the Hotel Barclay, the Navy Secretary expressed feeling victimized by members of the Navy staff, especially those working in OP-23. Matthews complained that he was uninformed regarding important Navy issues and rhetorically asked, "He [Denfeld] tells me nothing, . . . is that right?" Nimitz replied that when he was CNO working under Forrestal (before Forrestal became secretary of defense), he fully informed his boss every morning.[274] Frustrated, it was clear that Matthews was seeking his next step. He eventually laid his cards on the table, asking Nimitz, "How can I get rid of him?" While the Fleet Admiral held Denfeld in high esteem, he was now split between his fondness for a colleague and his commitment to the nation at large. Nimitz counseled Matthews that if he really could not work with Denfeld, he should consult with Truman. The president, as commander in chief, had the power to replace anyone in uniform. Additionally, knowing the assurances Vinson provided those testifying in front of the subcommittee, Nimitz warned Matthews not to reference Denfeld's testimony but to base his request upon the CNO's endorsement of Bogan's letter.[275] With this, the die was cast, and Denfeld's days were numbered.

WB-50 No. 44-62214, the aircraft that detected Joe-1 in 1949. It now sits ignominiously in a flooded gravel pit at Eielson Air Force Base, Alaska, and is known as the "Lady of the Lake." How the aircraft came to rest here is unknown. *(USAF photo)*

31 October 1949

Washington Evening Star

Sherman Flying Here for Talk on Top Navy Post

31 More Warships Ordered Laid Up in Economy Program

By John A. Giles

Speculation that Vice Admiral Forrest P. Sherman will be named Chief of Naval Operations increased today as Admiral Sherman headed toward Washington for conferences with Secretary of the Navy Matthews.

Admiral Sherman, commander of the Sixth Task fleet operating in the Mediterranean, is expected here by tomorrow. He boarded a Pan-American plane for the flight to this country, the Associated Press reported from London, after leaving his fleet at Beirut, Lebanon.

It was likely that Mr. Matthews himself ordered Admiral Sherman here for a conference before a final decision is made on a successor to Admiral Denfeld as Chief of Naval Operations.

Denfeld Still Undecided.

Admiral Denfeld, ousted by Mr. Matthews, still has not made up his mind on whether to accept another Navy assignment or to retire, it was reported this morning.

In another Navy development, the department announced last night that it was going to lay up

During Target Practice

By the Associated Press

RIVIERA BEACH, Md., Oct. 31.—A day of target practice ended in death yesterday for a 23-year-old Baltimore soldier on a week-end pass.

Ann Arundel County police said Frank A. Monte was accidentally shot when his companion's pistol jammed and then went off when attempts were made to clear it.

Monte, who was stationed at Aberdeen Proving Ground, died of a chest wound before he could be taken to a Baltimore hospital.

His younger brother and two other young men were with him. Police said the youth who owned the gun, 17-year-old John Gardiner, became panicky after the mishap and dismantled the foreign-make automatic pistol.

Editorial cartoon, *Washington Evening Star*, 31 October 1949. In the public realm there was plenty to worry about. Note that the headlines in the background do not reflect the emerging argument regarding the development of thermonuclear weapons. *(John L. Sullivan Papers, Harry S. Truman Presidential Library)*

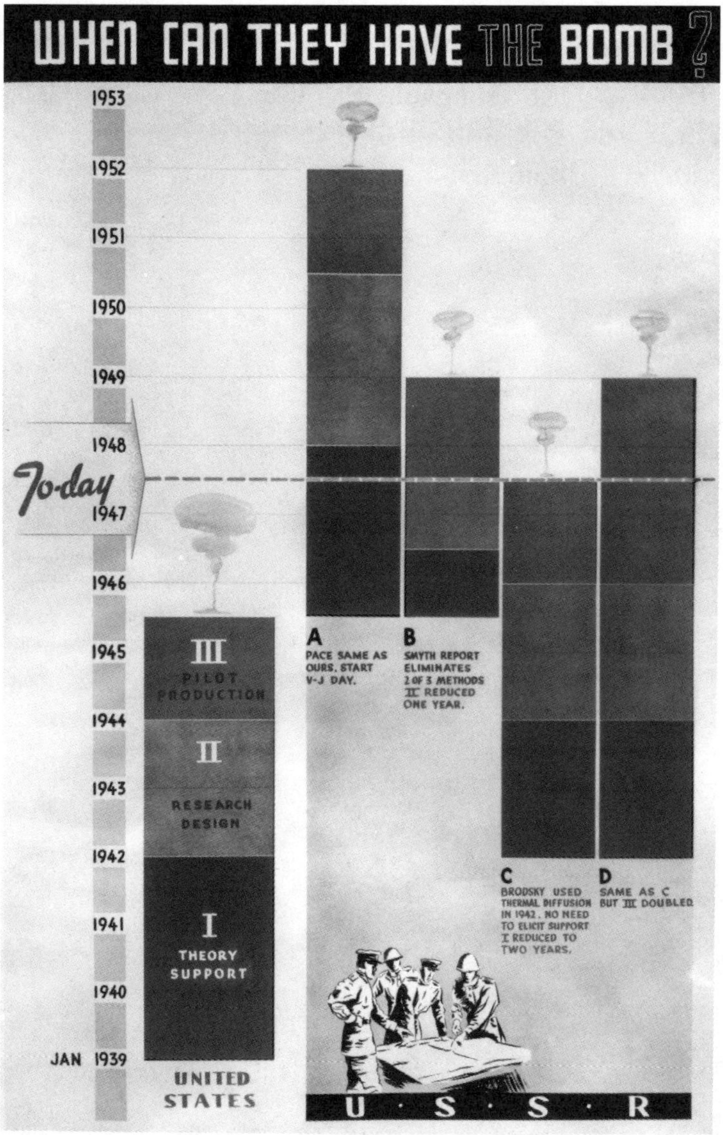

When Can They Have the Bomb? This graphic depicts the four scenarios Gen. Carl Spaatz articulated in his testimony to the Senate in June 1947 regarding Soviet atomic capability. *(Gen. Hoyt Vandenberg Papers, Manuscripts Division, Library of Congress)*

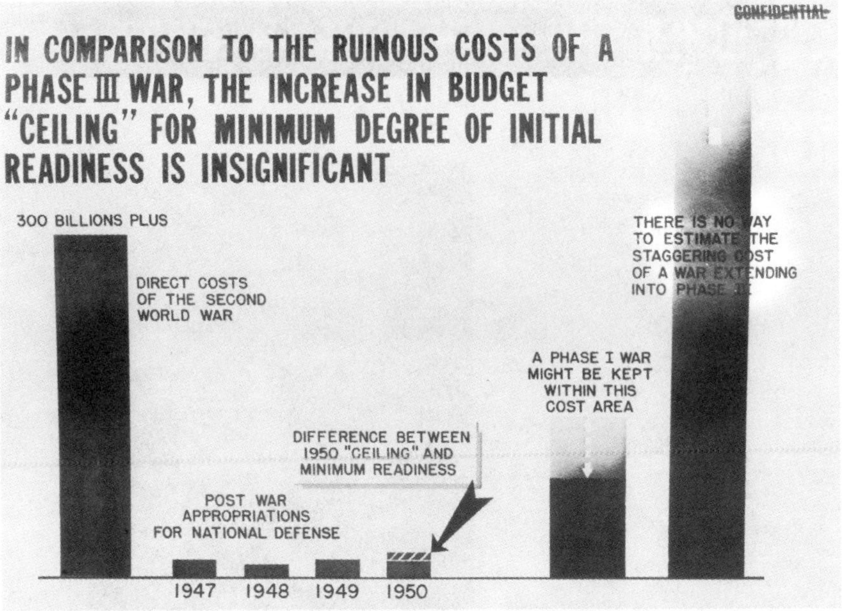
CONFIDENTIAL
IN COMPARISON TO THE RUINOUS COSTS OF A PHASE III WAR, THE INCREASE IN BUDGET "CEILING" FOR MINIMUM DEGREE OF INITIAL READINESS IS INSIGNIFICANT
300 BILLIONS PLUS
DIRECT COSTS OF THE SECOND WORLD WAR
DIFFERENCE BETWEEN 1950 "CEILING" AND MINIMUM READINESS
POST WAR APPROPRIATIONS FOR NATIONAL DEFENSE
A PHASE I WAR MIGHT BE KEPT WITHIN THIS COST AREA
THERE IS NO WAY TO ESTIMATE THE STAGGERING COST OF A WAR EXTENDING INTO PHASE
1947
1948
1949
1950

During the budget battles following World War II, the military struggled to maintain readiness in hopes of preventing a future large-scale conflict. *(Gen. Hoyt Vandenberg Papers, Manuscripts Division, Library of Congress)*

BK-010

The B-50 "Lucky Lady II" (*bottom*) on its nonstop, around-the-world flight. Covering 23,000 miles, it required four inflight refuelings. Early aerial refueling methods used a grapple-line looped-hose system as pictured in use here. *(USAF photo)*

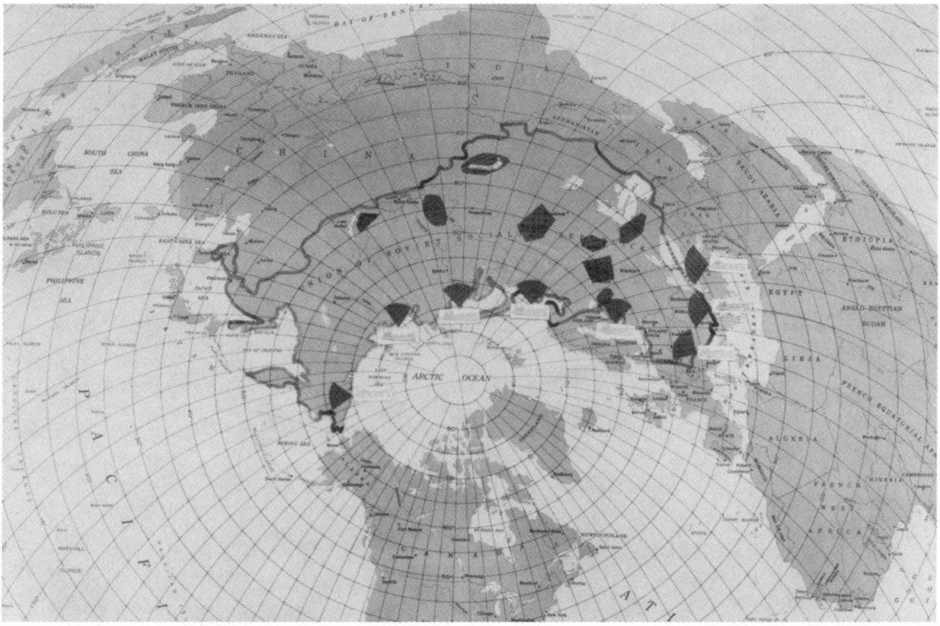

In this polar view of the globe, the shaded areas in the Soviet Union are targeted industrial locations. The triangular shapes near the coastlines depict USAF claims of the extent of naval-aircraft reach from carriers. *(Gen. Hoyt Vandenberg Papers, Manuscripts Division, Library of Congress)*

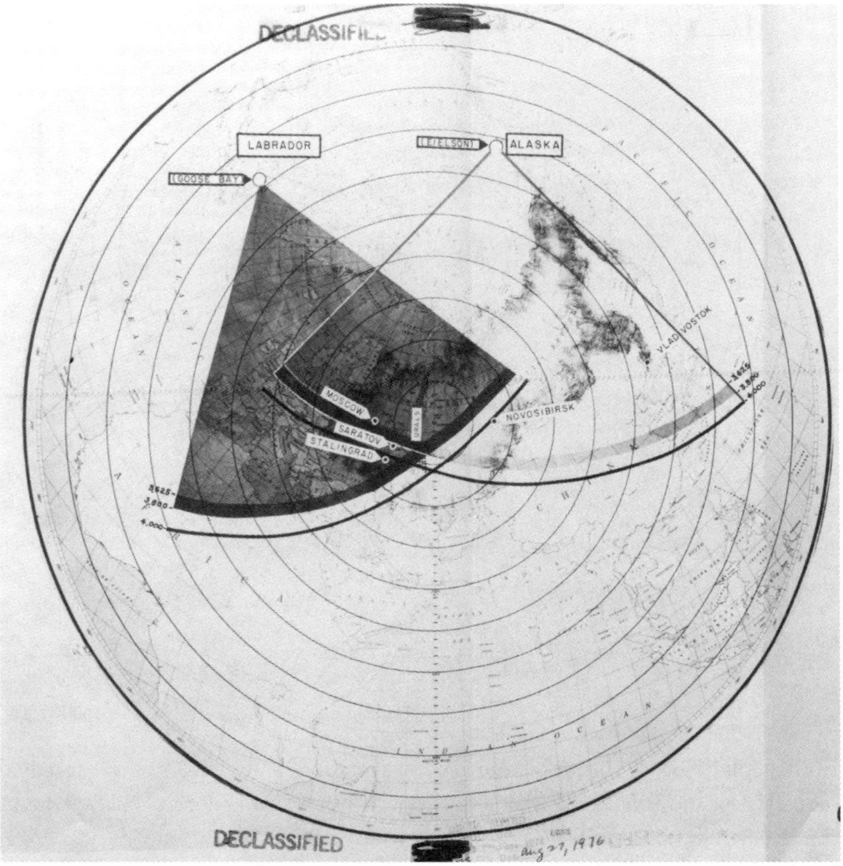

B-36 range fans depicting how far into the Soviet Union the bomber could fly from bases in Goose Bay, Canada, and Eielson Air Force Base, Alaska. *(Gen. Hoyt Vandenberg Papers, Manuscripts Division, Library of Congress)*

The B-36 Peacekeeper bomber. Seen as an interim solution until jet bombers became available, it was the symbol of SAC and an icon of American airpower at the time. *(USAF photo)*

The AJ-1 Savage nuclear attack aircraft on the flight deck of a Navy carrier. It was a problematic design, but with it the Navy could claim to have an atomic-capable delivery system. *(Naval History and Heritage Command)*

A nuclear-weapon-capable P2V3C takes off from USS *Ben Franklin*. Using rocket-assisted takeoff and having to be craned on board, it was hardly an efficient nuclear-delivery platform. *(Naval History and Heritage Command)*

Model of the proposed USS *United States* (CVA 58) in a testing pool. The flush-deck carrier was canceled shortly after its keel plates were laid. Its demise was a lightning rod for naval aviators in their early rivalry with the Air Force. *(Naval History and Heritage Command)*

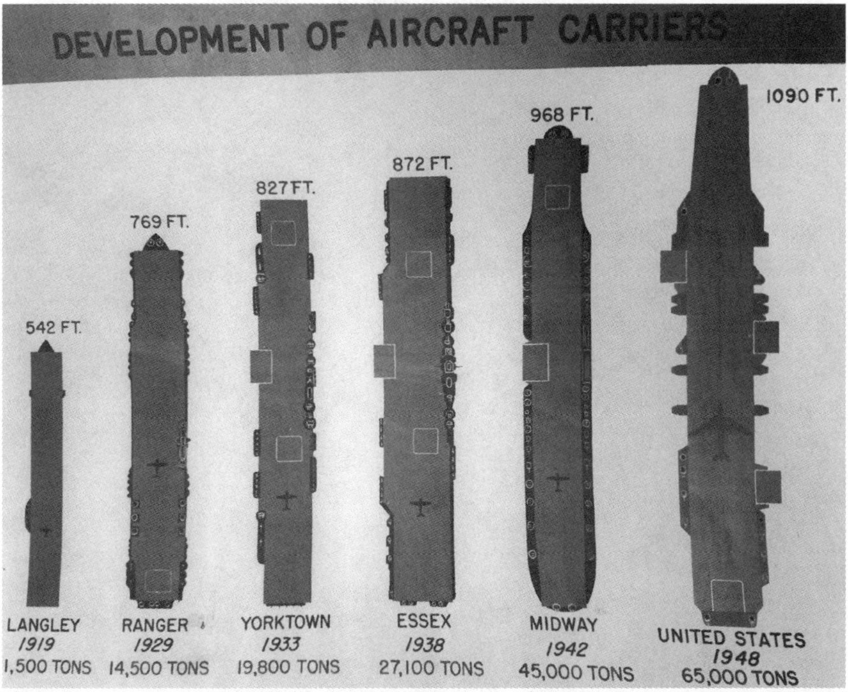

Development of Aircraft Carriers. This chart depicts a size comparison of CVA 58 to previous carrier classes. *(John L. Sullivan Papers, Harry S. Truman Library)*

Cdr. Tom Davies and the nose art of the P2V "The Turtle." The Navy chose the animal in reference to the Aesop fable regarding the race between the tortoise and the hare. Just visible above the turtle's backside is a rabbit's foot as a swipe at the Air Force. *(Naval History and Heritage Command)*

Editorial cartoon, *Washington Evening Star*, 14 September 1949. It comments on Capt. John Crommelin's charges that the other two services were conspiring against the Navy. *(Naval History and Heritage Command)*

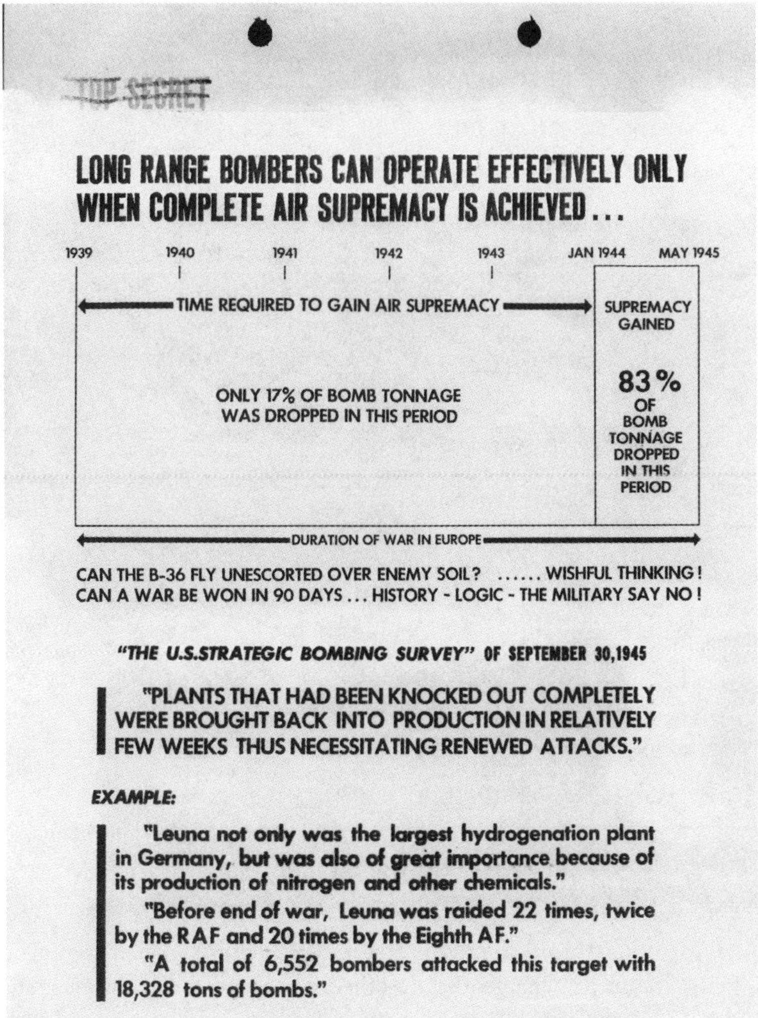

TOP SECRET

LONG RANGE BOMBERS CAN OPERATE EFFECTIVELY ONLY WHEN COMPLETE AIR SUPREMACY IS ACHIEVED . . .

1939 1940 1941 1942 1943 JAN 1944 MAY 1945

TIME REQUIRED TO GAIN AIR SUPREMACY

SUPREMACY GAINED

ONLY 17% OF BOMB TONNAGE WAS DROPPED IN THIS PERIOD

83% OF BOMB TONNAGE DROPPED IN THIS PERIOD

DURATION OF WAR IN EUROPE

CAN THE B-36 FLY UNESCORTED OVER ENEMY SOIL? ...... WISHFUL THINKING !
CAN A WAR BE WON IN 90 DAYS . . . HISTORY - LOGIC - THE MILITARY SAY NO !

"THE U.S.STRATEGIC BOMBING SURVEY" OF SEPTEMBER 30,1945

"PLANTS THAT HAD BEEN KNOCKED OUT COMPLETELY WERE BROUGHT BACK INTO PRODUCTION IN RELATIVELY FEW WEEKS THUS NECESSITATING RENEWED ATTACKS."

EXAMPLE:

"Leuna not only was the largest hydrogenation plant in Germany, but was also of great importance because of its production of nitrogen and other chemicals."

"Before end of war, Leuna was raided 22 times, twice by the RAF and 20 times by the Eighth AF."

"A total of 6,552 bombers attacked this target with 18,328 tons of bombs."

This Navy graphic seeks to refute the efficacy of strategic bombing based on the findings of the U.S. Strategic Bombing Survey. The Air Force claimed the B-36 could operate in hostile airspace without fighter escort. The Navy argued otherwise. *(Naval History and Heritage Command)*

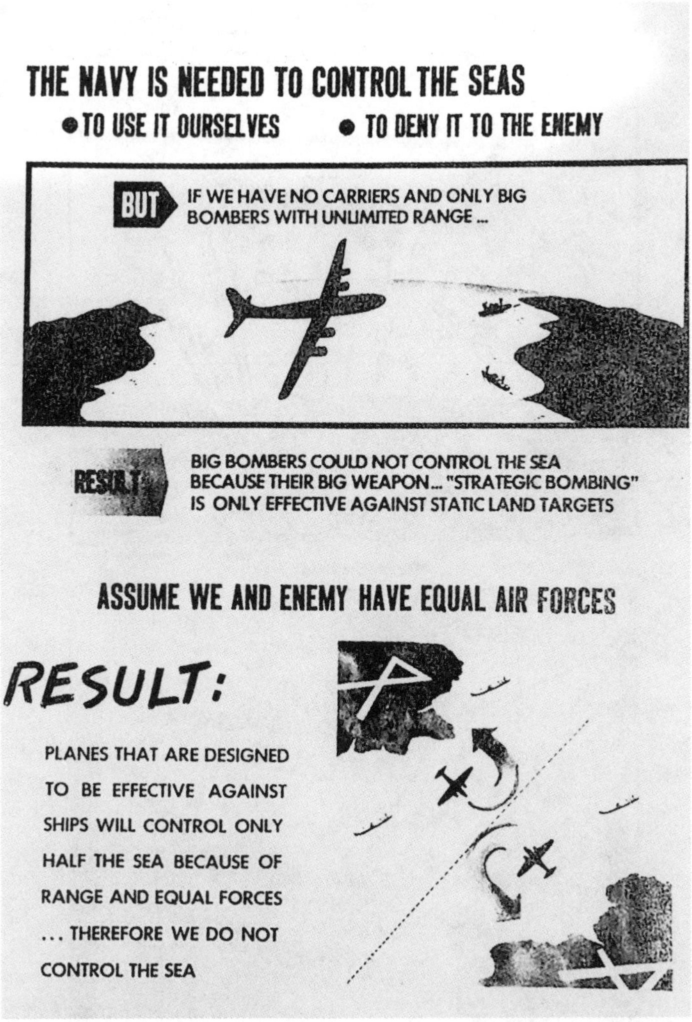

THE NAVY IS NEEDED TO CONTROL THE SEAS
● TO USE IT OURSELVES
● TO DENY IT TO THE ENEMY
BUT
IF WE HAVE NO CARRIERS AND ONLY BIG BOMBERS WITH UNLIMITED RANGE ...
RESULT
BIG BOMBERS COULD NOT CONTROL THE SEA BECAUSE THEIR BIG WEAPON... "STRATEGIC BOMBING" IS ONLY EFFECTIVE AGAINST STATIC LAND TARGETS
ASSUME WE AND ENEMY HAVE EQUAL AIR FORCES
RESULT:
PLANES THAT ARE DESIGNED TO BE EFFECTIVE AGAINST SHIPS WILL CONTROL ONLY HALF THE SEA BECAUSE OF RANGE AND EQUAL FORCES ... THEREFORE WE DO NOT CONTROL THE SEA

This Navy graphic highlights its argument regarding strategic airpower's inability to control and protect sea lines of communication. *(Naval History and Heritage Command)*

COMMENTS ON THE 'PENTAGON BATTLE'

Bishop in The St. Louis Star-Times

"Undeclared war."

These editorial cartoons depict the public perception of the arguments between the Navy and Air Force in October 1949. *(Francis Matthews Papers, Harry S. Truman Library)*

This March 1950 USAF advertisement ran on the page opposite of Admiral Denfeld's article in *Collier's* magazine. Its placement was possibly more than just coincidence.

A MiG-15 first-generation Soviet fighter. Encountering the jet-powered interceptor was an unpleasant surprise for American pilots during the Korean War. This particular aircraft was flown by a defecting North Korean pilot to Kimpo Airfield outside of Seoul. It resides today at the National Museum of the U.S. Air Force at Wright-Patterson Air Force Base near Dayton, Ohio. *(USAF photo)*

When testimony resumed on 17 October, Denfeld was followed by Marine Corps generals Clifton Cates and Alexander Vandergrift. Falling under the Department of the Navy, the Corps was not immune to the current row. Both of these men had a stake in the discourse, as Marine aviation was also at risk of losing a large part of its structure in the current environment. Since amphibious warfare was the primary mission of the service, aviation was seen by the Marines as a key component to the air-ground concept that figured prominently in its doctrines. While often viewed as a superfluous expense by its foes in Washington, the Corps once again had to prove its own worth as a standalone military organization.

With a post–World War II air- and atomic-centric vision of future war, the Marines were once again considered extraneous. Indicative of this sentiment was a quip from Air Force lieutenant general Frank Armstrong to a group of naval officers in Norfolk, Virginia: "Now as for the Marines, you know what they are. They are a small fouled up army talking Navy lingo. We're going to put those Marines in the Regular Army, and make efficient soldiers out of them."[276] With this context, the Marines were suspicious of unification and saw the current measures by the Air Force as yet another effort to downgrade their formations and roles. With the Marines' testimony before the subcommittee in full support of their Navy brethren, the first part of the October proceedings ended.[277]

The next day, 18 October, the USAF began its defense of the B-36 and the concept of strategic bombing. Tuesday's rebuttal testimony started off with Air Force Secretary Symington. Perhaps as a positive omen for this response, on the same weekend Matthews met with Nimitz, a Gallup poll found that 74 percent of American's believed the USAF would play the most important part in winning the next world war.[278] For Symington this second set of hearings was more a nuisance than anything else. The August session had already cleared his name, exonerated the B-36 procurement process, and proved the uncooperative nature of the Navy regarding unification. In his October statement he argued that the USAF was merely executing its roles and missions as assigned by the JCS and had purchased the B-36 as an approved program of record. Regarding it procurement, Symington pointed out that money allocated for additional bombers was approved through the normal budgetary process, with an official notification submitted to Secretary Forrestal on 28 January 1949. In support of his argument, the secretary reminded the committee that under federal law, such expenditures required both the president's and the secretary of defense's approval. He went on to note that the decision to buy the B-36 required Navy approval, with the JCS fully informed. Furthermore, he argued that claiming the USAF "went over the head of the Secretary of Defense [for the B-36] was not only untrue—[but] it just doesn't make sense."[279]

Symington also refuted the charge that the USAF was putting too much emphasis on strategic bombing. Providing actual numbers, the secretary claimed that for FYs 1949, 1950, and 1951, the USAF was buying 5,309 planes. Of that total, only 154, or 2.9 percent, of those airframes were B-36s.[280] With these and other figures, Symington rejected the idea that the USAF was putting all its "eggs in one basket."[281] He reported that the total expenditures of funds for the B-36 represented only 16.3 percent of all aircraft purchases for the same FYs.[282] He also rebuffed the idea that the B-36 would cost $1 billion, that calling it a "billion dollar-blunder," as specified by Admiral Radford, was indeed erroneous.[283]

Additionally, the secretary made deliberate reference to *The Strategic Bombing Myth*, the pamphlet that had surfaced before the August hearings. In addressing this anonymously produced document, he argued that it was more dangerous than Worth's earlier "anonymous report." For Symington, the pamphlet not only attacked USAF methods, principles, and objectives but also mislead members of the subcommittee about the combined-bomber-offensive.[284] Challenging the data articulated in the pamphlet, Symington presented the 23 August letter from Frank D'Olier, chairman of the USSBS, specifically countering many of its points.[285] To further emphasize this, the secretary not only read D'Olier's letter aloud but also made copies of it available to the subcommittee members and the press.

When addressing the B-36's ability to conduct its assigned mission, Symington rejected the rumor that the USAF claimed that the bomber was "invulnerable." He proffered that such a claim was "sheer non-sense" and that the plane was the best material solution available at this time. In countering the claim that the USAF alone was pushing the national security agenda, the secretary argued that national war plans were not a result of a single service's decision but were developed with the three services working together for the defense of the nation at large.[286] Regarding the idea of a "quick, easy painless war" as claimed from earlier testimony, Symington argued the deterrent effect of atomic weapons and that this application was the best method to safeguard American lives while crippling an enemy.[287] In closing the Air Force secretary made a thinly veiled swipe at the Navy, claiming that these public hearings needlessly provided the nation's enemies technical and operational details of U.S. defense capabilities, shortfalls, and overall military strategy.[288]

Following the Air Force secretary, Air Force Chief of Staff Hoyt Vandenberg testified later the same day, echoing many of the points made by his superior. He, too, rejected the idea that the USAF was putting all its "eggs in one basket" and testified as to the strength of SAC and the entire service. Vandenberg argued that SAC composed only 29 percent of regular USAF strength and that only 5 percent of the service's aircraft were B-36s.[289] He testified that in case of a full-scale mobilization of the nation, SAC constituted less than 20 percent of the total force. In this same perspective B-36s composed only 3 percent of the service's air fleet.[290] Furthermore, he addressed SAC percentages in terms of manpower allocations, showing similar figures.

Vandenberg argued that all the services had their voices heard in the current structure but admitted that "all voices cannot prevail."[291] He connected the argument of strategic plans, stating the use of atomic weapons were in concert with, and at the direction of, the members of the JCS, both as individual representatives of their particular service and as a collective body. Underscoring this statement, Vandenberg reiterated that SAC received its assignments from the JCS and not the USAF alone. As a result, missions assigned to it came not from those wearing sky blue uniforms, but by joint instruction comprising all services.[292] What he did not tell the subcommittee was that almost all strategic planning for a bombing campaign was generated by the planners at SAC, then forwarded to the JCS. According to Lieutenant General LeMay, and contrary to what the air chief of staff was claiming, there was very little guidance coming out of the JCS or Washington regarding targeting or bombing strategy. As for the strategic air offensive, the SAC commander claimed that most of the planning was done internally, with little outside influence, at least until

LeMay's departure in 1957.[293] Although LeMay overstated this claim, up to this point SAC was the lead agent for atomic-war planning.

Concerning the overall concept of bombing, the air chief of staff argued that the concept was sound. He further noted that the testimonies given the past few days by the naval-service representatives were rife with "inadequate evaluation of incomplete information." When addressing the larger issue of morality and the atomic offensive, Vandenberg claimed that the deterrent value justified the force and that this capability was "the greatest equalizing factor in the balance of military power between a potential enemy [the USSR] and the western democracies and could only be received with contempt or despair by those who have joined together for common defense."[294] For him, the atomic air threat put the Soviet Union on the defensive and forced the Communist state to expend resources to counter strategic bombers. As a result of its ever-present threat, the USAF thus precluded offensive action on part of the USSR. Furthermore, by focusing on strategic applications, Vandenberg believed it might negate the requirement for tactical aviation. He even suggested it was folly to fight a conventional war with an enemy on the ground "in equal [terms] man-to-man, body-to-body, gun-to-gun. . . . [That] offered us the prospect of only a defensive war."[295] If the United States was going to fight a war, Vandenberg believed, it was in its best interests not to get bogged down in a conventional fight against the mass of the Red Army but to leverage the nation's distinct strategic-air advantage. In this argument he specifically made reference to the long, costly, bloody, and ultimately futile ground campaigns in Russia by both Napoleon and Hitler.[296] This kind of warfare, given the new technological environment, was "militarily unsound."[297]

On the topic of the B-36, Vandenberg bristled at the idea that the bomber could not do its assigned job. He testified that the USAF had its most experienced crews conducting long-range bombing operations, with or without escorts, in all kinds of weather regardless of enemy opposition.[298] While that statement certainly was true, it did not necessarily mean the concept was valid nor did it actually address the issue over the B-36's effectiveness. He reiterated his support for his aircrews and his full confidence that they could do their jobs.[299] Additionally, in a pointed quip directed at the naval officers who had testified earlier, he stated, "This process of assertion and counter assertion cannot fail to confuse and deeply disturb the public. . . . [T]he public should take the glib assertions . . . and put those beside known facts or contrary statements."[300] For him, the naval officers did the nation a disservice by eroding confidence in the USAF and by bringing to light many technical and operational data points that might be exploited by an adversary.[301]

Vandenberg expressed confidence in his crews and SAC's ability to conduct its wartime mission. But what he did not tell the subcommittee was that an internal USAF report had identified significant deficiencies within his service, especially when compared to the Navy. During 17–26 August 1949, the Third Division Inspector General (IG) from Kelly Air Force Base, Texas, sent personnel on a routine visit to the 3170th Special Weapons Group at Kirtland Air Force Base, New Mexico. The 3170th was responsible for developing and testing atomic weapons and their associated aircraft for the USAF. During this inspection, officers found unqualified USAF personnel with worn-out or unmodified aircraft unable to carry atomic weapons. Then problems occurred once the unit finally received three B-36s for test evaluations. While flying at an altitude of 45,000 feet, ten propeller blades collapsed on one aircraft, and in another mission four engines were rendered inoperative due to oil issues. While these deficiencies did not affect the testing overall, the IG noted that they "indicate technical limitations" for the B-36. More importantly, the report specifically stated, "the B-36 is not, at present, a satisfactory bomber above 40,000 ft."[302]

In its conclusion the report made special mention of Navy personnel becoming increasingly more competent with atomic weapons, as many Navy veterans were now in key positions in the AEC. The IG expressed concern that the Navy might even surpass the Air Force in technical expertise with atomic munitions by warning, "The Atomic Energy Commission which has ex-Navy personnel in key positions, observes all the tests conducted by the Air Force. . . . [A]t present the Air Force . . . is both inefficient and deficient when compared with the Navy."[303]

Given this situation, a week later a memorandum from the deputy inspector, Lt. Gen. St. Clair Street, to Vandenberg reported much of the same. On 8 September the IG forwarded the following "inescapable" conclusions:

> The Air Force is not competent at the present time to perform its function as the primary agent for the delivery of the atomic bomb.

> An incredible lack of initiative is prevalent in Headquarters US Air Force toward establishing and maintaining our position as the chosen instrument for the waging of atomic warfare.
>
> Kirtland Air Force Base, instead of being in the forefront as the contact point between the Air Force and the Atomic Energy Commission, is a sorry spectacle of neglect in both material and equipment.
>
> Through neglect or disinterest, the Air Force has acquiesced in the placing of Navy personnel in almost every key position in the atomic weapons organization.[304]

Perhaps more relevant to the October discussions was another comment in the memo: "The capabilities of the Air Force atom bomb aircraft do not now meet the maximums claimed for them in recent public discussion." More importantly, addressing the deficiencies of the B-36 as a weapons carrier, the IG stated the USAF should "recast the supply system to fit the bomb rather than try to force the bomb into the present system."[305]

Reflective of this report was an operation conducted by SAC earlier that year. When LeMay assumed command in October 1948, he was skeptical of its readiness and operational capability. Assessing his new charge, in January 1949 he directed a mock attack on Dayton, Ohio, by his command's B-29/50 and B-36 fleet. The crews were given a picture of the city and directed to attack at the combat altitude of 30,000 feet using radar bombing procedures. The results were disastrous. Many aircrews aborted for technical or weather reasons. Of the 303 bombers that actually made it over the "target," two-thirds of simulated drops were more than 7,000 feet off target—far from the established USAF standard of 3,000 feet.[306] According to LeMay, "Not one airplane finished the mission as briefed. Not one."[307] He complained further of "aborts all over the place, [and that the] equipment didn't work, the crews didn't work, nothing worked."[308] As far as he was concerned, it was "just about the darkest night in American aviation history."[309] The results of the simulated Dayton attack combined with the IG report were hardly supportive of Vandenberg's statements before Congress both in the August and the October hearings. Had naval officers known of this lack of competence and performance on the part of SAC and the USAF atomic endeavor, they might have easily validated their claims regarding the B-36 and atomic strategic bombing. Fortunately for the USAF, these deficiencies remained largely hidden from the other services and the general public.

General Bradley, the newly appointed chairman of the JCS, testified on 19 October. His comments were the most aggressive of the pro-USAF rebuttals. He directly refuted almost every charge by the Navy contingent and accused them of not accepting the "decisions of the authorities established by law. . . . [They] have done infinite harm to our national defense . . . and the confidence of the people in their government." Regarding the expenditures for the respective services, Bradley testified that each service received roughly an equal share of the defense budget but argued that this was more coincidence than deliberate, warning that these percentages might change given national security requirements. He went on to defend the concept of strategic bombardment, arguing that "when properly applied" it could affect enemy national morale and its war-making potential.[310] The general argued that American war plans were not solely based upon an atomic "blitz," as charged by Admiral Radford, who misrepresented and "obscure[d] the real facts."[311] He came to the defense of the B-36, the USAF's ability to execute its assigned missions, and the aircrews' skills. It is unknown if he had knowledge of the existing deficiencies in the service's atomic endeavors as specified by LeMay or the Air Force IG. But like Denfeld, Bradley also endorsed the idea of waiting for the WSEG findings to help determine the efficacy of strategic bombing.[312]

Getting his dander up, the JCS switched to thinly veiled ad hominem arguments. He called into question the issue regarding Navy morale as articulated in the Bogan letter. Bradley took a deliberate jab at the admirals, arguing, "Senior officers decrying the low morale of their forces evidently do not realize that esprit of the men is but a mirror of their confidence in their leadership."[313] Very pointedly, he called into question Denfeld's military experience. The CNO's war record was hardly comparable with other members of the JCS, as he had served largely in staff billets in noncombat commands for most of World War II, whereas all the other members of the JCS had commanded in battle for an extended period or during specific campaigns. Bradley here took a direct personal swipe at the CNO's lack of experience by, after citing the combat experience of other members of the JCS during the war, purposely remarked, "I was not associated with Admiral Denfeld's [combat record] during the war. I am not familiar with his experiences."[314] Such comments were certainly impolite and indiscreet, given both the company and the venue. Navy friendly journalist Hanson Baldwin classified Bradley's remarks as "pretty poor pool."[315]

The JCS chairman also went so far as to charge the Navy with undermining the nation's security by questioning strategic plans, making their own assertions over other experts, and distorting the American perspective regarding war.[316] While he claimed to support the Navy and naval aviation, the general chided the service by use of a football analogy: "This is no time for 'fancy dans' who won't hit the line with all they have on every play, unless they can call the signals. Each player on this team—whether he shines in the spotlight of the backfield or eats dirt in the line—must be an All American."[317] In these statements Bradley made his emotional punch, painting the Navy officers as individuals more concerned with their reputations rather than being team players. Afterward one reporter wrote, "When Omar Bradley finished his biting, indignant statement there was stunned silence in the committee room. . . . [F]rom a military standpoint he has all but blasted the Navy admirals' case. And before the week was out, torpedoed by the testimony of other non-Navy men, the Navy's arguments were little more than just afloat."[318]

After Bradley's statements, the remaining testimonies paled in comparison. Secretary Johnson was next, but he and Vinson remained cordial despite the representative's past complaints of the secretary's fiscal and managerial abilities. With Bradley's stinging rebuke of the Navy, Johnson did not need to pile on. He did, however, testify that he had saved taxpayer dollars, as was his mandate, in a small exchange with Vinson. But in support of the USAF argument, Johnson testified that the "2 to 1 vote in the Joint Chiefs of Staff [as articulated by the naval officers] . . . is a fallacy from start to finish."[319] He attempted to downplay his authority and that of the service chiefs, claiming that the JCS "recommends to" the secretary, and "when appropriate the President himself does the deciding."[320] While a true statement, this was hardly indicative of the decision to cancel CVA 58. Finally, like Denfeld and Bradley before, the defense secretary also looked forward to the WSEG findings to clarify the issue at hand: "It is our hope through the WSEG, to bring the capabilities of various weapons systems, including the B-36, out of the area of inter-service controversy and into the area of fact."[321]

While other prominent figures testified following Johnson, the tension and drama were over. At 1250 on 21 October, the committee closed its proceedings. Overall, the Navy again made a poor showing for itself. Distortions, oversights, and errors undermined what was a legitimate claim regarding its marginalization. But factual data and a coordinated effort on the part of the Air Force successfully parried the (true and untrue) claims of the Navy. Had the naval service conducted their preparations and coordinated testimonies like their USAF counterparts, they may have made a more convincing argument.[322] Despite Matthews' lukewarm defense, naval aviators did indeed have a case to make, but they executed it poorly.

In the final report of the B-36 investigation, the subcommittee demurred and declined to proceed with further examination. Regarding the remaining issues on their list of tasks, the report concluded, "such questions had to be considered solely on their own merits."[323] As far as Congress was concerned, the admission of Worth in August fulfilled the main requirements of Resolution 234. Regarding the latest debate, for those who sided with the Navy in their testimony, retribution and a reckoning were in their immediate futures. Despite the assurances in the halls of Congress that the hearings would not result in revenge or reprisals, across the Potomac River in the Pentagon, the truth was very different.

Although the hearings were concluded, this did not mean the situation in the Pentagon had abated. Controversy still remained as to the nature of the nation's defense. The USAF apparently won another round in the public unification fight, but with the changing geopolitical environment, a complete review of U.S. national security policy was now envisioned. Perhaps the most important result of the October hearings was not the discourse between the two rival services and their respective leadership but the questions raised concerning the nation's overall military strategy. In its final report the congressional committee equivocated by formally stating, "The committee . . . draws a general conclusion on the issue which does not attempt to resolve the controversy by 'finding' in favor of one strategic concept as opposed to another."[324] It found relevance in both arguments from the October session, which gave the Navy a "victory" of sorts. The members came to the conclusion that "both sides are correct . . . that the Navy does not fully comprehend the problem incident to large scale land warfare. . . . Conversely [the committee] agrees that strategic bombing experts . . . cannot be expert in naval strategy and measures necessary to insure command of the seas."[325]

The committee took no further action regarding the B-36 program and declined to reverse the cancellation of USS *United States*. In addition, members reinforced their support for unification but proffered changes to the JCS that might alleviate future controversy. What was more important was that the committee determined that a wholesale review of national strategy was needed and made the case for such an effort multiple times in its formal findings:

> The decision belongs primarily within the National Security Council. . . . [T]he need for an astute appraisal by the National Security Council of present strategic planning reference atomic warfare, again for the reason that military considerations alone should not resolve the question of when and how this nation will resort to atomic warfare. . . .
>
> The Secretary of Defense should initiate a study in the National Security Council on the relationship to national objectives of atomic warfare and present strategic planning for the use of atomic weapons. . . . [T]he nation can no longer afford lackadaisical planning or complacency as to its defenses.[326]

During the conduct of the hearings, all those testifying placed great stock in the ongoing WSEG study and looked forward to its findings.[327] But those conclusions were still months away. With a potential release in early 1950, many looked to use the assessment's results to underscore their arguments. Despite the unfortunate timing of the WSEG results in relation to the October hearings, the first full month of autumn 1949 sowed the seeds for a review of national security policy. The arguments between the two services, combined with the explosion of Joe-1 and the weeks-old "loss" of China, primed the pump for a new approach to national security. Concurrently, as these events unfolded, another issue came to the fore, one that would cause even more debate and argument over military strategy.

Expansion and the "Super"

While the October hearings were going full bore, a secret yet equally contentious discussion was just beginning. This debate was not between the services, about budgets, or regarding who should have what roles in national defense. This discourse was about the need for larger, more powerful weapons given the Soviet explosion of Joe-1. Although the United States already had plans for the use of atomic weapons, the Kazakhstan detonation spurred interest in a next-generation weapon, previously a low priority given the Americans atomic monopoly.

Since the end of the war, the plutonium-based MK III Fat Man implosion design remained the standard atomic ordnance in the U.S. arsenal. The Little Boy gun-type assembly design was largely discounted as a waste of scarce fissionable material. Four years after the Nagasaki attack, an improved implosion-based bomb was only now coming into production in late 1949 after its successful testing at Eniwetok in 1948. Called the MK IV, it had better aerodynamics than the MK III, allowed for inflight insertion of atomic components, a new fusing-firing system, and more importantly allowed for mass production. While the MK IV was an upgrade in atomic munitions, the Soviet discovery of weaponized fission brought to the fore the question of developing deadlier and more destructive bombs.

The idea of a thermonuclear reaction had been around since the early 1930s. In 1939 physicist Hans Bethe suggested that this type of reaction was the explanation for the sun's light and radiating heat. While existing in nature, could man obtain the capacity to create it? A thermonuclear reaction transforms isotopes of hydrogen (deuterium and tritium) into helium, resulting in a process called fusion.[328] This process involves bringing together lighter nuclei atoms to make a heavier product, in the process creating even larger yields of explosive energy. The biggest problem with creating such an event by a man-made device was the natural tendency of the two light nuclei's electrostatic repulsion of each other. Yet with enough pressure and heat, this tendency could be overcome, resulting in limitless explosive power. The challenge was generating enough heat and energy to counter the repulsive forces.

One possible way to create sufficient force for fusion to occur was the detonation of a fission reaction (termed a "booster") that would create the conditions for a thermonuclear (fusion) event.[329] As a result, a thermonuclear weapon might include two types of events, one based on fission and the other on fusion. If this two-stage design worked, early estimates of such an explosion were impressive, as the "Super" (as the thermonuclear bomb was called) might be capable of producing the equivalent of 300 million tons of TNT compared to the 100,000 tons produced by a fission reaction. Early estimates surmised that while a fission-based bomb would destroy an area of eighteen square miles, the Super could lay waste to four thousand square miles (a severe overestimation).[330] With this much explosive energy, scientists saw this as a "quantum leap" in nuclear technology.

Edward Teller, considered the father of the thermonuclear bomb, credited famed physicist Enrico Fermi for triggering his curiosity in this new possibility during lunch at Columbia University one day in September 1941.[331] A Hungarian-born refugee, Teller was a rabid anti-Communist with a curious, ingenious mind that matched his unbounded energy.[332] In 1943 a number of physicists at the Los Alamos Scientific Laboratory (LASL), including Teller, began looking at the idea of atomic fusion. With the difficulty during the war of obtaining certain materials like tritium, combined with other major theoretical stumbling blocks, LASL focused on fission, with fusion merely an academic endeavor. Regardless of its secondary status, work on fusion continued throughout 1945, even after V-J Day. In a 31 October 1945 letter to Fermi, Teller suggested that work on fusion be continued, estimating that a weapon could be built in as little as five years.[333] In March 1946, at a fusion conference at LASL, the gathered scientists came to the unanimous conclusion that a "super bomb" was possible.[334] In addition to a weapon, some believed that such a reaction might have peacetime applications. Besides Teller, perhaps the most important attendee of the conference was Klaus Fuchs.[335]

While only a theoretical possibility, given the postwar environment and the U.S. fission (atomic) monopoly, there was little motivation to explore fusion.[336] Most of the research done within the AEC after the war was based upon refining the MK III weapon (resulting in the MK IV) and testing the effects of an atomic blast on military equipment. While the United States maintained its monopoly, that did not mean the AEC ignored thermonuclear technology wholesale. Within the AEC was a group of prominent physicists and scientists who had worked in the wartime MED. As part of their postwar duties, they were now members of what was called the General Advisory Committee (GAC). The GAC included scientists such as Oppenheimer, Fermi, James Conant, and Isidor Rabi. The committee was specifically established to provide technical advice and input to the AEC on atomic-related matters. At various meetings in the immediate postwar years, the GAC strongly recommended continuing research in the area of fusion.[337] Not only did they wish to continue looking into thermonuclear applications from an academic and research standpoint, but they also thought that such work would be a healthy stimulus to LASL following the war.[338]

Although many believed that such technology was feasible, most within the AEC and the military were not worried about a potential enemy having the facilities or resources to leverage a thermonuclear reaction. Moreover, because the knowledge was so theoretical and fragmented, the GAC even suggested that such research be classified only as "secret" as opposed to "top secret."[339] With a downgrade in classification, members hoped to expand the audience of those having access to such information and thereby facilitate the development of the technology.

But others were not as sure about the technical ignorance of the Soviet Union. One of the first commissioners of the AEC, Lewis Strauss, was wary of Communist resourcefulness and warned, "It would be prudent to proceed upon the assumption that the thermonuclear rather than the fission weapon had always been the Russian goal and that they might not only be parallel with us but even ahead of us."[340] By 1948, members of the GAC believed that part of a thermonuclear device, the booster, might be ready to test in the next two to five years.[341] By 1949, physicists Stanislaw Ulam, John von Neumann, Luis Alvarez, and Ernest Lawrence, among many others, made significant progress in thermonuclear theory.[342] Despite the GAC's long-range plans for fusion, the detection of Joe-1 became a catalyst for an invigorated American effort. Since the Soviets had broken the code on atomic fission years ahead of schedule, what proof was there that they were not already working on thermonuclear applications? Even more ominously, since the United States did not place fusion as the priority for postwar AEC efforts, could the Soviets now be ahead?[343]

On the same day the president announced the Soviet explosion, Congress' Joint Committee on Atomic Energy (JCAE) held the first of many meetings with AEC commissioners addressing American atomic production. Over the course of six days, those in attendance devised twenty-three possible ways to increase production of atomic weapons. Some suggestions included increasing the staff at LASL; building a K-31 gaseous-diffusion plant at Oak Ridge, Tennessee; expansion plans for the "DR reactor" at Hanford, Washington; and bringing in the DuPont Company to assist in the efforts.[344] In addition to these, another recommendation was to initiate an "all out" hydrogen bomb effort.[345] Later in the session a JCAE memo argued that "the atomic arms race . . . makes the primacy in developing a thermonuclear super-weapon a dominant consideration."[346] While some theoretical work had been ongoing, the JCAE was now suggesting it was time to step up the effort regarding fusion research.

On 5 October, four days after Mao proclaimed the PRC on the steps of the Forbidden City by Tiananmen Square and the same day that Carl Vinson opened the October hearings on the B-36, Commissioner Strauss forwarded a memo to his fellow AEC members advocating development of the Super in light of Joe-1.[347] In the short but powerful note, Strauss not only expressed his support for an expansion of fission-bomb production but also thought it time for a "quantum jump in our planning." The commissioner strongly encouraged his peers to support an "intensive effort in the development of thermonuclear weapons."[348] In this effort Strauss argued that even an increase in the atomic arsenal was not enough to regain the advantage in the new balance of power vis-à-vis the USSR.[349] In closing, he further requested that the GAC be called into session to obtain members' views regarding this proposal. When JCAE Chair Brien McMahon first read Strauss's letter, he told his assistant William Borden, "we're going all out on the H-bomb, nothing is going to stand in the way."[350]

As the idea regarding fusion and the Super gained momentum, the president was still awaiting an answer to his earlier July request regarding the expansion of the atomic stockpile. In his midsummer tasking Truman asked the secretaries of state and defense along with AEC Chair Lilienthal to study the efficacy of an increase in atomic-material production. Given earlier discussions, an increase was an imperative for many, and the presidential request was more a formality than an actual query. A month later, given the events in Kazakhstan and the sniffing out of radioactive material by 1st Lt. Robert Johnson's WB-29, it seemed obvious that by early fall the AEC needed to increase production. Before having read Strauss' 5 October note, JCAE Chair McMahon inserted himself into the process by writing Truman on 28 September encouraging approval for an expansion and reminding him that only a small fraction of U.S. military expenditures were devoted to atomic munitions.[351] This small number was ironic, given that existing and emerging war plans increasingly relied upon atomic weapons, and the stockpile was hardly sufficient to support the envisioned bombing campaigns.

Days later, on 7 October, as Admiral Radford was testifying before the B-36 committee, in a separate session with the JCAE, Air Force Secretary Symington, along with General Vandenberg and Lieutenant General LeMay, testified as to their dissatisfaction with the number of available atomic weapons.[352] Probably the most startling was the testimony of the SAC commander. As head of the unit designated to execute much of the campaign, LeMay testified to Congress that he had not even looked at the stockpile figures. When queried as to his knowledge of the current inventory of atomic weapons, he replied that he "preferred not to."[353] In June 1948 the stockpile composed some fifty MK III fissionable cores accompanying fifty-three nonfissionable assemblies.[354] But by late 1949, estimates placed the atomic stockpile at approximately 200 weapons, while the approved war plan, codenamed Offtackle, required some 220 bombs, with a reattack requirement of 72 more.[355] While the deficiency of only a few dozen bombs may seem insignificant, those numbers do not reflect the bombs loaded in aircraft that might be shot down, lost, or miss their assigned targets. As a result of these eventualities in a combat environment, the deficiency in available bombs might be more pronounced.

But indicative of the disjointed nature in the early atomic enterprise, the three departments tasked by Truman to study the expansion submitted individual positions that then were pieced together. Instead of sitting down and cobbling together a response as a single entity, DoD, AEC, and DoS submitted separate reports. Secretary Johnson forwarded DoD's stance regarding only the requirement of weapons, Chairman Lilienthal addressed the ability of the AEC to produce the additional requirements to meet the military need, and DoS focused solely on the international implications of such a move.[356] The idea of integrating their ideas into one formal response was an illustration of the federal turf wars of the time.

A little over a week after McMahon sent his letter to the president, Truman received an answer to his expansion query. The 10 October report was a fait accompli. The three departments were all supportive of a stepped-up atomic-energy program. The basis for their findings were many, including the efficiency of atomic weapons over conventional bombs, better access to more raw materials (uranium) and an increasingly efficient refinement process, the continued strained relationship with the USSR and the need to defend Western Europe, the possible vulnerability of atomic-production facilities to enemy attack, the lack of international control of atomic technology, and the inherent flexibility such weapons provided to military planners.[357] Understandably, the Soviet attainment of atomic technology figured prominently. In response to the discovery of Joe-1, their report justified the production acceleration: "From a military standpoint, the Joint Chiefs of Staff are of the opinion that the recent atomic explosion in the USSR underlines the military necessity of increased weapons production, and thus strongly reinforces and supports the justification and urgency of their previous [June] recommendations. . . . [T]he expansion is not considered untimely, . . . particularly in view of the recent atomic explosion in the USSR."[358] The AEC now had the capacity to increase production, and capital investment would reduce the unit cost of fissionable material. While Lilienthal stayed within his area of expertise and reported that the commission could support such an increase, privately he questioned the wisdom of such a move: "More and better bombs. Where will this lead—that is, whether this will lead to something good—is difficult to see. We keep saying we have no other course; what we should say is; We are not bright enough to see any other course."[359]

While focusing on military applications, the three heads also saw a peaceful use of fissionable materials that might also be an economic boon. In closing, their report clearly drew connections to current national security policy (as expressed by NSC 20/4), which focused on the "containment" of Communism and the Soviet Union. As a result, atomic weapons provided a deterrent effect, keeping the Russian "bear" at bay. Lastly, and in direct contradiction to Budget Director Frank Pace's earlier suggestions, the report did not endorse reducing the military budget commensurate with the AEC increase.[360] In a rare statement of unity, all three supported an increase in funding without an associated reduction.

Three days later, on 13 October, the JCAE issued its own report to Congress, stating, "Russia's ownership of the bomb, years ahead of anticipated date, is a monumental challenge to American boldness, initiative and effort." The next day it met with various military leaders who endorsed an expansion of the expansion effort and a "stepped up hydrogen program."[361] Furthermore, making the idea of expansion more palatable, the AEC cost figure of $500 million was adjusted, with the new cost estimate reduced to $319 million spread out over three years.[362] While this looked to be cheaper than first proposed, the timing of requesting additional funding was problematic. Given Truman's fiscal frugality, the proposed amount had not been included in the current budget. For the president to fully support this increase required a supplemental appropriations request. On 14 October the JCAE unanimously requested notification by the president if a funding deficiency needed immediate forwarding.[363] Many, of course, wanted to begin immediately.

Not surprising, and convinced that international control of atomic weapons was never going to happen, on 19 October Truman formally approved the expansion. But his approval was not all that was hoped by those looking for more weapons—especially Strauss. The president only authorized the AEC $30 million to study the feasibility of the project, with the funding coming from current appropriations. In his official statement the next day, Truman announced his authorization to initiate the construction with the current funds available, but he would not recommend increased monies until next year's budget.[364] While the president in essence agreed on the necessity, he failed to respond with the immediacy some required. Disappointed but undaunted, Strauss wrote to Lilienthal and urged that the AEC expedite the planned K-31 reactor and the DR waterworks.[365] Furthermore, the president tasked Secretary Johnson to review atomic-weapons targeting and strategic planning. With this

Truman was telling DoD to do a complete review of its atomic strategy and requirements.[366] This was something Lilienthal had been requesting for months.

There was a more strategic and thoughtful consideration to Truman's initial modest response to expansion. As the president made his decision, JCAE Chair McMahon leaked that the AEC had approved the K-31 plant and the modification for the DR waterworks. Though the two groups approved these expansions, funding them was another issue. Even though the president decided against submitting a budget supplement, approval of these expansions by the two atomic agencies at least gave the appearance of action as a result of the Soviet success. According to Gordon Dean, another AEC member, the president was furious at McMahon for this disclosure. After the surprise of Joe-1, Dean wrote that Truman's ire at McMahon came from the belief that the chief executive "did not want the Russians to think we [were] afraid of them."[367] In the opinion of some, the timing of such a request was especially poor given international events.[368] The president evidently was looking to exhibit a more staid response to Joe-1 than to appear panicked. Supporting this supposition that America was in a state of shock was a mention in the Russian newspaper *Pravda.* Supposedly, JCS Chairman Bradley was so worried about the Soviet bomb that he had been suffering from insomnia since first learning of the Russian success, an accusation Bradley flatly refuted.[369]

While the president only authorized a study regarding atomic expansion and directed a review of atomic-weapon requirements, he was about to run straight into an even larger issue regarding thermonuclear technology. While so far an unproven concept by man's hands, sides were already beginning to form about the need for such a program. Given the move to expand the atomic stockpile, should the United States commit even more resources to a speculative effort? The MED had cost $2 billion. Would the Super effort require the same large fiscal commitment? Perhaps the biggest obstacle in developing a hydrogen-based fusion bomb was not the technical hurdles, but the moral implications of the technology.

Because a potential thermonuclear bomb was speculative, could scientific research create such an event? Even with the promise of a quantum leap in technology and given the envisioned requirements to create a fusion reaction, the device might be so large and heavy that it may only be deliverable by train or ship.[370] One physicist's guess estimated the weight for such a weapon at ten tons.[371] Another scientist joked, "it can't be gotten to a target except by ox cart"—hardly a feasible offensive option given the air-centric war envisioned.[372] Although some intellectual foundations were laid by late 1949, the feasibility of the Super at this time was as unknown as fission was in 1930. Those aware of the technical challenge gave themselves a "better than a 50 percent" chance.[373] One of the early concerns was the amount of tritium required. Production of the essential heavy hydrogen isotope might possibly exceed the capacity of the reactors designated to produce plutonium for fission-based weapons.[374]

Regardless of the issues of feasibility, Strauss was not the only one worried about the recent Soviet achievement. In California physicists Luis Alvarez and Ernest Lawrence of the Berkeley Radiation Lab looked to bolster American efforts as a response to Joe-1. Getting in touch with Teller at LASL, the two men flew to New Mexico to discuss the possibility of fusion.[375] On 7 October Teller informed his visitors of the progress made in the past few years and claimed that, with enough funding and support, a fusion reaction was possible.[376] Emboldened with this information, Alvarez and Lawrence flew to Washington the next day to meet with members of the JCAE and the Military Liaison Committee (MLC). In a two-day whirlwind visit, they met with AEC physicist Paul Fine, Brig. Gen. James McCormack (head of Military Applications, AEC), Ken Pitzer (head of Research, AEC), Rep. Carl Hinshaw (R-CA), JCAE Chair McMahon, the AEC commissioners, and the newly appointed MLC chairman, William Webster.[377] None of the AEC commissioners were interested in their proposals except Strauss.

Invited to lunch with Hinshaw and McMahon on the ninth, the two physicists called the representatives' attention to the fact that Russian scientist Peter Kapitza was one of the world's leading experts in light elements (that is, hydrogen).[378] Painting a picture of doom and fearing America one day being held hostage to a Soviet fusion weapon, Alvarez and Lawrence worried that the Russians might possibly be ahead technologically and widening their lead. The Berkeley scientists were also concerned that the Soviets may just proceed to thermonuclear research, that their success at fission might only be a waypoint toward fusion. Alvarez and Lawrence easily sold Hinshaw on the idea of pursuing thermonuclear technology.[379]

But the same could not be said of their meeting with AEC Chair Lilienthal the next day. Lilienthal was disinterested in the topic altogether. Alvarez described his apathy regarding thermonuclear weapons as "shocking" and noted the AEC chair "did not even want to talk about the program. He turned his chair around and looked out the window. . . . [W]e could hardly get into a conversation with him."[380] After the meeting Lilienthal recorded, "Ernest Lawrence and Louis [*sic*] Alvarez in here drooling over the [Super]. Is this all we have to offer?"[381] Given his concerns over the existence of atomic weaponry and his inherent suspicions of the military, Lilienthal's position is hardly surprising. For him, atomic weapons and the military were to be held on a tight leash, and his mistrust of those in uniform reverberated throughout the AEC.

Before the two scientists departed Washington, they also met with other members of the AEC who, at the time, appeared to support their position. Leaving on 11 October, the two headed to New York to visit Isidor Rabi, a noted physicist at Columbia University and member of the GAC. Greeting the two men warmly, Rabi was intellectually interested in what they had to say about thermonuclear technology. But after the discussion he remained uncommitted regarding his support despite the theoretical intrigue and scientific challenge.[382] Nevertheless, leaving for home, Alvarez and Lawrence believed they had found Fermi another advocate for their position. Upon their return home they started looking for the best minds to help. Days later, on 13 October, the secretary general of the GAC, John Manley, echoed much of the same sentiment Alvarez and Lawrence espoused by writing his colleagues at LASL regarding the Soviet success: "[LASL] should admit at least to its own personnel that the current laboratory program has not been geared to such an event [Joe-1] in 1949. Rather it has been tacitly assumed that this event would not occur before 1952. . . . At the very least, therefore, the Laboratory should consider that it has lost some three years of time."[383] Although Manley eventually became an opponent of Super development, for those who were in favor of it and envisioned the threat posed by the Soviets, his concerns resonated.

While Strauss was an early proponent of the Super, it became apparent that his fellow commissioners were not as enthusiastic, even after Alvarez and Lawrence's visit. AEC Chair Lilienthal was already highly suspicious of atomic weapons and was loath to increase the danger posed by such technology.

Furthermore, given his cold reception to Lawrence and Alvarez, there was probably very little that might have change his mind. Looking for insight on this issue and on matters regarding expansion, on 11 October Lilienthal wrote Oppenheimer to request the GAC's opinions.[384] Supportive of a discussion, and as chair of the GAC, Oppenheimer replied that the committee could meet in Washington at the end of October. In the meantime on the seventeenth, Senator McMahon wrote to members of the AEC to encourage their support for the Super, arguing, "American efforts along this line should be as bold and urgent as our original atomic enterprise."[385] In addition to encouraging support for the Super, the JCAE chair was still smarting over the president's decision not to provide supplemental funding for proposed atomic expansion until next year. As far as Truman was concerned, the JCAE was always looking for more atomic bombs and oversimplified atomic-weapons issues.[386] In his disappointment over this delay of funds, McMahon corresponded with the members of the AEC in hopes they would help expedite K-31 and the DR waterworks funding in the next congressional session. He expressed to the commissioners that his committee understood that the "current situation dictates unusual and even extraordinary steps."[387] The senator hoped Congress would too.

Perhaps more pressing for Strauss and his support for the Super was a development coming from the FBI. During the summer the bureau believed that atomic secrets were passed to the Soviets by a British member of LASL. Through the Venona Project, which looked for evidence of Soviet espionage, Fuchs' name was uncovered in September in an encrypted 1944 KGB message addressing the process of gaseous diffusion. Days later the FBI began investigating the scientist and his espionage efforts at LASL.[388] By October preliminary conclusions about Fuchs took shape, with discussions about him occurring between MED chief Groves and Strauss.[389] On 19 October the commissioner met with FBI Director J. Edgar Hoover and requested a detailed report of British efforts at LASL. Interestingly, Fuchs had remained in the United States after the war into the spring of 1946. As a result, he not only attended the thermonuclear conference held in that season but also had access to the thermonuclear work done at laboratory.[390] If he shared this information with the Soviets, they might already be further ahead technologically than previously thought.[391] Since this had proven true with fission, the same might be true regarding fusion—a logical assumption. While still an ongoing investigation, the suspicion of Fuchs combined with the success of Joe-1 helped serve as a catalyst for Strauss' thermonuclear advocacy. Strauss was not alone in his assessment of possible Soviet infiltration of the AEC.[392] AEC Commissioner Gordon Dean also echoed this sentiment, writing, "I think we must recognize that if there is one place where Communists will attempt to infiltrate it is the atomic energy program."[393] As the proof of Fuchs' espionage came to light, Strauss and other Americans believed U.S. atomic parity with the Soviets might now be an illusion; given the events in Kazakhstan, America might now be behind.

Acceding to Lilienthal's request, the GAC met in Washington from 28 through 30 October. The agenda not only focused on a debate regarding a "crash effort" for the Super but also planned to address the adequacy of the current atomic enterprise in national defense. Yet even before the committee convened, there were clues as to how members felt. In an informal session earlier, Teller along with physicist Hans Bethe met with Oppenheimer in his office at Princeton. During the meeting the former head of LASL showed the two physicists a letter from fellow GAC member James Conant regarding a fusion-based bomb. Conant's words left no doubt as to his opinion: "Over my dead body."[394] Additionally, on 24 October Teller met with Fermi, another GAC member, in Chicago. While Teller was effusive over the idea of thermonuclear weapons, Fermi was largely noncommittal and barely reacted to his peer's enthusiasm.[395] While certainly not a definitive response, his lack of response was a possible barometer. Although interesting from an academic and intellectual standpoint, the use of such advances for more powerful weapons was not viewed by many on the committee as a positive development.

Members of the GAC were all renowned scientists and physicists, with most having contributed to the wartime MED. Other relevant parties were also invited to attend part of the deliberations, including Kennan from the DoS; JCS Chairman Bradley; Brigadier General McCormack of the MLC; director of the ongoing WSEG, Lt. Gen. John Hull; Vice Chief of Air Force Operations Lt. Gen. Lauris Norstad; and veteran of the first atomic attack Rear Adm. William Parsons.[396] The first session on 28 October was informal and largely filled with discussions regarding the role of atomic energy in the global environment and discourse on technical feasibility of fusion research.[397] The next day, the formal start of the GAC meeting, military members provided input as to the utility of the Super. Perhaps the most important comment came from JCS Chairman Bradley. He claimed that the effect of a thermonuclear weapon would come not so much from its physical results as from its potential psychological power.[398] Yet with this statement Bradley did not necessarily claim that there was a military need for the Super. Would a bomb with this much power have a practical military purpose? Would megatons worth of explosive force have a role to play in a strategic campaign? There were no real answers to these questions. While the testimony before the special committee regarding the B-36 and the "revolt" had just ended a week earlier, the reverberations were still being felt. Lilienthal noted that during this initial GAC discourse, he did not think the military fully understood the implications of a potential weapon and were "too busy with the inter-service row."[399]

That afternoon GAC members Conant and Hartley Rowe made their voices heard, arguing against the Super, with one quipping, "We [already] built one Frankenstein." For Lilienthal, the idea that this new potential weapon provided "security" was a weak argument. In private he wrote, "What happened to 'deterrent' (regarding fission based weapons) hadn't we seen how thin these arguments had proved in the past; why would it be different in the future?" Echoing this sentiment was Conant: "This whole discussion makes me feel [like] I was seeing the same film . . . for a second time."[400] As the discussion continued into Sunday, a trend emerged. Although the technical challenge was clearly an obstacle, the assembled scientists felt the idea of thermonuclear weapons was immoral. Given the size of a potential blast and the damage it would cause, there was no doubt that whatever its military target was, a Super would certainly slaughter vast numbers of civilians.[401] In the scientists' minds this weapon was aimed not so much at a potential enemy force as to an entire society or civilization—hence enacting a genocide.[402]

The remainder of Sunday was devoted to drafting a formal GAC response. Organized into three parts, the report's first section related to national defense and security, the second related to the Super and its use as a weapon, and the final part provided recommendations or opinions from individual GAC members. In the first part the committee endorsed the increase in fissionable materials and the investment in infrastructure. In response to Truman's fiscal calculations, and after Strauss's 17 October letter to GAC membership, the committee recommended that the upgrades be considered by their contributions to national security and scientific endeavor rather than by any sheer fiscal considerations. Furthermore, the membership endorsed the idea of developing tactical nuclear weapons and increasing attention regarding delivery platforms. In this the payload size and capacity of the delivery aircraft needed to be more of a consideration. Lastly, the GAC endorsed building a reactor that would generate large amounts of free neutrons. In such a development, the members recognized its utility in the conversion of U235 to plutonium, testing various reactor components, a secondary facility for polonium initiators for MK IIIs, and possible production of radiological-warfare agents.[403] Interestingly, they also believed that such a reactor might be used to produce tritium for booster components of a potential thermonuclear device.[404]

The second part of the GAC report made the greatest impression. In complete unanimity the committee rejected the idea of going forward with the Super.[405] While the technological obstacles were significant, those scientific hurdles were largely second to the moral and ethical implications. The members believed that use of such a weapon made the extermination of civilian populations now a national policy.[406] From the technical perspective, they saw the lack of available tritium a concern. Additionally they worried about the behavior of the weapon under the extreme conditions required for fusion. Since a thermonuclear event required a booster, members were troubled about the inability to measure the elements of the reaction relating to testing and development.[407] To a degree, these two rationales were connected. In the report the GAC stated, "It is notable that there appears to be no experimental approach short of an actual test which should substantially add to our conviction that a given model will or will not work. . . . Thus we are faced with a development which cannot be carried to the point of conviction without the actual construction and demonstration of the essential elements of the weapon in question." Members understood that the Super was so theoretical that it could not be proven as a workable weapon unless they actually built one—and they were unanimous that the weapon should never be built. While somewhat circular logic, the report also stated that the Super should never be produced, that mankind was better off without it. It declared, too, that before such a weapon was produced, the world's political climate required significant change.[408] All members of the GAC thought the United States should not commit to the bomb's development.[409] As if that point was not strong enough, the report clearly stated, "there are no known or foreseen non-military applications of this development."[410]

The last part of the report included two opinion pieces. The forwarded document contained both the majority and the minority reports. While all GAC members agreed that the Super should not be built based upon moral and ethical grounds, a differing of opinion came about regarding renouncement of the weapon. The larger group, composed of Conant, Rowe, Cyril S. Smith, Lee A. DuBridge, Oliver E. Buckley, and Oppenheimer, believed that the United States needed an unqualified commitment renouncing such a weapon or its development.[411] Even if the Soviets developed a thermonuclear device, these men believed America should take the moral high ground and avoid such a weapon with a "renounce and announce" strategy. If required, the United States could effectively retaliate with its existing fissionable weapons. The minority report, subscribed to by Fermi and Rabi, believed that such a commitment was conditional. In their opinion, a public pledge should be made committing the United States to the rejection of the Super while inviting other nations to make the same commitment. But the minority opinion was pragmatic in that the U.S. rejection was contingent upon the response from the nations of the world, notably the Soviet Union.[412] While certainly more flexible in response, if other nations rejected such a pledge, then what? The two scientists were vague in what action the United States should take if the USSR failed to ascribe to the pledge.

By late Sunday afternoon the report was drafted. While the GAC was unanimous in agreement about the Super, this was only one organization's position. Many more arguments and opinions had yet to be heard. Even though its opinion mattered, would it be enough to sway the AEC, the JCAE, other elements of the federal government, and especially the chief executive? None of the GAC members could answer these questions and realized that men of lesser scientific acumen would hold greater influence. Of particular importance was Senator McMahon and Commissioner Strauss, who both saw America under direct threat from the Soviet explosion and whose hawkish views were popular in many quarters. AEC Chair Lilienthal was, of course, pleased with the GAC's stated position. He now hoped his commissioners would follow suit with renunciation.

On Halloween, the day after the GAC session concluded, the AEC chair called his fellow commissioners to discuss the report. As a courtesy he also informed McMahon, who was all too eager to meet with the commissioners once he heard the GAC's findings.[413] Meeting in Lilienthal's office that evening, the senator expressed his fatalistic opinion, arguing that war with the USSR was inevitable and the nation's best bet was to "blow them [the Soviets] off the face of the earth, quick, before they do the same to us." Writing in his diary, the AEC chair thought the JCAE chair's thinking was "pretty discouraging.... [McMahon thinks] the whole world revolves about the exploding atom—and that's the whole of it."[414] Thinking the GAC members naïve and simplistic, McMahon was incensed with their report. He complained to Teller, "it [the GAC position] makes me sick."[415] Strauss, too, was displeased and looked to express his concerns when the commissioners met. Talking with Oppenheimer, he was amazed that the GAC thought the Soviets would be willing to renounce thermonuclear weapons and not decline such an opportunity.[416]

McMahon took matters into his own hands and wrote the president the next day. The JCAE chair recognized the GAC position and reminded the president that the AEC would soon forward its own position on the Super. He informed Truman that a subcommittee of the JCAE was already engaged in meetings with scientists at LASL and Berkeley, learning of the possibilities of fusion.[417] One of the committee's representatives described a presentation by the director of the Weapons Lab, Norris Bradbury, as "wonderful," and other JCAE members came away with great enthusiasm, hoping to give the program the highest priority.[418] For McMahon and many within the joint committee, an expeditious start on the Super was in the country's best interests and a national security imperative. Closing his letter, the senator asked for a meeting with the president and wondered if he was inclined not to pursue the weapon.[419] McMahon hoped for the chance to plead his case as the others, in his opinion, subverted an effort to safeguard the nation. The president responded quickly the next day: "After I study the matter . . . I'll be glad to talk. . . . It is a situation that I don't like[,] to put it bluntly."[420]

On the same day McMahon wrote the president, Lilienthal visited the secretary of state. Acheson, too, was concerned and disturbed that the United States, and more specifically the Truman administration, was placing too much emphasis on atomic weapons.[421] Given the recent events over the B-36 and the USS *United States*, it was not hard to make the connection. Furthermore, with arguments between the two military services serving as a backdrop, concerns over Joe-1, the loss of China, and now discussion over thermonuclear weapons, the PPS realized it might be time to initiate a wholesale review of U.S. foreign policy.[422] But even any preliminary review still had a ways to go, as influential events continued to unfold over the coming months.

Current PPS head Kennan was opposed to the idea of the Super and looked for a more measured response to the recent Soviet success.[423] As the first head of PPS, Kennan was the chief architect of the "containment" strategy underlying American foreign policy during the Cold War. He had laid its intellectual foundations and now hoped for some kind of international control. Kennan argued with Acheson regarding the problem of the Super, as building the weapon might not provide the "Russians any ray of light" regarding an arms race, only the promise of escalation.[424] Before going ahead with the project, Kennan believed that the United States should solemnly reexamine the principle of "first use" of the Super or any other weapon of mass destruction. For him, their use would not result in any real victory or advance security but would only lead to "deterioration" of civilization and the eventual decline of mankind. Understanding that retention of such weapons was still a requirement, Kennan hoped an international understanding might someday lead to a reduction in their numbers or possible elimination entirely.[425] With these thoughts, he started to part ways, philosophically at least, with Acheson.

On 3 November, meeting in Lilienthal's office in the afternoon, the AEC members expressed their views, with the preliminary tally decidedly against the Super, 4 to 1.[426] Commissioners Lilienthal and Henry Smith were pleased with the GAC opinion and were hopeful that this issue over fusion might pave the way for international control. Commissioner Dean was opposed to the "renounce and announce" strategy but offered a third alternative. He proposed a rather fanciful idea that the president contact the Kremlin through secret diplomatic channels and come to some kind of mutual renouncement agreement.[427] Alternatively, Commissioner Strauss remained staunchly supportive of the Super, as he proposed questions about the amount of time and effort required for such a weapon, whether the military actually had a need for such a bomb, and wondered what the DoS's position might be.[428] He recommended that these queries be forwarded to the president as "a complete package," suggesting that interdepartmental (DoS and DoD) perspectives needed inclusion as well.[429]

Yet in a subsequent meeting of the AEC in the afternoon of 7 November, and after a morning meeting with members of the GAC, Dean changed his mind and came around to support Strauss' position.[430] Commissioner Sumner Pike finally made his position known and casted his lot against development. Pike's calculus against the Super was threefold. He argued that the cost of tritium was "fantastically high," that the military had not stated a need for such a weapon, and that smaller (fission) bombs were much more efficient.[431] As a result, the AEC was now split 3 to 2. Having no consensus, the commissioners submitted a disjointed response to the president. DoD and DoS still had not provided any input regarding the Super, thus undermining Strauss' "complete package" proposal. Instead, the commissioners forwarded a response that included their individual views (to include even some GAC members), the submitted GAC report, and a summary of the technical data regarding the proposed weapon.[432]

Formally submitted on 9 November, the AEC report included a cover letter mentioning that it had not been shared with DoD or DoS but would be made available to them if desired.[433] The technical narrative included numerous estimates claiming that the Super was 100 to 1,000 times as powerful as the Little Boy bomb; the Russians were capable of building such a weapon; there was a better than even chance of them actually building it; and the explosion of perhaps ten of these bombs might pollute the earth's atmosphere. The report also warned of a new arms race between the United States and USSR. In line with most of the AEC and GAC thinking, it referred to the Super as "a tool for mass destruction beside which the fission atomic bomb would seem puny even if the latter's efficiency were increased to the foreseeable limit."[434] After framing these larger contexts, the report included the individual comments of both the majority and minority views.

Two days earlier, during the commissioners meeting on 7 November, Lilienthal left his office for a scheduled noon appointment at the White House to tender his resignation as AEC chair.[435] For the past year he had been under scrutiny regarding his management and oversight of security in the commission. With the Cold War beginning to heat up, Lilienthal was painted as a Communist sympathizer and accused of failing to properly vet AEC employees. A subsequent inquiry cleared him of the charges, with the final report finding no instances of violations.[436] Yet in his position as AEC chair, Lilienthal had constantly butted heads with the man he had replaced, Major General Groves. After congressional hearings on AEC security and the attacks on his character, Lilienthal succumbed to the political pressure despite his exoneration.[437] His 21 November letter of resignation stated, "I shall leave with reluctance, but deeply gratified . . . from your special knowledge of the sound condition of the country's atomic program."[438]

Arriving early for his noon appointment, Lilienthal found the president in a jovial mood, with Truman discussing an upcoming New York state election. After the chair submitted his resignation, the president remarked how hard it would be to find a replacement and sympathized with him regarding this questioning of his character. With the president now tasked to find a suitable successor, he asked Lilienthal to stay on until that person was named.[439] In the context of who was considered suitable for the post, the president said, "We don't want someone who will let that Joint Committee [JCAE] run things; we don't want a military-minded civilian, he must be someone who sees the necessary military setting, how it fits in. . . . [W]e're going to use this [atomic energy] for peace and never use it for war—I've always said this, and you'll see."[440] Lilienthal replied that the AEC was currently in the process of submitting its report regarding the Super. In an attempt to prepare for a future row regarding the decision, he told the president that he wanted to hand him the AEC's position on the program before McMahon's JCAE and other scientists tried to "blitz" the White House for a quick decision.[441] To this the president reportedly grinned wide and replied, "I don't blitz easily."[442]

Denfeld's Demise

As the various organizations and committees were all beginning their deliberations about the future of thermonuclear technology, a bombshell of another kind was developing. Although Representative Vinson's select committee eventually took no real action regarding the B-36 or provided any definitive guidance on military strategy, there were still consequences over what had occurred before members of Congress during October. Within twenty-four hours of the select committee's adjournment, speculation about the future of CNO Denfeld was already hitting the newspapers. The interservice tussle that raised so many questions regarding strategic approach, methodology, and the budget was now coming down to discussions over personal loyalty and allegiance.

Although General Bradley's stinging comments were still fresh in everyone's mind, the JCS chairman downplayed his pointed testimony—especially the attacks directed at Denfeld. Days later Bradley was called out by House Majority Leader John McCormack (D-MA) to withdraw his statement about the Navy's "fancy dans" and his attack on Denfeld, calling them "disrespectful."[443] The press also made much out of Bradley's comments about the admiral's combat record; when pressed by Hanson Baldwin regarding the general's thinly veiled disparagement, he replied, "If I made a mistake I am sorry."[444] Yet given the tone of his delivery, combined with Bradley's often abrasive personality, the general probably felt little remorse. Days later both the CNO and JCS chairman attended a meeting together. When asked if the session was "harmonious," Bradley simply replied, "sure . . . it was just a normal meeting."[445] While he tried to downplay any ill will, the general's harsh words during his testimony were nothing compared to what was awaiting the CNO after the hearings.

Given his earlier meeting with Fleet Admiral Nimitz in New York on 14 October, Secretary of the Navy Matthews felt confident in his plan to remove Denfeld. With all kinds of speculation swirling around as the hearings closed, days later, on 27 October, the secretary wrote the president asking permission to fire Denfeld. Even though Chairman Vinson specifically directed during the hearings that he would not tolerate any reprisals against witnesses, the removal of the CNO, according to Matthews at least, had already been underway.[446] As Nimitz suggested, to justify actions taken against the CNO, the Navy Secretary claimed that his confidence in Denfeld had waned even before the hearings commenced. In his three-page letter requesting the CNO's removal, the Navy Secretary argued that the two men "were [at one time] in complete agreement on all important questions affecting . . . the Department of the Navy. I felt sure that such a harmonious relationship would continue."[447] A few paragraphs later, however, Matthews stated that his relations with Denfeld had "finally become such that I find it increasingly difficult to work with him in the harmonious relationship which should prevail between the occupants of th[ese] two official positions."[448] Avoiding any mention of the CNO's testimony, he asked to "transfer" the admiral to "other important duties."[449] Interestingly, the secretary was not relieving the CNO of his duties as a naval officer, just those of his current position.

Truman's response was both quick and brief. That same day he approved Matthews' recommendation and authorized him to transfer Denfeld.[450] At his regularly scheduled press conference that day, the president announced his decision. Unceremoniously, Denfeld was notified of his removal by Vice Adm. John Price, who heard the news from a reporter. Coming into the CNO's office, Price announced, "Admiral, the President has just relieved you as Chief of Naval Operations." Reportedly, Denfeld's response was a strangely calm "Is that so?"[451] No official from the Navy Secretary's office or the White House attempted to contact the admiral privately. According to accounts, Denfeld was not angry about the news, just frustrated with its handling. The admiral reportedly took the news "like the man he was." Despite the brave face, he was supposedly hurt that Truman failed to at least call him personally.[452]

Over the following days Denfeld received heartfelt sympathy from his supporters in the Navy, with many expressing anger and frustration. Receiving telegrams and letters, subordinates encouraged the admiral to "fight for what you think is right."[453] Baldwin offered his support, writing in a personal letter, "Even though you have been sacrificed the end result may be—in terms of aroused public opinion—the national gain. . . . All the Baldwin's deeply admire your stand and are rooting for you."[454] As for Denfeld himself, he commented, "For thirty-odd years I've been sticking to my guns . . . and if they want to kick me out, I am still sticking to my guns."[455] Conversely, Matthews received letters of protest from Navy supporters, with one decrying the secretary's methods, poor handling of the unification process, and alleged slurring of the prestige of the Navy.[456]

As suggested by Nimitz, and in an attempt to keep in spirit with Vinson's statement regarding the protection of congressional witnesses, Matthews' request pointed to the release of Vice Admiral Bogan's letter and Denfeld's endorsement as the rationale for his action. The Navy Secretary argued that it was in a meeting on 4 October when he felt the CNO's "usefulness . . . had tarnished."[457] That was the same day Bogan's letter became public due to Captain Crommelin's subversion. With this document making headline news, the CNO and the Navy Secretary conferred regarding the fallout. In the CNO's mind the 4 October meeting was cordial, even friendly, as Denfeld claimed Matthews went so far to ask if they could call each other by their first names.[458] As a result, he had no indication then that his usefulness had tarnished. In his statements to the press following the CNO's removal, Matthews denied that Denfeld's ouster was an act of reprisal despite the optics of the move.[459]

This opaque reasoning was again echoed in a radio interview Matthews gave days later on Halloween. When asked about the firing of the CNO, he answered, "it would not be possible for us to function harmoniously as secretary and CNO in view of the developments which transpired and therefore it was necessary to have somebody as CNO who believed in the things I believe in."[460] The secretary vaguely denied that it was Denfeld's testimony alone that got him fired, but rather a culmination of events, comments, and sentiments. With the embarrassment of Worth at the August hearings, Crommelin's two publically insubordinate acts, and the CNO's strong endorsement of the Bogan letter, a number of events had indeed transpired in the weeks before Denfeld's October testimony. Interestingly, on the same day, Truman contacted Nimitz in New York, asking the Fleet Admiral to return to active service and serve as CNO once again. Nimitz turned down the offer, replying that there were plenty of younger, capable officers available to fill the position. When pressed by the president as to whom he would suggest, Nimitz gave Truman two names; one of them was Forrest Sherman. For Nimitz, Sherman was not only younger but also less politically active. Conveniently, Sherman, a naval aviator, had already been summoned by Matthews to return to the United

States from his current posting in Lebanon as commander of U.S. Naval Forces, Mediterranean.[461]

If Matthews' strategy was to get Navy leadership underfoot and in line publically, his choice for the next CNO was a good one. At a press conference the day before he was sworn in, Sherman was guarded with his answers. Regarding the latest decisions on the Navy's budget and recent cutbacks, the incoming CNO stated he was 100 percent behind the new unification law. All of his answers were fairly safe, given the current environment, and mild in content. When queried about the requirement of USS *United States*, the admiral plainly responded, "I'd rather not comment on that problem until I am more familiar with what's gone on in connection with it." Asked what he would have said if he had testified in the recent B-36 hearings, Sherman's retort was as anemic as the rest of his answers: "I would have had very little to say."[462]

Regardless of the events in both August and September, it was hard not make the connection between Denfeld's testimony and his removal. The embarrassment of Worth and Crommelin might have been enough to call into question the CNO's leadership. But some historians speculate that Bogan's letter and Denfeld's ringing endorsement of its sentiments, once made public, were truly the Navy Secretary's final straw, not the CNO's testimony. Had such an emotionally charged document not made it into the public eye, the two men might have continued in their professional relationship despite Worth and Crommelin. Yet Denfeld's testimony and the manner in which he opened his remarks probably gave Matthews the justification he required. In his view Denfeld became just another "revolting admiral."[463] When questioned on the *Meet the Press* television program on 28 January 1950, Matthews repeatedly argued that Denfeld was not fired but offered a reassignment. But members of the press continued questioning the action, insinuating that it was indeed retribution. The Navy Secretary consistently replied that his decision was made before the hearing took place and was not based upon the CNO's testimony.[464] Given Denfeld's account of their 4 October meeting, it is hard to accept Matthews' answers.

In a letter to Representative McCormack, who earlier chastised Bradley for his pointed comments, Denfeld questioned Matthews' motives over his removal. The admiral wrote that he found it strange that only months earlier he had been considered fully qualified for reappointment, while in his dismissal he was told he was removed for "lack of qualification." He also mentioned how he was viewed as a "rebel" against unification by Matthews but was held "in the highest esteem," according to the secretary's own description. While certainly hurt and disappointed with his removal, Denfeld responded that he was "proud of what I have done. I can live with my conscious and myself for the rest of my life and know that I have been honest and told the truth."[465]

Denfeld would go on later to tell his side of the story in a series of three featured articles in *Collier's*, appropriately titled "Why I Was Fired." Appearing in the March and April 1950 issues, the admiral not only described the nature of his removal but also echoed much of the sentiment naval officers expressed in the congressional hearings. Speculating this was the real reason he was fired, Denfeld addressed the furtive nature of the cancellation of CVA 58, the danger in creating an unbalanced military, and putting too much emphasis on strategic bombing. He believed he "was removed as Chief of Naval Operations . . . for criticizing, among other things, this heavy bomber thinking."[466] In his opinion "the Air Force saw the danger that the Navy would encroach on its prime mission. Accordingly our brother fliers and their zealous lay supporters went to work to 'sink' the USS *United States*."[467] Highlighting the importance of naval power, Denfeld argued that using the oceans as maneuver space provided flexibility for military operations ashore and maintaining the nation's ever important sea lines of communication.

The first featured article was published 18 March 1950, with advertisements and cartoons inserted within its pages. In a touch of irony, on page sixty-three, opposite from the admiral's continued commentary, was an advertisement encouraging young men to apply for the USAF. Given that nature of the interservice squabble during the previous years, the ad placement raises suspicions that it was a deliberate act by an unnamed USAF advocate. For those interested in national defense, the irony was probably obvious.

Members of the select committee were "keen[ly] disappointed" at the actions taken by Matthews. Despite what the Navy Secretary wrote in his letter to Truman justifying removing the CNO, they rejected it. To them his removal was in retaliation for his frank and honest opinions regarding the plight of the Navy and his views on the future of American defense.[468] The members viewed this act as a "reprisal" and saw it setting a dangerous precedent. Such retaliation against Denfeld might have implications for future congressional inquiries, as those testifying would no longer feel protected. Regardless of their dismay, the select committee recused itself from any further actions regarding this particular chapter of the interservice rivalry. With the final report of its findings published on 1 March, congressional concerns for the outgoing CNO already seemed a moot point—Denfeld retired the same day.

Days after Truman's announcement regarding the CNO's relief, on 2 November Admiral Sherman was sworn in as Denfeld successor in the Navy Secretary's office. One reporter described the setting as having "an atmosphere of repressed hostility and resentment [hanging] heavily in the room."[469] Present at the swearing in of Sherman, Denfeld was gracefully congratulatory, shaking his successor's hand and wishing him good luck. Sherman made a short speech, but it was far from inspirational. After the ceremony and looking forward to a sixty-day leave to his home in Massachusetts and then to vacation in Miami, Denfeld left the Pentagon.[470] On his way down the outside stairs, his path was lined by hundreds of Navy and Marine Corps personnel applauding and showing their appreciation for his bold stand. He received similar treatment the Saturday before Sherman's swearing in from Naval Academy midshipmen during the annual Navy–Notre Dame football game. Reportedly 3,000 midshipmen, accompanied by some 62,000 spectators, rose to their feet and applauded their appreciation for his singular act of courage.[471]

Since Secretary Matthews' letter to Truman specifically asked that Denfeld be "transferred," the admiral was subsequently offered the position as commander in chief, U.S. Naval Forces Eastern Atlantic and Mediterranean, based in London.[472] While Matthews tried to soften the blow with this assignment, tantamount to a demotion, the admiral sublimely refused. In his written response of 14 December, Denfeld quoted Matthews' words back to him: "I was in your opinion, not loyal to my superiors and did not have 'respect for authority.' . . . [I]t could conceivably happen that other nations having read of this public accusation, would not have the necessary respect for and confidence in me." He went on to request retirement after forty years of service. In his last act of defiance, his letter included a postscript, stating, "In view of the fact that your letter to the president . . . as well as the announcement that I was being offered the London assignment, have been given to the press, I most respectfully urge the text of this letter also be made public."[473] Denfeld wanted a full public accounting of his removal.

Yet it was not only Denfeld whose career suffered. Crommelin was still under house arrest and notified on 24 October that he could submit a written explanation as to why he compromised a classified document.[474] Reportedly, the content of his response might determine if the captain would be court-martialed for his actions and violation of military law. Given his temperament and passion, Crommelin probably looked forward to a court-martial so he could fully martyr himself publicly, much the same way as Billy Mitchell did in 1925. But after Sherman took office, the admiral came to the conclusion that the Navy needed to move on. Prosecuting Crommelin would only make for more publicity regarding the current row and give the captain another venue for argument. Furthermore, given his outstanding war record and service to the nation, court-martialing Crommelin might indeed make him a hero again to the aviation community and the Navy at large. With these thoughts in mind, the new CNO gave the captain a letter of reprimand and exiled him to San Francisco to work on the staff of the commander, Western Sea Frontier.[475] In his reprimand Sherman wrote, "To the degree you deliberately ignored your responsibilities to your naval superiors and disregarded the well understood privacy of confidential and privileged communications, you brought into question your fitness to exercise a position of trust and confidence."[476] The letter effectively terminated Crommelin's chances of ever achieving flag rank. On 22 February 1950 he was ordered by Sherman to refrain from making any public statements criticizing defense officials. Ever the rebel, Crommelin refused and was subsequently furloughed by April, returning to his home in Alabama.[477]

Adding to the list of casualties was OP-23. Earlier, in a surprise raid on 27 September, division files were seized and its offices secured by the Navy IG, as Marine guards stood by and detained the staff in their Pentagon offices.[478] Even before the October hearings, OP-23 was already a victim. Matthews surmised that the division was guilty of leaking information to the press regarding the proposal to delay the hearings. As a result he called for an immediate IG investigation. After searching the files and questioning the staff for two days, no incriminating evidence was found warranting further punitive action.[479]

Claiming that its "principal functions had been completed," one of Sherman's first acts as CNO was disbanding OP-23, dispersing its staff of twelve officers and seventeen men to other assignments.[480]

Matthews took further retaliatory action by personally striking Captain Burke's name from the promotion list for admiral. This was an illegal act in itself, as the secretary was required to forward the promotion list to the president without edit.[481] Given Burke's impressive war record and combat decorations, the former OP-23 head was a sure bet for flag-grade rank in a peacetime navy. When Burke received news of Matthews' actions, he requested a thirty-day leave and left Washington. Depressed and thinking his career was over, the captain prepared himself for retirement despite his impressive combat record, having been awarded the Navy Cross, Silver Star, and a host of other decorations. But when the modified list was forwarded to the White House for approval, Truman's naval aide caught wind of Burke's removal and informed the president of the illegality of the situation. The press also got wind of it, soon after which both Matthews and Defense Secretary Johnson were on their way to the White House to answer for Burke's removal.[482] Chastened, the civilian secretaries placed the captain's name back on the list.

While he was exiled to a job clearly out of the public eye for a time, Burke's career continued.[483] Once the Korean War broke out, Matthews' and Johnson's frugal policies became political liabilities, and they were eventually removed from office. After the North Korean attack in June 1950, the nation found the Army unprepared for conventional, sustained ground combat. In this newest conflict, tactical airpower played a significant role, as atomic weapons took a back seat. Johnson never won the White House and returned to practicing law, with Matthews resigning in 1951 and taking an ambassadorship to Ireland. But after the crisis passed, Burke continued his career unabated. In an ironic twist he became CNO six years later, in August 1955, jumping over a number of other senior officers for the position.

After all the tumult regarding the latest Air Force–Navy fight, those in the naval service were sullen, given strategic airpower's apparent second victory. With the cuts the Navy was forced to endure under Johnson, *Washington Times* columnists surmised, "Wartime control of the Mediterranean has probably now been cast away. . . . The Security of the United States and safety of the free world are being impaired daily; yet smart talk of the economy is all the explanation we get."[484] Shortly after the hearings Johnson made an official visit to Europe. Stopping in London, the defense secretary attended a cocktail party held in his honor. During the event, he claimed the Vinson Committee trouble was "all settled" and went on to argue, "We're going ahead and we're going to build up the Air Force. . . . I'm a great friend of the Air Force."[485] Again, given the dark humor that often accompanies military service, a clever Navy wordsmith drafted an ironic jeremiad titled "A New Prayer for the Navy in 1949 A. D. (After Denfeld)." Of similar cadence to the Roman Catholic "Hail Mary," it reads,

> Our Father, who art in Washington
> Truman be thy name
> Thy Navy's done . . . the Air Force won
> On the Atlantic as on the Pacific
> Give us this day our appropriations
> And forgive us our accusations
> As we forgive our accusers
> And lead us not into temptation but
> Deliver us from Matthews and Johnson
> For thine is the power, O' B-36,
> The Air Force forever and ever,
> Airmen.[486]

McMahon's Monologue

With the GAC and AEC reports forwarded to the president, the overall sentiment was decidedly against building the Super. As the technical hurdles were an obstacle, calling into question even the feasibility of a thermonuclear weapon, most of the men involved in the current discussions opposed development largely from a humanitarian perspective. For a majority of the GAC and AEC membership, creating the Super would take mankind down a wrong path and might eventually lead to genocide or possibly even the extermination of the human race. For them, hydrogen bombs did not provide any more security than fission weapons, and members questioned if the technology had any real military (or civilian) value. But for men like Senator McMahon and Commissioner Strauss, weapons such as the Super were required to counter an immoral and irrepressible enemy like the Soviet Union. For these men and the many of their ilk, this technological endeavor was part of a larger life-and-death struggle between good and evil.

Up until November 1949, any government discussion of the Super or thermonuclear technology was either classified or kept in a largely academic setting, removed from the public spotlight. Yet the idea of developing a thermonuclear bomb soon spilled into the public realm. With television broadcasting becoming a standard form of communication in the United States, some politicians were quick to leverage the new medium. On 1 November, the day after the GAC meeting concluded, in a broadcast on the DuMont television network in New York, JCAE member Sen. Edwin Johnson (D-CO) argued there was too little security and secrecy regarding the American atomic enterprise.[487] Believing the release of the Smyth Report in 1945 was a mistake, the senator ironically and unintentionally undercut his own argument, blurting out that American scientists were already working on a weapon that was "6-times the effectiveness of the bomb we dropped on Nagasaki." He went on to say that they want to make a device that was "1000 times the effect of the Nagasaki weapon."[488] While arguing about lax security in the AEC, Senator Johnson had just committed his own severe breach in public. The quip went largely unnoticed at the time but was reported in the *Washington Post* on 18 November.[489] As a result of that article, the proverbial cat was out of the bag as other newspapers picked up the story. Interestingly, the headline of the *Washington Post* the day before had announced "One A-Bomb Could Cripple Washington; AEC Advises Dispersal of US Govt," with an accompanying aerial photo of potential blast radii on the front page.[490]

While Johnson's statement was somewhat inaccurate regarding the current state of the technology, the news indeed brought part of the debate into public view. Furious over the security breach, Truman fired off an angry letter to the senator.

Furthermore, the president's ire might also be tied to his desire to not look panicked as a result of Joe-1. Apart from the senator's televised gaffe, the *Washington Post* article included a statement from Johnson that the nation was already looking for Anglo-Canadian assistance in developing the Super.[491] While the claim of Canadian assistance was completely false, Lilienthal, too, was incensed, surmising that Johnson was trying to deflect some of his guilt from his earlier broadcast error.[492]

Despite their minority status, proponents of the Super were not done advocating for the advancement in technology and weaponry. Days after Lilienthal submitted the various reports to the president, McMahon arrived at LASL for a briefing on thermonuclear technology. Given presentations from various scientists, he came away with an even stronger feeling regarding the need for the Super. During the session, Teller briefed the senator and was not only effusive about the promise of the technology but also firmly committed to the idea of the Super despite his scientific peers' moral and humanitarian objections.[493] On 21 November, the day after his visit to LASL and the date of Lilienthal's letter of resignation, McMahon drafted a seven-page letter to Truman rationalizing the need for the Super.

Now armed with the information from LASL and Teller, McMahon latest tome was very specific, presenting quite skillfully why the United States needed the Super. The recent Soviet success was indeed a national crisis, a danger that he believed "cannot . . . be exaggerated." Having visited various AEC sites and getting briefings on current nuclear progress, McMahon was enthusiastic about overcoming the technical hurdles. In his opening argument the senator explained the economy and efficiency of fusion-based weapons compared to that of fission-based devices. He surmised that "23 current-type fission bombs would be needed to duplicate the effect of one super which [might] destroy 150 square miles; about 143 fission bombs would be needed to equal the effect of one super that destroyed 1,000 square miles." Understanding Truman's fiscal concerns and frugal nature, McMahon also proffered that the development of the Super might only cost $200–$300 million, less than one-sixth of what the United States spent on the wartime Manhattan Project. He argued that only a small percentage was spent on atomic weapons currently, and that for FY 1950 it was less than 1 percent (one-fortieth of total military spending) of the national budget. Admitting his lack of understanding of military strategy, the senator claimed that the use of fusion bombs might be effective against an enemy's large industrial centers, therefore freeing up the stockpile of fission weapons for use against military targets and smaller industrial areas. For McMahon, the shock of such a combination of fusion and fission weapons would leave "the opponent . . . unable to retaliate in force."[494]

Interestingly, the JCAE chair argued that precision bombing would not be as important as it had been in previous conflicts. Referencing conventional-bombing practices and the use of fission weapons, McMahon stated that an aircrew might even miss the target by "ten miles or more and still serve the purpose of its intended [mission]."[495] With megatons worth of explosive firepower, bomb placement on or near a target would now be less important. Given what we now know about SAC's poor capabilities and targeting performance at that time, this point was indeed valid.[496] Despite early estimates that a Super might be so big that it would have to be delivered by "ox cart," McMahon was under the impression that a fully developed thermonuclear weapon's weight and size would be less than the maximum payload of a B-36. He believed the Super might be easier to deliver and less taxing on the nation's strategic bombers.[497] Instead of using large numbers of aircraft carrying conventional and smaller fission-based bombs, the nation might require fewer aircraft or gain efficiencies in airframe management.

Regarding the morality of the weapon, McMahon also had a response. He proposed that a leaflet campaign to warn populations of an impending raid might preclude needless civilian deaths. Furthermore, if the warning was heeded, fleeing refugees might make for a logistical and transportation problem on enemy road networks. Perhaps the senator's strongest answer to the moral dilemma was his practical view of bombing itself: "There is no moral dividing line that I can see between a big explosion which causes heavy damage and many smaller explosions causing equal or still greater damage."[498] He compared the firebombing of Tokyo in March 1945 to the August Hiroshima attack. What was the difference between either the source of ignition or the levels of devastation between the two? More were killed initially by the conventional firebombing raid than by the initial blast effect of Little Boy.[499] For the victims, he argued, the type of bomb made no real difference. This line of reasoning was also used by atomic-weapon proponents in the Interim Committee of 1945, which advised Truman regarding Little Boy and Fat Man. In the senator's opinion, "the notion that our possession of this weapon would harm our moral position makes no sense."[500]

In the later pages of his letter, the senator reminded the president that his first duty "consists in doing what is necessary to win." Harkening to the potential danger of Soviet advancements, he noted that not only had the Soviets captured German scientists to assist them in their nuclear endeavors but they also had their own talent, such as Peter Kapitza and his expertise with liquid deuterium, as physicists Alvarez and Lawrence had warned in October.[501] McMahon hinted that development of the Super would be a good bargaining chip to encourage some kind of mutual agreement between the United States and USSR. This was not the first time for such a suggestion. In June 1946 a proposal was drafted by American financier and statesman Bernard Baruch by which atomic materials and knowledge would be handled by an international organization. With this international control of fissionable materials and their associated technology, all nations would then agree to forgo future weapons development. Given the American monopoly at the time, the Soviet Union rejected what was referred to as the "Baruch Plan" unless the United States dismantled its weapons programs first. Thereafter, this peaceful gesture gave way to Cold War concerns. Now if the American Super effort was made public, it could serve as a tipping point leading to international controls on such weapons, despite the earlier dismissal of the Baruch Plan. In the last sentence of his discourse, the senator declared, "Thus the horror and revulsion which the super inspires in moral beings might be harnessed and made to generate a world-wide pressure of public opinion upon the Kremlin to accept a sane and worthwhile control plan."[502]

In addition to McMahon's lengthy epistle, Commissioner Strauss penned a letter to Truman also arguing for Super development. Written days later, on 25 November, Strauss' message was more concise but still numbered four pages. He also thought the Super should be given the highest priority, although only after its requirement as a weapon was validated by DoD and the issue considered by DoS regarding international implications. Strauss laid out a comprehensive argument, surmising that the idea of a Super had a "50-50 chance" and that such technology was within Russian technical competence. Like others he feared that the Soviet Union was already ahead of the United States in developing the weapon. Strauss suggested that a thermonuclear bomb provided a certain amount of efficiency in affecting an army occupying a large area.[503]

The commissioner claimed in his conclusions that the real threat was not so much the weapon itself as it was human behavior. Along this line of reasoning, Strauss wrote, "Its [the Super's] unilateral renunciation by the United States could very easily result in its unilateral [*sic*] possession by the Soviet government. I am unable to see any satisfaction in that prospect."[504] For him, it was reasonable to expect the Soviets to develop such a weapon, so it only made sense that the United States develop a similar capability. As Strauss saw it, the moral answer was the defense of the United States.[505] While certainly willing to let other elements of the federal government review both the need and implications of the Super, Strauss clearly rejected the opinions forwarded by his fellow commissioners and by the GAC scientists regarding the weapon's inherent moral implications.

Hoping to get ahead of the agencies denouncing the Super, DoS staffer R. Gordon Arneson claimed that Strauss was "running around town, running around the country drumming up support for this thing [the Super]. . . . It was very strange. He was all for it. He was getting all the support he could find."[506] In this effort the commissioner arranged for an audience with Defense Secretary Johnson. Using some of the same rhetoric from his letter to Truman, Strauss convinced the secretary of the Super's requirement.[507] Calling in those DoD members who attended the earlier GAC meeting, Johnson explained to his subordinates that he had every reason to believe the Soviets were working on an "H-bomb" and emphasized the necessity for an American effort. While at least one officer present dissented, he was quickly admonished with the response, "It's a fundamental law of defense that you always have to use the most powerful weapons you can produce." With this, Johnson ordered MLC chair Robert LeBaron to prepare a report regarding the military utility of the Super and the requirement for an "all out, crash H-bomb program."[508]

On 19 November, after receiving Strauss' letter and meeting with Senator McMahon, Truman established a working group to evaluate the matter. The president directed a three-member review panel to include Secretary of State Acheson, outgoing AEC chair Lilienthal, and Secretary of Defense

Johnson.[509] Called the "Z Committee," the president looked for perspectives on the international implications of developing the weapon and if a valid military requirement existed. With this, Truman was giving his decision some thought and looked for further insight from other government agencies, not just the AEC. While these three men were called upon to deliver a response, much of the work was done by a subcommittee that included the likes of NSC executive secretary Souers, Paul Nitze of the DoS, and MLC chair LeBaron for DoD.[510] This arrangement probably facilitated the process, as Lilienthal and Johnson's relationship was already an acrimonious one. The two had met earlier in the year to discuss atomic production and the stockpile. While already possessing opposing personalities, during that first meeting Lilienthal came away with the distinct impression that Johnson, "an able man . . . feeling his oats, and . . . riding high," looked to the AEC as merely "munition makers" who only filled orders established by the military.[511]

What Lilienthal, Acheson, and Truman did not know was, before the president even established the Z Committee, Secretary Johnson already ordered LeBaron to prepare the DoD position after the meeting with Strauss. In drafting the paper the military determined that "possession of a thermonuclear weapon by the USSR without such possession by the United States would be intolerable."[512] This served as the basis for the military's argument. For DoD, a Soviet monopoly of thermonuclear capability would imperil a morally superior United States. Despite Lilienthal's earlier thought, wondering "what happened to deterrence (regarding fission based weapons)," for the JCS, who also weighed in, possession of a thermonuclear weapon added to the U.S. deterrent effect despite the Super's perceived failures by the AEC chair. On 10 November, the day after Lilienthal presented the AEC and GAC positions to Truman, the JCS directed the Joint Strategic Survey Committee to study the issue. As that panel began its deliberations, the MLC forwarded its already drafted position regarding the Super. Finding this report acceptable, and in lieu of generating another similar one, the committee forwarded the MLC results to the JCS on 17 November.[513] In both tone and temperament, the MLC paper echoed the arguments of the Super's proponents. Like McMahon's reasoning, the MLC saw the value of the weapon's efficiency in attacking the few Soviet cities housing major population and manufacturing centers while freeing up both fission and conventional bombs for smaller targets. What was useful about the report was the introduction of metrics to determine this utility. Serving as the basis for the formal JCS submission to Secretary Johnson on 23 November, it provided context to the destructive potential of the Super and proffered that such a weapon would have an effective radius of some sixty-five miles.[514] While the numbers were slightly different than what McMahon proposed in his latest letter, the scale and scope were indeed similar. The MLC's positions were adopted as the official submission by Johnson and DoD to the Z Committee.

While this committee was just getting organized and its representatives preparing their respective positions, the GAC met again at the beginning of December. Underscoring their earlier position, this meeting produced no change from the October session.[515] In fact it only solidified the earlier position, as additional views from three other prominent scientists also rejected thermonuclear weapons. GAC member Rowe submitted, "A democracy, of the type in which I firmly believe, cannot in my opinion, be strengthened by possession of a super-bomb."[516] He was not alone in this, as Fermi and Buckley also submitted similar written statements. Concurrently, and reflective of the national sentiment, a recent Gallup poll found that 45 percent of Americans thought that Russian possession of the atomic bomb made another war more likely, with only 28 percent believing the opposite.[517]

With the passing of the winter solstice and the end of autumn, the three formal members of the Z Committee met for the first time on 22 December. Chaired by Acheson in his office, he stated that the session was not to be a decision meeting but an opportunity to exchange ideas and to "think together."[518] Yet two of the agencies already came prepared to deliver their respective positions despite Acheson's diplomatic tone. Predictably, with the MLC-drafted report in hand, Johnson gave the DoD view in favor of the weapon. Conversely, with fresh reinforcement from the latest GAC meeting, Lilienthal of the AEC came prepared to argue against the Super. But Acheson had yet to articulate a strong position for either side. The lunchtime meeting, lasting some two hours, largely reflected the existing strained relationship between Lilienthal and Johnson and turned into a philosophical discourse.[519] While Lilienthal was appreciative of Acheson's tactful manner and attempted mediation, the AEC chair had no affinity for his DoD counterpart. Writing in his diary after the meeting, Lilienthal referred to Johnson in disparaging terms, including "strong man," "man of heroic mould [*sic*]," and "big boy," while using an equally unflattering term for General Bradley, mentioning him as the "schoolmasterish-looking guy."[520] With the attitude reflected in such language, it is hardly surprising that the meeting yielded little progress.

The argument between them was not necessarily based upon their respective positions on the Super, but addressed if the issue at hand was solely a military question or one linked to larger implications of the international community and potential weapons control. For Johnson, the issue was not related to U.S. foreign relations or the possibility of enacting international controls at all but was strictly based upon defensive implications and maintaining a continued deterrent effect. Conversely, Lilienthal looked more from a moral standpoint for the "course of mankind" and the opportunity to prevent an international arms race.[521]

Acheson eventually sided with Lilienthal, arguing that a study of the broader implications was in order. He also questioned the value of the speculative thermonuclear effort, as it might only result in a technological dead end. As secretary of state he saw a diplomatic opportunity emerging that might be an opening for revisiting international controls. Johnson seemed open to this position if, and only if, the Soviets agreed to some form of weapons control.[522] But for him, JCS chairman Bradley, and MLC chair LeBaron, the Super question was "a technical matter with no necessary relevance to the broader [policy] questions."[523] For them, this was a simple matter of national defense.

The meeting broke up with no conclusions, thoughts about how to proceed further, or potential solutions. Despite Johnson's acerbic tone and combative nature, Lilienthal was optimistic. He saw that the requirement for continued discourse as a positive with no definitive decisions made.[524] But Acheson was less optimistic and actually disappointed with the outcome by describing the session as "a head on confrontation between Louis Johnson and David Lilienthal . . . that produced nothing new or helpful to the president."[525] After this meeting, Acheson began to see the requirement of building the Super if only to check Soviet expansion and maintain the global balance of power. The three men would not meet again on the issue except for a brief discussion in the old Army-Navy building the morning before briefing the president on 31 January 1950. Any further exchange of ideas, thoughts, or studies on the Super would all take the form of correspondence between departments or staffers, with no real discourse between the Z Committee members themselves. Despite their differing views, it would all come to a head on the last day in January.

Autumn Draws to a Close

With the winter solstice, the tumultuous autumn of 1949 came to an end. From late summer to early winter, in the span of one season, the balance of global military power shifted, the geopolitical landscape seismically altered, the nature of American military power and its overall strategy questioned, and a moral dilemma regarding nuclear applications in the offing. While these were the result of long-running efforts or were seen as future inevitabilities, they all came to a head in a short period of time. As the trees lost their fall foliage and colder air began to replace the pleasant sweater weather of autumn, the season ahead looked bleak. Many strategists began asking questions about the future of American national security policy. The events of the autumn of 1949 posed many questions that now required answers.

No longer possessing an atomic monopoly, facing a Communist-controlled China, the military at an impasse over grand strategy, and learning about the potential of thermonuclear weapons, many officials felt that a wholesale change in national security policy was in order. Given the new international environment, the United States required a fresh outlook and a break from the military traditions the nation had observed since its inception. Americans were forced to face an emerging reality. While certainly a global military and economic power, the United States could no longer maintain a small, unprepared military requiring months and years to prepare and mobilize for war, protected by two giant moats on either coast. In the very near future the Soviets would have intercontinental bombers possibly capable of carrying megatons worth of destruction only a few hours away from American airspace and cities. Like no time before, the continental United States was now vulnerable to a significant enemy attack.

In addition to these varied events, another situation developed quietly in the DoS at Foggy Bottom. Kennan's erudite and measured approaches at the

PPS were well received, with his ideas holding great sway with his bosses, both Marshall and his successor, Acheson. Yet during this same autumn period, Kennan began to withdraw from the staff and increasingly spent his time holed up alone writing in a small office he kept at the Library of Congress.[526] Nitze, who was only recently brought in as deputy for the PPS, noticed this change in his boss's demeanor. Kennan became chagrined with the unfolding events and looked for more thoughtful solutions. Hoping to avoid an arms race, he looked for more pragmatic solutions. Conversely, Nitze became steadily involved with the Pentagon and military-related issues, increasingly drawn to a more martial way of thinking.[527] Thus, during the autumn of 1949, the dynamics of the PPS began to shift, with Nitze becoming more and more influential both within the office and, more importantly, with Acheson. By November he was the influencing element within the PPS. While already looking for a break after two very long years as PPS head, in December Kennan decided that a leave of absence was required.[528]

Before he was announced as Kennan's successor effective 1 January 1950, Nitze was already being briefed by Teller regarding the possibility of the Super. The new PPS lead began thinking that not only would the nation need such a capability if the Russians had it but also, in order to contain the Soviets, the nation would need more than just nuclear weapons. For Nitze, this problem required something more than just the Super, something that provided more flexibility, promised additional options, and did not necessarily default to atomic weapons alone. His thinking would set the United States on a new national security path for decades.

With the passing season, a new reality emerged. The United States would embark on something wholly different in the American experience, laying the framework for a significantly larger military force, including both conventional and nuclear weapons, as part of a permanent overseas presence. This new path for national security would be outlined by Nitze soon after his ascension as PPS head. While events would still unfold in the upcoming winter of 1949–50, the stage was already set for the introduction of wholesale changes. With coming events like the Korean War to spur the implementation of these changes, the seeds for NSC 68 and its wide-ranging effects had already germinated.

—3—
WINTER

Months had passed since the WSEG started assessing the latest U.S. war plan, Offtackle. Although its study began in September 1949, the plan was not officially approved by the Joint Staff until 8 December. Despite its pending approval, Offtackle served as the base scenario for the group's evaluation. Up until this effort, the only analysis of the atomic offensive was the inconclusive Harmon Report published the previous May. That effort studied the Trojan war plan, and the report's lukewarm results were a disappointment to strategic bombing advocates. Despite the findings, the report helped stimulate the AEC's production of atomic munitions and fissionable material. Many hoped the more in-depth WSEG analysis would help validate the concepts of atomic-bombing strategy.

In the interim, during the Super discussions in November, Truman asked to see the published Harmon Report. Perhaps not wishing to prejudice the chief executive's opinion with its tepid results, Defense Secretary Johnson suggested that the president wait until the more thorough WSEG study was completed.[1] Accepting the advice, Truman remained a tabula rasa regarding the war plans. Many thought the report would help determine whether the B-36 or the USS *United States* was the best foundation for American military strategy.

WSEG Report No. 1

The finished report, comprising nine chapters and eleven enclosures, was simply titled "Evaluation of Effectiveness of Strategic Air Operations." With the formal submission dated 8 February 1950, preliminary briefs were conducted in mid-January.[2] While the JCS received its brief from the WSEG director, Lieutenant General Hull, on 19 January, Truman received his presentation days later, on the twenty-third, with Johnson, Secretary of State Acheson, Air Force Secretary Symington, and various other cabinet members present.[3] Knowing full well the reception of the earlier briefing, JCS chairman General Bradley tried to manage presidential expectations. Before Hull even began speaking, Bradley cautioned Truman that the JCS had not necessarily endorsed the findings and considered it a useful planning tool.[4]

The report specifically dealt with SAC's ability to carry out the planned aerial offensive while considering estimated Soviet defensive capabilities, USAF logistics limitations, bombing accuracy, and both aircraft and aircrew performance. With this, the WSEG attempted to determine the feasibility of strategic bombing vis-à-vis Offtackle and did not compare naval strike capabilities to that of the USAF. Thus, the report was not a comparative analysis of the two schools of thought. Furthermore, it did not address the bombing campaign's effect on Soviet war-making capabilities or on its will to wage war. The group deferred to the previously published Harmon Report for those larger strategic answers.[5] Because of these parameters, the WSEG report served only to evaluate USAF claims and capabilities. Superseding Trojan, the Offtackle scenario envisioned a global conflict, with a Soviet offensive thrusting into Western Europe accompanied by a secondary effort toward the Middle East's oil reserves. To counter this, Offtackle was a four-phase plan targeting twenty-six Soviet war-making industries with some 220 atomic bombs (with seventy-two planned reattacks) on 104 urban centers.[6] Given the events of the past autumn, the group pragmatically included the recent geopolitical developments of a "Red" China under Mao and an atomic-equipped Soviet Union.[7] While exaggerating Soviet capabilities, the WSEG staff assumed both sides would use atomic ordnance in support of military objectives. In the American aerial offensive, these would not only be used to destroy Soviet war-making capability and infrastructure but also be used in what was referred to as the "retardation mission" aimed directly against Russian ground capabilities.[8] While not directly targeting Soviet ground formations, the retardation mission looked to destroy or impair the Red Army's operational-level capabilities. The plan's ultimate goal was to reduce Soviet power and influence outside its borders, wrestle domestic political control from the Communist Party, and destroy the Russian ability to conduct offensive operations.[9]

Using the planned USAF force structure of 1 May 1950, the evaluation assumed an offensive using 570 medium bombers (B-29s and B-50s) combined with 54 of SAC's new B-36 heavy bombers.[10] The atomic-delivery portion of the war plan required 300 bombers and a total of 6,000 sorties in the first phase of the operation, with 17,610 tons of high-explosive bombs and 292 atomic weapons.[11] The older B-29s and B-50s would strike 86 percent of the targets in the initial phase, with the new B-36s attacking the remaining 14 percent.[12] In order to maximize the psychological effect of the aerial campaign, most of the planned atomic strikes were scheduled within the first thirty days of a conflict.[13] The B-29s and B-50s would operate from bases in the United Kingdom and, in a two-pronged approach, penetrate Soviet airspace through the Baltic states and the Black Sea. Each atomic-equipped medium bomber would be accompanied by two to four additional aircraft.[14] Concurrently, the B-36 fleet would operate from airfields in Alaska, North Dakota, and Canada.[15] Its targets were far beyond the range of the B-29 and B-50 medium bombers. Given the B-36's extended-range capabilities, its planned targets were located deep in the interior of the Soviet Union. Once they dropped their ordnance over the Soviet Union, they were to fly on to planned bases in Asia and the Middle East. Carrier assets were included in the offensive, though only as a secondary effort supporting the USAF offensive.[16]

The WSEG estimated that 70–85 percent of the USAF's atomic-armed aircraft would succeed in their mission. But the expected losses were placed at 30 percent for night operations and 50 percent during the day.[17] One of the loss-scenario evaluations reviewed a four-day massed operation with 1,221 sorties flown delivering 153 bombs. Staffers estimated that, with a competent Soviet integrated air defense, this would cost 222 aircraft, with an additional 27 damaged beyond repair. In this scenario the overall loss rate was 55 percent.[18] When adjusted for a less competent defense and a dispersed attack, the loss rate was estimated at 41 percent.[19] Additionally, the WSEG estimated that losses for unescorted reconnaissance missions were unsustainable.[20] Such exceedingly high loss rates surpassed the USAAF's deadly experiences during the darkest days of World War II. This high attrition of unescorted bombers was a central argument of naval aviation advocates during the October hearings. Furthermore, sustaining a bomber offensive in both crews and aircraft over an extended period under such conditions would have been difficult if not impossible.[21] Although the published plan was designed to provide a "Sunday punch" to the Soviet war machine in the opening days of a conflict, the estimated losses based upon the WSEG study precluded bomber operations in subsequent phases of Offtackle.

Interestingly, the study concluded that the loss rates of the B-29 and B-50 medium bombers were similar to those of the B-36 heavies.[22] According to the evaluation, the B-36's size made it easier to hit while its increased altitude and speed provided no real advantage over the current fleet—especially given estimated Soviet defenses. WESG personnel came to the conclusion that whatever security from ground-based fire the B-36 achieved in altitude it lost by presenting a larger target.[23] Knowing full well that this would alienate the USAF and possibly deter the service from supporting further group efforts, evaluators asked SAC to help develop their analysis. WSEG members met with LeMay at his headquarters at Offutt Air Force Base, Nebraska, hoping not only to gain further insight and help with their analysis but also to deliberately tip their hand about the likely results. The unveiling of unexpected bad news at such a high level would cause ill will and resentment among various parties. Group members thought that if they could get SAC to assist in the analysis, it might provide the USAF an opportunity to prepare a response and prevent the service chief and secretary from being blindsided.[24] Acquiescing to the WSEG request, SAC allowed evaluators to fly in the B-36 to gain an appreciation of the aircraft, its roles, and its mission profiles. While these representatives did get a firsthand appreciation of the plane, it might not have been what the USAF anticipated. According to one WSEG evaluator during his first flight,

> [A] report came in that the radar dish wasn't rotating and a little later, one of the six engines was acting up. . . . [T]he radar dish was frozen, so we couldn't make the simulated bombing run. As for the ailing

> engine, the controls were new and complicated, so the crew decided to shut down the engine. . . . I learned that each engine had a control device with four vacuum tubes; if any one of the tubes broke down or burned out, the engine was out of commission. . . . [W]hen we touched down, . . . we fishtailed erratically down the runway instead of a smooth stop. We then learned that a second engine had failed just before we landed. . . . I began to feel the B-36 was just too full of new gadgets to be a dependable piece of military equipment. . . . [I]t was not the most convincing demonstration.[25]

While the B-36 did have improved performance over the older bombers when operating at full capacity, the WSEG determined that the cost and complexity of the new aircraft could hardly be justified.[26] The findings did not provide the black-and-white answer some hoped and instead required interpretation and contextual understanding. The value of a specific point was sometimes in the eyes of the beholder. With many aware of the B-36's existing issues, some felt the report shed a favorable light on the controversial aircraft. As Hull finished his brief to Truman, Johnson reportedly stated, "There, I told you they'd say the B-36 is a good plane." But the president, according to one account, looked "disgusted and snapped, No dammit they said just the opposite!"[27]

The WESG study also identified Offtackle's infeasibility given current military staffing and structure. Evaluators identified a number of shortfalls in equipment, logistics, and intelligence. They also found significant problems with the number of aircraft and crews available, suitable forward bases, fuel accessibility, supporting airlift, and bomber maintenance and repair capabilities.[28] Strategic reserves of fuel were also inadequate and reportedly "seriously out of balance."[29] In addition, the number of medium bombers was too small given missions and expected attrition rates. When looking at the 6,000 sorties the plan called for in the first three months, the number was three times larger than SAC's current capabilities.[30] Furthermore, the conventional, high-explosive campaign was twice the size of the atomic requirement and accounted for two-thirds of the logistics demands. The lack of current intelligence on the proposed targets and the unknown strength of Soviet integrated air defenses was also a problem.[31] The report was emphatic on this point: "Grave deficiencies exist on enemy capability. These deficiencies must be corrected in order to improve the basis for future planning and evaluation."[32] Of the 123 targets SAC planned to strike in the opening phases of the campaign, it had prestrike reconnaissance on only 60 sites.[33] In a SAC conference held months later, attendees learned that the Offtackle plan required four reconnaissance wings to support the plan, but the USAF currently only had one operational.[34]

Additionally, while radar and antiaircraft artillery were key components of an integrated air defense, what the Americans did not know at the time was the capabilities of a new Soviet jet interceptor. The issue of B-36 interception and survivability from aerial attack was highlighted by naval aviation advocates during the October hearings. They argued that their own fighters could readily intercept the lumbering bomber at 40,000 feet. What the Soviet capabilities at interception where at this time could only be speculated. But a little over a year later, American B-29 aircrews over Korea would learn about the new MiG-15 and its stunning performance and effectiveness at point interception. In fact, so effective were the MiG-15s during the Korean War that B-29s sent to bomb targets in North Korea were eventually relegated to nighttime raids and required fighter escort.[35] Had the WSEG known about the MiG-15s effectiveness at the time of its analysis, the survival rates articulated in the study may have been much lower.[36]

Once the Korean War began, the MiG-15's capabilities had serious implications for the larger SAC mission, with LeMay confessing, "The fact that you have had a B-29 formation practically shot out of the air has serious implications, not only for the United States, but among our Allies and enemies as well."[37] Soon after the North Korean invasion of June 1950, WSEG director Hull suggested a group of B-36s fly from U.S. bases to strike targets in Korea. With such missions, the group could gather actual combat data on the performance and vulnerability of the bomber during nonstop intercontinental missions.[38] Someone, it is unclear who, rejected the suggestion. Given the B-29's later experience over Korea, the USAF claims of B-36 survivability during the October testimonies was overly optimistic.

While some of the report validated a number of the Navy's earlier contentions about strategic bombers and bombing, it did not necessarily invalidate the concept as an application. The WSEG determined that significant damage to Soviet infrastructure would occur, with many target sets destroyed or at least significantly damaged, precluding further use. But the identified vulnerability of Air Force bombers echoed the Navy's earlier argument. Furthermore, with the deficiencies in medium-bomber numbers and the inability to sustain the planned sortie rate, the USAF was woefully ill equipped. This deficiency in airframes might have been mitigated through the use of naval aviation. Having sea-based air platforms certainly provided dynamic tasking and operational flexibility for U.S. forces. A sea-based strike capability was a unique Navy feature unmatched by the Air Force.

With the WSEG findings, the feasibility of the Offtackle plan as a whole was in question. One of the findings suggested a reexamination of the entire targeting process.[39] This was something Lilienthal had been calling for ever since the military increased its atomic-bomb requirements the previous spring. Matching AEC bomb production to approved target lists would help in its production planning of fissionable materials. But the commission also required the military to do its homework regarding bomb requirements. Instead of using all the bombs in the atomic inventory just because they were there, the USAF had to determine which targets were worthy of atomic ordnance.

The report also shed some light on the interservice rivalry. While the bombers appeared to be more vulnerable than the USAF claimed, much interpretation of the findings was still required. While the Navy might have been justified in its arguments regarding execution, the planned bombing campaign could be an effective military application. Even though many hoped the WSEG would provide the definitive answer to the questions raised in October, the best it provided was potential effects, identification of deficiencies, and data points for further analysis.

"Sands Were Running Out of the Glass"

At the beginning of 1950, the question about the Super was still up for discussion. With the GAC rejecting the idea of its development and the Z Committee's 22 December meeting amounting to little more than a philosophical argument between Secretary Johnson and Chairman Lilienthal, much debate was still required. The congressional Joint Committee on Atomic Energy (JCAE) advocacy for development of the technology contrasted with the split vote within the AEC. As a result there was no consensus in the federal government. While the debate continued behind closed doors, word about the thermonuclear weapon got out. In a *Washington Post* editorial by Joseph and Stewart Alsop published on 2 January 1950, the public learned of the Super discussions among the various committees, panels, and groups in government. The Republican-leaning Alsops were remarkably accurate in their account, given the classified nature of the debate. They correctly wrote that Lilienthal had "no taste for being a merchant of death" and based his arguments upon a humanitarian consideration, much like the GAC had in their October meeting. The Alsop brothers described the debate in ominous fashion, writing, "Thus dustily and obscurely, the issues of life and death are settled nowadays: [in] dingy committee rooms are the scenes of debate; harassed officials are the disputants; all the proceedings are highly classified; yet the whole future hangs, perhaps, upon the outcome. . . . Yet this must be done since deeper issues are involved, which have been far too long concealed from the country."[40] The next day JCAE chairman Senator McMahon sent a copy of the article to the president, warning him, "we might well expect an attack from certain sources on the grounds of '[an] unnecessary delay.'"[41] For McMahon, the longer the discussion took, the greater the danger. Truman's response avoided the timing issue: "I don't know where the 'Sop Sisters' got their information but evidently somebody thinks it's proper to talk to such lying scoundrels. I don't."[42]

Like McMahon, Commissioner Strauss was concerned over the lack of a quick decision. Three months had passed since the Super question came to the fore and almost six since Joe-1. Because developing the new weapon could take as long as two years, many believed the United States was wasting time debating the issue while the Soviets might already be working on a fusion weapon.[43] Those supportive of the Super thought that time was of the essence. With the end of the holiday season, Congress reconvened on 3 January, and the JCAE met in closed session on 9 January, still awaiting the DoD position on the Super. Secretary Johnson, who remained supportive of the weapon, had Military Liaison Committee (MLC) chairman LeBaron and JCS chairman Bradley verbally provide Strauss with the substance of the forthcoming JCS statement.[44] Yet even before the report was briefed, the tide was already turning. During a closed session, one member of the JCAE stated what was becoming largely evident to many aware of the discussion: "it is inconceivable that this country would get itself into a position where the Soviet Union might have [the thermonuclear bomb] and we would be left without it."[45]

Days later, on 13 January, the JCS forward their position regarding the Super, dividing the response into five categories, "general, military value, diplomatic value, psychological value, [and] moral value."[46] The primary lingering question to this point was whether such a weapon had military value. Could the Super have wartime application or was it just a device of terror and genocide? Regarding its value, the JCS reported that they did not feel the need for a "crash" development program but thought the United States should determine the technical feasibility of fusion.[47] Furthermore, and more practically, no one knew if such a device could even be delivered by air. Some estimates suggested that it would be extraordinarily large compared to other atomic or conventional munitions. Given an early estimate that a fusion bomb might weigh as much as ten tons, the weapon would be too big for a bomber, making it deliverable only by ship. Along this line of reasoning, the JCS believed that concurrent studies on the means of delivery also needed consideration.[48] Regarding its military value, the Joint Chiefs thought that the weapon offered a possible deterrent effect. In addition, they did not foresee research for this project adversely affecting the recently approved plan that called for increased fissionable-material production.[49] Further, the JCS saw diplomatic value in the endeavor because it could create an opportunity for disarmament or arms-control negotiations with the USSR.

On the larger issue of morality, the Joint Chiefs thought that U.S. allies would accept the development of the Super as a necessity. America was a trusted agent, and the nation's allies would understand that the bomb was not for unilateral aggrandizement but for securing collective world peace. The report's closing perhaps carried the greatest weight: "In addition, it is difficult to escape the conviction that in war it is folly to argue whether one weapon is more immoral than another. For in the larger sense, it is war itself which is immoral, and the stigma of such immorality must rest upon the nation which initiates hostilities."[50] Although Secretary Johnson was supposed to be working with his fellow Z Committee members from DoS and the AEC and on joint recommendation, instead, with his usual zeal, he forwarded the JCS report to Truman directly without waiting for Acheson's or Lilienthal's input or review.[51]

With this Johnson was getting ahead of counterparts who possibly differed in opinion. His aggressive political maneuver might have been the most important one. Upon receiving the report Truman read through the JCS position without waiting for the Z Committee's collective report. After reviewing the document, the president supposedly determined that it "made a lot of sense and he was inclined to think that was what we should do."[52] Meanwhile, on 20 January, both General Bradley and MLC chair LeBaron briefed the JCAE on the formal report, recommending thermonuclear research go forward.[53]

One of the technical considerations affecting the Super was the lack of tritium. The isotope is rare on earth, and any deposits available were formed naturally billions of years earlier. For man-made fusion, building a large supply of the tritium isotope was a major practical hurdle. But on the same day General Bradley appeared before the JCAE, Dr. Lawrence Hafstad, director of reactor development with the AEC, testified on possible ways to make the isotope, including the use of existing reactors at Hanford, Washington. With this kind news, the JCAE became more optimistic about the possibility of a fusion reaction.[54] Combined with briefings received by JCAE members at LASL, in addition to Teller's enthusiasm, this information helped promulgate a feeling of possibility within the joint committee. When compounded by the possible threat of a Soviet thermonuclear bomb, it made the case for an American effort more attractive.

Members of the JCAE were already aware of the GAC's moral views on the matter. Yet during the joint committee's deliberations, McMahon parried the GAC's moral justifications against the Super by arguing that the scientists were "beyond their area of competence."[55] As the end of January approached, both the JCAE and the JCS were now in favor of thermonuclear development. Other organizations and opinions had countered the negative conclusions of the GAC and AEC with compelling counterarguments.

On 19 January, during a phone conversation between Acheson and Rear Adm. Sidney Souers, the executive secretary of the NSC, the secretary of state replied that he had met with all the experts that Lilienthal requested and was fully cognizant of the relevant issues. After all the consultations and discussions, Acheson came to the conclusion, "we should advise the president to go ahead and find out about the feasibility of the matter."[56] In reporting back to

Truman, Acheson suggested that the Z Committee needed to provide him with "a straightforward paper and an honest one; not glossing over some of the problems or letting the President think the problems are less than they are."[57]

As the JCAE continued its discussions and hearing testimony, the press became increasingly aware of the thermonuclear debate. Although Senator Johnson's November on-air security indiscretion was followed by the *Washington Post* article and then the Alsop brothers' editorial, very little else was said publicly. But on 15 January a Sunday-evening radio broadcast by Drew Pearson mentioned the topic, squarely placing it in the public forum. Two days later the *New York Times* posted a front-page headline, "US Hydrogen Bomb Delay Urged Pending Bid to Soviets."[58] That same day the newspaper ran an article on the development of a Soviet aircraft capable of carrying an atomic bomb.[59] Subsequent articles concerning the topic were also published in the following days, with one even addressing LeBaron and Bradley's briefing to the JCAE on 20 January.[60] Such reporting worried Strauss, who had earlier penned a letter to the president on 16 January expressing his concerns over disinformation about the Super in the public forum.[61] For the AEC commissioner, the worry was that potential public sentiment against the weapon might develop based upon inaccurate or false reporting.

But the tide continued to turn in support of the Super. On 27 January the AEC commissioners testified on the matter in front of the JCAE. Lilienthal began outlining the sequence of events about the Super and the conclusions drawn up to this point. While much of the discussion was based upon technical matters, potential weapon yields, deuterium-tritium production, and the like, near the end of the session, the individual AEC members were free to express their opinions.[62] Strauss had plenty to say and made a number of key points in his testimony. He reported that the Super was feasible, stating "there appears to be a 50-50 chance of it being successful," that "thermonuclear weapons were not outside the [Russian] field of technical competence," and that there was no likelihood the Soviets would be morally dissuaded from building their own device.[63] Furthermore, the commissioner argued that thermonuclear technology was no secret, having been discussed years earlier, and that development of such a weapon might take less time than had the fission bomb.[64] He also believed that the Soviets might already be developing thermonuclear weapons, warning that "the sands were running out of the glass."[65] After making his points, Strauss finished by providing some personal insight: "[These] were the conclusions I reached, and that was a couple of months ago, . . . and I have thought a lot about it, I might say almost constantly since and I haven't been able to change my opinion."[66] While Strauss was certainly emphatic and deliberate, his remarks might not have been the most important testimony during the session.

A change in temperament about the Super within the commission began to emerge when Commissioners Summer Pike and Gordon Dean both testified before the joint committee. They now stated that the AEC provided only opinions to the president and did not really have the justification or authority to tell LASL to start research on the weapon.[67] This was a softening of their November position on the matter.[68] Second-guessing his earlier decision, Dean was then supported by Strauss. Providing further amplification, Strauss reminded the committee that he supported the measure from the beginning and added, "we had started making them [atomic weapons] first and that in any case if the Russians were making them we could only maintain our lead in some arithmetical difference since our relative lead [would] most likely be reduced."[69]

More interesting, Lilienthal was missing from part of the session because he had a scheduled meeting with the president. Thus, the AEC chair could provide no input regarding Dean's or Pike's statements. Commissioner Henry Smyth, too, seemed to vacillate by stating that his rejection of the Super in November was now subject to change. He explained that how he felt back in the autumn might be different compared to how he felt "at this time."[70] With their latest statements, it appeared that the balance of votes within the AEC might shift. With this possible change in its recommendation, Oppenheimer and the other members of the GAC looked to be the only group standing against the Super. From what had looked like a complete rejection of the program only months ago, might now turn into general agreement.

In addition to the DoD, the JCAE, and the emerging AEC position, Acheson at the DoS now developed his own opinion on the matter. While Lilienthal hoped that the secretary would be an ally in arguing against the Super, the DoS was already leaning toward development of the weapon by the time 1950 was ushered in.[71] Acheson realized that international control of the technology was a chimera, now believing the Soviets would never agree to such conditions given their new success. Furthermore, many came to believe that even if the Soviets assented to swear off thermonuclear technology, there were no assurances that they would abide by such an agreement. Earlier in December 1949, R. Gordon Arneson, Acheson principal advisor on atomic matters, determined that possession of a thermonuclear device by the Soviets "would cause severe damage not only to our military posture, but [also] to our foreign policy position."[72] Reflective of this opinion, Acheson recalled a discussion he had with Oppenheimer: "I listen[ed as] carefully as I know how, but I don't understand what Oppie is trying to say. How can you persuade a paranoid adversary to disarm by example?"[73] As evidence of the department's inclinations, even before the Z Committee's testy meeting that month, Nitze already drafted a position paper advocating the Super. This eventually served as the foundation for the Z Committee's submission to Truman in January 1950.[74]

Nitze's plan suggested that the president direct the AEC to investigate the feasibility of fusion, delay any decision on weapons development, review national security policies given the Soviet bomb, and keep such discourse classified.[75] With these considerations, hope for any kind of international weapons control began to fade.[76] In the view of DoS, if the United States did not develop the weapon, then other nations would, certainly the Russians.[77] Regarding potential Soviet weapons development, Arneson later recalled, "with the kind of people in charge of the Soviet Union, you couldn't expect anything else."[78]

At a press conference on 27 January, Truman was asked if another attempt at international control of atomic weapons in the United Nations was planned. To this he only replied, "I can't comment on that. I am doing everything I possibly can to get the international control of atomic energy. I have been working at it ever since I became President."[79] Regardless of Truman's staid response, the reporter's question showed that the topic of thermonuclear weapons was now fully in the public realm. That same day reporter Alfred Friendly of the *Washington Post* wrote a column titled "Urey, Baruch, and Others Urge Going Ahead with Project for Super Weapon." In the short article Friendly noted that at the news conference, Truman acknowledged the existence of the thermonuclear-bomb issue publically for the first time. Before then he had responded to any questions about the Super with an invariable "no comment."[80]

On the morning of 31 January, the three Z committee members (Acheson, Johnson, and Lilienthal), accompanied by various staffers, assembled for the second time. Gathering in NSC executive secretary Souers' office in the old State Department building across from the White House at 1030, Acheson took charge of the meeting.[81] What the Alsop brothers described in their 2 January editorial about "dingy committee rooms" as the locations for such debates, proved prophetic. Souers' conference room with dirty brownish-yellow walls was spartan in accommodation.[82] Acheson stated that many staff papers and studies had been written about the Super, with no real decisions made. But wasting no time, he took the first real step by announcing four recommendations for the committee to consider. They were almost identical to those drafted by Nitze earlier in December 1949:

1. That the President direct the Atomic Energy Commission to proceed to determine the technical feasibility of a thermonuclear weapon. . . .
2. That the President defer his decision regarding the production of weapons pending the reexamination of the nation's objectives in peace and war. . . .
3. That the President direct the Secretary of State and Defense [to] undertake a review of national strategic plans in light of the Soviet fission bomb and possible thermonuclear capability. . . .
4. That no further information on this topic be made [public] without approval of the President.[83]

After announcing these points, Acheson handed out a draft presidential press release. After reviewing the material, Johnson spoke first. The defense secretary concurred with Acheson's proposal but suggested omitting the decision deferring production of the weapons until feasibility had been determined.[84] This suggestion allowed the president more flexibility in determining weapons requirements and when such a device might be made. His point would later prove prescient. Johnson also proposed three more suggestions: that the public statement be shorter, that the president mention an absence of international control of atomic weapons as a consideration, and that the statement be in written form and not a live press briefing.[85] By providing a written release over a verbal announcement, Johnson hoped to make the decision appear insignificant, "to play it down, [to] make it just one of those things."[86] Looking for consensus, Acheson agreed to the changes with Lilienthal acquiescing, thus avoiding the acrimony of the earlier December meeting.[87]

Lilienthal, knowing he was defeated, stated that he tried to abide "in the spirit and letter of the law providing for civilian control of atomic weapon development."[88] In his role as the AEC chair, he argued that military requirements had largely been beyond his concern; given the issue at hand, he argued that the nation now needed real inquiry into some basic issues: What is the best way to further our common defense and security? Should the United States reconsider its dependence on the atomic bomb as a matter of foreign policy? Does this situation provide a unique opportunity to promote a better strategy than "a headlong rush to war of mass destruction weapons"?[89] With the October approval to increase fissionable-weapons production, combined with planned research into fusion, the AEC chair thought an overall study of national security was in order. In Lilienthal's mind the nation needed to do some collective soul-searching regarding defense and the lengths it was willing to go to secure victory. While Acheson agreed verbally, others in attendance probably also saw merit in Lilienthal's statements. Regardless of the AEC chair's concerns, given the emerging Cold War environment and the apparent successes of international Communism, for those assembled, there was no alternative regarding the Super.

Now with the JCAE leaning strongly toward development, public awareness of the Super, and fear over encroaching Communism, domestic political considerations were now a factor in the decision. With these relevant political concerns, Acheson told the committee, "We must protect the president."[90] Perhaps one of the most telling observations about the current domestic political and security environment was a commentary by Acheson noted in Lilienthal's diaries:

> This kind of war—strategic bombing—[was] not a useful means of effecting national policy, in a democracy. [It] [d]oesn't break the will of [an enemy] population, [it] destroys them. So [it] can only be considered to effect sheer survival, not winning, i.e. achieving national purpose.
>
> Two years ago we were winning. Now [with] China, things going [the] other way. China may—possibly—be partial undoing.

> Atom can't be dealt with separately anymore; [its] part of [an] overall settlement.[91]

Agreeing to the changes, all three members of the Z Committee signed the document, with Acheson surprised by Lilienthal's willing signature.[92] But having signed, Lilienthal asked Acheson if he could say a few words in the Oval Office when they met with the president. The meeting adjourned at 1230. After months of deliberation, position papers, and reports, the final-decision conference lasted only two hours.

Johnson already had an appointment with the president that afternoon. Stating "the heat was on in Congress and every hour counted in getting the matter disposed of," the defense secretary suggested the committee use that time to present its findings.[93] Given their proximity to the White House, the Z Committee, escorted by NSC executive secretary Souers, left the dingy conference room and walked across the street to meet with Truman.

Making their way into the Oval Office at 1235, Acheson handed the president the committee's recommendation.[94] As he requested earlier in the morning, Lilienthal made his last-ditch plea for his position, stating that this course of action was not the wisest and that others were still available. He argued further that such actions magnified our military weakness, as the nation was becoming increasingly dependent upon atomic weapons.[95] But Truman cut the AEC chair short and interjected that they might have had a longer, quieter examination of the Super issue if Senator Johnson had not made his unguarded public comment back in November.[96] Regarding the recommendation, the president inquired, "Can the Russians do it?" The group collectively nodded, with Souers simply commenting that "there wasn't much time." Truman replied, "We have no other choice, we'll go ahead."[97] The men left the Oval office, concluding a meeting that lasted only seven minutes.[98]

That afternoon the White House released the president's formal announcement to the American public:

> It is part of my responsibility as Commander-in-Chief of the armed forces to see to it that our country is able to defend itself against any possible aggressor. Accordingly I have directed the Atomic Energy Commission to continue its work on all forms of atomic weapons,

> including the so-called hydrogen or super-bomb. Like all other work in the field of atomic weapons, it is being and will be carried forward on a basis consistent with the overall objective of our program for peace and security.
>
> This we shall continue to do until a satisfactory plan for international control of atomic energy is achieved. We shall also continue to examine all those factors that affect our program for peace and this country's security.[99]

With this announcement, Truman beat the JCAE to the punch, as McMahon had yet to publish the joint committee's formal findings. The senator found out about the coming announcement soon after the lunchtime decision. Lilienthal informed him of the news by phone just as the McMahon concluded the JCAE's latest session. Days later on the floor of the Senate, McMahon lauded the decision, claiming, "American renunciation of the hydrogen bomb would mean embracing the folly of 'disarmament by example.' Our friends abroad would shrink away from us seeing that we had lost [the] power to defend the United States, much less to help defend Europe."[100] While obviously disappointed that the JCAE's recommendation was now largely immaterial and perfunctory, McMahon could still revel in the fact that his efforts in Congress had played a role in the decision.

With Truman's statement, the American public was now officially informed of the Super debate. Given the current security environment, most were supportive of the decision. Only days later, when asked about the decision to research fusion, 77 percent of Americans surveyed who knew about the H-bomb believed that the nation should make the weapon. Furthermore, 45 percent of those surveyed did not think America should try to work out an agreement regarding the atom bomb with the Soviet Union before trying to make an H-bomb. Conversely, 48 percent agreed that the United States should seek an agreement. More telling was that 70 percent of those asked did not think that an agreement with the Russians over atomic-weapons limitations would succeed.[101] Given these numbers, Truman made the correct political decision, reflecting American domestic security concerns. When queried months later in March, 68 percent of Americans believed the USSR would use a thermonuclear bomb on the United States, with 69 percent approving the development of such weapons by the United States.[102]

Regarding the decision, the press as a whole was largely equivocal. While many saw the necessity for the weapon, several raised the moral issue and weapons-control debate. Some editorials argued that there was not enough information to really make a judgment on the matter, but now that the decision was made to go forward, the American people should be fully informed on the progress.[103] There was no major condemnation of the decision, but there was no celebration either. One editorial noted that the president had "a Hobson's choice. He could not, for the security of the nation, have decided otherwise than he did. He nevertheless has assumed an enormous responsibility. It required great courage."[104] Americans generally agreed with McMahon's statement on the floor of the Senate days later, in which he proclaimed, "He [Truman] had no choice, and his decision under the present circumstances [was] right."[105] They came to see the possibility of thermonuclear weapons as part of a new reality, just as they had come to accept fission-based ones. In this new reality a nuclear sword of Damocles was forever suspended above the growing sprawl of postwar suburbia.

While the public statement grabbed the headlines, more important was Truman's formal tasking to both Johnson and Acheson. In addition to instructing the AEC to continue work on thermonuclear technology, the president also directed the secretaries of state and defense to "undertake a re-examination of our objectives in peace and war and of the effect of these objectives on our strategic plans."[106] The second paragraph of the Acheson's draft was key. In essence Truman was directing a wholesale review of national security goals and objectives much like Lilienthal requested in the last Z Committee meeting. This directive was also reflected in results of the B-36 and the unification investigations done by the subcommittee of the House Armed Services Committee the previous autumn. While Truman ordered the review officially on 31 January, the formal report from the House committee regarding the B-36, published on 1 March, also specifically called for "an astute appraisal by the National Security Council of present strategic planning reference atomic warfare."[107] While Lilienthal may have lost the battle over the Super, he possibly won the argument. As Kennan withdrew from

Washington to serve as a special envoy in South America, Nitze and the PPS Office began the review of American national defense policy. The blossom that became NSC 68 was planted in October 1949 and fully germinated at the end of January 1950.

Coups de Grâce

As the Super discussion came to a conclusion, other events during that same two-week period also exacerbated existing domestic concerns. The weekend before Truman's approval of the program, Alger Hiss' second trial came to an end. Charged with perjury from his 1948 testimony before the House Un-American Activities Committee (HUAC), on 21 January 1950 Hiss was found guilty on two counts.[108] A longtime DoS representative who served as an American diplomat to the nascent United Nations, Hiss became a lightning rod concerning Communist infiltration into the federal government. In 1947 Hiss left DoS and served as president of the Carnegie Endowment for International Peace. But Whitaker Chambers, a writer and a former member of the Communist Party, testified before the HUAC in August 1948 that Hiss was not only a party member but also a spy who passed secrets to Soviet agents. Rumors of his Communist affiliation existed before Chamber's testimony but were largely ignored by his DoS superiors. Although Hiss refuted the claim, corroborating evidence from other sources surfaced. In an effort to clear his name, Hiss appeared before the HUAC in December 1949, proclaiming he was not a Communist nor had he ever met Chambers.

Typewritten notes, microfilm, and secret drop-offs were all part of the intrigue of a sensationalized trial. Rep. Richard Nixon (R-CA), chair of the HUAC and a virulent anti-Communist, sought to make a name for himself by vilifying and convicting Hiss. Although many disregarded Chambers' claims and called the whole issue a red herring, Nixon continued the investigation. Never actually found guilty of espionage due to the statute of limitations, Hiss was charged with perjury for his testimony before the committee. While his first trial ended in July 1949 in a hung jury, his second trial ended just before Truman's thermonuclear decision. Four days later Hiss was sentenced to five years in prison. Given the suspicions over Communist infiltration in the DoS as a result of the "loss of China" the previous summer, this verdict only added fuel to a smoldering fire.

Although Secretary of State Acheson supported Hiss publically, the case not only provided further "evidence" of Communist incursions but also underscored the emerging narrative of infiltration into the federal government. Stating he would not "turn his back on Hiss," Acheson himself became a target of Republican lawmakers and was vilified for his supposed harboring of Communists at DoS. As Major General Hurley claimed in his departure from China in 1945, many now feared Communist infiltration in Washington. In line with the prevailing sentiment of the anti-Communist periodical *Plain Talk*, the Hiss allegations only reinforced the assumption that Communists were everywhere and trying to destroy the American way of life. Such sentiment quickly manifested in draconian actions.

The timing of the Hiss verdict was coincidental but made a convenient backdrop for those looking for a more assertive national security effort. Additionally, barely a week afterward, an even bigger case of espionage became public. Tipped off by the FBI during the previous autumn, security and espionage investigators in the United Kingdom (predecessors to the modern-day MI-5 and MI-6) began tracking physicist Klaus Fuchs as he returned home. During questioning, the former member of the MED and attendee of the 1946 thermonuclear technology conference, finally confessed to spying for the Soviets. Arraigned on 3 February, when this news hit the papers in America, a shocked Senator McMahon commented, "we are in a hell of a mess."[109] Fuchs' arrest only underscored the existing suspicions of Communist incursion.

Some in Washington were already aware of the Fuchs investigation and the possibility of his espionage efforts. But such knowledge had little influence on the thermonuclear decision and was not even discussed in the Z Committee's 31 January meeting.[110] Truman was allegedly ignorant regarding Fuchs' activities until 1 February.[111] If he had he been aware of them, it probably would have only reinforced what he was thinking since receiving the JCS position paper from Defense Secretary Johnson on 19 January. As soon as this news broke, the question on everyone's mind was how much damage had been done. As to his assessment of Fuchs' assistance to the Russians, Oppenheimer warned, "I think the only safe assumption is to say that as far as we had gone, he knew everything we did. It seems this group of British scientists knew more about the

H-Bomb than our own people did." In a later meeting of the JCAE, McMahon declared that Fuchs took all LASL information on hydrogen bombs in 1946 and gave it to the Soviets. The AEC reached the same conclusion a month later at its 10 March meeting.[112]

In mid-February Brig. Gen. Herbert Loper and Maj. Gen. Kenneth Nichols of the MLC estimated Soviet atomic capabilities in light of Fuchs' confession. Their findings included

- Russian knowledge of basic nuclear physics is at least equivalent to our own.
- The theoretical basis for developing a thermo-nuclear weapon was firmly established by the USSR by 1945 at the latest and development kept pace with the fission type bomb.
- The USSR stockpile and current production capacity are equal or actually superior to our own, both in yield and numbers.
- The thermonuclear weapon may be in actual production.[113]

While many of these assumptions were erroneous and overstated the Soviet capability, such thinking was prevalent given the environment. The same week as the MLC memo, the CIA reported, "The USSR is mounting a new offensive in the cold war. This behavior is a reflection of the aggressive, self-confident, and even boastful Soviet attitude of recent months and is an effort to add new triumphs to the start of post war Communist success."[114]

Adding to the national security concerns in February 1950 were the claims of an obscure Wisconsin senator, Joseph McCarthy. In Wheeling, West Virginia, on 9 February, he claimed to have a list of 205 known Communists "working and shaping policy" in DoS. With this, McCarthy irresponsibly exacerbated fears over Communist infiltration. Echoing the sentiment of both Hurley and the publishers of *Plain Talk,* McCarthy took such fears to a new level, making the search for Communist sympathizers a sport within American political and social circles. His number of suspected Communist infiltrators was speculative at best and changed based upon the audience. But few were ever discovered. His efforts forced more than 2,000 people from their jobs in the federal service while he continued to smear, harass, and harangue anyone with any semblance of Communist affiliation—or more likely those deemed a political foe. While anti-Communist sentiment was an American phenomenon since the end of World War I, these events raised suspicions and enabled the rise of "McCarthyism."

With Fuchs' espionage, Secretary Johnson and the MLC were now motivated for an "all-out" hydrogen-bomb effort. Some had requested this kind of effort soon after hearing of the Joe-1 explosion. But the shared DoD and JCS position during the previous autumn rejected the idea of a "crash" program. Now because of Fuchs' help, the Soviets could be ahead of the West, and a crash program might be a logical and prudent response.[115] Additionally, Johnson's suggested change to Acheson's proposal on 31 January to give the president more freedom to develop thermonuclear weapons now looked like an act of pure clairvoyance. As a result, the AEC could look directly into developing a weapon as opposed to waiting for a presidential decision only after proving fusion's feasibility. Yet a study commission by the president for a "stepped up" program determined that "there were no known additional steps which might be taken for further acceleration of the test program."[116] By 1952 American scientists engineered the first man-made fusion event and two years later developed the first thermonuclear weapon. After these achievements, when queried as to who deserved credit for the U.S. thermonuclear success, Teller ironically replied, "Brien McMahon, Lewis Strauss, and Klaus Fuchs."[117]

Concerned with Communist plots everywhere, any support of the United Nations, internationalism, fluoridation, and some vaccinations were now seen as Bolshevik ploys to undermine American society. Hollywood and the entertainment industry were especially vulnerable, with dozens of skilled performers and writers "blacklisted" for their Communist affiliations. While the decision for a new national security review was formally approved by Truman on 31 January, his decision was also a reflection of American fears and the national zeitgeist of the time.

The Inception

As this trio of events unfolded in the public sphere, in February 1950 Nitze started the directed review of national security. Before leaving the PPS, Kennan, Nitze's predecessor and superior, increasingly looked for other options for dealing with the changing geopolitical balance. The author of the "long telegram" rejected the development of the Super and hoped for a more cooperative approach among rival nations. Kennan spent much of his last days at PPS drafting a position paper reflecting the idea.[118] In contrast, Nitze, ever the Wall Street investment banker, was less inclined to see the world through a cooperative lens and pursued a more hawkish unilateral approach. For Kennan, containment was more a regional commitment than a global one. He thought the United States needed to prioritize key areas of the world important to American interests and police them with military power. His policy also sought to deter international Communism by largely economic and political action, rather than defending against Soviet expansion everywhere militarily. This kind of thinking was becoming a minority view by 1950, especially after the events in the fall of 1949. As a result, Kennan's thoughtful perspectives grew fundamentally and philosophically opposed to those of Acheson.[119] Meanwhile, Nitze countered his former boss and developed a more defensively minded outlook as he rose in influence in the DoS. Kennan's final PPS draft reflected his less confrontational and more cooperative strategy, but the submission was rejected by Acheson. This reflected the leadership shift in PPS, as Acheson replaced Kennan with Nitze.[120]

Working with representatives from the Pentagon during the autumn, Nitze had already become increasingly convinced that the Super was a requirement. As Kennan saw it, Nitze was succumbing to the military way of thinking by always planning on the worst-case scenarios, not necessarily upon the most realistic ones.[121] Additionally, after obtaining a lecture from Teller on the principles of fusion, the new PPS lead's desire for pursuing the technology became acute.[122] One of the biggest problems Nitze had in starting his review of national security policy was Defense Secretary Johnson. Given that the president directed both the DoS and the DoD to conduct the review, Johnson needed to have a role in the discussion. Yet his uncooperative and confrontational style often precluded any DoD participation with Nitze. Johnson forbade any such involvement unless he personally approved it.[123] Despite a lack of interdepartmental coordination, Nitze began outlining the problem. As a starting point he framed the issue:

1. Risk of a general, all-out war initiated by the USSR, either by direct attack on us or on one or more of our principal allies.

2. Localized military aggression.
3. Loss of areas/positions of importance to the west through internal weakness, intimidation, or subversion.
4. A general weakening and splitting up of the cohesive will and power of coordinated action of the free world coalition which was beginning to take shape.[124]

While the previous policy of NSC 20/4 did not consider an atomic-capable Soviet Union, that document served as the basis for the new effort. What Nitze eventually decided was that the nation needed a more flexible response to Communism and its inroads around the globe. In his view atomic weapons and strategic bombers were seen as part of a deterrent effort, but the nation and the free world also needed the ability to counter Communist advances locally.[125] What was required was a buildup of the conventional military during peacetime in order to check Soviet aggression. Such an expansion required not only a substantial increase in DoD expenditures from its paltry levels under Johnson but also a break from the American tradition of only maintaining a small standing army. The 1949 DoD budget remained at $13 billion; however, Nitze's budget for defense increased almost fourfold to some $40–50 billion. Knowing Truman's and Johnson's positions on defense expenditures, Nitze deliberately left the projected DoD price tag off early versions of his proposals.[126] Fully understanding economics and a Keynesian at heart, Nitze held that such a buildup was affordable despite its ballooning cost.[127] For him, the American economy could well afford deficit spending for this new military requirement. With a new infusion of funding, the DoD could now have both fission- and fusion-based weapons along with a credible conventional capability, which would be able to handle smaller Soviet or Communist incursions wherever they might occur.[128]

Because of what transpired the previous autumn, Nitze argued that "a radical increase in power and strength of the free world was called for."[129] Inspired by a discussion with New York economist Alexander Sachs, he saw that the Communist bloc had fully aligned its "correlation of forces," a term referring to the totality of a nation's elements of power. Included in this was a state's diplomatic, information, military, and economic elements of power. At the beginning of 1950, the Soviet Union and its Communist allies were all seen as aligning their collective power against the West. According to Sachs, when the correlation of forces were in your favor, it was time to consolidate your gains and "nail them down."[130] Given Joe-1, China, and an stronger grip on Eastern Europe, international Communism was on the offensive. In order to counter this disposition, Nitze felt that the West needed to align and develop its own correlation of forces. Using this philosophical model, he went to work on developing a policy to regain the West's predominance in the global environ.

Despite Secretary Johnson's tight control on DoD participation, a number of military officers saw merit in Nitze's effort. While the services initially expected to gain a few divisions or air wings, as officers became familiar with PPS's efforts, they realized this was more than just an opportunity to gain around the margins; this was a chance for a complete revision of American military power and structure.[131] Working with the entire PPS staff, including John Ferguson, John Paton Davies, Robert Tufts, Bob Hooker, and Charles Burton Marshall, over the course of six weeks, Nitze drafted the proposed national security policy.[132] Combined with input from both official and unofficial representatives from the DoD, Maj. Gen. Truman Landon, Maj. Gen. Ray Maddocks, and Rear Adm. Thomas Robbins, the team forwarded the first draft of the proposed policy in March.[133] As Nitze gained Acheson's confidence, he daily briefed his boss. Conversely, Major General Landon avoiding briefing Johnson, as the defense secretary's contentious personality and unswerving focus on lowering expenditures might derail or influence the ongoing work.[134] The first draft was sent to Truman on 14 April, but little action was taken regarding the proposed documents recommendations. It would take another significant event to make the proposal a policy.

For Nitze, the year 1954 would be an important milestone in his policy review. Based on intelligence reports, he surmised that by then the Soviets would have a sizable atomic arsenal along with strategic bombers able to reach the continental United States. This atomic armada would also be backed up by formidable ground formations.[135] Unless the United States did something in the interim, the nation might lose its edge militarily. Nitze used a chess analogy to describe the American situation: "We had been playing a forward game with our advance pieces, backed up by our atomic queen. The Russians had castled long ago, gotten their rooks into position and were now deploying an atomic queen of their own. It was high time we got about the business of castling ourselves."[136] As the PPS director saw it, the nation needed to increase its general security and military strength as a way to counter the emerging Soviet threat. He was concerned not only with the military weakness of U.S. allies after the war but also with the impotence of the U.S. military. Because stimulating the peacetime economy was the priority, the Army had only a handful of divisions, with many only training formations; there was no production of ammunition or ground-combat vehicles; North American aviation was producing only six new F-86 fighters per month; and tactical aviation was woefully deficient, with only a few squadrons.[137]

Nitze and Kennan both saw air supremacy as a key factor in winning World War II. As a member of the USSBS, Nitze was keenly aware of the capabilities—and limitations—of airpower. Assuming the same requirement existed in the postwar world, under the budgetary constraints of the time, the only real offensive airpower the nation had was strategic in nature.[138] While the USAF testified that it had not "put all its eggs into the strategic basket" during the October hearings, in its current form Nitze feared that tactical aviation was insufficient to support a ground campaign. Given the results of the WSEG study, even the strategic force would have a difficult time executing an extended aerial offensive.

Cognizant of the WSEG work and the deficiencies it identified, Nitze understood how hollow the 1950 force structure was when compared to the proposed war plans. Even accepting overly optimistic USAF claims regarding the strategic offensive, if the military budget and structure were not increased, the United States was setting itself up for a doctrinal straightjacket in relation to strategy and warfare. With no other form of war-making capability available given the budget and staffing constraints, the nation would be forced to resort to waging atomic war. This was not the first time this sentiment was expressed, as Budget Director Frank Pace had voiced the same concern in the spring of 1949 in relation to the cost of the B-36.

Under this kind of scenario, if the United States committed itself to combat in Taiwan, there would be no credible military force available to counter a Soviet thrust into Western Europe.[139] If this occurred, the U.S. military might have sufficient resources to deter local aggression but not a credible defensive force elsewhere on the globe. The basic American strategy at that time was to use the stocks left over from World War II until new equipment was built and sent to forward locations. This scenario played out only months later when North Korean armor overran South Korea, initiating the Korean War. While this conflict saw some new equipment and innovations, like jet fighters, helicopters, and forward air controllers, much of the ground equipment used came from surplus stocks remaining from 1945.

Given the anticipated nature of future combat, the extended time to "spool up" production and forward equipment to contested regions was now a luxury the nation no longer had. Unlike the world wars, the United States had to maintain a military force sufficient at the very onset of hostilities. According to proponents of the new policy, the nation needed a credible standing military and had to have it in place by 1954. Events during the autumn of 1949 cultivated such thinking. Unfortunately, this change in policy and armaments came much too late for the U.S. troops in Korea in the upcoming summer.

Legacies

While NSC 68 would not become policy until after the North Korean invasion in June, the Communist offensive served as the impetus for the policy's eventual approval. Communist aggression on the Korean Peninsula only validated what most in the West were already thinking: global monolithic Communism threated Western democracies as it sought world domination through military aggression. Time eventually revealed the localized motivation of Kim Il Sung, with only a lukewarm approval Stalin, for the North Korean offensive. Yet in the early 1950s the democracies believed most, if not all, Communist nations were unified in an effort to undermine the West.

In the summer of 1950, as the NSC 68 draft languished in the staff offices around Washington, supporters of the proposed policy might have secretly expressed relief at the North Korean attack. Such aggressive action seemingly provided definitive proof of Communist designs for global domination. While some who worked on the draft policy were beginning to wonder if their efforts had been in vain, their concerns were alleviated when NSC 68 was officially approved in September 1950. A full year had passed since the explosion of Joe-1, but Korea provided the catalyst for the policy's eventual adoption. While motivations for its drafting occurred in late 1949, it took another nine months to officially respond to the previous autumn's events with a new national defense strategy.

Regardless of the delay, the document was a watershed event in American history. Setting the precedent for a large standing military, the United States was now breaking its historical pattern. After 1950, defense expenditures under the Truman administration grew threefold, from $14 billion to over $44 billion.[140] Many claimed the increase was excessive and thought NSC 68 provided a "holiday on defense spending" as the services clamored to increase structure, buy equipment, and fill their ranks.[141] At the end of 1950, SAC was a force of only 85,000 personnel and fewer than 1,000 aircraft. By the end of the next year, the command grew to 145,000 airmen with 1,200 warplanes. Three years later, in 1954, SAC's air fleet almost doubled, numbering some 2,100 airframes.[142] By the end of the Korean War, the Army, too, doubled in size from ten to twenty divisions, while the number of combat vessels in the Navy grew from 238 to 409. Total active-duty military personnel also doubled to more than 3.5 million Americans.[143]

This substantial increase in defense spending became a presidential issue as early as 1952, with Republican candidate Dwight Eisenhower campaigning against the "Democrats' profligacy" on defense spending.[144] During this campaign, he argued that "a bankrupt America is more the Soviet goal than an America conquered on the field of battle."[145] While NSC 68 focused on 1954 as the year of danger, Ike believed that the United States needed to plan for a potential defense budget for the "long haul" while looking to avoid protracted ground conflicts like Korea.[146] Once in office the Eisenhower administration developed NSC 162/2, the "New Look" and its associated concept of "Massive Retaliation" with nuclear weapons. With this policy, the United States clearly placed its defense strategy back into the strategic bombing basket instead of the more balanced approach Nitze proposed. While seemingly contrary to NSC 68 in strategy, the cost for the New Look was initially thought to be cheaper. Although Ike envisioned a cut in military spending during his presidency, New Look eventually ballooned the defense budget back to the levels of its NSC 68 predecessor.

Before World War II, American defense spending composed less than 1 percent of the nation's GDP. During the fight against the Axis powers, it grew to 43 percent of GDP. By 1948 it had dropped again to 8 percent, only to rise to a high of 16 percent during the initial years of NSC 68 and the Korean War. For much of the Cold War period, DoD budget allocations changed by only a few percentage points. While defense GDP allocations peaked at 16 percent in 1954, they fell to the low teens (12–13 percent) for the next ten years until the Vietnam War. For the next few decades, until the Soviet Union collapsed in 1991, the defense budget remained at approximately 8 percent of GDP.[147] The Obama administration hoped to cut the defense budget to 2.3 percent of GDP, making it the lowest allocation in the post–World War II era.[148] Regardless of the years or changes in presidential administration, American peacetime defense expenditures after 1950 dwarfed those of the interwar years of the 1920s and 1930s and in previous periods of the nation's history.

In June 1950 the United States had 1.5 million personnel in uniform. This was three times the number on active duty in 1940 and six times the average number during the interwar years (approximately 250,000 annually).[149] In 1954 the U.S. military had 3.2 million personnel and eventually retained approximately 2.7 million in uniform until 1964, when its commitment in Vietnam grew. During the conflict in Southeast Asia, DoD personnel strength rose again to 3.5 million but then dropped back to just over 2 million after 1972, where it remained for the rest of the Cold War.[150] Again, this number reflects a significant difference from the nation's previous history, as more citizens wore a military uniform during peacetime than ever before.

The autumn of 1949 still resonates in the American experience. Not only was it a confluence of diplomatic, military, and economic concerns, but it also laid the groundwork for a new military tradition. The events of that season served as the impetus for the questioning of the American military posture, leading to Truman's request for a wholesale review of national security policy. The results of this assessment not only increased the defense budget but also, and more importantly, laid the foundations for a large, peacetime standing military, breaking the American tradition of maintaining only a small-cadre military. The arguments over the efficacy of strategic bombing, atomic global balances of power, the establishment of another major Communist power, concern over domestic Communist infiltration, the imbedded argument of strategic-versus-tactical airpower, and the (im)morality of thermonuclear weapons were all on the table simultaneously. NSC 68 made the United States a very different nation, one that would now maintain military potency in conventional and atomic capabilities in both peace and war.

This sizable U.S. military force has increasingly become the "go-to" option in addressing American national interests abroad. The U.S. armed forces are still seen as a primary tool for American foreign policy, providing a range of response options. Whether it is combat operations, humanitarian efforts, a noncombatant-evacuation mission, or a show of force, the U.S. military maintains both size and capability that few nations, if any, can match. Despite its shrinking size in the post–Cold War era, it still remains the most capable, and expensive, military in the world. Until the nexus of events in late 1949, the idea of a large peacetime military funded by a substantial percent of the national budget was unfathomable. Since the inception of NSC 68, the use of military power, with its unique capabilities and formations, is now a major component in U.S. interactions in the global environment. A myriad of successive, and concurrent, events during the autumn of 1949 made it all possible.

Notes

Introduction

1. John F. Fuller, *Thor's Legions, Weather Support to the US Air Force and Army, 1937–1987* (Boston: American Meteorology Society, 1990), 246.
2. Fuller, 246–47; "A Real Lady," *Airscape*, Mar 15, 2016, https://airscapemag.com/2016/03/15/eielson-b29/ (accessed 9 Aug. 2017).
3. Fuller, *Thor's Legions*, 247.
4. "Real Lady."
5. "Real Lady." WB-29 44-62214 is currently submerged in a flooded gravel pit at Eielson Air Force Base, Alaska, where it is known as "The Lady of the Lake." Conflicting stories on how 62214 ended up in the lake abound. Recent dives into the wreck have produced no new information as to the plane's sad fate.
6. Kenneth W. Condit, *History of the Joint Chiefs of Staff: The Joint Chiefs of Staff and National Policy*, vol. 2, *1947–1949* (Washington, DC: Office of the Secretary of Defense, 1996), 279.
7. Lester Machta, "Finding the Site of the First Soviet Nuclear Test in 1949," *Bulletin of the American Meteorological Society* 73, no. 11 (Nov. 1992): 1798; Richard Hewlett and Francis Duncan, *Atomic Shield: A History of the United States Atomic Energy Commission*, vol. 2, *1947–1952* (Berkeley: University of California Press, 1990), 362–63.
8. Memorandum, Lewis Strauss to AEC Commissioners, 11 Apr. 1947, Monitoring of Soviet Tests, 1947–1956 Folder, Lewis Strauss Papers, Herbert Hoover Presidential Library, West Branch, IA (hereafter HHPL); A Chronology of the Thermonuclear Weapon Program to November 1952, Hydrogen Bomb 1951–1970 Folder, ibid.; Memorandum for Files, Subj.: History of Long-Range Detection Program, Atomic Energy Commission, 21 July 1948, Atomic Bomb Long Range Detection Folder, NSC Atomic File, Box 174, President's Secretary Files, Harry S. Truman Presidential Library, Independence, MO (hereafter HSTPL).

9. Intelligence Division, War Department, "Long Range Detection of Atomic Explosions," *Intelligence Review* 37 (24 Oct. 1946), 56.
10. T. A. Heppenheimer, "How to Detect an Atomic Bomb," *American Heritage* 21, no. 4 (Spring 2006).
11. Memorandum for Files, Subj.: History of Long-Range Detection Program, Atomic Energy Commission, 21 July 1948, Atomic Bomb Long Range Detection Folder, NSC Atomic File, Box 174, President's Secretary Files, HSTPL.
12. Robert A. Mann, *The B-29 Superfortress Chronology, 1934–1960* (Jefferson, NC: McFarland, 2009), 218; Lewis Strauss, *Men and Decisions* (New York; Doubleday, 1963), 214.
13. Doyle L. Northrup and Donald H. Rock, "The Detection of Joe I," Sept. 1966, Document 2 in "Detection of the First Soviet Nuclear Test, September 1949," National Security Archive, 9 Sept. 2019, https://nsarchive.gwu/briefing-book/nuclear-vault/2019-09-09/detection-first-soviet-nuclear-test-september-1949 (accessed 26 July 2016); Michael Gordin, *Red Cloud at Dawn: Truman, Stalin, and the End of the American Atomic Monopoly* (New York: Picador, 2009), 203; Machta, "Finding the Site of the First Soviet Nuclear Test," 1798.
14. Northrup and Rock, "Detection of Joe I"; Machta, "Finding the Site of the First Soviet Nuclear Test," 1798; Machta, "Finding the Site of the First Soviet Nuclear Test," 1798.
15. Heppenheimer, "How to Detect an Atomic Bomb"; Richard Rhodes, *Dark Sun: The Making of the Hydrogen Bomb* (New York: Simon and Schuster, 1995), 370–71.
16. Machta, "Finding the Site of the First Soviet Nuclear Test," 1798.
17. Northrup and Rock, "Detection of Joe I."
18. Doyle Northrup, "Detection of the First Soviet Nuclear Test on August 29, 1949," Air Force Technical Application Center, 1 Feb. 1962, Document 1 in "Detection of the First Soviet Nuclear Test, September 1949," National Security Archive, 9 Sept. 2019, https://nsarchive.gwu.edu/briefing-book/nuclear-vault/2019-09-09/detection-first-soviet-nuclear-test-september-1949 (accessed 26 July 2016); John Farquhar, *A Need to Know: The Role of Air Force Reconnaissance in War Planning, 1945–1953* (Maxwell AFB, AL: Air University Press, 2004), 116; Machta, "Finding the Site of the First Soviet Nuclear Test," 1798.
19. Northrup and Rock, "Detection of Joe I"; Rhodes, *Dark Sun*, 371.
20. Northrup, "Detection of the First Soviet Nuclear Test."
21. Air Force Technical Applications Center, "Long Range Detection Program," Commemorative Issue, Oct. 1997, pg. 11, www.foia.af.mil/shared/media/document/AFD-081007-010.pdf (accessed 25 July 2016; page removed), copy in author's possession. See also Mary Welch, "AFTAC Celebrates 50 Years of Long Range Detection," *Monitor*, Oct. 1997, p. 11.

22. Northrup and Rock, "Detection of Joe I"; Machta, "Finding the Site of the First Soviet Nuclear Test," 1798; Rhodes, *Dark Sun*, 371; Gordin, *Red Cloud at Dawn*, 204.
23. Northrup and Rock, "Detection of Joe I"; Machta, "Finding the Site of the First Soviet Nuclear Test," 1800.
24. Peter King and H. Friedman, Naval Research Laboratory, "Collection and Identification of Fission Products of Foreign Origin," 22 Sept. 1949, NSC–Atomic Series, Box 200, President's Secretary Files, HSTPL.
25. "An Interim Report of British Work on Joe," n.d., copy 2 of 6, NSC–Atomic Series, Box 199, President's Secretary Files, HSTPL; Hewlett and Duncan, *Atomic Shield*, 364–65; Gordin, *Red Cloud at Dawn*, 205; Stanley Bloomberg and Gwinn Owens, *Energy and Conflict: The Life and Times of Edward Teller* (New York: Putnam, 1976), 200.
26. This was an incredibly accurate estimate, as Tracerlab was only off by one hour. Heppenheimer, "How to Detect an Atomic Bomb"; Machta, "Finding the Site of the First Soviet Nuclear Test," 1802; Rhodes, *Dark Sun*, 372.
27. Northrup and Rock, "Detection of Joe I," 32.
28. V. Bush, J. Robert Oppenheimer, Robert Bacher, and W. S. Parsons to Gen. Hoyt Vandenberg, 20 Sept. 1949, Atomic Bomb Long Range Detection Program Folder, NSC–Atomic Series, Box 174, President's Secretary Files, HSTPL; Condit, *History of the Joint Chiefs of Staff*, 279; Hewlett and Duncan, *Atomic Shield*, 365.
29. U.S. Government, Statement by the President on Announcing the First Atomic Explosion in the USSR, September 23, 1949, *The Public Papers of the Presidents of the United States—Harry S. Truman, . . . 1949* (Washington, DC: U.S. Government Printing Office, 1964), 485; Strauss, *Men and Decisions*, 215.
30. James Shepley and Clay Blair Jr., *The Hydrogen Bomb: The Men, the Menace, the Mechanism* (New York: David McKay, 1954), 19.
31. David Halberstam, *The Fifties* (New York; Ballentine, 1993), 26.
32. Correspondence, Col. John Schwartz, USAF, Executive Director of Intelligence, to Commanding General, Air Material Command, Subj: Estimate of Soviet Capabilities in the Field of Atomic Energy, 13 July 1949, National Security Archive, https://nsarchive.gwu.edu/document/19581-national-security-archive-doc-10-document-4 (accessed 26 Oct. 2021); Hewlett and Duncan, *Atomic Shield*, 362.
33. Joint Nuclear Energy Intelligence Committee, "Status of the USSR Atomic Energy Project—1 July 1949," Document 10 in "Detection of the First Soviet Nuclear Test, September 1949," National Security Archive, 9 Sept. 2019, https://nsarchive.gwu.edu/briefing-book/nuclear-vault/2019-09-09/detection-first-soviet-nuclear-test-september-1949 (accessed 26 July 2016); Strauss, *Men and Decisions*, 212.

34. Paul H. Nitze, "Certain Foreign Policy Alternatives, 1949–1953," 17 Oct. 1953, speech at Conference of Business Economists, Folder 5, Speeches, Statements, and Writings File, Box 193, Paul Nitze Papers, Manuscripts Division, Library of Congress, Washington, DC (hereafter LOC).
35. Foreign Reaction to Announcement of Atomic Explosion, Russian Folder 176-4, National Security: Atomic Energy, President's Secretary File, HSTPL; Shepley and Blair, *Hydrogen Bomb*, 21.
36. Steven L. Reardon, *History of the Office of the Secretary of Defense: The Formative Years, 1947–1950* (Washington, DC: Historical Office of the Secretary of Defense, 1984), 312 (hereafter, Reardon, *Formative Years*).
37. John M. Curatola, *Bigger Bombs for a Brighter Tomorrow: The Strategic Air Command and American War Plans at the Dawn of the Atomic Age, 1945–1950* (Jefferson, NC: McFarland, 2015), 30.
38. Thomas Etzold and John Lewis Gaddis, eds., *Containment: Documents on American Policy and Strategy, 1945–1950* (New York: Colombia University Press, 1999), 204.
39. "U.S. Objectives with Respect to the USSR to Counter Soviet Threats to US Security," NSC 20/4, in U.S. Department of State, *Foreign Relations of the United States*, vol. 1 (Washington, DC: U.S. Government Printing Office, Department of State, 1948), 663–69.
40. "U.S. Objectives with Respect to the USSR."
41. "U.S. Objectives with Respect to the USSR."
42. "U.S. Objectives with Respect to the USSR."
43. Samuel R. Williamson and Steven L. Rearden, *The Origins of US Nuclear Strategy, 1945–1953* (New York: St. Martin's, 1993), 95.
44. Reardon, *Formative Years*, 339.
45. Reardon, 350.
46. Paul H. Nitze, *From Hiroshima to Glasnost: At the Center of Decision* (New York: Grove Weidenfeld, 1989), 87.
47. George Gallup, *The Gallup Poll on Public Opinion 1935–1971*, 3 vols. (New York: Random House, 1972), 1:897.
48. Gallup, 899, 906.
49. Gallup, 857. Other responses were: unemployment, 16 percent; high cost of living, 11 percent; high cost of government waste, 9 percent; labor-management problems, 6 percent; housing, 5 percent; recession, 5 percent; and others or no opinion, 18 percent.
50. Dinah Walker, "Trends in U.S. Military Spending," Council on Foreign Relations, 15 July 2014, https://www.cfr.org/report/trends-us-military-spending (accessed 13 Apr. 2020).

51. Reardon, *Formative Years*, 387.
52. Drew Pearson, "End of the Marines? Summary of Remarks from General Frank Armstrong," *Washington Post,* 20 Mar. 1947, AAF Information Program B-36 Folder, Chief of Naval Operations (CNO), Organizational Research and Policy Division (OP-23) Papers, 1932–1949, Box 174, Naval History and Heritage Command, Washington, DC (hereafter NHHC).
53. Unnamed Newspaper Clipping, "Public Would Give Air Force Top Priority," 18 Oct. 1942, Scrapbook vol. 2 Folder, Box 1, Robert Lovett Papers, HSTPL.
54. Gallup, *Gallup Poll on Public Opinion*, 1:897.
55. Murray Green, Draft of "The B-36 Controversy in Retrospect," n.d., Box 102, Curtis E. LeMay Papers, LOC.
56. Omar Bradley, *A General's Life: An Autobiography*, with Clay Blair (reprint, Lexington, MA: Plunkett Lake, 2019), 508.
57. Christian Brahmstedt, ed., *Defense's Nuclear Agency, 1947–1997* (Washington, DC: Defense Threat Reduction Agency, U.S. Department of Defense, 2002), 58.
58. Hewlett and Duncan, *Atomic Shield*, 48.
59. Brien McMahon to Harry Truman, 21 Nov. 1949, Atomic Energy Bulk Dates, 1946–1949, File, Box 10, Subject File, Naval Aide to the President File, HSTPL.
60. Harry S. Truman to Sidney Souers, 26 July 1949, Sidney Souers Folder 173-9, NSC Reports, Subject File, President's Secretary Files, HSTPL.
61. Brien McMahon to Harry Truman, 30 May 1952, with attachment, "The Scale and Scope of Atomic Production: A Chronology of Leading Events," 30 Jan. 1952, Thermonuclear Folder 177-2, Atomic Weapons Box 177, National Security Atomic, Subject File, President's Secretary Files, HSTPL.
62. Memorandum, Lewis Strauss to D. Lilienthal, S. Pike, H. Smyth, and G. Dean, 5 Oct. 1949, Hydrogen Bomb Folder 1949, Lewis Strauss Papers, HHPL; Hewlett and Duncan, *Atomic Shield*, 373.
63. Rhodes, *Dark Sun*, 381.
64. David McCullough, *Truman* (New York: Simon and Schuster, 1992), 742.
65. As referenced in John Patrick Diggins, *The Proud Decades: America in War and Peace, 1941–1960* (New York: W. W. Norton, 1988), 64.
66. Arthur Krock, "Kremlin Casts Shadow on Most US Affairs," *New York Times*, 25 Dec. 1949, in Lisle A. Rose, *The Cold War Comes to Main Street* (Lawrence: University Press of Kansas, 1999), 22.
67. Rose, 26.
68. Arnold Offner, *Another Such Victory: President Truman and the Cold War, 1945–1953* (Stanford, CA: Stanford University Press, 2002), 202–3.
69. Gallup, *Gallup Poll Public Opinion*, 1:881.
70. Gallup, 907.

71. Halberstam, *The Fifties*, 7.
72. Offner, *Another Such Victory*, 266.
73. Halberstam, *The Fifties*, 10.
74. Elaine Tyler May, *Homeward Bound—American Families in the Cold War Era* (New York: Basic Books, 1999), xvii, xx.
75. "World Role for US," *New York Times*, 2 Mar. 1947.
76. Paul Nitze, interviewed by Richard D. McKinzie, 5, 6 Aug. 1975, Oral History Interviews, HSTPL, https://www.trumanlibrary.gov/library/oral-histories/nitzeph1 (accessed 12 Feb. 2018).
77. Carl von Clausewitz, *On War*, ed. Michael Howard and Peter Paret (Princeton, NJ: Princeton University Press, 1984), 89.

Chapter 1. Summer

1. David Holloway, *Stalin and the Bomb: The Soviet Union and Atomic Energy, 1939–1956* (New Haven, CT: Yale University Press, 1994), 213; Richard Rhodes, *Dark Sun: The Making of the Hydrogen Bomb* (New York: Simon and Schuster, 1995), 365; Jim Baggott, *The First War of Physics: The Secret History of the Atomic Bomb, 1939–1949* (New York: Pegasus, 2010), 450; Igor Golovin, "Kurchatov, a Man and His Work," trans. (from Russian) L. C. Ronson and P. A. Farmer, Culham Laboratory, Kurchatov Folder, Lewis Strauss Papers, Herbert Hoover Presidential Library, West Branch, IA (hereafter HHPL), chap. 16.
2. Michael Gordin, *Red Cloud at Dawn: Truman, Stalin, and the End of the Atomic Monopoly* (New York: Picador, 2009), 172; Baggott, *First War of Physics*, 450.
3. Gordin, *Red Cloud at Dawn*, 216; Golovin, "Kurchatov," chap. 16.
4. Nikita Khrushchev, *Khrushchev Remembers*, trans. and ed. Strobe Talbott, ed. Edward Crankshaw (Boston: Little, Brown, 1970), 251; Rhodes, *Dark Sun*, 182.
5. Holloway, *Stalin and the Bomb*, 218; Yuli Khariton and Yuri Smirnov, "The Khariton Version," *Bulletin of Atomic Scientists* 49, no. 4 (May 1993): 29; Nicholas Thompson, *The Hawk and the Dove: Paul Nitze, George Kennan, and the History of the Cold War* (New York: Henry Holt, 2009), 99; Gerard J. DeGroot, *The Bomb: A Life* (Cambridge, MA: Harvard University Press, 2004), 147; Baggott, *First War of Physics*, 451. The accounting itself may be apocryphal, but given the history of Beria and his methodologies, there is little doubt that something similar would have resulted had the test been a failure.
6. Holloway, *Stalin and the Bomb*, 218.
7. Amy Knight, *Beria, Stalin's First Lieutenant* (Princeton, NJ: Princeton University Press, 1993), 137.
8. Gordin, *Red Cloud at Dawn*, 164, 172; Baggott, *First War of Physics*, 448; Golovin, "Kurchatov," chap. 16. The bomb was also known as Reaktvnyi dvigatel Stalina–1 (RDS-1), which translates as "Stalin's Rocket Engine." But there were also other

names associated with the device—"Russia does it itself" (Rossiia delaet sama), "Rocket Engine S," "device 501," and "I-200."

9. Gordin, *Red Cloud at Dawn*, 177.
10. Holloway, *Stalin and the Bomb*, 216; Rhodes, *Dark Sun*, 367. Golovin, "Kurchatov," chap. 16. But Golovin claims, "There was none of the jubilant wild confusion that had broken out among the scientists in the United States."
11. Knight, *Beria*, 139.
12. Holloway, *Stalin and the Bomb*, 216.
13. Khariton and Smirnov, "Khariton Version," 29; DeGroot, *The Bomb*, 147; Rhodes, *Dark Sun*, 368.
14. Rhodes, *Dark Sun*, 367; DeGroot, *The Bomb*, 145.
15. Knight, *Beria*, 139; DeGroot, *The Bomb*, 145; Rhodes, *Dark Sun*, 367. According to Michael Gordin, Beria's anger was pointed at no one in particular. *Red Cloud at Dawn*, 176.
16. Khariton and Smirnov, "Khariton Version," 26; Gordin, *Red Cloud at Dawn*, 143; DeGroot, *The Bomb*, 140–41.
17. Kate Brown, *Plutopia: Nuclear Families, Atomic Cities, and the Great Soviet Union and American Plutonium Disasters* (Oxford; Oxford University Press, 2013), 109; Golovin, "Kurchatov," chap. 16.
18. As quoted in Gordin, *Red Cloud at Dawn*, 143.
19. Gordin, *Red Cloud at Dawn*, 144.
20. Khrushchev, *Khrushchev Remembers*, 362.
21. Baggott, *First War of Physics*, 428.
22. Khariton and Smirnov, "Khariton Version," 26; DeGroot, *The Bomb*, 136, 140; Baggott, *First War of Physics*, 427.
23. Rhodes, *Dark Sun*, 365; Golovin, "Kurchatov," chap. 16; Gordin, *Red Cloud at Dawn*, 166–67; Baggott, *First War of Physics*, 450.
24. Holloway, *Stalin and the Bomb*, 217; DeGroot, *The Bomb*, 145; Rhodes, *Dark Sun*, 365.
25. Memorandum, Central Intelligence Agency, Subj: Briefing for the Combined Chiefs of Staff Planners, 27 Sept. 1949, Intelligence File: CIA Memorandum, 1949, Box 213, President's Secretary Files, Harry S. Truman Presidential Library, Independence, MO (hereafter HSTPL).
26. Memorandum, Central Intelligence Agency, Subj: Briefing for the Combined Chiefs of Staff Planners, 27 Sept. 1949; "Estimate of the Effects of the Soviet Possession of the Atomic Bomb upon the Security of the United States and upon the Probabilities of Direct Soviet Military Action," 6 Apr. 1950, Document 11 in "U.S. Intelligence and the Detection of the First Soviet Nuclear Test, September 1949," ed. William Burr, National Security Archive, 22 Sept. 2009, https://nsarchive.gwu.edu/nukevault/ebb286/ (accessed 21 Apr. 2017).

27. DeGroot, *The Bomb*, 140; Baggott, *First War of Physics*, 362–63, 374; Golovin, "Kurchatov," chap. 12.
28. DeGroot, *The Bomb*, 140; Cynthia C. Kelly, ed., *The Manhattan Project: The Birth of the Atomic Bomb in the Words of Its Creators, Eyewitnesses, and Historians* (New York: Black Dog and Leventhal, 2007), 257; Golovin, "Kurchatov," chap. 12; Rhodes, *Dark Sun*, 29; DeGroot, *The Bomb*, 140.
29. Holloway, *Stalin and the Bomb*, 87; Rhodes, *Dark Sun*, 48, 106–7; Thompson, *Hawk and the Dove*, 98.
30. Holloway, *Stalin and the Bomb*, 87; Rhodes, *Dark Sun*, 106–8; Kelly, *Manhattan Project*, 257.
31. Released in 1941, the MAUD Report was a purely theoretical document based upon British research. Yet its value lay not only in its technological thesis in leveraging the fissionable qualities of uranium but also in the conclusion that an atomic bomb was indeed feasible. It provided a level of specificity that had not been articulated before regarding the requirements of an atomic-bomb program. The report comprised two volumes, the first dealing with atomic weapons, the second addressing the use of atomic power for industrial and other peaceful purposes.
32. Golovin, "Kurchatov," chap. 17; Rhodes, *Dark Sun*, 73; Baggott, *First War of Physics*, 17.
33. Gordin, *Red Cloud at Dawn*, 71.
34. R. H. Hillenkoetter, Memorandum to the President, "Estimate of the Status of Russian Atomic Energy Project," 6 July 1948, Document 3 in "U.S. Intelligence and the Detection of the First Soviet Nuclear Test, September 1949," ed. William Burr, National Security Archive, 22 Sept. 2009, https://nsarchive.gwu.edu/nukevault/ebb286/ (accessed 17 July 2016).
35. USAF Executive Directorate of Intelligence, "Estimate of Soviet Capabilities in the Field of Atomic Energy," 13 July 1949, Document 4, ibid. (accessed 26 July 2016); James Shepley and Clay Blair Jr., *The Hydrogen Bomb: The Men, the Menace, the Mechanism* (New York: David McKay, 1954), 13.
36. USAF Executive Directorate of Intelligence, "Estimate of Soviet Capabilities," 13 July 1949.
37. AC/AS-2 Comments at General Spaatz's Briefing of the Senate Committee, 12 June 1947 Binder, Box 47, Gen. Hoyt Vandenberg Papers, Manuscripts Division, Library of Congress, Washington, DC (hereafter LOC).
38. Golovin, "Kurchatov," chap. 15; Baggott, *First War of Physics*, 420–21; Rhodes, *Dark Sun*, 275.
39. Joint Committee on Atomic Energy, "Report of the Central Intelligence Agency," 17 Oct. 1949, Document 25 in "Detection of First Soviet Nuclear Test, September 1949," ed. William Burr, National Security Archive, 9 Sept. 2019,

https://nsarchive.gwu.edu/document/19596-national-security-archive-doc-25-document-12 (accessed 27 Oct. 2021).

40. Khariton and Smirnov, "Khariton Version," 20. The site was also known by other names, including Base 112, Site 550, and simply "the installation."
41. Holloway, *Stalin and the Bomb*, 197; DeGroot, *The Bomb*, 138; Baggott, *First War of Physics*, 419.
42. DeGroot, *The Bomb*, 143.
43. John Farquhar, *A Need to Know: The Role of Air Force Reconnaissance in War Planning, 1945–1953* (Maxwell AFB, AL: Air University Press, 2004), 37.
44. Memorandum for the Executive Secretary, NSC, Subj: Atomic Energy Program of the USSR, 20 Apr. 1949, Atomic Energy–Russia Folder, Box 176, NSC File, President's Secretary Files, HSTPL.
45. Joint Committee on Atomic Energy, "Report of the Central Intelligence Agency," 17 Oct. 1949.
46. Department of Energy, *Manhattan District History*, bk. 1, vol. 1, pg. 1.4, OpenNet System, https://www.osti.gov/opennet/manhattan_district.jsp (accessed 1 May 2017).
47. Gordin, *Red Cloud at Dawn*, 103–4; Brown, *Plutopia*, 84–85; Rhodes, *Dark Sun*, 182.
48. Gordin, *Red Cloud at Dawn*, 103–4; William J. Wilcox, *K-25: A Brief History of the Manhattan Project's "Biggest" Secret* (Oak Ridge, TN, 2008), 2–4, 7. Wilcox's publication is an expanded version of eighteen articles on the history of the K-25 that appeared in the *Oak Ridge Observer* in 2008.
49. Vincent C. Jones, *United States Army in World War II, Special Studies, Manhattan: The Army and the Atomic Bomb* (Washington, DC: Center for Military History, 1988), 10; Wilcox, *K-25*, 2, 25.
50. Holloway, *Stalin and the Bomb*, 173; Nicolaus Riehl, *Stalin's Captive: Nicolaus Riehl and the Soviet Race for the Bomb*, trans. and ed. Fredrick Seitz (Washington, DC: American Chemical Society, 1996), 95.
51. Knight, *Beria*, 133; Holloway, *Stalin and the Bomb*, 84.
52. Holloway, *Stalin and the Bomb*, 91–93; Rhodes, *Dark Sun*, 80.
53. Rhodes, *Dark Sun*, 71; Holloway, *Stalin and the Bomb*, 91; Golovin, "Kurchatov"; Brown, *Plutopia*, 97.
54. DeGroot, *The Bomb*, 128; Rhodes, *Dark Sun*, 137.
55. Kelly, *Manhattan Project*, 258.
56. Khariton and Smirnov, "Khariton Version," 22; DeGroot, *The Bomb*, 128; Holloway, *Stalin and the Bomb*, 138.
57. Khariton and Smirnov, "Khariton Version," 25; Rhodes, *Dark Sun*, 107; Charles R. Loeber, *Building the Bombs: A History of the Nuclear Weapons Complex* (Albuquerque: Sandia National Laboratories, 2002), 67.

58. Rhodes, *Dark Sun*, 60; Holloway, *Stalin and the Bomb*, 78; Kelly, *Manhattan Project*, 257; Golovin, "Kurchatov."
59. Holloway, *Stalin and the Bomb*, 78; Rhodes, *Dark Sun*, 46, 60; DeGroot, *The Bomb*, 130–31; Riehl, *Stalin's Captive*, 75.
60. DeGroot, *The Bomb*, 131; Holloway, *Stalin and the Bomb*, 96; Gordin, *Red Cloud at Dawn*, 31; Golovin, "Kurchatov."
61. Joint Committee on Atomic Energy, "Report of the Central Intelligence Agency," 17 Oct. 1949; DeGroot, *The Bomb*, 131; Golovin, "Kurchatov"; Rhodes, *Dark Sun*, 82.
62. U.S. Congress, Joint Committee on Atomic Energy, *Soviet Atomic Espionage*, Apr. 1951 (Washington, DC: U.S. Government Printing Office, 1951), 1, 3, 5; Rhodes, *Dark Sun*, 193.
63. Untitled and undated document, NSC File 176-4, Box 176, Subject File, President's Secretary Files, HSTPL.
64. Robert Chadwell Williams, *Klaus Fuchs, Atom Spy* (Cambridge MA; Harvard University Press, 1987), 119–20.
65. Memorandum for the Secretary of Defense, 20 Feb. 1949, File 176-4, Atomic Energy–Russia Folder, NSC File, Subject File, President's Secretary Files, HSTPL; Rhodes, *Dark Sun*, 80.
66. Williams, *Klaus Fuchs*, 79; Rhodes, *Dark Sun*, 118; Joint Committee on Atomic Energy, *Soviet Atomic Espionage*, 15; Stanley A. Blumberg and Gwinn Owens, *Energy and Conflict: The Life and Times of Edward Teller* (New York: Putnam, 1976), 228.
67. Joint Committee on Atomic Energy, *Soviet Atomic Espionage*, 7.
68. Rhodes, *Dark Sun*, 54, 57; Williams, *Klaus Fuchs*, 14, 16, 18–19, 23; Loeber, *Building the Bombs*, 62; Joint Committee on Atomic Energy, *Soviet Atomic Espionage*, 8, 17.
69. Williams, *Klaus Fuchs*, 29; Holloway, *Stalin and the Bomb*, 83; Loeber, *Building the Bombs*, 62.
70. Joint Committee on Atomic Energy, *Soviet Atomic Espionage*, 20.
71. Williams, *Klaus Fuchs*, 38–40; Kelly, *Manhattan Project*, 257; Loeber, *Building the Bombs*, 62–63; Joint Committee on Atomic Energy, *Soviet Atomic Espionage*, 16, 20.
72. Williams, *Klaus Fuchs*, 38–40; Holloway, *Stalin and the Bomb*, 80, 84; Kelly, *Manhattan Project*, 257.
73. Holloway, *Stalin and the Bomb*, 83.
74. Loeber, *Building the Bombs*, 62–63; Joint Committee on Atomic Energy, *Soviet Atomic Espionage*, 21.

75. Holloway, *Stalin and the Bomb*, 222; DeGroot, *The Bomb*, 128; Rhodes, *Dark Sun*, 74; Kelly, *Manhattan Project*, 236; Joint Committee on Atomic Energy, *Soviet Atomic Espionage*, 13, 14.
76. Williams, *Klaus Fuchs*, 61; Rhodes, *Dark Sun*, 57–58.
77. Rhodes, *Dark Sun*, 63; Williams, *Klaus Fuchs*, 61.
78. Jeremy Bernstein, *Nuclear Weapons: What You Need to Know* (Cambridge: Cambridge University Press, 2008), 250; Joint Committee on Atomic Energy, *Soviet Atomic Espionage*, 17. The account goes on to state that Fuchs did accept money but only to help support a sick family member.
79. David Halberstam, *The Fifties* (New York: Ballantine, 1993), 90; Joint Committee on Atomic Energy, *Soviet Atomic Espionage*, 14.
80. Williams, *Klaus Fuchs*, 76; Joint Committee on Atomic Energy, *Soviet Atomic Espionage*, 14.
81. Williams, *Klaus Fuchs*, 7.
82. Correspondence RE: Day of Trinity, Research Materials (Rough Notes), Box 1, Lansing Lamont Papers, HSTPL.
83. Williams, *Klaus Fuchs*, 45; Joint Committee on Atomic Energy, *Soviet Atomic Espionage*, 13.
84. Holloway, *Stalin and the Bomb*, 106–7; Joint Committee on Atomic Energy, *Soviet Atomic Espionage*, 24.
85. Holloway, *Stalin and the Bomb*, 137; Williams, *Klaus Fuchs*, 79; Loeber, *Building the Bombs*, 65.
86. Bernstein, *Nuclear Weapons*, 248–49; Rhodes, *Dark Sun*, 193–95; Joint Committee on Atomic Energy, *Soviet Atomic Espionage*, 7.
87. Khariton and Smirnov, "Khariton Version," 23.
88. Khariton and Smirnov, 23; Brown, *Plutopia*, 100; Baggott, *First War of Physics*, 370.
89. Kelly, *Manhattan Project*, 258; Rhodes, *Dark Sun*, 38, 42.
90. Kelly, *Manhattan Project*, 258.
91. Leslie Groves, *Now It Can Be Told: The Story of the Manhattan Project* (New York: Da Capo, 1962), 230–34, 248. Included in this effort was the aim to keep atomic assets from falling into the hands of the French. Ibid., 224–29; Holloway, *Stalin and the Bomb*, 174; Rhodes, *Dark Sun*, 155–56; Loeber, *Building the Bombs*, 44–45.
92. Normal M. Naimark, *The Russians in Germany: A History of the Soviet Zone of Occupation 1945–1949* (London: Belknap, 1995), 236; Loeber, *Building the Bombs*, 45.
93. Gordin, *Red Cloud at Dawn*, 73–74. The Swedes supposedly had the remaining 3 percent.

94. Naimark, *Russians in Germany*, 235; Gordin, *Red Cloud at Dawn*, 75.
95. Naimark, *Russians in Germany*, 235.
96. Gordin, *Red Cloud at Dawn*, 126.
97. Naimark, *Russians in Germany*, 236.
98. Caitlin E. Murdock, "A Gulag in the Erzgebirge? Forced Labor, Political Legitimacy, and Eastern German Uranium Mining in the Early Cold War," *Central European History Society of the American Historical Association* 47 (2014): 797; František Šedivý, *Uran für die Sowjetunion Mit einer Einführung von František Bártik* (Lepzing, Germany: Evangelische Verlaganstalt, 2015), 7.
99. Naimark, *Russians in Germany*, 238; Šedivý, *Uran für die Sowjetunion*, 16.
100. Naimark, *Russians in Germany*, 240–46; Murdock, "Gulag in the Erzgebirge?," 801.
101. Naimark, *Russians in Germany*, 242; "Legacy of Ashes: The Uranium Mines of Eastern Germany," *New York Times*, 19 Mar. 1991.
102. Gordin, *Red Cloud at Dawn*, 125; Rhodes, *Dark Sun*, 214.
103. Kevin Dietrich, "Remembering the Notorious 'Uranium Gulag,'" *The Cotton Boll Conspiracy* (blog), 7 Mar. 2014, https://southcarolina1670.wordpress.com/2014/03/07/remembering-the-notorious-uranium-gulag/ (accessed 2 May 2017).
104. Naimark, *Russians in Germany*, 248; Murdock, "Gulag in the Erzgebirge?," 810.
105. Murdock, "Gulag in the Erzgebirge?," 803.
106. Holloway, *Stalin and the Bomb*, 127.
107. Holloway, 127; DeGroot, *The Bomb*, 132.
108. Golovin, "Kurchatov."
109. War Department, Intelligence Division, "Analysis of Stalin's Address to Moscow Constituency," *Intelligence Review* no. 2, 21 Feb. 1946, p. 29, Combined Arms Research Library Archives, Fort Leavenworth, KS (hereafter CARL); DeGroot, *The Bomb*, 137.
110. Steven L. Reardon, *History of the Office of the Secretary of Defense: The Formative Years, 1947–1950* (Washington, DC: Office of the Secretary of Defense, 1984), 5 (hereafter Reardon, *Formative Years*).
111. Khariton and Smirnov, "Khariton Version," 27; Holloway, *Stalin and the Bomb*, 148.
112. DeGroot, *The Bomb*, 134; Holloway, *Stalin and the Bomb*, 132; Baggott, *First War of Physics*, 362; Rhodes, *Dark Sun*, 178.
113. War Department, Intelligence Division, "Soviet Measures to Stimulate Scientific Research and Development," *Intelligence Review* no. 40, 14 Nov. 1946, CARL.
114. Holloway, *Stalin and the Bomb*, 133; DeGroot, *The Bomb*, 133–34.
115. The number of dead is in stark contrast to the number of dead for the United States, which stands at 400,000 people. War Department, Intelligence Division,

"Strategic Weakness of the Soviet War Potential," *Intelligence Review* no. 41, 21 Nov. 1946, pp. 37–38, CARL; George Kennan, "Russia—Seven Years Later," n.d., p. 1, Subject File, Soviet Union, Box 4, Frank Roberts Papers, HSTPL.

116. Brown, *Plutopia*, 91.
117. War Department, Intelligence Division, "Strategic Weakness of the Soviet War Potential," 37–38.
118. Brown, *Plutopia*, 85.
119. Kennan, "Russia—Seven Years Later," 5.
120. Timothy Dunmore, *Soviet Politics, 1945–1953* (New York: St. Martin's, 1984), 45; Kennan, "Russia—Seven Years Later," 3.
121. War Department, Intelligence Division, "The Economy of the USSR," *Intelligence Review*, no. 30, 5 Sept. 1946, p. 39, CARL.
122. Dunmore, *Soviet Politics*, 45; Kennan, "Russia—Seven Years Later," 3–4.
123. War Department, Intelligence Division, "Soviet Measures to Stimulate Scientific Research and Development," 38.
124. War Department, Intelligence Division, 39.
125. War Department, Intelligence Division, 40.
126. Holloway, *Stalin and the Bomb*, 172.
127. Riehl, *Stalin's Captive*, 35; Groves, *Now It Can Be Told*, 245.
128. Groves, *Now It Can Be Told*, 245.
129. Riehl, *Stalin's Captive*, 91.
130. Holloway, *Stalin and the Bomb*, 110, 173.
131. Rhodes, *Dark Sun*, 178.
132. Holloway, *Stalin and the Bomb*, 137.
133. Khariton and Smirnov, "Khariton Version," 27; Rhodes, *Dark Sun*, 182. DeGroot, *The Bomb*, 136. But this is not to imply that Beria was unanimously lauded by the team of scientists working on the project. At least one prominent Soviet physicist, Peter Kapitza, complained about Beria to Stalin. In a letter dated 3 October 1945, he argued that Beria's management style was problematic and harmful to the atomic effort. As a result, Kapitza was removed from the project in 1946 and later lost his position as head of the Institute of Physical Problems.
134. Rhodes, *Dark Sun*, 44; Brown, *Plutopia*, 92–93.
135. Brown, *Plutopia*, 84, 86.
136. Baggott, *First War of Physics*, 432.
137. Knight, *Beria*, 6, 112.
138. Knight, 4.
139. Khrushchev, *Khrushchev Remembers*, 541.
140. Rhodes, *Dark Sun*, 182.
141. Khariton and Smirnov, "Khariton Version," 26; Baggott, *First War of Physics*, 361; DeGroot, *The Bomb*, 136.

142. Khariton and Smirnov, "Khariton Version," 26.
143. Baggott, *First War of Physics*, 421.
144. Knight, *Beria*, 93.
145. Baggott, *First War of Physics*, 361.
146. Brown, *Plutopia*, 108.
147. Brown, 109.
148. Department of Energy, *Manhattan District History*, bk. 1, vol. 1, OpenNet System, https://www.osti.gov/opennet/manhattan_district.jsp (accessed 15 Mar. 2017); Wilcox, *K-25*, 2–3.
149. George F. Kennan, *The Kennan Diaries*, ed. Frank Constigliola (New York: W. W. Norton, 2014), 226.
150. Reardon, *Formative Years*, 24.
151. The U.S. Army Air Force came into existence in 1941. Prior to this it was known as the U.S. Army Air Corps and before that the Air Service. For purposes of brevity I will refer to any antecedent of the Air Force as either the USAAF or USAAC.
152. Jeffery Barlow, *The Revolt of the Admirals, The Fight for Naval Aviation, 1945–1940* (Washington, DC: Brassey's, 1998), 4.
153. Robert Futrell, *Ideas, Concepts, and Doctrine: Basic Thinking in the United States Air Force, 1907–1960* (Maxwell AFB, AL: Air University Press, 1989), 66.
154. Futrell, 76.
155. Irving Brinton Holley, *United States Army in World War II, Special Studies: Buying Aircraft: Material Procurement for the Army Air Forces* (Washington, DC: Office of the Chief of Military History, 1964), 480–84.
156. Futrell, *Ideas, Concepts, and Doctrine*, 81.
157. Futrell, 87.
158. Futrell, 81.
159. Futrell, 91.
160. Futrell, 92.
161. Herman S. Wolk, *Planning and Organizing the Postwar Air Force, 1943–1947* (Washington, DC: Office of Air Force History, 1984), 219.
162. Actually, the USAAF asked Stimson to forward the request to Roosevelt.
163. U.S. Strategic Bombing Survey, *Summary Report (Pacific War)* (reprint, Maxwell AFB, AL: Air University Press, 1987), 50.
164. Minority Report to Secretary of War, Military Analysis Division (Anderson Report), 11 July 1946, in *The United States Strategic Bombing Survey*, 10 vols. (reprint, New York: Garland, 1976), 7:2.
165. "Annual Message to the Congress on the State of the Union," 6 Jan. 1947, *The Public Papers of the Presidents of the United States: Harry S. Truman, . . . 1947* (Washington, DC: U.S. Government Printing Office, 1962), 12.

166. Paul Hammond, *Super Carriers and B-36 Bombers: Appropriations, Strategy, and Politics* (Indianapolis: Bobbs-Merrill, 1963), 22.
167. Hammond, *Super Carriers and B-36 Bombers*, 22.
168. Murray Green, "The B-36 Controversy in Retrospect," n.d., Box 102, Curtis E. LeMay Papers, LOC.
169. Richard F. Haynes, *The Awesome Power: Harry S. Truman as Commander in Chief* (Baton Rouge: Louisiana State University Press, 1971), 100; David McCullough, *Truman* (New York: Simon and Schuster, 1992), 741.
170. David Bruce Dittmer, "The Firing of Admiral Denfeld: An Early Casualty of the Military Unification Process" (master's thesis, University of Nebraska–Omaha, 1995), 42.
171. McCullough, *Truman*, 402.
172. Stuart Symington, interviewed by James R. Fuchs, 29 May 1981, Oral History Interviews, HSTPL, https://www.trumanlibrary.gov/library/oral-histories/symton (accessed 4 Mar. 2019).
173. Barlow, *Revolt of the Admirals*, 48; Hammond, *Super Carriers and B-36 Bombers*, 23.
174. Barlow, *Revolt of the Admirals*, 309; Hammond, *Super Carriers and B-36 Bombers*, 23.
175. Air University, Bibliography Problem #4, Required Reading, 3 Oct. 1946, Army Air Force Information Program Folder B-36, Box 174, CNO, Organizational Research and Policy Division Papers, 1932–1949 (hereafter OP-23 Papers), Naval History and Heritage Command, Washington, DC (hereafter NHHC).
176. James E. Van Zandt, "Weakening Our National Security Can Please None Save the Kremlin," Extension of Remarks in the House of Representatives, 14 Apr. 1949, NME Folder 48-49 (2 of 5), Box 11, John L. Sullivan Papers, HSTPL.
177. Reardon, *Formative Years*, 396.
178. Reardon, *Formative Years*, 396; Kenneth Condit, *History of the Joint Chiefs of Staff: The Joint Chiefs of Staff and National Policy*, vol. 2, *1947–1949* (Washington, DC: Office of Joint History, 1996), 94–96.
179. Louis Denfeld, "The Only Carrier the Air Force Ever Sank," *Collier's*, 25 Mar. 1950, p. 47.
180. Robert J. Donovan, *Tumultuous Years: The Presidency of Harry S. Truman, 1949–1953* (New York: W. W. Norton, 1982), 58; Condit, *History of the Joint Chiefs of Staff*, 99.
181. Reardon, *Formative Years*, 341.
182. Reardon, 338–39.
183. Melvyn Leffler, *A Preponderance of Power: National Security, the Truman Administration, and the Cold War* (Stanford, CA: Stanford University Press, 1992), 304–5.

184. Hammond, *Super Carriers and B-36 Bombers*, 18; Reardon, *Formative Years*, 341–42.
185. Hammond, *Super Carriers and B-36 Bombers*, 19; Reardon, *Formative Years*, 341–42.
186. Hammond, *Super Carriers and B-36 Bombers*, 18; Condit, *History of the Joint Chiefs of Staff*, 124.
187. Spaatz Board Report, n.d., Atomic Bomb Project File, Policy File Series, Lauris Norstad Papers, Box 20, Dwight Eisenhower Presidential Library, Abilene, KS.
188. Speech made by Lt. Gen. Curtis E LeMay in Omaha, NE, 14 Dec. 1948, File VI 2-A Extracts from Speeches and Articles for the B-36, Box 95, LeMay Papers, LOC.
189. Wolk, *Planning and Organizing the Postwar Air Force*, 219.
190. AC/AS-2 Comments at General Spaatz's Briefing of the Senate Committee, 12 June 1947.
191. Headquarters Eighth Air Force Report, 2 Mar. 1949, Diary Folder, Box 103, LeMay Papers, LOC; Phillip S. Meilinger, "The Admirals' Revolt: Lessons for Today," *Parameters*, Sept. 1989, p. 86; Newspaper Article, *New York Herald Tribune*, 3 Mar. 1949, Newspaper Clippings 1948–1949 Folder [2 of 2], Box 1, Robert Landry Papers, HSTPL.
192. "B-50 Circles World Non Stop in 94 Hours Refueled 4 Times in Air LeMay It Could Deliver Atom Bomb Anywhere," *New York Herald Tribune*, 3 Mar. 1949, Newspaper Clippings 1948–1949 Folder [2 of 2], Box 1, Landry Papers, HSTPL.
193. Green, "B-36 Controversy in Retrospect," 7.
194. Green, 8.
195. Green, 9.
196. Green, 11.
197. "History of B-36 Procurement," Box 102, LeMay Papers, LOC, 1-2.
198. Walter S. Moody, *Building a Strategic Air Force* (Washington, DC: Air Force History and Museum Program, 1996), 100.
199. Moody, *Building a Strategic Air Force*, 100–101; "History of B-36 Procurement," LeMay Papers, 8-1.
200. Moody, *Building a Strategic Air Force*, 100–101; "History of B-36 Procurement," LeMay Papers, 8-1.
201. Statement of Arthur W. Radford before the Armed Services Committee of the House of Representatives Investigating the B-36 and Related Matters, Adm. Arthur Radford (10/7/49) File, Box 44, Francis Matthews Papers, HSTPL.
202. Don Pyeatt and Dennis Jenkins, *Cold War Peacemaker: The Story of Cowtown and the Convair B-36* (Manchester: Crecy, 2010), 70.
203. Daily Diary, 26 May 1949, Diary File, Box 103, LeMay Papers, LOC.

204. Elliot V. Converse III, *Rearming for the Cold War, 1945–1960* (Washington, DC: Office of the Secretary of Defense, 2011), 221, 225; U.S. Congress, House, *Investigation of the B-36 Bomber Program: Report of the Committee on Armed Services, . . . Pursuant to H. Res. 234 . . .* (Washington, DC: U.S. Government Printing Office, 1950), 17.
205. U.S. Congress, House, *Investigation of the B-36 Bomber Program*, 17.
206. U.S. Congress, House, 17.
207. Frank Pace Jr., Memorandum for the President, Subj: Atomic Warfare and B-36 Procurement Program from, 5 Apr. 1949, Subject File, NSC-Atomic, Atomic Energy Budget File, Box 174, President's Secretary Files, HSTPL.
208. Converse, *Rearming for the Cold War*, 346. The origins of the design are a classic "chicken and egg" argument. Some sources claim the aircraft was designed to carry the bomb, others that the design was modified to carry it.
209. Barlow, *Revolt of the Admirals*, 134.
210. Converse, *Rearming for the Cold War*, 349.
211. Converse, 350.
212. Steeljaw, "Naval Aviation Centennial: Neptune's Atomic Trident (1950)," *U.S. Naval Institute Blog*, 6 Feb. 2011, https://blog.usni.org/posts/2011/02/06/naval-aviation-centennial-neptunes-atomic-trident-1950 (accessed 17 Aug. 2017); Meilinger, "Admirals' Revolt," 86; Jerry Miller, *Stockpile and the Story behind 10,000 Strategic Nuclear Weapons* (Annapolis, MD: Naval Institute Press, 2010), 11.
213. Converse, *Rearming for the Cold War*, 350.
214. Steeljaw, "Naval Aviation Centennial: Neptune's Atomic Trident (1950)."
215. Converse, *Rearming for the Cold War*, 352.
216. Steeljaw, "Naval Aviation Centennial: Neptune's Atomic Trident (1950)."
217. Converse, *Rearming for the Cold War*, 351.
218. Converse, 6.
219. Green, "B-36 Controversy in Retrospect," 19.
220. Green, "B-36 Controversy in Retrospect," 6; AC/AS-2 Comments at General Spaatz's Briefing of the Senate Committee, 12 June 1947.
221. Hammond, *Super Carriers and B-36 Bombers*, 36.
222. Memorandum, Capt. Lynch/Lt. Cdr. Howard to Capt. Arleigh Burke, "Summary Position of the Navy," Attachment 2, 10 Oct. 1949, Summary Reports on B-36 Investigation, G-10 Folder, Box 169, OP-23 Papers, NHHC.
223. Daily Diary, 19 Sept. 1949, Diary File, Box 103, LeMay Papers, LOC.
224. Hammond, *Super Carriers and B-36 Bombers*, 2.
225. Hammond, 3.
226. D. Clark to Mr. Beauregard, Memo for CVA 58, 19 May 1949, Aircraft Carrier File, Box 10, Sullivan Papers, HSTPL.

227. U.S. Government, President's Air Policy Commission, *Survival in the Air Age: A Report* (Washington, DC: U.S. Government Printing Office, 1948), v.
228. U.S. Government, President's Air Policy Commission, 24–25, 31.
229. Hammond, *Super Carriers and B-36 Bombers*, 24; Green, "B-36 Controversy in Retrospect," 19; Robert K. Walsh, "The 70 Group Air Force," *Washington Evening Star*, 13 May 1948, Newspaper Clipping 1948–1949 Folder [1 of 2], Box 1, Landry Papers, HSTPL.
230. Donovan, *Tumultuous Years*, 53.
231. Reardon, *Formative Years*, 43; Donovan, *Tumultuous Years*, 60; Symington, interviewed by Fuchs, 29 May 1981.
232. Reardon, *Formative Years*, 43; James C. Olson, *Stuart Symington: A Life* (Columbia: University of Missouri Press, 2003), 175.
233. Reardon, *Formative Years*, 43; Olson, *Stuart Symington*, 175; Barlow, *Revolt of the Admirals*, 174; E. B. Potter, *Admiral Arleigh Burke* (New York: Random House, 1990), 319; Walter Isaacson and Evan Thomas, *The Wise Men: Six Friends and the World They Made* (New York: Simon and Shuster, 1986), 468–69.
234. Leffler, *Preponderance of Power*, 270; Robert S. Allen and William V. Shannon, *The Truman Merry-Go-Round* (New York: Vanguard, 1950), 449; Donovan, *Tumultuous Years*, 60.
235. Leffler, *Preponderance of Power*, 270; Eugene Zuckert, interviewed by Jerry N. Hess, 27 Sept. 1971, Oral History Interviews, HSTPL, https://www.trumanlibrary.gov/library/oral-histories/zuckert (accessed 4 Mar. 2019).
236. Isaacson and Thomas, *Wise Men*, 458.
237. Donovan, *Tumultuous Years*, 61; Isaacson and Thomas, *Wise Men*, 445.
238. Barlow, *Revolt of the Admirals*, 175–74.
239. Donovan, *Tumultuous Years*, 61; Isaacson and Thomas, *Wise Men*, 445.
240. Reardon, *Formative Years*, 46; Potter, *Admiral Arleigh Burke*, 319; McCullough, *Truman*, 738.
241. Lewis Strauss, interviewed by Jerry N. Hess, 16 June 1971, Oral History Interviews, HSTPL, https://www.trumanlibrary.gov/library/oral-histories/strauss; Richard Pfau, *No Sacrifice Too Great: The Life of Lewis L. Strauss* (Charlottesville: University Press of Virginia, 1984), 105.
242. Reardon, *Formative Years*, 47.
243. Allen and Shannon, *Truman Merry-Go-Round*, 446–47; "Master of the Pentagon," *Time*, June 6, 1949.
244. Reardon, *Formative Years*, 44; "Master of the Pentagon."
245. Reardon, *Formative Years*, 44; John Huston, ed., *American Airpower Comes of Age: General Henry H. "Hap" Arnold's War Diaries* (Maxwell AFB, AL: Air University Press, 2002), 56; Zuckert, interviewed by Hess, 27 Sept. 1971.

246. Huston, *American Airpower Comes of Age*, 56.
247. Holley, *United States Army in World War II, Special Studies: Buying Aircraft*, 175, 177.
248. Allen and Shannon, *Truman Merry-Go-Round*, 447.
249. Reardon, *Formative Years*, 48; Holley, *United States Army in World War II, Special Studies: Buying Aircraft*, 175.
250. Paolo E. Coletta, *The United States Navy and Defense Unification, 1947–1953* (East Brunswick, NJ: Associated University Press, 1981), 127.
251. "Master of the Pentagon."
252. Coletta, *United States Navy and Defense Unification*, 127.
253. "Master of the Pentagon."; Symington, interviewed by Fuchs, 29 May 1981.
254. Donovan, *Tumultuous Years*, 62.
255. Reardon, *Formative Years*, 411.
256. Dittmer, "Firing of Admiral Denfeld," 55.
257. Olson, *Stuart Symington* 179; "Master of the Pentagon."
258. G. L. Russel, Memorandum for the Secretary of the Navy, Subj: Legislative History of the Authority for the Construction of the Flush Deck Carrier, 24 Apr. 1949, Aircraft Carrier File, Box 10, Sullivan Papers, HSTPL; Denfeld, "Only Carrier the Air Force Ever Sank," 33, 46.
259. Hammond, *Super Carriers and B-36 Bombers*, 27; John L. Sullivan, Letter of Resignation as Secretary of the Navy, 26 Apr. 1949, appendix to Sullivan, interviewed by Jerry N. Hess, 27 Mar., 13 Apr. 1972, Oral History Interviews, HSTPL, https://www.trumanlibrary.org/oralhist/sullivan.htm (accessed 6 Sept. 2017).
260. Sullivan, Letter of Resignation, 26 Apr. 1949; Barlow, *Revolt of the Admirals*, 184; David Lawrence, "Johnson Seen Defying Congress by Halting Work on New Carrier," *Washington Evening Star*, 25 Apr. 1949, Aircraft Carrier File, Box 10, Sullivan Papers, HSTPL; Statement of Louis E. Denfeld before the Armed Services Committee, House of Representatives, Investigating the B-36 and Related Matters, 13 Oct. 1949, Adm. Louis E. Denfeld File, House Armed Services Committee Investigation of the B-36 and Related Matters (Oct. 10–17), Box 56: House Armed Services Committee Investigation of B-36 and Related Matters, Matthews Papers, ibid.; Denfeld, "Only Carrier the Air Force Ever Sank," 33, 46; Sullivan, Letter of Resignation, 26 Apr. 1949.
261. Dittmer, "Firing of Admiral Denfeld," 60.
262. Memorandum for the Secretary of the Air Force, Subj: Position of the USAF with Reference to the Super-Carrier, 9 Feb. 1949, Navy vs. Air Force File, Box 52, Vandenberg Papers, LOC.
263. Reardon, *Formative Years*, 411.

264. CNO Louis Denfeld, Memorandum for the Secretary of Defense, Subj: The USS *United States*, 22 Apr. 1949, Navy vs Air Force File, Box 52, Subject File, Vandenberg Papers, LOC.
265. Denfeld, "Only Carrier the Air Force Ever Sank," 33.
266. Chief of Staff U.S. Army, Memorandum for the Secretary of Defense, Subj: Construction of the Super Aircraft Carrier USS *United States*, 22 Apr. 1949, Navy vs. Air Force File, Box 52, Vandenberg Papers, LOC.
267. Memorandum for the Secretary of Defense, Subj: CVA-58 Project, 23 Apr. 1949, Navy vs. Air Force File, Box 52, Vandenberg Papers, LOC.
268. Memorandum for the Secretary of the Air Force, 9 Feb. 1949, Vandenberg Papers, LOC.
269. Hammond, *Super Carriers and B-36 Bombers*, 27–28.
270. Memorandum for the Secretary of Defense, 26 Apr. 1949, Navy vs. Air Force File, Box 52, Subject File, Vandenberg Papers, LOC.
271. Condit, *History of the Joint Chiefs of Staff*, 142; Memorandum for the Secretary of Defense, 26 Apr. 1949.
272. Memorandum for the Secretary of Defense, 26 Apr. 1949.
273. Memorandum for the Secretary of Defense, 26 Apr. 1949; Condit, *History of the Joint Chiefs of Staff*, 174–75.
274. Hammond, *Super Carriers and B-36 Bombers*, 28; Omar Bradley, *A General's Life: An Autobiography*, with Clay Blair (reprint, Lexington, MA: Plunkett Lake, 2019), 502; Reardon, *Formative Years*, 412; Denfeld, "Only Carrier the Air Force Ever Sank," 46; Sullivan, Letter of Resignation, 26 Apr. 1949.
275. Dittmer, "Firing of Admiral Denfeld," 62; Hammond, *Super Carriers and B-36 Bombers*, 28; Potter, *Admiral Arleigh Burke*, 320; Arleigh Burke, interviewed by Maurice Matloff, Historical Office of the Secretary of Defense, 9 Nov. 1983, https://history.defense.gov/Portals/70/Documents/oral_history/OH_Trans_BurkeArleigh11-9-1983.pdf?ver=2014-05-28-124343-427 (accessed 27 Oct. 2021).
276. Denfeld, "Only Carrier the Air Force Ever Sank," 47; Barlow, *Revolt of the Admirals*, 184; Sullivan, Letter of Resignation, 26 Apr. 1949; Statement of Louis E. Denfeld, before the Armed Services Committee, House of Representatives,13 Oct. 1949; Bradley, *General's Life*, 502.
277. Barlow, *Revolt of the Admirals*, 184; Lawrence, "Johnson Seen Defying Congress by Halting Work on New Carrier," 25 Apr. 1949; Statement of Louis E. Denfeld before the Armed Services Committee, House of Representatives, 13 Oct. 1949; Denfeld, "Only Carrier the Air Force Ever Sank," 33, 46; Sullivan, Letter of Resignation, 26 Apr. 1949.
278. Dittmer, "Firing of Admiral Denfeld," 62; Hammond, *Super Carriers and B-36 Bombers*, 28; Denfeld, "Only Carrier the Air Force Ever Sank," 46; Statement of Louis E. Denfeld before the Armed Services Committee, House of

Representatives, 13 Oct. 1949; Jeffrey Barlow, *From Hot War to Cold: The U.S. Navy and National Security Affairs, 1945–1955* (Stanford, CA; Stanford University Press, 2009), 212; Sullivan, Letter of Resignation, 26 Apr. 1949; Robert L. Dennison, interviewed by Jerry Hess, 6 Oct. 1971, Oral History Interviews, HSTPL, https://www.trumanlibrary.org/oralhist/dennisn2.htm (accessed 11 Feb. 2019).

279. Barlow, *From Hot War to Cold*, 213.
280. "Johnson Hints He Forced Out John Sullivan," *New York Herald Tribune*, 22 Oct. 1949, Aircraft Carrier File, Box 10, Sullivan Papers, HSTPL.
281. Sullivan, Letter of Resignation, 26 Apr. 1949.
282. "Master of the Pentagon," *Time*, 6 June 1949.
283. Barlow, *From Hot War to Cold*, 213; Potter, *Admiral Arleigh Burke*, 320.
284. "Rowboat Sailor," *Time*, May 23, 1949.
285. "Rowboat Sailor"; Dittmer, "Firing of Admiral Denfeld," 67.
286. Dittmer, "Firing of Admiral Denfeld," 71.
287. "Rowboat Sailor."
288. Barlow, *Revolt of the Admirals*, 206; Coletta, *United States Navy and Defense Unification*, 154; Dittmer, "Firing of Admiral Denfeld," 71; Potter, *Admiral Arleigh Burke*, 320.
289. Coletta, *United States Navy and Defense Unification*, 154; Allen and Shannon, *Truman Merry-Go-Round*, 468.
290. Burke, interviewed by Matloff, 9 Nov. 1983, 13.
291. Coletta, *United States Navy and Defense Unification*, 154.
292. Hanson Baldwin, "The Super Carrier II," *New York Times*, 29 Apr. 1949, Aircraft Carrier File, Box 10, Sullivan Papers, HSTPL.
293. Lawrence, "Johnson Seen Defying Congress by Halting Work on New Carrier," 25 Apr. 1949.
294. "A New Maginot Line—Extension of Remarks of Hon. Henry J. Latham of New York in the House of Representatives, Tuesday, May 17, 1949," *Congressional Record*, 17 May 1949, National Military Establishment File (4 of 5), Box 11, Sullivan Papers, HSTPL.
295. Donovan, *Tumultuous Years*, 65.
296. "History of B-36 Procurement," 23-5.
297. Potter, *Admiral Arleigh Burke*, 312.
298. Barlow, *Revolt of the Admirals*, 168–69; Potter, *Admiral Arleigh Burke*, 312–13, 318.
299. Green, "B-36 Controversy in Retrospect," 19.
300. Burke, interviewed by Matloff, 9 Nov. 1983, 8.
301. Barlow, *Revolt of the Admirals*, 171; Potter, *Admiral Arleigh Burke*, 322.
302. Potter, *Admiral Arleigh Burke*, 322.
303. "O'Kay Louis Drop Your Gun," copy in Aircraft Carrier File, Box 10, Sullivan Papers, HSTPL.

304. Barlow, *Revolt of the Admirals*, 208. Barlow, *From Hot War to Cold*, 215.
305. Barlow, *Revolt of the Admirals*, 208.
306. The aircraft's name eventually became known as the "Truculent Turtle." Truculent was intended to mean pugnacious or determined. The turtle was chosen as the nose art as a reference to the Aesop fable of the race with the hare; in this case the hare was the Air Force and the turtle represented the Navy. To add further insult to the Air Force, the turtle even had a lucky rabbit's foot trailing him.
307. Hammond, *Super Carriers and B-36 Bombers*, 30; Barlow, *Revolt of the Admirals*, 208; Green, "B-36 Controversy in Retrospect," 20; Reardon, *Formative Years*, 413; Dittmer, "Firing of Admiral Denfeld," 98; Potter, *Admiral Arleigh Burke*, 321; Meilinger, "Admiral's Revolt," 89.
308. Hammond, *Super Carriers and B-36 Bombers*, 30; Moody, *Building a Strategic Air Force*, 302; Phillip S. Meilinger, *Bomber: The Formation and Early Years of Strategic Air Command* (Maxwell AFB, AL: Air University Press, 2012), 145.
309. The term "Baltimore Whore" refers to the Martin Aircraft Company being based in that city, while the plane's short wings seemingly provided no visible means of support.
310. "The Great Bomber Fly Off," *Wings* 29, no. 3 (June 1994): 18–21.
311. "Great Bomber Fly Off," 21.
312. John C. Fredriksen, *The B-45 Tornado: An Operational History of the First American Jet Bomber* (Jefferson, NC: McFarland, 2009), 5–6; Michael E. Brown, *Flying Blind: The Politics of the US Strategic Bomber Program* (Ithaca, NY: Cornell University Press, 1992), 77; "Great Bomber Fly Off," 15. There is a small disparity between Fredriksen and Brown regarding the range of the proposed design, with Brown claiming that the Air Force required a range of 2,500 miles.
313. "Great Bomber Fly Off," 16; Fredriksen, *B-45 Tornado*, 6.
314. Fredriksen, *B-45 Tornado*, 10.
315. Brown, *Flying Blind*, 83.
316. Fredriksen, *B-45 Tornado*, 17.
317. Fredriksen, *B-45 Tornado*, 17; Brown, *Flying Blind*, 81.
318. Fredriksen, *B-45 Tornado*, 17; Brown, *Flying Blind*, 81.
319. "Great Bomber Fly Off," 24, 44, 47–50; Fredriksen, *B-45 Tornado*, 17.
320. Moody, *Building a Strategic Air Force*, 239.
321. Olson, *Stuart Symington* 184; Green, "B-36 Controversy in Retrospect," 20.
322. Olson, *Stuart Symington*, 184.
323. Green, "B-36 Controversy in Retrospect"; Barlow, *From Hot to Cold War*, 216.
324. "Worth Called," *Army-Navy Journal* 87, no. 4, 24 Sept. 1949, p. 103; Proceedings from the Naval Court of Inquiry into the Circumstances Surrounding Preparation of Anonymous Document Furnished Member of Congress Concerning

Contracts for B-36 Aircraft and Other Matters, 21 Sept. 1949, H-1 B-36 Naval Court Inquiry Folder, Box 169, OP-23 Papers, NHHC.

325. Jeffrey Barlow, "Nation Aviation's Most Serious Crisis," *Naval History* 25, no. 6 (Dec. 2011); Coletta, *United States Navy and Defense Unification*, 170; Hammond, *Super Carriers and B-36 Bombers*, 30–31, Green, "B-36 Controversy in Retrospect," 20–22; Reardon, *Formative Years*, 415; Dittmer, "Firing of Admiral Denfeld," 98; Barlow, *Revolt of the Admirals*, 207–9; "Worth Called," 103.
326. Burke, interviewed by Matloff, 9 Nov. 1983, 11–12.
327. Copy of the Anonymous Document Introduced into the Record Hearings, 13 Aug. 1949, B-36 File Investigation Committee, Armed Services, House of Representatives Report, Oct. 1949, Box 10, Sullivan Papers, HSTPL.
328. Copy of the Anonymous Document.
329. "It's a Lie," *Time*, 13 June 1949.
330. Copy of the Anonymous Document, 13 Aug. 1949.
331. The B-49 had its own problems during its troubled development. Poor control characteristics, limited bomb load, and awkward internal design were at the top of a long list of engineering issues. The program was canceled more for the technical maladies of the cutting-edge aircraft than for any other reason.
332. Copy of the Anonymous Document.
333. Copy of the Anonymous Document.
334. Proceedings from the Naval Court of Inquiry, 21 Sept. 1949; Bradley, *General's Life*, 507.
335. U.S. Congress, House, *Investigation of the B-36 Bomber Program*, 2; Reardon, *Formative Years*, 414; Olson, *Stuart Symington*, 180; "B-36 Defense Policy Investigations," CQ Almanac 1949, *Congressional Quarterly*, 5th ed., http://library.cqpress.com/cqalmanac/cqal149-1400649 (accessed 1 Oct. 2017).
336. "The Attack Opens," *Time*, 6 June 1949.
337. U.S. Congress, House, *Investigation of the B-36 Bomber Program*, 1; Hammond, *Super Carriers and B-36 Bombers*, 31; Barlow, *From Hot War to Cold*, 220.
338. Barlow, *From Hot War to Cold*, 221; Meilinger, "Admirals Revolt," 88; U.S. Congress, House, *Investigation of the B-36 Bomber Program*; Symington, interviewed by Fuchs, 29 May 1981.
339. U.S. Congress, House, *Investigation of the B-36 Bomber Program*, 2; Hammond, *Super Carriers and B-36 Bombers*, 31; Dittmer, "Firing of Admiral Denfeld," 95; Barlow, *Revolt of the Admirals*, 217; U.S. Congress, House, *Unification and Strategy: A Report of Investigation by the Committee on Armed Services House of Representatives*... (Washington, DC: U.S. Government Printing Office, 1950), 7.
340. Dittmer, "Firing of Admiral Denfeld," 95; U.S. Congress, House, *Investigation of the B-36 Bomber Program*, 32–33; Condit, *History of the Joint Chiefs of Staff*, 177–78.

341. Statement of Arthur W. Radford before the Armed Services Committee of the House of Representatives Investigating the B-36 and Related Matters, Adm. Arthur Radford (10/7/49) File, Box 44, Matthews Papers, HSTPL.
342. Dittmer, "Firing of Admiral Denfeld," 96; Hammond, *Super Carriers and B-36 Bombers*, 32; Barlow, *Revolt of the Admirals*, 218; Andrew L. Lewis, "The Revolt of the Admirals," Air Command and Staff College Paper, Air University, Maxwell AFB, AL, 1988; Condit, *History of the Joint Chiefs of Staff*, 180.
343. Barlow, *Revolt of the Admirals*, 218.
344. Hammond, *Super Carriers and B-36 Bombers*, 32; Dittmer, "Firing of Admiral Denfeld," 96.
345. Hammond, *Super Carriers and B-36 Bombers*, 32.
346. Memorandum to Mr. Symington, General Vandenberg, and General Norstad, Subj: The Super-Carrier Study, 11 Apr. 1949, Navy vs. Air Force File, Box 52, Vandenberg Papers, LOC.
347. Copy of the Anonymous Document, 13 Aug. 1949.
348. David Alan Rosenberg, "American Atomic Strategy and the Hydrogen Bomb Decision," *Journal of American History* 66, no. 1 (June 1979): 72; Rosenberg, "The Origins of Overkill: Nuclear Weapons and American Strategy, 1945–1960," *International Security* 7, no. 4 (Spring 1983): 16; Condit, *History of the Joint Chiefs of Staff*, 169; Samuel R. Williamson and Steven L. Reardon, *The Origins of US Nuclear Strategy, 1945–1953* (New York: St. Martin's, 1993), 104; L. Douglas Keeney, *General Curtis LeMay and the Countdown to Nuclear Annihilation* (New York; St. Martin's, 2011), 55–56; Meilinger, *Bomber*, 151.
349. Thomas Etzold and John Lewis Gaddis, eds., *Containment: Documents on American Policy and Strategy, 1945–1950* (New York; Columbia University Press, 1978), 361–62; Condit, *History of the Joint Chiefs of Staff*, 169; Moody, *Building a Strategic Air Force*, 295; Meilinger, *Bomber: The Formation and Early Years of Strategic Air Command*, 151.
350. Etzold and Gaddis, *Containment*, 363; Condit, *History of the Joint Chiefs of Staff*, 169.
351. Etzold and Gaddis, *Containment*, 364; Condit, *History of the Joint Chiefs of Staff*, 169.
352. Etzold and Gaddis, *Containment*, 361–63; Condit, *History of the Joint Chiefs of Staff*, 168–69; Arnold Offner, *Another Such Victory: President Truman and the Cold War, 1945–1953* (Stanford, CA: Stanford University Press, 2002), 359.
353. "Evaluation of the Effect Resulting from the Strategic Air Offensive [Harmon Report]," in Etzold and Gaddis, *Containment*, 324; David Kunsman and Douglas Lawson, *A Primer on U.S. Nuclear Policy*, Sandia Report SAND 2001-0053 (Albuquerque: Sandia National Laboratories, 2001), 23; Meilinger, *Bomber*, 151–52.

354. Rosenberg, "American Atomic Strategy and the Hydrogen Bomb Decision," 77–78; "Evaluation of the Effect Resulting from the Strategic Air Offensive [Harmon Report]," 361; Rosenberg, "Origins of Overkill," 16; Williamson and Reardon, *Origins of US Nuclear Strategy*, 104.
355. Harry Truman, *Years of Trial and Hope* (Garden City, NY: Doubleday, 1956), 305.
356. Rosenberg, "American Atomic Strategy and the Hydrogen Bomb Decision," 73; Kunsman and Lawson, *Primer on U.S. Nuclear Policy*, 24; Moody, *Building a Strategic Air Force*, 295; Bradley, *General's Life*, 501.
357. Bradley, *General's Life*, 501.
358. Meilinger, *Bomber*, 152.
359. Bradley, *General's Life*, 501.
360. Converse, *Rearming for the Cold War*, 30; John Ponturo, *Analytical Support for the Joint Chiefs of Staff: The WSEG Experience, 1948–1976* (Arlington, VA: Institute for Defense Analysis International Studies Division, 1979), xii.
361. Ponturo, *Analytical Support for the Joint Chiefs of Staff*, 34.
362. Ponturo, 41.
363. Converse, *Rearming for the Cold War*, 30; Ponturo, *Analytical Support for the Joint Chiefs of Staff*, 71.
364. *The Strategic Bombing Myth*, [1949], National Military Establishment, Folder 5 of 5, Box 12, Sullivan Papers, HSTPL.
365. Green, "B-36 Controversy in Retrospect," 29.
366. Frank D'Olier to Louis Johnson, 23 Aug. 1949, B-36 Investigation (Folder 2), Box 42, Vandenberg Papers, LOC; Green, "B-36 Controversy in Retrospect," 30.
367. D'Olier to Johnson, 23 Aug. 1949.
368. D. V. Gallery, "An Admiral Talks Back to the Airmen," *Saturday Evening Post* 221, no. 52, 25 June 1949, p. 25.
369. Potter, *Admiral Arleigh Burke*, 321.
370. Gallery, "An Admiral Talks Back to the Airmen," 138.
371. Potter, *Admiral Arleigh Burke*, 321.
372. Reardon, *Formative Years*, 371.
373. Reardon, *Formative Years*, 373; Barlow, *From Hot War to Cold*, 224.
374. Barlow, *From Hot War to Cold*, 224.
375. Barlow, 222.
376. Dittmer, "Firing of Admiral Denfeld," 97; Barlow, *From Hot to Cold War*, 223.
377. Dittmer, "Firing of Admiral Denfeld," 97; Barlow, *From Hot War to Cold*, 224, 226; Condit, *History of the Joint Chiefs of Staff*, 180.
378. Hammond, *Super Carriers and B-36 Bombers*, 40.

379. "Report to the President of the United States from the Atomic Energy Commission January 1–April 1, 1947," 3 Apr. 1947, AEC Folder, Box 175, NSC Reports, President's Secretary Files, HSTPL.
380. Williamson and Reardon, *Origins of US Nuclear Strategy*, 63–64; Rosenberg, "American Atomic Strategy and the Hydrogen Bomb Decision," 65; "Report to the President of the United States from the Atomic Energy Commission January 1–April 1, 1947," 3 Apr. 1947; Christian Brahmstedt, ed., *Defense's Nuclear Agency, 1947–1997* (Washington, DC: Defense Threat Reduction Agency, U.S. Department of Defense, 2002), 12; Keeney, *15 Minutes*, 34.
381. James Abrahamson and Paul Carew, *Vanguard of American Deterrence: The Sandia Pioneers, 1946–1949* (Westport, CT: Praeger, 2002), 20; Rhodes, *Dark Sun*, 212; Keeney, *15 Minutes*, 34.
382. Abrahamson and Carew, *Vanguard of American Deterrence*, 41–42.
383. Keeney, *15 Minutes*, 39.
384. Gregg Herken, *The Winning Weapon: The Atomic Bomb in the Cold War, 1945–1950* (Princeton, NJ: Princeton University Press, 2014), 239; Keeney, *15 Minutes*, 39.
385. Brien McMahon to Harry S. Truman, 30 May 1952, Attachment: "The Scale and Scope of Atomic Production—A Chronology of Leading Events," Atomic Weapons: Thermonuclear Folder 177-2, Box 177, NSC Reports, Atomic Subject File, President's Secretary Files, HSTPL, 12 (hereafter Attachment: Scale and Scope of Atomic Production).
386. Brahmstedt, *Defense's Nuclear Agency*, 12; Necah S. Furman, "Sandia National Laboratories: A Product of Postwar Readiness, 1945–1950" (report, Sandia National Laboratories, Albuquerque, NM, 1988), 11.
387. David Alan Rosenberg, "US Nuclear Stockpile, 1945 to 1950," *Bulletin of Atomic Scientists* 38, no. 5 (May 1982): 26; Furman, "Sandia National Laboratories," 17.
388. Attachment: Scale and Scope of Atomic Production, 3.
389. Furman, "Sandia National Laboratories," 17.
390. It can be assumed that the number was provided orally and not in written form as evidenced in the document. Rosenberg, "Origins of Overkill," 14; "Report to the President of the United States from the Atomic Energy Commission, January 1–April 1, 1947," 3 Apr. 1947; Rosenberg, "US Nuclear Stockpile 1945 to 1950," 26; Reardon, *Formative Years*, 439; Loeber, *Building the Bombs*, 81.
391. JSPG 496/4, "Broiler," 11 Feb. 1948, p. 2, in *America's Plans for War against the Soviet Union, 1945–1950*, ed. Steven T. Ross and David Alan Rosenberg, vol. 13, *Evaluating the Air Offensive: The WSEG I Study* (New York: Garland, 1990), Annex A, 14; Rosenberg, "Origins of Overkill," 16; Rosenberg, "American Atomic Strategy and the Hydrogen Bomb Decision," 76.

392. Rosenberg, "American Atomic Strategy and the Hydrogen Bomb Decision," 66; "Report to the President of the United States From the Atomic Energy Commission January 1–April 1, 1947," 3 Apr. 1947; Williamson and Reardon, *Origins of US Nuclear Strategy*, 34; Rosenberg, "US Nuclear Stockpile 1945 to 1950," 15; Brahmstedt, *Defense's Nuclear Agency*, 6, 11; DeGroot, *The Bomb*, 159.
393. Attachment: Scale and Scope of Atomic Production, 3.
394. Attachment: Scale and Scope of Atomic Production, 5.
395. Attachment: Scale and Scope of Atomic Production.
396. Attachment: Scale and Scope of Atomic Production, 6.
397. Attachment: Scale and Scope of Atomic Production, 7; Rosenberg, "US Nuclear Stockpile 1945 to 1950," 26. There appears to be a discrepancy between the two documents, however, the Rosenberg article is more exacting, given that the HSTPL document gives no specific numbers.
398. Attachment: Scale and Scope of Atomic Production, 8; Rosenberg, "American Atomic Strategy and the Hydrogen Bomb Decision," 71.
399. Attachment: Scale and Scope of Atomic Production, 8; Keeney, *15 Minutes*, 56.
400. Atomic Energy Commission, Thermonuclear Weapons Program Chronology, App., p. 131, Hydrogen Bomb Folder 1950, Lewis Strauss Papers, HHPL; Attachment: Scale and Scope of Atomic Production.
401. Attachment: Scale and Scope of Atomic Production, 8; Condit, *History of the Joint Chiefs of Staff*, 284.
402. Report to the President of the United States by the Special Committee of the National Security Council on the Proposed Acceleration of the Atomic Energy Program, 10 Oct. 1949, Atomic Energy: Expansion of Atomic Energy Program Folder, Atomic Energy: Advisory Committee and Atomic Energy Plans, Box 174, NSC Reports, Subject File, President's Secretary Files, HSTPL.
403. Reardon, *Formative Years*, 443.
404. Atomic Energy Commission, Thermonuclear Weapons Program Chronology, App., p. 131; Attachment: Scale and Scope of Atomic Production.
405. Richard Hewlett and Francis Duncan, *Atomic Shield: A History of the United States Atomic Energy Commission*, vol. 2 (Berkeley: University of California Press, 1990), 183.
406. David E. Lilienthal, *The Journals of David E Lilienthal*, vol. 2, *The Atomic Energy Years, 1945–1950* (New York: Harper and Row, 1964), 553.
407. Attachment: Scale and Scope of Atomic Production, 12.
408. Offner, *Another Such Victory*, 359; Truman, *Years of Trial and Hope*, 304.
409. Correspondence, White House to Mr. Souers, 26 July 1949, Reports: Sidney Souers File, Folder 173-9, Box 175, NSC Reports, Subject File, President's Secretary Files, HSTPL; Executive Office of the President NSC Memorandum for the

President, 10 Oct. 1949, Expansion of the Atomic Energy Program Folder 175-11, ibid.; Condit, *History of the Joint Chiefs of Staff*, 284; Williamson and Reardon, *Origins of US Nuclear Strategy*, 104; Reardon, *Formative Years*, 443.

410. White House to Mr. Souers, 26 July 1949; Attachment: Scale and Scope of Atomic Production, 12.
411. White House to Mr. Souers, 26 July 1949.
412. U.S. Congress, House, *Unification and Strategy Report of Investigation by the Committee on Armed Services House of Representatives*... (Washington, DC: U.S. Government Printing Office, 1950), 7.
413. Moody, *Building a Strategic Air Force*, 3002–3.
414. Hammond, *Super Carriers and B-36 Bombers*, 32; Barlow, *Revolt of the Admirals*, 226.
415. "History of B-36 Procurement: Presented to the House Armed Services Committee by Major General F. H. Smith Jr.," Subject File: B-36 Procurement, Box 119, Nathan Twining Papers, LOC, 10-2.
416. "History of B-36 Procurement," Twining Papers, 10-4.
417. "History of B-36 Procurement," LeMay Papers, 10-3.
418. U.S. Congress, House, *Investigation of the B-36 Bomber Program*, 15. The studies Smith used were the Finnletter Commission Report and the Hinshaw-Brewster Report.
419. Robert K. Walsh, "The 70 Group Air Force," *Washington Evening Star*, 13 May 1948; Newspaper Clippings 1948–1949 Folder [1 of 2], Box 1, Landry Papers, HSTPL.
420. U.S. Congress, House, *Investigation of the B-36 Bomber Program*, 22–23.
421. U.S. Congress, House, 7, 10.
422. Moody, *Building a Strategic Air Force*, 102–3; Barlow, *From Hot War to Cold*, 225; U.S. Congress, House, *Investigation of the B-36 Bomber Program*, 14.
423. Barlow, *From Hot War to Cold*, 225; U.S. Congress, House, *Investigation of the B-36 Bomber Program*, 14; Barlow, *Revolt of the Admirals*, 227.
424. "History of B-36 Procurement," LeMay Papers, 10-2.
425. Curtis LeMay and MacKinlay Kantor, *Mission with LeMay* (Garden City, NY: Doubleday, 1965), 475.
426. "Man in the First Plane," *Time*, 4 Sept. 1950; Olson, *Stuart Symington*, 186.
427. U.S. Congress, House, *Investigation of the B-36 Bomber Program*, 26–29.
428. U.S. Congress, House, 28.
429. Olson, *Stuart Symington*, 186.
430. Transcript of Stuart Symington Testimony to the House Armed Services Committee, Investigation Folder [1 of 2], Box 6, Symington Papers, HSTPL.
431. Transcript of Symington Testimony, 26.

432. Newspaper clipping, "Symington's Show," *Washington Post*, 16 Aug. 1949, Investigation Folder [1 of 2], Box 6, Symington Papers, HSTPL.
433. Olson, *Stuart Symington*, 186.
434. "Navy Aide Admits B-36 Memo; Surprise Witness Says He Acted Alone on Tip That Began Inquiry," *Washington Evening Star*, 24 Aug. 1949, Subject File, B-36 Clippings (1 of 2), Dan A. Kimball Papers, HSTPL; Olson, *Stuart Symington*, 188.
435. "Navy Aide Admits B-36 Memo," 24 Aug. 1949; "The B-36 Bombs the Black Paper," *Newsweek*, 5 Sept. 1949, p. 14.
436. "B-36 Bombs the Black Paper," 14.
437. "B-36 Bombs the Black Paper," 14.
438. "Meet the Author," National Affairs Section, *Time*, 5 Sept. 1949; "Navy Aide Admits B-36 Memo," 24 Aug. 1949; Barlow, *From Hot War to Cold War*, 227; "B-36 Bombs the Black Paper," 14; Olson, *Stuart Symington*, 188; Symington, interviewed by Fuchs, 29 May 1981.
439. "Navy Aide Admits B-36 Memo," 24 Aug. 1949; Proceedings from the Naval Court of Inquiry, 21 Sept. 1949, 3.
440. Green, "B-36 Controversy in Retrospect," 25.
441. "Meet the Author," 5 Sept. 1949; "B-36 Bombs the Black Paper," 14; Barlow, *Revolt of the Admirals*, 232.
442. "Meet the Author," 5 Sept. 1949.
443. "Navy Aide Admits B-36 Memo," 24 Aug. 1949.
444. "Meet the Author," 5 Sept. 1949; Proceedings from the Naval Court of Inquiry into the Circumstances Surrounding Preparation of Anonymous Document Furnished Member of Congress Concerning Contracts for B-36 Aircraft and Other Matters, 22 Sept. 1949, H-1 B-36 Naval Court Inquiry Folder, Box 169, OP-23 Papers, NHHC; "The Black Paper," *Newsweek*, 5 Sept. 1949.
445. Statement by Glenn L Martin, Chairman of the Board, the Glenn L. Marin Company, Baltimore, MD, before U.S. Navy Court of Inquiry, Washington, DC, 8 Sept. 1949, H-1 B-36 Naval Court of Inquiry Folder, Box 169, OP-23 Papers, NHHC.
446. Appointment Letter, Secretary of the Navy, Francis Matthews, to Adm. Thomas C. Kinkaid, Subj: Court of Inquiry into the Circumstances Surrounding Preparation of Anonymous Document Furnished Member of Congress Concerning Contracts for B-36 Aircraft and Other Matters, 25 Aug. 1949, H-1 B-36 Naval Court Inquiry Folder, Box 169, OP-23 Papers, NHHC.
447. U.S. Congress, House, *Investigation of the B-36 Bomber Program*, 32–33; Reardon, *Formative Years*, 415; Olson, *Stuart Symington*, 189; Potter, *Admiral Arleigh Burke*, 321–22; Barlow, *From Hot to Cold War*, 227; Barlow, *Revolt of the Admirals*, 232; Meilinger, *Bomber*, 145.

448. U.S. Congress, House, *Investigation of the B-36 Bomber Program*, 32–33.
449. Floyd Odlum to Francis Matthews, 30 Aug. 1949, B-36 Investigation (Folder 2), Box 42, Vandenberg Papers, LOC.
450. Floyd Odlum to Louis Johnson, 30 Aug. 1949, B-36 Investigation (Folder 2), Box 42, Vandenberg Papers, LOC.
451. Memorandum, W. Stuart Symington for Secretary Johnson, 24 Aug. 1949, Louis Johnson File, Box 6, Symington Papers, HSTPL.
452. Editorial Clipping, n.d., Loose document, Box 42, Vandenberg Papers, LOC.
453. Hanson Baldwin, "The Unheard Opposition," *New York Times*, 14 Aug. 1949, p. 30; Meilinger, "Admirals' Revolt," 86.

Chapter 2. Autumn

1. Proclamation of the Central People's Government of the PRC, 1 Oct. 1949 [source: *People's Daily*, 2 Oct. 1949], *Selected Works of Mao Tse-tung*, https://www.marxist.org/reference/archive/mao/selectedworks (accessed 12 Feb. 2018); Kevin Peraino, *A Force So Swift: Mao, Truman, and the Birth of Modern China, 1949* (New York: Crown, 2017), 210–11; Ryan Grauer, *Commanding Military Power* (Cambridge: Cambridge University Press, 2016), 99; Kenneth Condit, *History of the Joint Chiefs of Staff: The Joint Chiefs of Staff and National Policy*, vol. 2, *1947–1949* (Washington, DC: Office of Joint History, 1996), 254–55.
2. "Democratic Leadership," *Time*, 3 Oct. 1949.
3. "The Chinese People Have Stood Up," 21 Sept. 1949, Opening Address of Mao Tse-Tung, Chairman of the Chinese Communist Party at the First Plenary Session of the Chinese People's Political Consultative Conference, *Selected Works of Mao Tse-tung*, https://www.marxist.org/reference/archive/mao/selectedworks (accessed 12 Feb. 2018).
4. Paul H. Nitze, interviewed by Richard D. McKinzie, 5, 6 Aug. 1975, Oral History Interviews, Harry S. Truman Presidential Library, Independence, MO (hereafter HSTPL), https://www.trumanlibrary.gov/library/oral-histories/nitzeph1 (accessed 12 Feb. 2018); by Paul H. Nitze, "The Relation of the Political End to the Military Objective," 28 Oct. 1954, speech at Maxwell Air Force Base, AL, Folder 6, Speeches, Statements, and Writing File, Box 193, Paul Nitze Papers, Manuscripts Division, Library of Congress, Washington, DC (hereafter LOC); Nitze, "Certain Foreign Policy Alternatives 1949–1953," 17 Oct. 1953, speech at Conference of Business Economists, Folder 5, ibid.; Nitze, address at National Security Orientation Conference, Pentagon, 30 Nov. 1940, ibid.
5. Albert C. Wedemeyer, *Wedemeyer Reports!* (New York: Henry Holt, 1958), 323; Jay Taylor, *The Generalissimo: Chiang Kai-shek and the Struggle for Modern China* (Cambridge, MA: Harvard University Press, 2009), 323.

6. Taylor, *Generalissimo*, 182; U.S. Department of State, *China White Paper: August 1949* (reprint, Stanford, CA: Stanford University Press, 1967), 31 (hereafter *China White Paper*).
7. *China White Paper*, 37.
8. Jonathan D. Spence, *The Gate of Heavenly Peace: The Chinese and Their Revolution (1895–1980)* (New York: Penguin, 1981), 237; *China White Paper*, 43; Richard Bernstein, *China 1945: Mao's Revolution and America's Fateful Choice* (New York: Knopf, 2014), 26.
9. Spence, *Gate of Heavenly Peace*, 238; Gary J. Bjorge, *Moving the Enemy: Operational Art in the Chinese PLA's Huai Hai Campaign*, Leavenworth Paper 22 (Ft. Leavenworth, KS: Combat Studies Institute Press, 2003), 12.
10. James Sheridan, *China in Disintegration: The Republican Era, 1912–1949* (New York: Free Press, 1975), 149.
11. Taylor, *Generalissimo*, 55.
12. Nancy Bernkopf-Tucker, *China Confidential: American Diplomats and Sino-American Relations, 1946–1996* (New York: Columbia University Press, 2001), 12.
13. *China White Paper*, 12.
14. Taylor, *Generalissimo*, 90.
15. Taylor, 90; Bernstein, *China 1945*, 26–27.
16. Sheridan, *China in Disintegration*, 220–24.
17. Sheridan, 225.
18. Sheridan, 230.
19. Kitamura Minoru and Lin Siyun, *The Reluctant Combatant: Japan and the Second Sino-Japanese War*, trans. Connie Prener (Lanham, MD: University Press of America, 2014), 15; *China White Paper*, 46; Sheridan, *China in Disintegration*, 254–55; Charles F. Romanus and Riley Sunderland, *United States Army in World War II: The China-Burma-India Theater*, vol. 1, *Stilwell's Mission to China* (Washington, DC: Center for Army History, 2002), 5.
20. *China White Paper*, 46.
21. *China White Paper*, 47; Minoru and Siyun, *Reluctant Combatant*, 26; Sheridan, *China in Disintegration*, 254–55; Taylor, *Generalissimo*, 127–35; Bernstein, *China 1945*, 29; Mark Selden, *China in Revolution; The Yenan Way Revisited* (Armonk, NY: M. E. Sharpe, 1995), 93; Department of State, Office of Public Affairs, Information Memorandum No. 50, 24 May 1949, Foreign Relations–China Folder, Box 59, George Elsey Papers, HSTPL, 2.
22. Tsou Tang, *America's Failure in China, 1941–1950*, 2 vols. (Chicago; University of Chicago Press, 1963), 1:128.
23. Selden, *China in Revolution*, 109.

24. Taylor, *Generalissimo*, 169; Minoru and Siyun, *Reluctant Combatant*, 67; Sheridan, *China in Disintegration*, 257; Bernstein, *China 1945*, 36.
25. Sheridan, *China in Disintegration*, 257, Minoru and Siyun, *Reluctant Combatant*, 54–55; Bernstein, *China 1945*, 16; Wedemeyer, *Wedemeyer Reports*, 326.
26. Bernkopf-Tucker, *China Confidential*, 14; Tang, *America's Failure in China*, 1:88–93; U.S. State Department, *United States Relations with China, with Special Reference to the Period 1944–1949*, vol. 1 (St. Clair Shores, MI: Scholarly Press, 1971), 60–61; Barbara Tuchman, *Stilwell and the American Experience in China, 1911–1945* (New York: Macmillan, 1970), 388–90.
27. Taylor, 208; Bernkopf-Tucker, *China Confidential*, 13.
28. *China White Paper*, 69–70.
29. U.S. State Department, *United States Relations with China*, 61.
30. Bernstein, *China 1945*, 24; Bernkopf-Tucker, *China Confidential*, 13; Taylor, *Generalissimo*, 244.
31. *China White Paper*, 68; U.S. Department of State, *United States Relations with China*, 68.
32. Dean Acheson, "China White Paper Fair and Honest Record, Statement," *Department of State Bulletin*, 5 Sept. 1949, Foreign Relations–China Folder, Box 59, Elsey Papers, HSTPL; Department of State, Office of Public Affairs, Information Memorandum No. 50, p. 5.
33. Ronald Spector, *In the Ruins of Empire: The Japanese Surrender and the Battle for Postwar Asia* (New York: Random House, 2008), 248–49; U.S. State Department, *United States Relations with China*, 311.
34. Sheridan, *China in Disintegration*, 262; Selden, *China in Revolution*, 101, 132.
35. Minoru and Siyun, *Reluctant Combatant*, 67; Sheridan, *China in Disintegration*, 263; Selden, *China in Revolution*, 131; Jiajing Wu, "The Marshall Mission and KMT-CCP Negotiations after World War II" (master's thesis, Michigan State University, 1984; UMI Dissertation Information Service), 17.
36. Bjorge, *Moving the Enemy*, 42.
37. Bernkopf-Tucker, *China Confidential*, 16, 30; Mark A. Stoler, *George C. Marshall: Soldier Statesman of the American Century* (New York: Prentice Hall, 1989), 145–46; Bernstein, *China 1945*, 28, 42; Barbara Gooden-Mulch, "A Chinese Puzzle: Patrick J. Hurley and the Foreign Service Officer Controversy" (PhD diss., University of Kansas, 1972), 641; Robert J. Donovan, *Tumultuous Years: The Presidency of Harry S. Truman, 1949–1953* (New York: W. W. Norton, 1982), 67; Condit, *History of the Joint Chiefs of Staff*, 236; Summary Report of Vice President Wallace's Visit to China, 10 July 1944, Foreign Relations–China Folder, Box 59, Elsey Papers, HSTPL, 2.

38. Wedemeyer, *Wedemeyer Reports*, 335–36; Department of State, Office of Public Affairs, Information Memorandum No. 50, pp. 7, 9.
39. Ross Y. Koen, *The China Lobby in American Politics* (New York: Harper and Row, 1974), 34.
40. S. C. M. Payne, *The Sino-Japanese War of 1894–1894: Perceptions, Power, and Primacy* (New York: Cambridge University Press, 2004), 240–41; Department of State, Office of Public Affairs, Information Memorandum No. 50, p. 7.
41. Sheridan, *China in Disintegration*, 285.
42. Spector, *In the Ruins of Empire*, 26; Department of State, Office of Public Affairs, Information Memorandum No. 50, p. 4.
43. Stoler, *George C. Marshall*, 136.
44. Tang, *America's Failure in China*, 1:114; *China White Paper*, 68–69; Stoler, *George C. Marshall*, 145; U.S. Department of State, *United States Relations with China*, 59.
45. Tang, *America's Failure in China*, 1:117; *China White Paper*, 69; Stoler, *George C. Marshall*, 136, 145.
46. Wedemeyer, *Wedemeyer Reports*, 342; Donovan, *Tumultuous Years*, 67.
47. Arnold Offner, *Another Such Victory: President Truman and the Cold War, 1945–1953* (Stanford, CA: Stanford University Press, 2002), 311; Ṭaylor, *Generalissimo*, 242–43; Bernstein, *China 1945*, 44.
48. Rana Mitter, *Forgotten Ally: China's World War II, 1937–1945* (Boston: Houghton, Mifflin, Hardcourt, 2013), 345.
49. Daniel Kurtz-Phelan, *The China Mission: George Marshall's Unfinished War, 1945–1947* (New York: W. W. Norton, 2018), 12; Jonathan Fenby, *Chiang Kai Shek China's Generalissimo and the Nation He Lost* (New York: Carroll and Graf, 2003), 437; Mitter, *Forgotten Ally*, 347.
50. Kurtz-Phelan, *China Mission*, 12.
51. Offner, *Another Such Victory*, 312; "Marshall in China," *Washington Post*, 16 Sept. 1950, unattributed clipping, Foreign Relations–China Folder, Box 59, Elsey Papers, HSTPL; Department of State, Office of Public Affairs, Information Memorandum No. 50, p. 5.
52. Tang, *America's Failure in China*, 1:141–42; Stoler, *George C. Marshall*, 146; Bernkopf-Tucker, *China Confidential*, 14.
53. Mitter, *Forgotten Ally*, 347.
54. Bernstein, *China 1945*, 222–23.
55. Bernkopf-Tucker, *China Confidential*, 30, 32, 46–47; Warren I. Cohen, "Whose Afraid of Alfred Kohlberg?," *Reviews in American History* 3, no. 1 (Mar. 1975): 119; Summary Report of Vice President Wallace's Visit to China, 10 July 1944, p. 3; Department of State, Office of Public Affairs, Information Memorandum No. 50, p. 7.

56. Bernkopf-Tucker, *China Confidential*, 21.
57. Tang, *America's Failure in China*, 1:322.
58. Kenneth Shewmaker, *Americans and Chinese Communists, 1927–1945* (Ithaca, NY: Cornell University Press, 1971), 121–25; Department of State, Office of Public Affairs, Information Memorandum No. 50, p. 10.
59. Tang, *America's Failure in China*, 1:144; Koen, *China Lobby*, 71; Ellen Schrecker, *The Age of McCarthyism: A Brief History with Documents*, 2nd ed. (Boston: Bedford/St. Martin's, 2002), 75.
60. Wu, "Marshall Mission and KMT-CCP Negotiations," 4; Stoler, *George C. Marshall*, 147; Bernkopf-Tucker, *China Confidential*, 23; Summary Report of Vice President Wallace's Visit to China, 10 July 1944.
61. *China White Paper*, 88.
62. *China White Paper*, 90.
63. *China White Paper*, 90–92.
64. U.S. Department of State, *United States Relations with China*, 87; O. Edmund Clubb, interviewed by Richard D. McKinzie, 26 June 1974, Oral History Interviews, HSTPL, https://www.trumanlibrary.gov/library/oral-histories/clubb (accessed 2 Dec. 2018).
65. Bernstein, *China 1945*, 230–31; Bernkopf-Tucker, *China Confidential*, 30; Wu, "Marshall Mission and KMT-CCP Negotiations," 288; Stanley D. Bachrack, *The Committee of One Million: "China Lobby" Politics, 1953–1971* (New York: Columbia University Press, 1976), 25–26; Acheson, "China White Paper Fair and Honest Record, Statement"; Department of State, Office of Public Affairs, Information Memorandum No. 50, pp. 7, 9; Department of State Press Release, "Remarks at the National Press Club by Secy State Acheson, January 12, 1950," Acheson Sec of State Dean, Remarks at Natl Press Club Folder, Box 57, Francis Matthews Papers, HSTPL.
66. Bernstein, *China 1945*, 229.
67. Bernstein, 231.
68. Gooden-Mulch, "Chinese Puzzle," 249; Clubb, interviewed by McKinzie, 26 June 1974.
69. U.S. Department of State, *Foreign Relations of the United States: Diplomatic Papers, 1945*, vol. 7, *The Far East, China* (Washington, DC: U.S. Government Printing Office, 1978), 472.
70. Wu, "Marshall Mission and KMT-CCP Negotiations," 4; Spector, *In the Ruins of Empire*, 71; Taylor, *Generalissimo*, 327; Stoler, *George C. Marshall*, 147; Marc Gallicchio, "About Face: General Marshall's Plan for the Amalgamation of Communist and Nationalist Armies in China," in *George C. Marshall's Mediation*

Mission to China, December 1945–January 1947, ed. Larry Bland (Lexington, VA: George C. Marshall Foundation, 1998), 392; Offner, *Another Such Victory*, 320.

71. Gooden-Mulch, "Chinese Puzzle," 647–48.
72. Bachrack, *Committee of One Million*, 27; Tang, *America's Failure in China*, 2:464–71; Schrecker, *Age of McCarthyism*, 75.
73. Bernkopf-Tucker, *China Confidential*, 15; Tang, *America's Failure in China*, 2:437.
74. As quoted in Offner, *Another Such Victory*, 307, 326, 329. See also Pauley to Truman, 14 Feb. 1950, President's Secretary Files, Box 173, HSTPL; David E. Lilienthal, *The Journals of David E. Lilienthal*, vol. 2, *The Atomic Energy Years, 1945–1950* (New York: Harper and Row, 1964), 525.
75. Offner, *Another Such Victory*, 114.
76. Offner, 115; Spector, *In the Ruins of Empire*, 70–71; Gooden-Mulch, "Chinese Puzzle," 251.
77. Offner, *Another Such Victory*, 307, 320.
78. Bernstein, *China 1945*, 345; Wu, "Marshall Mission and KMT-CCP Negotiations," 5; Taylor, *Generalissimo*, 327.
79. Harry S. Truman, *Memoirs*, vol. 2 (Garden City, NY: Doubleday, 1956), 66–67.
80. Wu, "Marshall Mission and KMT-CCP Negotiations," 4; Raymond H. Myers, "Frustration, Fortitude, and Friendship: Chiang Kai-shek's Reaction to Marshall's Mission," in Bland, *George C. Marshall's Mediation Mission*, 169; Tang, *America's Failure in China*, 2:438; Department of State, Office of Public Affairs, Information Memorandum No. 50.
81. Bernkopf-Tucker, *China Confidential*, 24–25.
82. Wedemeyer, *Wedemeyer Reports*, 363; Department of State, Confidential Release No. 9, Personal Statement by General Marshall, American War Production Mission in China, 7 Jan. 1947, 3rd Trip Folder, Box 1, Edwin Locke Papers, HSTPL.
83. "Statement by the President: United States Policy toward China," 15 Dec. 1945, Public Papers, HSTPL, https://www.trumanlibrary.gov/library/public-papers/216/statement-president-united-states-policy-toward-china (accessed 1 Feb. 2018); *China White Paper*, 133–34; Donovan, *Tumultuous Years*, 71.
84. Koen, *China Lobby*, 75; "Marshall in China," Elsey Papers, HSTPL; Department of State, Office of Public Affairs, Information Memorandum No. 50, p. 5.
85. Campbell Craig and Fredrik Logevall, *America's Cold War: The Politics of Insecurity* (Cambridge, MA: Harvard University Press, 2009), 104.
86. Alfred Kohlberg, "The Lie Marches On," in *Plain Talk: An Anthology from the Leading Anti-Communist Magazine of the 1940s*, ed. Isaac Don Levine (New Rochelle, NY: Arlington House, 1976), 140.

87. "Statement by the President: United States Policy toward China," 15 Dec. 1945.
88. Offner, *Another Such Victory*, 320–21; Department of State, Office of Public Affairs, Information Memorandum No. 50.
89. Bernkopf-Tucker, *China Confidential*, 14; Wu, "Marshall Mission and KMT-CCP Negotiations," 12–13; Offner, *Another Such Victory*, 344.
90. Bernkopf-Tucker, *China Confidential*, 15; *China White Paper*, 116–17; Offner, *Another Such Victory*, 344.
91. Bjorge, *Moving the Enemy*, 15; *China White Paper*, 312.
92. *China White Paper*, 136; Stoler, *George C. Marshall*, 148; Department of State, Confidential Release No. 9, 7 Jan. 1947, p. 2.
93. *China White Paper*, 136; Department of State, Confidential Release No. 9, 7 Jan. 1947, p. 2.
94. *China White Paper*, 143; Stoler, *George C. Marshall*, 149; Tang, *America's Failure in China*, 2:413–14; Offner, *Another Such Victory*, 322; Department of State, Office of Public Affairs, Information Memorandum No. 50, p. 6.
95. *China White Paper*, 145; Stoler, *George C. Marshall*, 148.
96. *China White Paper*, 151.
97. *China White Paper*, 181; Tang, *America's Failure in China*, 2:428; Condit, *History of the Joint Chiefs of Staff*, 236.
98. Bernkopf-Tucker, *China Confidential*, 25; Dean Acheson, "Letter of Transmittal," *China White Paper*, xiii; "Marshall in China," Elsey Papers, HSTPL.
99. Wu, "Marshall Mission and KMT-CCP Negotiations," 4; Stoler, *George C. Marshall*, 149–50; Offner, *Another Such Victory*, 326; Wedemeyer, *Wedemeyer Reports*, 376; "Marshall in China," Elsey Papers, HSTPL.
100. Marshall quoted in Stoler, *George C. Marshall*, 150.
101. Henry P. Van Dusen, "An American Policy for China," in Levine, *Plain Talk* (anthology), 102.
102. Koen, *China Lobby*, xxi, 29.
103. Joseph C. Keeley, *The China Lobby Man: The Story of Alfred Kohlberg* (New Rochelle, NY: Arlington, 1969), 24–25; Koen, *China Lobby*, 50.
104. Levine, *Plain Talk*, xii; Schrecker, *Age of McCarthyism*, 76.
105. Keeley, *China Lobby Man*, 199; Koen, *China Lobby*, 50.
106. Levine, *Plain Talk*, xiii.
107. Keeley, *China Lobby Man*, 114–15.
108. Schrecker, *Age of McCarthyism*, 76; Koen *China Lobby*, 28; Richard D. Weigle, interview by Richard D. McKinzie, 11 June 1973, Oral History Interviews, HSTPL, https://www.trumanlibrary.gov/library/oral-histories/weigle (accessed July 5, 2018).
109. Donovan, *Tumultuous Years*, 75.

110. Department of State, Office of Public Affairs, Information Memorandum No. 50, p. 2.
111. Tang, *America's Failure in China*, 2:467; Schrecker, *Age of McCarthyism*, 76.
112. Walter H. Judd, interviewed by Jerry Ness, 13 Apr. 1970, Oral History Interviews, HSTPL, https://www.trumanlibrary.gov/library/oral-histories/judd#note (accessed 2 July 2018).
113. Donovan, *Tumultuous Years*, 75; Kohlberg, "The Lie Marches On," 141; Judd, interview by Ness, 13 Apr. 1970.
114. Tang, *America's Failure in China*, 2:449.
115. Kohlberg, "The Lie Marches On," 139.
116. Clare Boothe Luce, "The Mystery of Our China Policy," in Levine, *Plain Talk*, 148.
117. Bernkopf-Tucker, *China Confidential*, 39–41.
118. Wedemeyer, *Wedemeyer Reports*, 371.
119. Wedemeyer, 372.
120. Wedemeyer, 388; Condit, *History of the Joint Chiefs of Staff*, 238.
121. A. C. Wedemeyer, "Report to the President," 1947, in Wedemeyer, *Wedemeyer Reports*, 476–77.
122. Wedemeyer, 476–77; Offner, *Another Such Victory*, 328; Tang, *America's Failure in China*, 2:363; Condit, *History of the Joint Chiefs of Staff*, 238.
123. Lyman P. Van Slyke, introduction to *China White Paper.*
124. Offner, *Another Such Victory*, 327; Tang, *America's Failure in China*, 2:461; "Why the China Mission Failed," *US News and World Report*, 29 Sept. 1949, Magazine Clipping, Foreign Relations–China Folder, Box 59, Elsey Papers, HSTPL.
125. Tang, *America's Failure in China*, 2:453; Condit, *History of the Joint Chiefs of Staff*, 236.
126. Tang, *America's Failure in China*, 2:463.
127. Special Message to the Congress of the United States on the Need for Assistance to China, 18 Feb. 1948, Public Papers of Harry S. Truman, 1945–1953, HSTPL, https://www.trumanlibrary.gov/library/public-papers/31/special-message-congress-need-assistance-china (accessed 7 June 2018); Condit, *History of the Joint Chiefs of Staff*, 239; Department of State, Office of Public Affairs, Information Memorandum No. 50, p. 8.
128. Tang, *America's Failure in China*, 2:428; Koen, *China Lobby*, 75; "Marshall in China," Elsey Papers, HSTPL.
129. *China White Paper*, 322; Grauer, *Commanding Military Power*, 110.
130. Tang, *America's Failure in China*, 1:322; Grauer, *Commanding Military Power*, 99.
131. Ed Cray, *General of the Army: George C. Marshall, Soldier and Statesman* (New York: Cooper, 1990), 674.

132. Memorandum, Dean Acheson, Acting Secretary of State, to W. W. Butterworth, Far East Affairs, 7 June 1949, Documents on Diplomatic Aspects Pt. 2, 1942, Box 2 [of 3], Foreign Affairs File, China 1948, Subject File, 1940–1953, President's Secretary Files, HSTPL.
133. Mao Tse-tung, *Selected Military Writings* (Pretorian, 2011), 96.
134. Donovan, *Tumultuous Years*, 74.
135. As referenced in Donovan, *Tumultuous Years*, 75.
136. Luce, "Mystery of Our China Policy," 151.
137. Donovan, *Tumultuous Years*, 76; Keith D. McFarland and David L. Roll, *Louis Johnson and the Arming of America: The Roosevelt and Truman Years* (Bloomingdale: Indiana University Press, 2005), 254–55; Melvin Leffler, *A Preponderance of Power: National Security, the Truman Administration, and the Cold War* (Stanford, CA: Stanford University Press, 1992), 292.
138. B. B. Hickenlooper to Miss Carolyn T. Menke, 4 Jan. 1949, Foreign Relations Committee, Countries, China, Republic of, 1949 Folder, Bourke B. Hickenlooper Papers, Herbert Hoover Presidential Library, West Branch, IA (hereafter HHPL).
139. John McCormack to Harry Truman, ? July 1949, Documents on Diplomatic Aspects, pt. 2, 1942, China 1948 Folder, Box 2 [of 3], Foreign Affairs File, Subject File 1940–1953, President's Secretary Files, HSTPL.
140. Harry Truman to John McCormack, personal and confidential, n.d., Documents on Diplomatic Aspects, pt. 2, 1942, China 1948 Folder, Box 2 [of 3], Foreign Affairs File, Subject File 1940–1953, President's Secretary Files, HSTPL.
141. Offner, *Another Such Victory*, 336.
142. Bernkopf-Tucker, *China Confidential*, 61.
143. Bernkopf-Tucker, 62.
144. Van Slyke, introduction to *China White Paper.*
145. Statement by the President, 4 Aug. 1949, Foreign Relations–China Folder, Box 59, Elsey Papers, HSTPL.
146. Dean Acheson, Letter of Transmittal, 30 July 1949, in *China While Paper*, iii.
147. Van Slyke, introduction to *China White Paper.*
148. William Rintz, "The Failure of the China White Paper," *Constructing the Past* 11, no. 1 (2009): 79.
149. Rintz, 79.
150. Rintz, 80; Acheson, "China White Paper Fair and Honest Record, Statement."
151. Walter Judd to B. B. Hickenlooper, 25 Aug. 1945, Foreign Relations Committee, Countries, China, Republic of, General 1949 Folder, Hickenlooper Papers, HHPL; Acheson, "China White Paper Fair and Honest Record, Statement."
152. Koen, *China Lobby*, 167; Rintz, "Failure of the China White Paper," 80.
153. Koen, *China Lobby*, 165, 170.

154. Van Slyke, introduction to *China White Paper.*
155. Koen, *China Lobby*, 58.
156. Van Slyke, introduction to *China White Paper*; "Marshall in China," Elsey Papers, HSTPL.
157. Van Slyke, introduction to *China White Paper.*
158. DoS Letter, Dean Acheson to President Truman, 10 Mar. 1949, Documents on Diplomatic Aspects, pt. 2, 1942, China 1948 Folder, Box 2 [of 3], Foreign Affairs File, Subject File 1940–53, President's Secretary Files, HSTPL.
159. W. Walton Butterworth, interviewed by Richard D. McKenzie and Theodore A. Wilson, 6 July 1971, Oral History Interviews, HSTPL, https://www.trumanlibrary.gov/library/oral-histories/butter (accessed 2 July 2018); Clubb, interviewed by McKinzie, 26 June 1974.
160. Open Letter, Alfred Kohlberg to Pres. Harry S. Truman, 30 Nov. 1950, Foreign Relations Committee Countries, Chinese Lobby 1945–52+1961 Folder, Hickenlooper Papers, HHPL.
161. Koen, *China Lobby*, 15.
162. NSC 37/8, "The Position of the United States with Respect to Taiwan," 6 Oct. 1949, Folder 180-1, NSC Reports, Box 180, mtgs. 47–49, Subject File, President's Secretary Files, HSTPL, 2.
163. NSC 37/8, 3.
164. NSC 37/8, 4.
165. NSC 37/8, 6.
166. Donovan, *Tumultuous Years*, 86.
167. Donovan, *Tumultuous Years*, 86; Bernkopf, *China Confidential*, 40; Memorandum of Conversation with the President, 21 Nov. 1949, Acheson Papers—Secretary of State File, HSTPL, https://www.trumanlibrary.gov/library/personal-papers/memoranda-conversations-file-1949-1953/october-november-1949-0?documentid=33&pagenumber=5 (accessed 1 Nov. 2021).
168. "Record of Round-Table Discussion by Twenty-Five Far East Experts with the Department of State on 'American Policy toward China,' October 6, 7, 8, 1949," Records of Round Table Discussions Folder, China Documents on Diplomatic Aspects, pt. 2, 1942, Folder 2 [of 3], Box 151, Foreign Affairs File, Subject File 1940–53, President's Secretary Files, HSTPL.
169. "Record of Round-Table Discussion by Twenty-Five Far East Experts with the Department of State on 'American Policy toward China,' October 6, 7, 8, 1949"; Weekly Review, Soviet Designs in Communist China, 23 Nov. 1949, Policy Information Committee, Department of State, Foreign Relations–China Folder, Box 59, Elsey Papers, HSTPL; John Patrick Diggins, *The Proud Decades: America in War and Peace, 1941–1960* (New York: W. W. Norton, 1988), 88.

170. "Record of Round-Table Discussion by Twenty-Five Far East Experts with the Department of State on 'American Policy toward China,' October 6, 7, 8, 1949."
171. "Marshall in China," Elsey Papers, HSTPL.
172. Joseph R. McCarthy, *America's Victory from Retreat: The Story of George Catlett Marshall* (New York: Devin Adair, 1951) 115, 170–71.
173. "Record of Round-Table Discussion by Twenty-Five Far East Experts with the Department of State on 'American Policy toward China,' October 6, 7, 8, 1949," 3.
174. Tang, *America's Failure in China*, 2:516; Offner, *Another Such Victory*, 336.
175. Tang, *America's Failure in China*, 2:516; Offner, *Another Such Victory*, 337.
176. Harry Truman to Maury Maverick, 22 Nov. 1949, Documents on Diplomatic Aspects, pt. 2, 1942, Box 2 [of 3], Foreign Affairs File, China 1948, Subject File, 1940–1953, President's Secretary Files, HSTPL.
177. Department of Defense, Office of Public Information, Analysis Branch, B-36 Investigation, 30 Aug. 1949, B-36 Investigation (File 2), Box 42, Gen. Hoyt S. Vandenberg Papers, LOC; Omar Bradley, *A General's Life: An Autobiography*, with Clay Blair (reprint, Lexington, MA: Plunkett Lake, 2019), 508.
178. Paul Hammond, *Super Carriers and B-36 Bombers: Appropriations, Strategy, and Politics* (Indianapolis: Bobbs-Merrill, 1963), 46; Jeffrey Barlow, *The Revolt of the Admirals: The Fight for Naval Aviation, 1945–1950* (Washington, DC: Brassey's, 1998), 237; David Bruce Dittmer, "The Firing of Admiral Denfeld: An Early Casualty of the Military Unification Process" (master's thesis, University of Nebraska–Omaha, 1995), 110; Jeffrey Barlow, *From Hot War to Cold: The U.S. Navy and National Security Affairs, 1945–1955* (Stanford, CA: Stanford University Press, 2009), 228, 234.
179. David Alan Rosenberg, "American Atomic Strategy and the Hydrogen Bomb Decision," *Journal of American History* 66, no. 1 (July 1979): 72.
180. Hammond, *Super Carriers and B-36 Bombers*, 45; Paolo E. Coletta, *The United States Navy and Defense Unification, 1947–1952* (East Brunswick, NJ: Associated University Press, 1981), 235; McFarland and Roll, *Louis Johnson and the Arming of America*, 181.
181. Appointment Letter, Secretary of the Navy, Francis Matthews, to Adm. Thomas C. Kinkaid, Subj: Court of Inquiry into the Circumstances Surrounding Preparation of Anonymous Document Furnished Member of Congress Concerning Contracts for B-36 Aircraft and Other Matters, 25 Aug. 1949, H-1 B-36 Naval Court Inquiry Folder, Box 169, CNO, Organizational Research and Policy Division Papers, 1932–1949 (hereafter OP-23 Papers), Naval History and Heritage Command, Washington, DC (hereafter NHHC).

182. E. B. Potter, *Admiral Arleigh Burke* (Annapolis, MD: Naval Institute Press, 1990), 322; Phillip S. Meilinger, "The Admirals Revolt: Lessons for Today," *Parameters*, Sept. 1989, p. 90; David Stringer, "Roles, Missions, and Politics: The USAF and the B-36, 1945–50" (master's thesis, Air Command and Staff College, 1987), 13; Barlow, *Revolt of the Admirals*, 234; Steven L. Reardon, *History of the Office of the Secretary of Defense: The Formative Years, 1947–1950* (Washington, DC: Historical Office of the Secretary of Defense, 1984), 415 (hereafter Reardon, *Formative Years*); Proceedings from the Naval Court of Inquiry into the Circumstances Surrounding Preparation of Anonymous Document Furnished Member of Congress Concerning Contracts for B-36 Aircraft and Other Matters, 21 Sept. 1949, H-1 B-36 Naval Court Inquiry Folder, Box 169, OP-23 Papers, NHHC.
183. Proceedings from the Naval Court of Inquiry into the Circumstances Surrounding Preparation of Anonymous Document; Murray Green, "The B-36 Controversy in Retrospect," n.d., Box 102, Curtis E. LeMay Papers, LOC, 24.
184. Hanson Baldwin to Louis Denfeld, 10 Sept. 1949, Baldwin Folder, Box 2, ser. 2, Personal Correspondence, 1947–49, Louis Denfeld Papers, NHHC. This statement is in reference to the court-martial of Brig. Gen. Billy Mitchell in 1925. Mitchell's outspoken advocacy for airpower was deemed insubordinate, and he stood trial for his public comments. He was found guilty of the charges but resigned his commission. Once out of uniform Mitchell continued to advocate for airpower until his death in 1936 at the age of fifty-six. He is viewed as a martyr by airpower enthusiasts.
185. Rear Adm. James Ramage testimonial, *Tailhook*, n.d., quoted in "Rear Admiral John G. Crommelin (1902–1996)," http://www.crommelin.org/history/Biographies/Alabama/1902JohnGeraerdt/JohnCrommelin.htm (accessed 20 Sept. 2018). The "Big E" was the nickname of the USS *Enterprise* (CV 6).
186. Hammond, *Super Carriers and B-36 Bombers*, 42; Dittmer, "Firing of Admiral Denfeld," 105; Potter, *Admiral Arleigh Burke*, 322; Coletta, *United States Navy and Defense Unification*, 175; "Fat or Muscle?," *Time*, 5 Dec. 1949.
187. Barlow, *From Hot War to Cold*, 228; Hammond, *Super Carriers and B-36 Bombers*, 41; McFarland and Roll, *Louis Johnson and the Arming of America*, 181.
188. "Captain Crommelin's Statement," *Army-Navy Journal* 87, no. 3, 17 Sept. 1949, p. 51; Reardon, *Formative Years*, 415.
189. "Pentagon Wrecking Navy, Captain Says," unattributed newspaper clipping, B-36 Editorial Comments K-6, Sept. 1949, Box 170, OP-23 Papers, NHHC.
190. "Captain Charges General Staff Wrecks Navy, Calls B-36 Furor Attempt to Avert Destruction," *Washington Evening Star*, 11 Sept. 1949; "Revolt of the Admirals," *Time*, 17 Oct. 1949; "Pentagon Crippling Power of the Navy, Captain Says,

Risking His Career," *New York Times* 11 Sept. 1949, clipping, B-36 Editorial Comments K-6, Sept. 1949, Box 170, OP-23 Papers, NHHC; Green, "B-36 Controversy in Retrospect," 26; Potter, *Admiral Arleigh Burke*, 323.

191. "The Basic Difference," n.d., Summary Reports on B-36 Investigation G-10 folder, Box 169, OP-23 Papers, NHHC.

192. "Basic Difference"; Memorandum, Captain Lynch and Lieutenant Commander Howard to Captain Burke, Subj: Summary of Points and Navy Recommendations, 20 Oct. 1949, Summary Reports on B-36 Investigation G-10 Folder, Box 169, OP-23 Papers, NHHC; "The Air Force and Army's Turn," *New York Herald Tribune*, 18 Oct. 1947.

193. "Basic Difference"; "Trends in Unification."

194. "Praises Mr. Worth," *Army-Navy Journal* 87, no. 4, 24 Sept. 1949, p. 103.

195. "Praises Mr. Worth"; "Now It's Crommelin's Revolt," *Washington Daily News*, 11 Sept. 1949; "Revolt of the Admirals"; "Pentagon Wrecking Navy, Captain Says"; "Pentagon Crippling Power of the Navy."

196. "Captain Crommelin's Statement"; "Charges 'General Staff' Wrecks Navy, Calls B-36 Furor Attempt to Avert Destruction"; "I Can't Stand It Any Longer," *Time Magazine*, 26 Sept. 1949; "Now It's Crommelin's Revolt."

197. "Praises Mr. Worth"; "Captain Charges General Staff Wrecks Navy"; "Pentagon Crippling Power of the Navy."

198. "Praises Mr. Worth"; Hammond, *Super Carriers and B-36 Bombers*, 42; "I Can't Stand It Any Longer," *Time*, 26 Sept. 1949; Coletta, *United States Navy and Defense Unification*, 171.

199. "Praises Mr. Worth"; Hammond, *Super Carriers and B-36 Bombers*, 42.

200. Coletta, *United States Navy and Defense Unification*, 172; Hammond, *Super Carriers and B-36 Bombers*, 42; "Pentagon Boots Navy Capt. Who Blasted USAF," *Washington Daily News*, 15 Sept. 1949, newspaper clipping, 1949 Unification and Crommelin Controversy Folder, Box 68, Matthews Papers, HSTPL.

201. "I Can't Stand It Any Longer"; Dittmer, "Firing of Admiral Denfeld," 106–7.

202. "Navy 'Promotes' Crommelin, Then Has Its Mind Changed," *Washington Times Herald*, 16 Sept. 1949, newspaper clipping, B-36 Editorial Comments K-6, Sept. 1949, Box 170, OP-23 Papers, NHHC.

203. "I Can't Stand It Any Longer"; Dittmer, "Firing of Admiral Denfeld," 106–7; Hammond, *Super Carriers and B-36 Bombers*, 42; McFarland and Roll, *Louis Johnson and the Arming of America*, 181.

204. Hammond, *Super Carriers and B-36 Bombers*, 43; Barlow, *Revolt of the Admirals*, 236; Dittmer, "Firing of Admiral Denfeld," 107; Coletta, *United States Navy and Defense Unification*, 172; "Secretary's Order," *Army-Navy Journal* 87, no. 4, 24 Sept. 1949, p. 103.

205. Hammond, *Super Carriers and B-36 Bombers*, 44; Coletta, *United States Navy and Defense Unification*, 177; "Revolt of the Admirals"; Louis Denfeld, "Why I Was Fired," *Collier's*, 18 Mar. 1950.
206. Hammond, *Super Carriers and B-36 Bombers*, 45.
207. Hammond, 45; Coletta, *United States Navy and Defense Unification*, 175–76.
208. Coletta, *United States Navy and Defense Unification*, 181; Dittmer, "Firing of Admiral Denfeld," 118.
209. Barlow, *Revolt of the Admirals*, 243; Coletta, *United States Navy and Defense Unification*, 179; Dittmer, "Firing of Admiral Denfeld," 117; Hammond, *Super Carriers and B-36 Bombers*, 45.
210. Coletta, *United States Navy and Defense Unification*, 178–80; Barlow, *From Hot War to Cold*, 235; Barlow, *Revolt of the Admirals*, 243; Hammond, *Super Carriers and B-36 Bombers*, 45; McFarland and Roll, *Louis Johnson and the Arming of America*, 181–82.
211. Hammond, *Super Carriers and B-36 Bombers*, 45.
212. Hammond, 45; Barlow, *Revolt of the Admirals*, 244.
213. Barlow, *Revolt of the Admirals*, 244.
214. McFarland and Roll, *Louis Johnson and the Arming of America*, 182; Coletta, *United States Navy and Defense Unification*, 179; Hammond, *Super Carriers and B-36 Bombers*, 45–46; Barlow, *From Hot War to Cold*, 235; Barlow, *Revolt of the Admirals*, 244; Dittmer, "Firing of Admiral Denfeld," 116; Phillip S. Meilinger, *Bomber: The Formation and Early Years of Strategic Air Command* (Maxwell AFB: Air University Press, 2012), 146.
215. Green, "B-36 Controversy in Retrospect," 26; *Army-Navy Journal* 87, no. 6, 8 Oct. 1949, p. 139; Meilinger, "Admirals Revolt," 90.
216. *Washington Post*, *New York Times*, and *Baltimore Sun*, 4 Oct. 1949, newspaper clippings, 1949 Unification and Crommelin Controversy Folder, Box 68, Matthews Papers, HSTPL.
217. Dittmer, "Firing of Admiral Denfeld," 118.
218. McFarland and Roll, *Louis Johnson and the Arming of America*, 182; Hammond, *Super Carriers and B-36 Bombers*, 50; Coletta, *United States Navy and Defense Unification*, 186; "Capt. Crommelin Returns to Duty," *Washington Daily News*, 8 Nov. 1949, clipping, Subject File: B36 Clippings, Dan A. Kimball Papers, HSTPL; "Evil Split in US High Command," *Washington Daily News*, 7 Oct. 1949, clipping, ibid.; "Today in Washington: Involves President Truman in Crommelin's Arrest, David Lawrence," *Pittsburgh Post-Gazette*, 8 Oct. 1949, clipping, ibid.; *Army Navy Journal* 87, no. 6, 8 Oct. 1949; Donovan, *Tumultuous Years*, 107.
219. Hammond, *Super Carriers and B-36 Bombers*, 46.

220. U.S. Congress, House, *Unification and Strategy: A Report of Investigation by the Committee on Armed Services House of Representatives . . .* (Washington, DC: U.S. Government Printing Office, 1950), 8.
221. Paul H. Nitze, interviewed by Richard D. McKinzie, 4 Aug. 1975, Oral History Interviews, HSTPL, https://www.trumanlibrary.gov/library/oral-histories/nitzeph2 (accessed 8 July 2016).
222. U.S. Congress, House, *Investigation of the B-36 Bomber Program: Report of the Committee on Armed Services, . . . Pursuant to H. Res. 234 . . .* (Washington, DC: U.S. Government Printing Office, 1950), 2; Hammond, *Super Carriers and B-36 Bombers*, 31; Dittmer, "Firing of Admiral Denfeld," 95; Barlow, *Revolt of the Admirals*, 217; *Army-Navy Journal* 87, no. 6, 8 Oct. 1949, 139.
223. U.S. Congress, House, *Unification and Strategy*, 10.
224. Statement of Secretary of the Navy Francis P. Matthews before the Armed Services Committee of the House of Representatives, 6 Oct. 1949, Matthews File, 10/6/49, Speech File, Box 55, Matthews Papers, HSTPL, 3, 7.
225. Statement of Secretary of the Navy Francis P. Matthews, 3.
226. Statement of Secretary of the Navy Francis P. Matthews, 3; "Revolt of the Admirals."
227. Statement of Secretary of the Navy Francis P. Matthews, 9–10.
228. Statement of Secretary of the Navy Francis P. Matthews, 8–9.
229. Statement of Secretary of the Navy Francis P. Matthews, 11.
230. Hanson Baldwin, "Navy Wars with Itself," *New York Times*, 8 Oct. 1949, clipping, Subject File: B36 Clippings, Kimball Papers, HSTPL; Barlow, *From Hot War to Cold*, 236; Hammond, *Super Carriers and B-36 Bombers*, 50; Coletta, *United States Navy and Defense Unification*, 185; Denfeld, "Why I Was Fired."
231. Bradley, *General's Life*, 507.
232. Statement of Arthur W. Radford before the Armed Services Committee of the House of Representatives Investigating the B-36 and Related Matters, Adm. Arthur Radford (10/7/49) File, Box 44, Matthews Papers, HSTPL; "Admiral Challenges Atomic Blitz Strategy," *Washington Post*, 8 Oct. 1949, clipping, Subject File: B36 Clippings, Kimball Papers, HSTPL; U.S. Congress, House, *Unification and Strategy*, 21; "Revolt of the Admirals."
233. Statement of Arthur W. Radford; "Defense Plan Is Phony Says Radford," *Washington Times-Herald*, 8 Oct. 1949, clipping, Subject File: B36 Clippings, Kimball Papers, HSTPL; "Revolt of the Admirals."
234. Statement of Arthur W. Radford; Baldwin, "Navy Wars with Itself." Claire Chennault was a proponent of pursuit aviation when stationed at the Air Corps Tactical School at Maxwell Field. His frustration with Air Corps intransigence regarding bombers caused him to leave the service.

235. Stuart Symington, interviewed by James R. Fuchs, 29 May 1981, Oral History Interviews, HSTPL, https://www.trumanlibrary.gov/library/oral-histories/symton (accessed 4 Mar. 2019).
236. Statement of Arthur W. Radford.
237. Statement of Arthur W. Radford.
238. Baldwin, "Navy Wars with Itself"; "Revolt of the Admirals."
239. Statement of Arthur W. Radford.
240. "Admiral Challenges Atomic Blitz Strategy."
241. "Defense Plan Is Phony Says Radford."
242. Hammond, *Super Carriers and B-36 Bombers*, 56.
243. "Navy Demands Jet vs. B-36 Test," *Washington Daily News*, 10 Oct. 1949, clipping, Subject File: B36 Clippings, Kimball Papers, HSTPL.
244. "LtCmdr E. W. Harrison USN," *Army-Navy Journal*, 87, no. 7, 15 Oct. 1949, p. 166, Subject File: B36 Clippings, Kimball Papers, HSTPL; "Navy Sinks Unification," *Washington Times-Herald*, 10 Oct. 1949, ibid.; U.S. Congress, House, *Unification and Strategy*, 22; Hammond, *Super Carriers and B-36 Bombers*, 55.
245. Statement of Fred Trapnell, Captain United States Navy, Commanding Officer U.S. Naval Air Test Center, Patuxent River, MD, before the Armed Services Committee of the House of Representatives Investigating the B-36 and Related Matters, Technical Statement Folder, Box 174, OP-23 Papers, NHHC.
246. "Captain F. M. Trapnell, USN," *Army-Navy Journal*, 15 Oct. 1949; Barlow, *Revolt of the Admirals*, 249; "Navy vs. AF: Banshee Can Lick 36; Can't Find It at Night," *Washington Daily News*, 18 Oct. 1949, Subject File: B36 Clippings, Kimball Papers, HSTPL; Statement of Fred Trapnell.
247. "Cmdr W. I. Martin," *Army-Navy Journal*, 15 Oct. 1949; U.S. Congress, House, *Unification and Strategy*, 22; Hammond, *Super Carriers and B-36 Bombers*, 55.
248. "Navy Sinks Unification," 49.
249. "Navy Sinks Unification"; "Navy Demands Jet vs. B-36 Test."; "Mr Abraham Hyatt," *Army-Navy Journal*, 15 Oct. 1949; "Johnson Attacks Navy Backers' 'Campaign of Terror' on Unification," *Washington Daily News*, 10 Oct. 1949, Subject File: B36 Clippings, Kimball Papers, HSTPL; Hammond, *Super Carriers and B-36 Bombers*, 55.
250. Hammond, *Super Carriers and B-36 Bombers*, 56; "Facts and Fears," *Time*, 24 Oct. 1949; Green, "B-36 Controversy in Retrospect," 27.
251. "Facts and Fears."
252. "The Navy Rebellion," *New York Herald Tribune*, 16 Oct. 1949, Subject File: B36 Clippings, Kimball Papers, HSTPL; Summary of Statement by Rear Adm. Ralph A. Ofstie, "Concept of Strategic Bombing," in Memorandum, Captain Lynch and Lieutenant Commander Howard to Captain Burke, Subj: Summary of

Points and Navy Recommendations, 20 Oct. 1949, Summary Reports on B-36 Investigation G-10 Folder, Box 169, OP-23 Papers, NHHC.

253. "Navy Rebellion"; Barlow, *Revolt of the Admirals*, 250; Statement of Gen. Omar Bradley, Chairman, Joint Chiefs of Staff, before the Armed Services Committee of the House of Representatives, General Omar Bradley Oct 19–20 File, Matthews Papers Box 57, HSTPL, 28.
254. "Navy Rebellion."
255. Thach gained fame during World War II by developing a fighter tactic known as the "Thach Weave," which helped counter the superior maneuverability of the Japanese "Zero" fighter. This tactic became a standard practice early in the Pacific War.
256. Summary of Technical Data by John S. Thach, Captain, United States Navy Staff, Naval Air Training Command, U.S. Naval Air Station Pensacola, Florida, before the Armed Services Committee of the House of Representatives Investigation of the B-36 and Related Matters, Technical Statements Folder B-36, Box 174 OP-23 Papers, NHHC.
257. Arleigh Burke to J. S. Thach, 30 Aug. 1949, A-18.1-3 Investigation (Vinson) Folder, Box 143, OP-23 Papers, NHHC.
258. Statement of Arleigh A. Burke, Captain USN, Assistant Chief of Naval Operations (Organizational Policy and Research Division), Navy Department, Washington, DC, before the Armed Services Committee of the House of Representatives Investigating the B-36 and Related Matters, House Armed Services Committee Investigation of the B-36 and Related Matters (Oct 10–17, 49) Folder, Box 56: House Armed Services Committee Investigation of B-36 and Related Matters, Matthews Papers, HSTPL.
259. Statement of Chester W. Nimitz, Fleet Admiral, U.S. Navy (Ret.) before the Armed Services Committee of the House of Representatives Investigating the B-36 and Related Matters, Fleet Admiral Chester W. Nimitz 10/13/49 File, Box 56: House Armed Services Committee Investigation of B-36 and Related Matters, Matthews Papers, HSTPL.
260. U.S. Congress, House, *Unification and Strategy*, 15, 22–23.
261. Statement of Chester W. Nimitz.
262. Denfeld, "Why I Was Fired."
263. "Facts and Fears"; Dittmer, "Firing of Admiral Denfeld," 127; Barlow, *From Hot War to Cold*, 238; Donovan, *Tumultuous Years*, 110.
264. Barlow, *Revolt of the Admirals*, 251–52; Barlow, *From Hot War to Cold*, 237; "Facts and Fears."
265. Hammond, *Super Carriers and B-36 Bombers*, 62.
266. Barlow, *From Hot War to Cold*, 237; Potter, *Admiral Arleigh Burke*, 325; Dittmer, "Firing of Admiral Denfeld," 132.

267. Statement of Louis E. Denfeld, Admiral United States Navy, Chief of Naval Operations, Navy Department, Washington, DC, before the Armed Services Committee of the House of Representatives Investigating the B-36 and Related Matters, Adm. Louis E. Denfeld 10/13/49 File, Box 56: House Armed Services Committee Investigation of B-36 and Related Matters, Matthews Papers, HSTPL; Hammond, *Super Carriers and B-36 Bombers*, 62.
268. Statement of Louis E. Denfeld.
269. Statement of Louis E. Denfeld.
270. Statement of Louis E. Denfeld. As mentioned earlier, the WSEG report was scheduled for January 1950.
271. "Facts and Fears."
272. McFarland and Roll, *Louis Johnson and the Arming of America*, 183; Coletta, *United States Navy and Defense Unification*, 192; Potter, *Admiral Arleigh Burke*, 326; "Facts and Fears"; Hammond, *Super Carriers and B-36 Bombers*, 63; Dittmer, "Firing of Admiral Denfeld," 143.
273. Denfeld, "Why I Was Fired," 62; Dittmer, "Firing of Admiral Denfeld," 144; "Denfeld Facing Ouster as Chief of Navy over B-36 Stand," *Washington Times-Herald*, 22 Oct. 1949.
274. E. B. Potter, *Nimitz* (Annapolis, MD: Naval Institute Press, 1976), 446.
275. Potter, 447.
276. "End of the Marines?," *Washington Post*, 20 Mar. 1947, AAF Information Program Folder B-36, Box 174, OP-23 Papers, NHHC.
277. Bradley, *General's Life*, 508.
278. Hammond, *Super Carriers and B-36 Bombers*, 63; "Public Would Give Air Force Top Priority," n.d., unattributed newspaper clipping, Scrapbook vol. 2 Folder [3 of 3], Box 1, Robert Lovett Papers, HSTPL; Green, "B-36 Controversy in Retrospect," 34; George H. Gallup, *The Gallup Poll on Public Opinion, 1935 1971*, 3 vols. (New York: Random House, 1972), 2:858–59.
279. Statement of W. Stuart Symington, Secretary of the Air Force before the Armed Services Committee of the House of Representatives Concerning the B-36 and Related Matters, W. Stuart Symington 10/18/49 Folder, Box 57, Matthews Papers, HSTPL, 3; "Symington Affirms B-36 Faith, Hits Critics," *Washington Post*, 19 Oct. 1949, Subject File: B36 Clippings, Kimball Papers, ibid.
280. Statement of W. Stuart Symington, 4–5; "Defends B-36 Bomber: Secretary Stuart Symington," *Army-Navy Journal*, 87, no. 8, 22 Oct. 1949; Hammond, *Super Carriers and B-36 Bombers*, 64.
281. Condit, *History of the Joint Chiefs of Staff*, 183; Meilinger, *Bomber*, 141, 146.
282. Statement of W. Stuart Symington; "Symington Affirms B-36 Faith, Hits Critics"; "Defends B-36 Bomber"; "Facts and Fears"; Meilinger, "Admirals Revolt," 91; U.S. Congress, House, *Unification and Strategy*, 32–33.

283. Statement of W. Stuart Symington; "Symington Affirms B-36 Faith, Hits Critics"; "Defends B-36 Bomber."
284. Statement of W. Stuart Symington; "Defends B-36 Bomber."
285. Statement of W. Stuart Symington, 15–18; "New Anonymous Navy Document Falsifies Data to Disparage B-36 Symington Tells Unification Probe," *Washington Evening Star*, 18 Oct. 1949, Subject File: B36 Clippings, Kimball Papers, HSTPL; *Army-Navy Journal* 87, no. 9, 22 Oct. 1949, p. 213.
286. Statement of W. Stuart Symington; Hammond, *Super Carriers and B-36 Bombers*, 65; "New Anonymous Navy Document Falsifies Data to Disparage B-36 Symington Tells Unification Probe."
287. Statement of W. Stuart Symington; "Defends B-36 Bomber"; "Navy's All Wet, Says Symington," *Washington Daily News*, 18 Oct. 1949, Subject File: B36 Clippings, Kimball Papers, HSTPL.
288. Statement of W. Stuart Symington; "Navy's All Wet, Says Symington"; "New Anonymous Navy Document Falsifies Data to Disparage B-36 Symington Tells Unification Probe"; "Symington Affirms B-36 Faith, Hits Critics."
289. Statement of Gen. Hoyt S. Vandenberg, Chief of Staff, United States Air Force, before the Armed Services Committee of the House of Representatives Concerning the B-36 and Related Matters, Gen. Hoyt S. Vandenberg File, House Armed Services Committee Investigation into the B-36 and Related Matters (Oct 18–21, 49), Box 57, Matthews Papers, HSTPL; "Air Force Chief Sees No Need for Big Carrier," *Washington Evening Star*, 19 Oct. 1949, Subject File: B36 Clippings, Kimball Papers, HSTPL.
290. Statement of Gen. Hoyt S. Vandenberg; "Air Force Chief Sees No Need for Big Carrier"; "Defends B-36 Bomber."
291. Statement of Gen. Hoyt S. Vandenberg; "Defends B-36 Bomber."
292. Statement of Gen. Hoyt S. Vandenberg; "Air Force Chief Sees No Need for Big Carrier"; "Defends B-36 Bomber"; Hammond, *Super Carriers and B-36 Bombers*, 65.
293. Richard Kohn and Joseph Harahan, eds., *Strategic Air Warfare: An Interview with Generals Curtis E. LeMay, Leon W. Johnson, David A. Burchinal, and Jack J. Catton* (Washington, DC: Office of Air Force History, 1988), 90.
294. Statement of Gen. Hoyt S. Vandenberg.
295. Kohn and Harahan, *Strategic Air Warfare*, 90; "Air Force Chief Sees No Need for Big Carrier."
296. Statement of Gen. Hoyt S. Vandenberg; "Air Force Chief Sees No Need for Big Carrier"; "Defends B-36 Bomber."
297. Statement of Gen. Hoyt S. Vandenberg.
298. Statement of Gen. Hoyt S. Vandenberg; "Air Force Chief Sees No Need for Big Carrier"; "Defends B-36 Bomber."

299. Statement of Gen. Hoyt S. Vandenberg; "Air Force Chief Sees No Need for Big Carrier"; "Defends B-36 Bomber."
300. Statement of Gen. Hoyt S. Vandenberg; "Air Force Chief Sees No Need for Big Carrier"; "Defends B-36 Bomber."
301. "Air Force Chief Sees No Need for Big Carrier"; Bradley, *General's Life*, 510.
302. Col. Ray Clark, USAF Inspector General, Third Division, Kelly AFB, TX, to Maj. Gen. St. Clair Street, 29 Aug. 1949, Joint Committee on Atomic Energy (JCAE) AFSWP [Armed Forces Special Weapons Project], 1947–1952 Folder, Hickenlooper Papers, HHPL.
303. Clark to Street, 29 Aug. 1949.
304. Memorandum for the Chief of Staff, USAF, from St. Clair Street, Deputy Inspector General, USAF, 8 Sept. 1949, Joint Committee on Atomic Energy (JCAE) AFSWP, 1947–1952 Folder, Hickenlooper Papers, HHPL.
305. Memorandum for the Chief of Staff, USAF, 8 Sept. 1949.
306. Walter S. Moody, *Building a Strategic Air Force* (Washington, DC: Air Force History and Museum Program, 1996), 233; L. Douglas Keeney, *General Curtis LeMay and the Countdown to Nuclear Annihilation* (New York; St. Martin's, 2011), 54–55.
307. Curtis LeMay and MacKinlay Kantor, *Mission with LeMay* (Garden City, NY: Doubleday, 1965), 433; Kohn and Harahan, *Strategic Air Warfare*, 79.
308. Kohn and Harahan, *Strategic Air Warfare*, 79.
309. LeMay and Kantor, *Mission with LeMay*, 433.
310. Statement of Gen. Omar Bradley.
311. Statement of Gen. Omar Bradley; U.S. Congress, House, *Unification and Strategy*, 21, 28.
312. Statement of Gen. Omar Bradley.
313. Statement of Gen. Omar Bradley; "Roles for All Services," *Army-Navy Journal* 87, no. 9, 22 Oct. 1949.
314. Statement of Gen. Omar Bradley; "The Incorrigible and the Indomitable," *Time*, 31 Oct. 1949; Barlow, *Revolt of the Admirals*, 262; Bradley, *General's Life*, 511.
315. Baldwin quoted in Coletta, *United States Navy and Defense Unification*, 199.
316. Statement of Gen. Omar Bradley; "Staff Chiefs Chairman Assails Top Admirals for Hurting Defense," *Washington Post*, 20 Oct. 1949, Subject File: B36 Clippings, Kimball Papers, HSTPL.
317. Statement of Gen. Omar Bradley; "The Incorrigible and the Indomitable"; "Staff Chiefs Chairman Assails Top Admirals for Hurting Defense"; Barlow, *Revolt of the Admirals*, 262; Barlow, *From Hot War to Cold*, 238; McFarland and Roll, *Louis Johnson and the Arming of America*, 184; Potter, *Admiral Arleigh Burke*, 326; Bradley, *General's Life*, 511.
318. "The Incorrigible and the Indomitable."

319. Statement of Louis Johnson, Secretary of Defense, before the Committee on Armed Services, House of Representatives, 21 Oct. 1949, Box 57, Matthews Papers, HSTPL; Hammond, *Super Carriers and B-36 Bombers*, 69–70.
320. Statement of Louis Johnson, 13.
321. Statement of Louis Johnson; John Ponturo, *Analytical Support for the Joint Chiefs of Staff: The WSEG Experience, 1948–1976* (Arlington, VA: Institute for Defense Analysis International Studies Division, 1979), 60.
322. Hammond, *Super Carriers and B-36 Bombers*, 77.
323. House Armed Services Committee Investigation of B-36 and Related Matters, p. 34, Matthews Papers, HSTPL.
324. U.S. Congress, House, *Unification and Strategy*, 19.
325. U.S Congress, House, 46.
326. U.S. Congress, House, 16–17, 54.
327. U.S. Congress, House, 24.
328. Atomic Energy Commission, Thermonuclear Weapons Program Chronology, Chronology Folder, Hydrogen Bomb Weapons Program 1950, Lewis Strauss Papers, HHPL, 4 (hereafter AEC Thermonuclear Weapons Program Chronology); U.S. Congress, Joint Committee on Atomic Energy, *The Hydrogen Bomb and International Control: Technical and Background Information* (Washington, DC: U.S. Government Printing Office, 1950), 1, 1948–1950 Folder, Joint Committee on Atomic Energy, Hickenlooper Papers, HHPL; James Shepley and Clay Blair Jr., *The Hydrogen Bomb: The Men, the Menace, the Mechanism* (New York: David McKay, 1954), 46.
329. U.S. Congress, Joint Committee on Atomic Energy, *Hydrogen Bomb and International Control*, 1, 3.
330. AEC Thermonuclear Weapons Program Chronology, 14.
331. Transcript, Edward Teller, interviewed by Jay Kenworth, 20 Sept. 1979, Enclosure with Teller to Carol Lynch, 9 Apr. 1987, National Security Archive, George Washington University Washington, DC; Stanley A. Blumberg and Gwinn Owens, *Energy and Conflict: The Life and Times of Edward Teller* (New York: Putnam and Sons, 1976), 109.
332. Shepley and Blair, *Hydrogen Bomb*, 41–43.
333. AEC Thermonuclear Weapons Program Chronology, 7–8.
334. Draft, "A Chronology of the Thermonuclear Weapon Program to November 1952," 14 Oct. 1953, Hydrogen Bomb 1951–1970 Folder, Strauss Papers, HHPL, 3 (hereafter Draft Chronology to 1952); Transcript, Teller, interviewed by Kenworth, 20 Sept. 1979; Reardon, *Formative Years*, 447; Shepley and Blair, *Hydrogen Bomb*, 55.

335. Shepley and Blair, *Hydrogen Bomb*, 55; Blumberg and Owens, *Energy and Conflict*, 228.
336. Blumberg and Owens, *Energy and Conflict*, 186; Richard Pfau, *No Sacrifice Too Great: The Life of Lewis Strauss* (Charlottesville: University Press of Virginia, 1984), 112.
337. Excerpts from GAC Meetings, 18 Oct. 1953, 2nd Meeting 2-4-47, General Advisory Committee 1947–53 Folder, Strauss Papers, HHPL, 1; Richard Hewlett and Francis Duncan, *Atomic Shield: A History of the United States Atomic Energy Commission*, vol. 2 (Berkeley: University of California Press, 1990), 373.
338. Excerpts from GAC Meetings, 18 Oct. 1953, 3rd Meeting 3-28-47, 5; Hewlett and Duncan, *Atomic Shield*, 376.
339. Excerpts from GAC Meetings, 18 Oct. 1953, 6th Meeting 10-3-47, 9.
340. Draft Chronology to 1952, 3.
341. Excerpts from GAC Meetings, 18 Oct. 1953, 10th Meeting 6-4-48, 14; AEC Thermonuclear Weapons Program Chronology, 7.
342. Hewlett and Duncan, *Atomic Shield*, 376; Richard Rhodes, *Dark Sun: The Making of the Hydrogen Bomb* (New York: Simon and Schuster, 1995), 382–83; Pfau, *No Sacrifice Too Great*, 112–13.
343. Lewis Strauss to the President, 25 Nov. 1949, enclosure 1, Atomic Energy Bulk Dates 1946–1949 File, Subject File, Box 10, Naval Aide to the President Files, HSTPL.
344. Brien McMahon to Harry S. Truman, 30 May 1952, Attachment: "The Scale and Scope of Atomic Production—A Chronology of Leading Events," Atomic Weapons: Thermonuclear Folder 177-2, Box 177, NSC Reports, Atomic Subject File, President's Secretary Files, HSTPL, 13 (hereafter Attachment: Scale and Scope of Atomic Production); AEC Thermonuclear Weapons Program Chronology, 20; Pfau, *No Sacrifice Too Great*, 112; Roger M. Anders, ed., *Forging the Atomic Shield*, 18.
345. Attachment: Scale and Scope of Atomic Production, 13.
346. AEC Thermonuclear Weapons Program Chronology, 20.
347. Draft Chronology to 1952, 2; Memorandum, Lewis Strauss to D. Lilienthal, S. Pike, H. Smyth, and G. Dean, 5 Oct. 1949, Hydrogen Bomb Folder 1949, Strauss Papers, HHPL; Pfau, *No Sacrifice Too Great*, 112–13.
348. Memorandum, Strauss to Lilienthal, Pike, Smyth, and Dean, 5 Oct. 1949; Hewlett and Duncan, *Atomic Shield*, 373; AEC Thermonuclear Weapons Program Chronology, 22; Anders, *Forging the Atomic Shield*, 35.
349. Memorandum, Strauss to Lilienthal, Pike, Smyth, and Dean, 5 Oct. 1949; Lewis Strauss, *Men and Decisions* (New York: Doubleday, 1963), 227.

350. Shepley and Blair, *Hydrogen Bomb*, 62. William Borden was a B-24 bomber pilot in the war and was impressed with the German V-2 rockets and the possible application of such technology in the future. He wrote a book, *There Will Be No Time*, published in 1946, addressing the perils of future warfare. Borden was brought to Washington by McMahon.
351. Attachment: Scale and Scope of Atomic Production, 13; Hewlett and Duncan, *Atomic Shield*, 371. But others claimed one-fortieth.
352. Attachment: Scale and Scope of Atomic Production, 14.
353. Attachment: Scale and Scope of Atomic Production, 14; Samuel R. Williamson and Steven L. Reardon, *The Origins of US Nuclear Strategy, 1945–1953* (New York: St. Martin's, 1993), 112.
354. Necah S. Furman, "Sandia National Laboratories: A Product of Postwar Readiness 1945–1950" (report, Sandia National Laboratories, Albuquerque, NM, 1988), 17.
355. Sources cite some 228 nonfissionable components that were available for implosion-type bombs, with another 12 for gun type. Yet the amount of fissionable components available remains classified to this point. By the next summer reports stated that the United States held 292 fissionable components and 688 nonfissionable components for all types. JCS 1952/11 Weapons Systems Evaluation Group, "Evaluation of Effectiveness of Strategic Air Operations," 10 Feb. 1950, in *America's Plans for War against the Soviet Union, 1945–1950*, ed. Steven T. Ross and David Alan Rosenberg, vol. 13, *Evaluating the Air Offensive: The WSEG I Study* (New York: Garland, 1990), 163; David Alan Rosenberg, "US Nuclear Stockpile, 1945 to 1950," *Bulletin of Atomic Scientists* 38, no. 5 (May 1982): 26.
356. Reardon, *Formative Years*, 444; Hewlett and Duncan, *Atomic Shield*, 370.
357. Report to the President of the United States by the Special Committee of the National Security Council on the Proposed Acceleration of the Atomic Energy Program, 10 Oct. 1949, Atomic Energy: Expansion of Atomic Energy Program Folder, Atomic Energy: Advisory Committee and Atomic Energy Plans, Box 174, NSC Reports, Subject File, President's Secretary Files, HSTPL, 1–4 (hereafter Proposed Acceleration of the Atomic Energy Program, 10 Oct. 1949); Reardon, *Formative Years*, 444.
358. Proposed Acceleration of the Atomic Energy Program, 5, 7.
359. Lilienthal, *Journals*, 577.
360. Proposed Acceleration of the Atomic Energy Program, 9.
361. Attachment: Scale and Scope of Atomic Production, 14.
362. Reardon, *Formative Years*, 444; Hewlett and Duncan, *Atomic Shield*, 371.
363. Attachment: Scale and Scope of Atomic Production, 14.
364. Statement by the President, 20 Oct. 1949, General File, Atomic Bomb Folder, Box 96, President's Secretary Files, HSTPL; Rhodes, *Dark Sun*, 386; Reardon,

Formative Years, 444–45; Hewlett and Duncan, *Atomic Shield*, 377, 380; Attachment: Scale and Scope of Atomic Production, 14.

365. Attachment: Scale and Scope of Atomic Production, 14.
366. Rosenberg, "American Atomic Strategy and the Hydrogen Bomb Decision," 78–79; Reardon, *Formative Years*, 445.
367. Anders, *Forging the Atomic Shield*, 17, 43; Hewlett and Duncan, *Atomic Shield*, 375.
368. Lilienthal, *Journals*, 577.
369. The article also reported that the general was indeed getting six hours of sound sleep every night. "Peaceful Sleep," *Washington Times-Herald*, 25 Oct. 1949, B-36 Clippings, Subject File, Kimball Papers, HSTPL.
370. AEC Thermonuclear Weapons Program Chronology, 21, 40; Hewlett and Duncan, *Atomic Shield*, 372.
371. AEC Thermonuclear Weapons Program Chronology, 92.
372. Blumberg and Owens, *Energy and Conflict*, 208.
373. Rosenberg, "American Atomic Strategy and the Hydrogen Bomb Decision," 79 (quote); Blumberg and Owens, *Energy and Conflict*, 216; Williamson and Reardon, *Origins of US Nuclear Strategy*, 115; Hewlett and Duncan, *Atomic Shield*, 385.
374. Hewlett and Duncan, *Atomic Shield*, 372, 376–77.
375. Transcript, Teller, interviewed by Kenworth, 20 Sept. 1979, 13; Reardon, *Formative Years*, 447; Hewlett and Duncan, *Atomic Shield*, 375; Blumberg and Owens, *Energy and Conflict*, 202–3; Pfau, *No Sacrifice Too Great*, 113; Shepley and Blair, *Hydrogen Bomb*, 60–61.
376. Reardon, *Formative Years*, 447; Hewlett and Duncan, *Atomic Shield*, 376; Rhodes, *Dark Sun*, 383; Pfau, *No Sacrifice Too Great*, 113.
377. Draft Chronology to 1952, 4; Reardon, *Formative Years*, 447; Hewlett and Duncan, *Atomic Shield*, 377; Blumberg and Owen, *Energy and Conflict*, 203; Pfau, *No Sacrifice Too Great*, 114; Shepley and Blair, *Hydrogen Bomb*, 61.
378. Rhodes, *Dark Sun*, 32; Shepley and Blair, *Hydrogen Bomb*, 62–63.
379. Hewlett and Duncan, *Atomic Shield*, 377; Draft Chronology to 1952, 4; Blumberg and Owens, *Energy and Conflict*, 202–3; Strauss, *Men and Decisions*, 228; Rhodes, *Dark Sun*, 384–85.
380. Blumberg and Owens, *Energy and Conflict*, 204; Hewlett and Duncan, *Atomic Shield*, 377; Shepley and Blair, *Hydrogen Bomb*, 64.
381. Lilienthal, *Journals*, 577.
382. Blumberg and Owens, *Energy and Conflict*, 205; Hewlett and Duncan, *Atomic Shield*, 378.
383. Draft Chronology to 1952, 4; Hewlett and Duncan, *Atomic Shield*, 378.

384. David Lilienthal to J. Robert Oppenheimer, 11 Oct. 1949, Hydrogen Bomb Folder, 1949, Strauss Papers, HHPL; AEC Thermonuclear Weapons Program Chronology, 23.
385. AEC Thermonuclear Weapons Program Chronology, 23.
386. Harry Truman, *Years of Trial and Hope* (New York: Doubleday, 1956), 298.
387. AEC Thermonuclear Weapons Program Chronology, 23–24.
388. David Holloway, *Stalin and the Bomb: The Soviet Union and Atomic Energy, 1939–1956* (New Haven, CT: Yale University Press, 1994), 301; Memorandum for Mr. Robert LeBaron, Chairman, Military Liaison Committee to the Atomic Energy Commission, from H. B. Loper, 16 Feb. 1950, NSC Atomic Energy File: Russian Folder, Box 176, President's Secretary Files, HSTPL.
389. Pfau, *No Sacrifice Too Great*, 115; Rhodes, *Dark Sun*, 412; Hewlett and Duncan, *Atomic Shield*, 312–13.
390. Holloway, *Stalin and the Bomb*, 296.
391. Pfau, *No Sacrifice Too Great*, 115; Blumberg and Owens, *Energy and Conflict*, 214; Holloway, *Stalin and the Bomb*, 302; Memorandum for LeBaron, from Loper, 16 Feb. 1950. In retrospect the information provided by Fuchs regarding fusion in 1946 proved to be erroneous and of little use to the Soviet development of a thermonuclear weapon.
392. Pfau, *No Sacrifice Too Great*, 117.
393. Anders, *Forging the Atomic Shield*, 45.
394. Blumberg and Owens, *Energy and Conflict*, 210; Rhodes, *Dark Sun*, 392.
395. Hewlett and Duncan, *Atomic Shield*, 380; Blumberg and Owens, *Energy and Conflict*, 217; Rhodes, *Dark Sun*, 393.
396. Memorandum to Dr. J. H. Manley, Subj: Thumbnail Sketches of Representatives of the Department of Defense Attending the GAC Meeting Saturday, 29 Oct. 1949, Atomic Energy Commission, GAC DoD Reps, 1949, Folder 1, Box 176, J. Robert Oppenheimer Papers, LOC; Blumberg and Owens, *Energy and Conflict*, 213; Hewlett and Duncan, *Atomic Shield*, 381; AEC Thermonuclear Weapons Program Chronology, 26.
397. Hewlett and Duncan, *Atomic Shield*, 381–82; Blumberg and Owens, *Energy and Conflict*, 214.
398. Hewlett and Duncan, *Atomic Shield*, 382; Pfau, *No Sacrifice Too Great*, 116; Lilienthal, *Journals*, 581; Rhodes, *Dark Sun*, 398; Gerard J. DeGroot, *The Bomb: A Life* (Cambridge, MA; Harvard University Press, 2004), 169; McFarland and Roll, *Louis Johnson and the Arming of America*, 219.
399. Lilienthal, *Journals*, 580; Shepley and Blair, *Hydrogen Bomb*, 74.
400. Lilienthal, *Journals*, 581.
401. AEC Thermonuclear Weapons Program Chronology, 30.

402. Excerpts from GAC Meetings, 17th Meeting, 10-29-49, Majority Report, 20; AEC Thermonuclear Weapons Program Chronology, 30; Offner, *Another Such Victory*, 360.
403. AEC Thermonuclear Weapons Program Chronology, 27; Hewlett and Duncan, *Atomic Shield*, 383; Pfau, *No Sacrifice Too Great*, 116; Blumberg and Owens, *Energy and Conflict*, 218; Excerpts from GAC Meetings, 17th Meeting, 10-29-49; Reardon, *Formative Years*, 448.
404. Excerpts from GAC Meetings, 17th Meeting, 10-29-49, 19; AEC Thermonuclear Weapons Program Chronology, 27; Rosenberg, "American Atomic Strategy and the Hydrogen Bomb Decision," 80.
405. AEC Thermonuclear Weapons Program Chronology, 27–28; Attachment: Scale and Scope of Atomic Production, 15; Draft Chronology to 1952, 4; Hewlett and Duncan, *Atomic Shield*, 384–85; Pfau, *No Sacrifice Too Great*, 116; Lilienthal, *Journals*, 581–83; Anders, *Forging the Atomic Shield*, 36, 59; Strauss, *Men and Decisions*, 228; Reardon, *Formative Years*, 448–49; Blumberg and Owens, *Energy and Conflict*, 211–12; Dean Acheson, *Present at the Creation: My Years in the State Department* (reprint, New York: W. W. Norton, 1987), 346.
406. AEC Thermonuclear Weapons Program Chronology, 29.
407. Excerpts from GAC Meetings, 17th Meeting, 10-29-49, 20.
408. David Kunsman and Douglas Lawson, *A Primer on U.S. Strategic Nuclear Policy*, Sandia Report SAND 2001-0053 (Albuquerque: Sandia National Laboratories, 2001), 27.
409. Excerpts from GAC Meetings, 17th Meeting, 10-29-49, 20a.
410. Draft Chronology to 1952, 5.
411. Excerpts from GAC Meetings, 17th Meeting, 10-29-49, 21; AEC Thermonuclear Weapons Program Chronology, 30; Hewlett and Duncan, *Atomic Shield*, 384.
412. Excerpts from GAC Meetings, 17th Meeting, 10-29-49, 2; AEC Thermonuclear Weapons Program Chronology, 31; Hewlett and Duncan, *Atomic Shield*, 384; Anders, *Forging the Atomic Shield*, 49; Pfau, *No Sacrifice Too Great*, 116.
413. Anders, *Forging the Atomic Shield*, 48; AEC Thermonuclear Weapons Program Chronology, 32.
414. Lilienthal, *Journals*, 584.
415. Blumberg and Owens, *Energy and Conflict*, 220; DeGroot, *The Bomb*, 170; Shepley and Blair, *Hydrogen Bomb*, 77.
416. Pfau, *No Sacrifice Too Great*, 116–17.
417. Brien McMahon to the President, 1 Nov. 1949, Atomic Energy Folder, Super Bomb, President's Secretary Files, HSTPL; Anders, *Forging the Atomic Shield*, 51.
418. Hewlett and Duncan, *Atomic Shield*, 390; McMahon to the President, 1 Nov. 1949; Shepley and Blair, *Hydrogen Bomb*, 68.

419. McMahon to the President, 1 Nov. 1949.
420. Memorandum, Harry S. Truman to Brien McMahon, 2 Nov. 1949, Atomic Energy Folder, Super Bomb, President's Secretary Files, HSTPL.
421. David McLellan, *Dean Acheson: The State Department Years* (New York: Dodd, Mead, 1976), 175; Acheson, *Present at the Creation*, 345; Walter Isaacson and Evan Thomas, *The Wise Men: Six Friends and the World They Made* (New York: Simon and Schuster, 1986), 486–87.
422. Isaacson and Thomas, *Wise Men*, 487; McLellan, *Dean Acheson*, 175; Acheson, *Present at the Creation*, 346.
423. R. Gordon Arneson, interviewed by Niel M. Johnson, 21 June 1989, Oral History Interviews, HSTPL, https://www.trumanlibrary.gov/library/oral-histories/arneson (accessed 27 Mar. 2019).
424. Isaacson and Thomas, *Wise Men*, 487.
425. George F. Kennan, *Memoirs, 1925–1950* (New York: Pantheon, 1967), 473–74.
426. Strauss, *Men and Decisions*, 228.
427. Anders, *Forging the Atomic Shield*, 49–50; Hewlett and Duncan, *Atomic Shield*, 386–87.
428. Memorandum from Lewis Strauss to Roy B. Snapp, 3 Nov. 1949, Hydrogen Bomb 1949 Folder, Strauss Papers, HHPL; Hewlett and Duncan, *Atomic Shield*, 387; Pfau, *No Sacrifice Too Great*, 117–19; Blumberg and Owens, *Energy and Conflict*, 221.
429. Memorandum from Strauss to Snapp, 3 Nov. 1949; AEC Thermonuclear Weapons Program Chronology, 32–33.
430. AEC Thermonuclear Weapons Program Chronology, 35–36.
431. Blumberg and Owens, *Energy and Conflict*, 222.
432. AEC Thermonuclear Weapons Program Chronology, 38–46; Draft Chronology to 1952, 5; Attachment: Scale and Scope of Atomic Production, 15; Hewlett and Duncan, *Atomic Shield*, 391; McFarland and Roll, *Louis Johnson and the Arming of America*, 220.
433. AEC Thermonuclear Weapons Program Chronology, 38.
434. AEC Thermonuclear Weapons Program Chronology, 40–41.
435. Lilienthal, *Journals*, 592.
436. U.S. Congress, Senate, *Investigation into the United States Energy Commission, Report of the Joint Committee on Atomic Energy* (Washington, DC: U.S. Government Printing Office, 1949), National Defense–Atomic Energy 1947–1949 Folder, Box 59, Elsey Papers, HSTPL; Shepley and Blair, *Hydrogen Bomb*, 7.
437. Statement by Sen. Bourke B. Hickenlooper at the Joint Committee Hearing on the Lilienthal Matter, 2 June 1949. AEC Commissioners, David E. Lilienthal, 1949–1954 Folder, Hickenlooper Papers, HHPL; Leslie Groves to Bourke Hickenlooper, 25 May 1949, AEC Groves 1946–49 Folder, ibid.

438. David Lilienthal to Harry S. Truman, 21 Nov. 1949, David E. Lilienthal, 1949 Folder, Strauss Papers, HHPL.
439. Harry Truman to David Lilienthal, 23 Nov. 1949, David E. Lilienthal, 1949 Folder, Strauss Papers, HHPL.
440. Hewlett and Duncan, *Atomic Shield*, 389; Lilienthal, *Journals*, 594; Rhodes, *Dark Sun*, 408.
441. Hewlett and Duncan, *Atomic Shield*, 389; Lilienthal, *Journals*, 594.
442. Lilienthal, *Journals*, 594.
443. "Defense," *Washington Times-Herald*, 25 Oct. 1949, B-36 Clippings, Subject File, Kimball Papers, HSTPL; Hammond, *Super Carriers and B-36 Bombers*, 67.
444. Bradley quoted in Barlow, *Revolt of the Admirals*, 262.
445. "Speculation Continues That Admiral Denfeld Will Be Forced Out," *Washington Evening Star*, 26 Oct. 1949, Subject Files, B-36 Clippings (2 of 2), Kimball Papers, HSTPL.
446. U.S. Congress, House, *Unification and Strategy*, 11.
447. Francis Matthews to Harry S. Truman, 27 Oct. 1949, Folder 1, Louis Denfeld, Correspondence File, Box 27, Matthews Papers, HSTPL.
448. Matthews to Truman, 27 Oct. 1949; U.S. Congress, House, *Unification and Strategy*, 14.
449. Matthews to Truman, 27 Oct. 1949; Hammond, *Super Carriers and B-36 Bombers*, 80; U.S. Congress, House, *Unification and Strategy*, 14.
450. Memorandum for the Secretary of the Navy from the President, 27 Oct. 1949, Louis E. Denfeld Folder, Box 27, Matthews Papers, HSTPL.
451. "Punishment," *Time*, 7 Nov. 1949.
452. Adm. Charles Donald Griffin, quoted in Coletta, *United States Navy and Defense Unification*, 208.
453. Denfeld, "Why I Was Fired."
454. Hanson Baldwin to Louis Denfeld, 28 Oct. 1949, B Folder, Box 7, Ser. 3 Post Relief Correspondence, 1949, Denfeld Papers, NHHC.
455. Donovan, *Tumultuous Years*, 112; McFarland and Roll, *Louis Johnson and the Arming of America*, 185.
456. Laura H. Ingalls to Secretary of the Navy, 27 Oct. 1949, Adm. Louis E. Denfeld (Folder 1), Box 27, Matthews Papers, HSTPL.
457. Matthews to Truman, 27 Oct. 1949.
458. Denfeld, "Why I Was Fired."
459. "Denfeld's Ouster Is Not Reprisal," *Washington Evening Star*, 29 Oct. 1949; "Sec. Johnson Calls Firing of Denfeld No Reprisal," *Washington Post*, 29 Oct. 1949, Subject Files, B-36 Clippings (2 of 2), Kimball Papers, HSTPL.
460. Telephone Interview with Mr. Bradbury, 31 Oct. 1949, Folder 1, Box 27, Matthews Papers, HSTPL.

461. Potter, *Nimitz*, 447–48.
462. Minutes of Press Conference Held by Secretary Francis P. Matthews and Vice Adm. Forrest P. Sherman, 1 Nov. 1949, Minutes of Press Conference Held by Sec Navy Matthews and VAdm Sherman 11/1/45 Folder, Box 52, Matthews Papers, HSTPL.
463. Dittmer, "Firing of Admiral Denfeld," 119–20.
464. Transcription from Recording of *Meet the Press*, 28 Oct. 1950, Transcription . . . *Meet the Press* Folder, Box 52, Matthews Papers, HSTPL.
465. Louis Denfeld to Rep. John McCormack, 1 Nov. 1949, McCormack Folder, Box 5, Ser. 2, Personal Correspondence 1947–1949, Denfeld Papers, NHHC.
466. Louis Denfeld, "The Nation Needs the Navy: Concluding 'Why I Was Fired,'" *Collier's*, 1 Apr. 1950.
467. Louis Denfeld, "The Only Carrier the Air Force Ever Sank: Continuing 'Why I Was fired,'" *Collier's*, 25 Mar. 1950.
468. U.S. Congress, House, *Unification and Strategy*, 53.
469. "Man in a Blue Suit," *Time*, 14 Nov. 1949.
470. "Denfeld's Off on Holiday," *Washington Post*, 16 Nov. 1949.
471. "Midshipmen Roar Approval of Admiral Denfeld at Game," *Washington Sunday Star*, 30 Oct. 1949; Subject Files, B-36 Clippings (2 of 2), Kimball Papers, HSTPL; "Punishment," *Time*, 7 Nov. 1949; Hammond, *Super Carriers and B-36 Bombers*, 80.
472. Louis Denfeld to Francis Matthews, 14 Dec. 1949, Denfeld Folder, Box 27, Correspondence File, Matthews Papers, HSTPL; Coletta, *United States Navy and Defense Unification*, 211.
473. Denfeld to Matthews, 14 Dec. 1949.
474. "Denfeld Tells Crommelin to Explain Actions," *Washington Post*, 25 Oct. 1949; "Court-Martial of Crommelin over Letter Pressed by Brass," *Washington Times-Herald*, 25 Oct. 1949, Subject Files, B-36 Clippings (2 of 2), Kimball Papers, HSTPL.
475. "Capt. Crommelin Returns to Duty," *Washington Daily News*, 8 Nov. 1949, Subject Files, B-36 Clippings (2 of 2), Kimball Papers, HSTPL; "Reprimand," *Time*, 21 Nov. 1949; Coletta, *United States Navy and Defense Unification*, 211.
476. Walter Winchell, "The Case for Crommelin," *Pittsburgh Sun-Telegraph*, 23 Nov. 1949, Subject Files, B-36 Clippings (2 of 2), Kimball Papers, HSTPL; "Reprimand," Time Magazine.
477. Hammond, *Super Carriers and B-36 Bombers*, 82.
478. Barlow, *Revolt of the Admirals*, 241–42; Potter, *Admiral Arleigh Burke*, 326; "Adm. Sherman Scuttles Navy Unity Snipers," *Washington Times-Herald*, 4 Nov. 1949, Subject Files, B-36 Clippings (2 of 2), Kimball Papers, HSTPL; Potter, *Admiral Arleigh Burke*, 326.

479. Barlow, *Revolt of the Admirals*, 242.
480. "Sherman Dissolves OP 23 Unit, Called Key to Fight by Navy," *Washington Post*, 4 Nov. 1949, Subject Files, B-36 Clippings (2 of 2), Kimball Papers, HSTPL; "OP-23 Disbanded," *Army-Navy Journal*, 87, no. 10, 5 Nov. 1949, p. 251, Subject Files, B-36 Clippings (2 of 2), Kimball Papers, HSTPL; Barlow, *Revolt of the Admirals*, 277–78.
481. Potter, *Admiral Arleigh Burke*, 328–30; "Stopped Cold," *Time*, 26 Dec. 1949.
482. Potter, *Admiral Arleigh Burke*, 329.
483. Potter, 330.
484. Joseph and Steward Alsop, quoted in "Fat or Muscle?," *Time*, 5 Dec. 1949.
485. Coletta, *United States Navy and Defense Unification*, 213.
486. "New Prayer for the Navy in 1949 AD (After Denfeld)," n.d., Misc. Correspondence and Speeches 1948–1949 Folder, Post Relief Correspondence 1949, Box 9, Denfeld Paper, NHHC.
487. "New A-Bomb Has 6 Times Power of 1st," *Washington Post*, 18 Nov. 1949; Strauss, *Men and Decisions*, 119; Hewlett and Duncan, *Atomic Shield*, 394.
488. "New A-Bomb Has 6 Times Power of 1st"; "Hydrogen Bomb Is New Threat," Washington Merry-Go-Round, *Washington Post*, 27 Nov. 1949; Blumberg and Owens, *Energy and Conflict*, 226; Hewlett and Duncan, *Atomic Shield*, 394; Acheson, *Present at the Creation*, 345–46.
489. "New A-Bomb Has 6 Times Power of 1st"; Strauss, *Men and Decisions*, 119; Blumberg and Owens, *Energy and Conflict*, 227.
490. "One A-Bomb Could Cripple Washington: AEC Advises Dispersal of U.S. Govt.," *Washington Post*, 17 Nov. 1949.
491. New A-Bomb Has 6 Times Power of 1st"; Lilienthal, *Journals*, 601.
492. Lilienthal, *Journals*, 601.
493. Hewlett and Duncan, *Atomic Shield*, 12–13.
494. Brien McMahon to Harry Truman, 21 Nov. 1949, Atomic Energy Folder, Naval Aide to the President File, 1945–1953, Box, 10, HSTPL.
495. McMahon to Truman, 21 Nov. 1949.
496. Neither Truman nor McMahon probably knew how bad SAC was regarding its accuracy and its average Circular Error Probable.
497. McMahon to Truman, 21 Nov. 1949.
498. McMahon to Truman, 21 Nov. 1949.
499. Of course, the number of dead from Hiroshima rose as radiation sickness and other long-term ailments associated with the bombing claimed many more lives. In this argument McMahon was only referencing the initial effects.
500. McMahon to Truman, 21 Nov. 1949.
501. McMahon to Truman, 21 Nov. 1949. As mentioned earlier, the German scientists associated with the Russian effort provided largely ancillary support to the

endeavor, with Soviet scientists largely in the lead. Despite this, McMahon's argument made the situation appear more dangerous. Also as mentioned earlier, Kapitza had quit the Soviet program in 1945.

502. McMahon to Truman, 21 Nov. 1949.
503. Lewis Strauss to Harry Truman, 25 Nov. 1949, Atomic Energy Bulk Dates 1946–1949 File, Box 10, Subject File, Naval Aide File, HSTPL; AEC Thermonuclear Weapons Program Chronology, 48.
504. Strauss to Truman, 25 Nov. 1949; AEC Thermonuclear Weapons Program Chronology, 49.
505. Pfau, *No Sacrifice Too Great*, 119.
506. Unattributed Interview with Gorden [*sic*] Arneson, Washington, DC, 11 July 1984, Atomic Energy Program and R. Gordon Arneson Corr. Folder [2 of 2], Subj. File, Box 1, Arneson Papers, HSTPL.
507. Shepley and Blair, *Hydrogen Bomb*, 80.
508. Shepley and Blair, 81.
509. Despite his letter of resignation, Lilienthal remained a member of the AEC until 15 February 1950 after asking and receiving approval from Truman in December 1949. His extension was based upon his membership in the Z Committee. Hewlett and Duncan, *Atomic Shield*, 394; Draft Chronology to 1952, 5; AEC Thermonuclear Weapons Program Chronology, 60; Reardon, *Formative Years*, 450; Rosenberg, "American Atomic Strategy and the Hydrogen Bomb Decision," 80; Strauss, *Men and Decisions*, 234; Condit, *History of the Joint Chiefs of Staff*, 293; DeGroot, *The Bomb*, 170; McFarland and Roll, *Louis Johnson and the Arming of America*, 220; Acheson, *Present at the Creation*, 346; Truman, *Years of Trial and Hope*, 309; ; Arneson, interviewed by Johnson, 21 June 1989. Acheson places the establishment of the Z Committee as 10 November.
510. Nitze, interviewed by McKinzie, 5 Aug. 1975.
511. Lilienthal, *Journals*, 509; McFarland and Roll, *Louis Johnson and the Arming of America*, 209.
512. Rosenberg, "American Atomic Strategy and the Hydrogen Bomb Decision," 81; Hewlett and Duncan, *Atomic Shield*, 395; Reardon, *Formative Years*, 449; Condit, *History of the Joint Chiefs of Staff*, 292; Pfau, *No Sacrifice Too Great*, 121.
513. Condit, *History of the Joint Chiefs of Staff*, 291; Rosenberg, "American Atomic Strategy and the Hydrogen Bomb Decision," 82; McFarland and Roll, *Louis Johnson and the Arming of America*, 220.
514. Condit, *History of the Joint Chiefs of Staff*, 291; Rosenberg, "American Atomic Strategy and the Hydrogen Bomb Decision, 82.
515. Excerpts from GAC Meetings, 18th Meeting, 12-3-49, 22; Draft Chronology to 1952, 5; Attachment: Scale and Scope of Atomic Production, 15; Hewlett and Duncan, *Atomic Shield*, 396; Anders, *Forging the Atomic Shield*, 63.

516. AEC Thermonuclear Weapons Program Chronology, 64.
517. Gallup, *Gallup Poll on Public Opinion*, 2:869. Seventeen percent believed it made no difference, and 10 percent had no opinion on the matter.
518. Lilienthal, *Journals*, 614; Hewlett and Duncan, *Atomic Shield*, 398; Acheson, *Present at the Creation*, 348; Reardon, *Formative Years*, 451.
519. Lilienthal, *Journals*, 614; Condit, *History of the Joint Chiefs of Staff*, 293; Rosenberg, "American Atomic Strategy and the Hydrogen Bomb Decision," 82; McFarland and Roll, *Louis Johnson and the Arming of America*, 220; Offner, *Another Such Victory*, 361; Acheson, *Present at the Creation*, 348; Rhodes, *Dark Sun*, 406.
520. Lilienthal, *Journals*, 614.
521. Condit, *History of the Joint Chiefs of Staff*, 293; Rosenberg, "American Atomic Strategy and the Hydrogen Bomb Decision," 82; Lilienthal, *Journals*, 614; Hewlett and Duncan, *Atomic Shield*, 398; Acheson, *Present at the Creation*, 348.
522. Hewlett and Duncan, *Atomic Shield*, 398; Rosenberg, "American Atomic Strategy and the Hydrogen Bomb Decision," 82; McFarland and Roll, *Louis Johnson and the Arming of America*, 220.
523. Hewlett and Duncan, *Atomic Shield*, 398; Rosenberg, "American Atomic Strategy and the Hydrogen Bomb Decision," 82.
524. Lilienthal, *Journals*, 614; Hewlett and Duncan, *Atomic Shield*, 398; McFarland and Roll, *Louis Johnson and the Arming of America*, 221; Reardon, *Formative Years*, 451.
525. Acheson, *Present at the Creation*, 348; McFarland and Roll, *Louis Johnson and the Arming of America*, 221; Reardon, *Formative Years*, 451.
526. Isaacson and Thomas, *Wise Men*, 481; Kennan, *Memoirs*, 472.
527. Isaacson and Thomas, *Wise Men*, 482–85; Kennan, *Memoirs*, 475.
528. Nicholas Thompson, *The Hawk and the Dove: Paul Nitze, George Kennan, and the History of the Cold War* (New York: Henry Holt, 2009), 105; Kennan, *Memoirs*, 465–66.

Chapter 3. Winter

1. Steven L. Reardon, *History of the Office of the Secretary of Defense: The Formative Years, 1947–1950* (Washington, DC: Historical Office of the Secretary of Defense, 1984), 408–9 (hereafter Reardon, *Formative Years*).
2. Walter S. Moody, *Building a Strategic Air Force* (Washington, DC: Air Force History and Museum Program, 1996), 306; John Ponturo, *Analytical Support for the Joint Chiefs of Staff: The WSEG Experience, 1948–1976* (Arlington, VA: Institute for Defense Analysis International Studies Division, 1979), 74; JCS 1952/11 Weapons Systems Evaluation Group, "Evaluation of Effectiveness of Strategic Air Operations," 10 Feb. 1950, in *America's Plans for War against the Soviet Union, 1945–1950*, ed. Steven T. Ross and David Alan Rosenberg,

vol. 13, *Evaluating the Air Offensive: The WSEG I Study* (New York: Garland, 1989), contents (hereafter WSEG, "Evaluation of Effectiveness of Strategic Air Operations").

3. Reardon, *Formative Years*, 409; Ponturo, *Analytical Support for the Joint Chiefs of Staff*, 74; Moody, *Building a Strategic Air Force*, 306; David Alan Rosenberg, "American Atomic Strategy and the Hydrogen Bomb Decision," *Journal of American History* 66, no.1 (July 1979): 83; WSEG, "Evaluation of Effectiveness of Strategic Air Operations," introduction.
4. Ponturo, *Analytical Support for the Joint Chiefs of Staff*, 74; Reardon, *Formative Years*, 409; Keith D. McFarland and David L. Roll, *Louis Johnson and the Arming of America: The Roosevelt and Truman Years* (Bloomingdale: Indiana University Press, 2005), 222.
5. WSEG, "Evaluation of Effectiveness of Strategic Air Operations," 157.
6. "Brief of Joint Outline Emergency War Plan (Offtackle) JSPC 877/59, May 26, 1949," in Thomas Etzold and John Lewis Gaddis, *Containment: Documents on American Policy and Strategy, 1945–1950* (New York: Columbia University Press, 1978), 332–33; "Proceedings, Commanders Conference, April 25, 26, & 27, 1950, Ramey Air Force Base, Puerto Rico, Top Secret, Excerpts," Document 3a, "Special Collection: Some Key Documents on Nuclear Policy Issues, 1945–1990," ed. William Burr, National Security Archive, 15 June 2007, https://nsarchive2.gwu.edu/nukevault/special/doc03a.pdf (accessed 2 Nov. 2021), 18; WSEG, "Evaluation of Effectiveness of Strategic Air Operations," 163.
7. "Brief of Joint Outline Emergency War Plan (Offtackle)," 324.
8. Moody, *Building a Strategic Air Force*, 309–10; WSEG, "Evaluation of Effectiveness of Strategic Air Operations," 163; "Proceedings, Commanders Conference," 18; David Kunsman and Douglas Lawson, *A Primer on U.S. Strategic Nuclear Policy*, Sandia Report SAND 2001-0053 (Albuquerque: Sandia National Laboratories, 2001), 26; Moody, *Building a Strategic Air Force*, 309.
9. "Brief of Joint Outline Emergency War Plan (Offtackle)," 327.
10. WSEG, "Evaluation of Effectiveness of Strategic Air Operations," 163; Kenneth Condit, *History of the Joint Chiefs of Staff: The Joint Chiefs of Staff and National Policy*, vol. 2, *1947–1949* (Washington, DC: Office of Joint History, 1996), 157, 188.
11. The number is seventy-two atomic bombs higher as it includes reattack in certain objectives. WSEG, "Evaluation of Effectiveness of Strategic Air Operations," 194.
12. WSEG, "Evaluation of Effectiveness of Strategic Air Operations," 164; "Presentation by the Strategic Air Command, Commanders Conference, Ramey Air Force Base, 25–26–27 April 1950, Top Secret, Excerpts," Document 3c, "Special Collection: Some Key Documents on Nuclear Policy Issues, 1945–1990," ed. William Burr, National Security Archive, 15 June 2007, https://nsarchive2.gwu

.edu/nukevault/special/doc03c.pdf (accessed 2 Nov. 2021); Reardon, *Formative Years*, 410.

13. "Evaluation of Effect on Soviet War Effort Resulting from the Strategic Air Offensive," in Etzold and Gaddis, *Containment*, 361; WSEG, "Evaluation of Effectiveness of Strategic Air Operations," 164.
14. "Presentation by the Strategic Air Command, Commanders Conference."
15. "Presentation by the Strategic Air Command, Commanders Conference"; WSEG, "Evaluation of Effectiveness of Strategic Air Operations," Enclosure F, 5; Moody, *Building a Strategic Air Force*, 272, 273, 276.
16. "Proceedings, Commanders Conference," 21.
17. Reardon, *Formative Years*, 409; Condit, *History of the Joint Chiefs of Staff*, 188; Moody, *Building a Strategic Air Force*, 307; Phillip S. Meilinger, *Bomber: The Formation and Early Years of Strategic Air Command* (Maxwell AFB: Air University Press, 2012), 153; Rosenberg, "American Atomic Strategy and the Hydrogen Bomb Decision," 83; WSEG, "Evaluation of Effectiveness of Strategic Air Operations," 159–60.
18. WSEG, "Evaluation of Effectiveness of Strategic Air Operations," 191.
19. WSEG, 190.
20. WSEG, 193.
21. Meilinger, *Bomber*, 164.
22. Reardon, *Formative Years*, 409; Philip Morse, *In at the Beginning: A Physicist's Life* (Cambridge, MA: MIT Press, 1977), 255; WSEG, "Evaluation of Effectiveness of Strategic Air Operations," 159.
23. WSEG, "Evaluation of Effectiveness of Strategic Air Operations," Enclosure H, 5.
24. Morse, *In at the Beginning*, 256.
25. Morse, 257.
26. Morse, 258.
27. Reardon, *Formative Years*, 410; Morse, *In at the Beginning*, 259.
28. WSEG, "Evaluation of Effectiveness of Strategic Air Operations," 158.
29. WSEG, 194.
30. WSEG, 195, Enclosure K, 3.
31. Moody, *Building a Strategic Air Force*, 312–13; WSEG, "Evaluation of Effectiveness of Strategic Air Operations," 159.
32. WSEG, "Evaluation of Effectiveness of Strategic Air Operations," 161.
33. "Presentation by the Strategic Air Command, Commanders Conference," 5; Morse, *In at the Beginning*, 253.
34. "Presentation by the Strategic Air Command, Commanders Conference," 5.
35. Conrad Crane, *American Airpower Strategy in Korea, 1950–1953* (Lawrence: University Press of Kansas, 2000), 87–88; Meilinger, *Bomber*, 240–41, 274.

36. Crane, *American Airpower Strategy in Korea*, 90.
37. Crane, 90.
38. Memorandum for the Joint Chiefs of Staff, from J. E. Hull, Subj: Heavy Bomber Operations, 21 July 1950, in WSEG, "Evaluation of Effectiveness of Strategic Air Operations."
39. WSEG, 161.
40. Joseph Alsop and Steward Alsop, "Matter of Fact," *Washington Post*, 2 Jan. 1950, newspaper clipping, NSC–Atomic Energy Super Bomb Folder, Subject File, Box 176, President's Secretary Files, Harry S. Truman Presidential Library, Independence, MO (hereafter HSTPL).
41. Brien McMahon to the President, 3 Jan. 1950, NSC–Atomic Energy Super Bomb Folder, Subject File, Box 176, President's Secretary Files, HSTPL.
42. Note, Truman to McMahon, 5 Jan. 1949, NSC–Atomic Energy Super Bomb Folder, Subject File, Box 176, President's Secretary Files, HSTPL.
43. Richard Pfau, *No Sacrifice Too Great: The Life of Lewis Strauss* (Charlottesville: University Press of Virginia, 1984), 121.
44. McFarland and Roll, *Louis Johnson and the Arming of America*, 221; Richard Hewlett and Francis Duncan, *Atomic Shield: A History of the United States Atomic Energy Commission*, vol. 2 (Berkeley: University of California Press, 1990), 400.
45. Brien McMahon to Harry S. Truman, 30 May 1952, Attachment: "The Scale and Scope of Atomic Production—A Chronology of Leading Events," Atomic Weapons: Thermonuclear Folder 177-2, Box 177, NSC Reports, Atomic Subject File, President's Secretary Files, HSTPL, 16 (hereafter Attachment: Scale and Scope of Atomic Production).
46. Atomic Energy Commission, Thermonuclear Weapons Program Chronology, Chronology Folder, Hydrogen Bomb Weapons Program 1950, Lewis Strauss Papers, Herbert Hoover Presidential Library, West Branch, IA, 79 (hereafter AEC Thermonuclear Weapons Program Chronology).
47. AEC Thermonuclear Weapons Program Chronology, 79; Hewlett and Duncan, *Atomic Shield*, 400; Robert J. Donovan, *Tumultuous Years: The Presidency of Harry S. Truman, 1949–1953* (New York: W. W. Norton, 1982), 154.
48. AEC Thermonuclear Weapons Program Chronology, 79; Hewlett and Duncan, *Atomic Shield*, 400.
49. AEC Thermonuclear Weapons Program Chronology, 81; Hewlett and Duncan, *Atomic Shield*, 400.
50. AEC Thermonuclear Weapons Program Chronology, 86; Hewlett and Duncan, *Atomic Shield*, 400.
51. Rosenberg, "American Atomic Strategy and the Hydrogen Bomb Decision," 82; McFarland and Roll, *Louis Johnson and the Arming of America*, 222; Condit,

History of the Joint Chiefs of Staff, 297; Donovan, *Tumultuous Years*, 154; Richard Rhodes, *Dark Sun: The Making of the Hydrogen Bomb* (New York: Simon and Schuster, 1995), 407.

52. McFarland and Roll, *Louis Johnson and the Arming of America*, 222; Donovan, *Tumultuous Years*, 154; Rhodes, *Dark Sun*, 407; Reardon, *Formative Years*, 452.
53. Attachment: Scale and Scope of Atomic Production, 16; Hewlett and Duncan, *Atomic Shield*, 401; Condit, *History of the Joint Chiefs of Staff*, 297; Roger M. Anders, ed., *Forging the Atomic Shield: Excerpts from the Office Diary of Gordon Dean* (Chapel Hill: University of North Carolina Press, 1987), 63.
54. Hewlett and Duncan, *Atomic Shield*, 401.
55. Hewlett and Duncan, 402.
56. Memorandum of Telephone Conversation between Admiral Souers and Secretary Acheson, 19 Jan. 1950, January 1950 Folder, Memorandum of Conversations File, Acheson Papers Box 66, HSTPL.
57. Memorandum of Telephone Conversation between Admiral Souers and Secretary Acheson, 19 Jan. 1950.
58. James Reston, "US Hydrogen Bomb Delay Urged Pending Bid to Soviet," *New York Times*, 17 Jan. 1950.
59. "Atom Bomb Plane Linked to Soviets," *New York Times*, 17 Jan. 1950.
60. "Bradley Consults with Atomic Group," *New York Times*, 20 Jan. 1950.
61. Lewis Strauss to Harry S. Truman, 16 Jan. 1950, Hydrogen Bomb 1950 Folder, Strauss Papers, Herbert Hoover Presidential Library, West Branch, IA (hereafter HHPL).
62. Anders, *Forging the Atomic Shield*, 63; Hewlett and Duncan, *Atomic Shield*, 404.
63. Draft, "A Chronology of the Thermonuclear Weapon Program to November 1952," 14 Oct. 1953, Hydrogen Bomb 1951–1970 Folder, Strauss Papers, HHPL, 6 (hereafter Draft Chronology to 1952); AEC Thermonuclear Weapons Program Chronology, 97–98.
64. AEC Thermonuclear Weapons Program Chronology, 97–98.
65. AEC Thermonuclear Weapons Program Chronology, 98.
66. AEC Thermonuclear Weapons Program Chronology, 98.
67. AEC Thermonuclear Weapons Program Chronology, 95.
68. Anders, *Forging the Atomic Shield*, 63; AEC Thermonuclear Weapons Program Chronology, 99–108.
69. AEC Thermonuclear Weapons Program Chronology, 97.
70. Anders, *Forging the Atomic Shield*, 63–64; Pfau, *No Sacrifice Too Great*, 121; Hewlett and Duncan, *Atomic Shield*, 404–5; AEC Thermonuclear Weapons Program Chronology, 108.
71. David S. McLellan, *Dean Acheson: The State Department Years* (New York: Dodd, Mead, 1976), 177; Hewlett and Duncan, *Atomic Shield*, 403.

72. McLellan, *Dean Acheson*, 175; Hewlett and Duncan, *Atomic Shield*, 403; Pfau, *No Sacrifice Too Great*, 121.
73. Walter Isaacson and Evan Thomas, *The Wise Men: Six Friends and the World They Made* (New York: Simon and Schuster, 1986), 487.
74. Reardon, *Formative Years*, 450–51; Paul H. Nitze, interview by Richard D. McKinzie, 5, 6 Aug. 1975, Oral History Interviews, HSTPL, https://www.trumanlibrary.gov/library/oral-histories/nitzeph3 (accessed 8 July 2019).
75. Reardon, *Formative Years*, 450–51.
76. Hewlett and Duncan, *Atomic Shield*, 403.
77. Isaacson and Thomas, *Wise Men*, 487; Thompson, 107; Hewlett and Duncan, *Atomic Shield*, 403; R. Gordon Arneson, interviewed by Niel M. Johnson, 21 June 1989, Oral History Interviews, HSTPL, https://wwwtrumanlibrary.gov/library/oral-histories/arneson (accessed 27 Mar. 2019).
78. Arneson, interviewed by Johnson, 21 June 1989.
79. President's News Conference, 27 Jan. 1950, Public Papers, HSTPL, https://trumanlibrary.gov/library/public-papers/23/presidents-news-conference (accessed 28 Mar. 2019).
80. Alfred Friendly, "Urey, Baruch, and Others Urge Going Ahead with Project for Super Weapon," *Washington Post*, 28 Jan. 1949.
81. "Declassified Version of Mr. Lilienthal's memorandum of January 31," 5 Mar. 1964, Dean Acheson Papers, HSTPL; AEC Thermonuclear Weapons Program Chronology, 108–9; McFarland and Roll, *Louis Johnson and the Arming of America*, 222, Hewlett and Duncan, *Atomic Shield*, 406; Attachment: Scale and Scope of Atomic Production, 16; Pfau, *No Sacrifice Too Great*, 121–22; Reardon, *Formative Years*, 452; James Shepley and Clay Blair Jr., *The Hydrogen Bomb: The Men, the Menace, the Mechanism* (New York: David McKay, 1954), 87; Dean Acheson, *Present at the Creation: My Years in the State Department* (reprint, New York: W. W. Norton, 1987), 348; Donovan, *Tumultuous Years*, 155; David E. Lilienthal, *The Journals of David E. Lilienthal*, vol. 2, *The Atomic Energy Years* (New York: Harper and Row, 1964), 623; Stanley A. Blumberg and Gwinn Owens, *Energy and Conflict: The Life and Times of Edward Teller* (New York: Putnam and Sons, 1976), 230.
82. Shepley and Blair, *Hydrogen Bomb*, 87.
83. Declassified Version of Mr. Lilienthal's memorandum of January 31; AEC Thermonuclear Weapons Program Chronology, 109; Hewlett and Duncan, *Atomic Shield*, 406; Reardon, *Formative Years*, 452; Condit, *History of the Joint Chiefs of Staff*, 298; Lilienthal, *Journals*, 624.
84. "Declassified Version of Mr. Lilienthal's memorandum of January 31"; AEC Thermonuclear Weapons Program Chronology, 109–11; McFarland and Roll, *Louis Johnson and the Arming of America*, 222–23; Hewlett and Duncan, *Atomic Shield*, 406–7; Lilienthal, *Journals*, 625.

85. "Declassified Version of Mr. Lilienthal's memorandum of January 31"; AEC Thermonuclear Weapons Program Chronology, 109–11; Lilienthal, *Journals*, 625; Hewlett and Duncan, *Atomic Shield*, 406; McFarland and Roll, *Louis Johnson and the Arming of America*, 222–23; Condit, *History of the Joint Chiefs of Staff*, 299.
86. "Declassified Version of Mr. Lilienthal's memorandum of January 31," 3.
87. AEC Thermonuclear Weapons Program Chronology, 109–11; Condit, *History of the Joint Chiefs of Staff*, 299; Hewlett and Duncan, *Atomic Shield*, 406–7.
88. "Declassified Version of Mr. Lilienthal's memorandum of January 31"; AEC Thermonuclear Weapons Program Chronology, 111; Hewlett and Duncan, *Atomic Shield*, 407.
89. "Declassified Version of Mr. Lilienthal's memorandum of January 31," 6; AEC Thermonuclear Weapons Program Chronology, 112; Hewlett and Duncan, *Atomic Shield*, 407; Lilienthal, *Journals*, 630.
90. "Declassified Version of Mr. Lilienthal's memorandum of January 31," 9; Lilienthal, *Journals*, 630; McFarland and Roll, *Louis Johnson and the Arming of America*, 223; Acheson, *Present at the Creation*, 348.
91. Lilienthal, *Journals*, 620–21.
92. Acheson, *Present at the Creation*, 349.
93. "Declassified Version of Mr. Lilienthal's memorandum of January 31," 11.
94. Harry Truman, *Memoirs*, vol. 2 (Garden City, NY: Doubleday, 1956), 309; Pfau, *No Sacrifice Too Great*, 122; McFarland and Roll, *Louis Johnson and the Arming of America*, 223; Hewlett and Duncan, *Atomic Shield*, 408; Shepley and Blair, *Hydrogen Bomb*, 88; Nicholas Thompson, *The Hawk and the Dove: Paul Nitze, George Kennan, and the History of the Cold War* (New York: Henry Holt, 2009), 108.
95. Lilienthal, *Journals*, 632; Donovan, *Tumultuous Years*, 156; Hewlett and Duncan, *Atomic Shield*, 408; Blumberg and Owens, *Energy and Conflict*, 230–31; McLellan, *Dean Acheson*, 178–79.
96. Lilienthal, *Journals*, 632; McFarland and Roll, *Louis Johnson and the Arming of America*, 223; Donovan, *Tumultuous Years*, 156; Hewlett and Duncan, *Atomic Shield*, 408; Blumberg and Owens, *Energy and Conflict*, 231; McLellan, *Dean Acheson*, 178–79.
97. Pfau, *No Sacrifice Too Great*, 122; Condit, *History of the Joint Chiefs of Staff*, 299; Lilienthal, *Journals*, 632; Attachment: Scale and Scope of Atomic Production, 16; Blumberg and Owens, *Energy and Conflict*, 231; Thompson, *Hawk and the Dove*, 109; Sara L. Sale, *The Shaping of Containment: Harry S. Truman, the National Security Council, and the Cold War* (St. James, NY: Brandywine, 1998), 124.
98. Lilienthal, *Journals*, 632; McFarland and Roll, *Louis Johnson and the Arming of America*, 223.

99. Statement by the President, 31 Jan 1950, Hydrogen Bomb 1950 Folder, Strauss Papers, HHPL.
100. Address of Sen. Brien McMahon, Chairman Joint Committee on Atomic Energy, 2 Feb. 1950, JCAE, Brien McMahon, 1950–1952 Folder, Bourke B. Hickenlooper Papers, HHPL.
101. George H. Gallup, *The Gallup Poll on Public Opinion 1935–1971*, 3 vols. (New York: Random House, 1972), 2:888.
102. Gallup, 895.
103. Summary of Columns and Editorials, 2 Feb. 1950, Hydrogen Bomb 1950 Folder, Strauss Papers, HHPL, 1.
104. "A Terrible Weapon and a Courageous Decision," *Fort Worth Star Telegram*, 2 Feb. 1950, Correspondence File C–Folder 1, Box 2, Stuart Symington Papers, HSTPL.
105. Speech of Hon. Brien McMahon in the Senate of the United States, "The Hydrogen Bomb: A Plan for Atomic Peace," 2 Feb. 1950, JCAE Hydrogen Bomb 1948–1950 Folder, Hickenlooper Papers, HHPL.
106. Harry S. Truman to Secretary of State and Defense, 31 Jan. 1950, Atomic Weapons: Thermonuclear Folder 177-1; Subject File–NSC Atomic; Box 177, President's Secretary Files, HSTPL.
107. U.S. Congress, House, *Unification and Strategy: A Report of Investigation by the Committee on Armed Services House of Representatives* . . . (Washington, DC: U.S. Government Printing Office, 1950), 17, 41.
108. "Hiss Guilty on Both Perjury Counts; Betrayal of U.S. Secrets Is Affirmed; Sentence Wednesday; Limit 10 Years," *New York Times*, 22 Jan. 1950.
109. Pfau, *No Sacrifice Too Great*, 124; Hewlett and Duncan, *Atomic Shield*, 314.
110. Reardon, *Formative Years*, 454n; Sale, *Shaping of Containment*, 127.
111. Sale, *Shaping of Containment*, 127.
112. Draft Chronology to 1952, 9.
113. Memorandum for Robert LeBaron, Chairman Military Liaison Committee to the Atomic Energy Commission, Subj: A Basis for Estimating Maximum Soviet Capabilities for Atomic Warfare, 16 Feb. 1950, NSC–Atomic Energy, Russia Folder, Subject File, Box 176, President's Secretary Files, HSTPL.
114. Central Intelligence Agency, "Review of the World Situation," 15 Feb. 1950, NSC Meetings File; Feb 16, 1950, 180-7 Folder; Subject File, Box 180, President's Secretary Files, HSTPL.
115. Hewlett and Duncan, *Atomic Shield*, 416.
116. Draft Report to the President by the Special Committee of the NSC on Development of Thermonuclear Weapons, NSC–Atomic Weapons, Thermonuclear Folder, Subject File, Box 177, President's Secretary Files, HSTPL.
117. Blumberg and Owens, *Energy and Conflict*, 213, 228.

118. Paul H. Nitze, interview by Richard D. McKinzie, 4 Aug. 1975, Oral History Interviews, HSTPL, https://www.trumanlibrary.gov/library/oral-histories/nitzeph2#oh3 (accessed 8 July 2019).
119. Nitze, interviewed by McKinzie, 4 Aug. 1975; Thompson, *Hawk and the Dove*, 113.
120. Melvin Leffler, *Preponderance of Power: National Security, the Truman Administration, and the Cold War* (Stanford, CA: Stanford University Press, 1992), 313.
121. Isaacson and Thomas, *Wise Men*, 495.
122. Isaacson and Thomas, 486; Nitze, interviewed by McKinzie, 5, 6 Aug. 1975.
123. Herman S. Wolk, "The Blueprint for Cold War Defense," *Air Force Magazine*, Mar. 2000, p. 66; Paul Nitze, "The Relation of the Political End to the Military Objective," Speech at the Air War College, 28 Oct. 1954, Speeches, Statements, and Writing File, Folder 6, Box 193, Paul Nitze Papers, Manuscripts Division, Library of Congress, Washington, DC (hereafter LOC).
124. Paul H. Nitze, Speech before the Student Conference, U.S. Military Academy, West Point, NY, 1–2 Dec. 1954, Speeches, Statements, and Writing File, Folder 6, Box 193, Nitze Papers, LOC; Paul H. Nitze, "Certain Foreign Policy Alternatives 1949–1953," Address at the Conference of Business Economist, 17 Oct. 1953, Folder 5, ibid.; Nitze, "Relation of the Political End to the Military Objective."
125. Isaacson and Thomas, *Wise Men*, 497; Thompson, *Hawk and the Dove*, 113.
126. Thompson, *Hawk and the Dove*, 111; Acheson, *Present at the Creation*, 374, 377.
127. Isaacson and Thomas, *Wise Men*, 496; Acheson, *Present at the Creation*, 377.
128. Isaacson and Thomas, *Wise Men*, 498; Acheson *Present at the Creation*, 376.
129. Paul H. Nitze, Address Delivered at the Pentagon's National Security Orientation Conference, 30 Nov. 1950, Speeches, Statements, and Writings File, Folder 5, Box 193, Nitze Papers, LOC.
130. Nitze, interviewed by McKinzie, 5, 6 Aug. 1975.
131. Nitze, interviewed by McKinzie, 5, 6 Aug. 1975; Thompson, *Hawk and the Dove*, 113.
132. Nitze, interviewed by McKinzie, 5, 6 Aug. 1975; Thompson, *Hawk and the Dove*, 112; Acheson, *Present at the Creation*, 373.
133. Nitze, interviewed by McKinzie, 5, 6 Aug. 1975.
134. McFarland and Roll, *Louis Johnson and the Arming of America*, 227; Thompson, *Hawk and the Dove*, 112.
135. Paul Nitze, "Relation of the Political End to the Military Objective"; McFarland and Roll, *Louis Johnson and the Arming of America*, 228; Isaacson and Thomas, *Wise Men*, 496.
136. Nitze, "Certain Foreign Policy Alternatives."
137. Nitze, Speech before the Student Conference, U.S. Military Academy, 1–2 Dec. 1954; Nitze, "Certain Foreign Policy Alternatives."

138. Nitze, "Relation of the Political End to the Military Objective." Some of these assumptions could be refuted by Air Force testimony from October 1949.
139. Nitze, interviewed by McKinzie, 5, 6 Aug. 1975.
140. Lawrence S. Wittner, *Cold War America: From Hiroshima to Watergate* (New York: Praeger, 1974), 79.
141. Allen R. Millett and Peter Maslowski, *For the Common Defense: A Military History of the United States of America*, rev. and expanded ed. (New York: Free Press, 1994), 513.
142. J. C. Hopkins, *The Development of Strategic Air Command, 1946–1981: A Chronological History* (Omaha, NE: Office of the Historian, Headquarters Strategic Air Command, 1982), 28.
143. Elliot V. Converse III, *Rearming for the Cold War, 1945–1960* (Washington, DC: Historical Office of the Secretary of Defense, 2011), 6.
144. Samuel Wells, "The Origins of Massive Retaliation," *Political Science Quarterly* 96, no. 1 (Spring 1981): 31.
145. Speech by Dwight Eisenhower, "Feast or Famine Defense Policy," *New York Times*, 26 Sept. 1952.
146. Warner R. Schilling, Paul Y. Hammond, and Glenn H. Snyder, *Strategy, Politics, and Defense Budgets* (New York: Columbia University Press, 1962), 390–92.
147. Dinah Walker, "Trends in US Military Spending," Council on Foreign Relations, 15 July 2014, https://www.cfr.org/report/trends-us-military-spending (accessed 13 Apr. 2020).
148. Walker; Comparatively, during the Cold War the Soviet Union's defense spending ranged at 12–20 percent of GDP. "Soviet Military Budget: $128 Billion Bombshell," *New York Times*, 31 May 1989, https://www.nytimes.com/1989/05/31/world/soviet-military-budget-128-billion-bombshell.html (accessed 13 Apr. 2020; subscription required).
149. Converse, *Rearming for the Cold War*, 6.
150. Defense Manpower Data Center, Office of the Secretary of Defense, U.S. Department of Defense, https://dwp.dmdc.osd.mil/dwp/app/dod-data-reports/workforce-reports (accessed 2 Nov. 2021).

Bibliography

Archival Sources

Combined Arms Research Library, Fort Leavenworth, KS
- Archival and Special Collections

Dwight David Eisenhower Presidential Library, Abilene, KS
- Lauris Norstad Papers

George Washington University, National Security Archives, Washington, DC
- Oral History Archives
- Virtual Reading Room

Harry S. Truman Presidential Library, Independence, MO
- Dean Acheson Papers
- George Elsey Papers
- Dan A. Kimball Papers
- Lansing Lamont Papers
- Robert Landry Papers
- Edwin Locke Papers
- Robert Lovett Papers
- Francis Matthews Papers
- Naval Aide to the President Files
- Oral Histories Interviews
- President's Personal Files
- President's Secretary Files
- Frank Roberts Papers
- John L. Sullivan Papers

Herbert Hoover Presidential Library, West Branch, IA
- Bourke B. Hickenlooper Papers
- Lewis Strauss Papers

Manuscripts Division, Library of Congress, Washington, DC
Curtis E. LeMay Papers
Paul Nitze Papers
J. Robert Oppenheimer Papers
Nathan Twining Papers
Hoyt Vandenberg Papers
Naval History and Heritage Command, Washington, DC
Chief of Naval Operations, Organizational Research and Policy Division Papers, 1932–1949
Louis Denfeld Papers

Published Primary Sources

Acheson, Dean. *Present at the Creation: My Years in the State Department.* Reprint. New York: W. W. Norton, 1987.

Anders, Roger, ed. *Forging the Atomic Shield, Excerpts from the Office Diary of Gordon Dean.* Chapel Hill: University of North Carolina Press, 1987.

Bradley, Omar. *A General's Life: An Autobiography.* With Clay Blair. Reprint. Lexington, MA: Plunkett Lake, 2019.

Brahmstedt, Christian, ed. *Defense's Nuclear Agency, 1947–1997.* Washington, DC: Defense Threat Reduction Agency, U.S. Department of Defense, 2002.

Clausewitz, Carl von. *On War.* Edited by Michael Howard and Peter Paret. Princeton, NJ: Princeton University Press, 1984.

Etzold, Thomas, and John Lewis Gaddis, eds. *Containment: Documents on American Policy and Strategy, 1945–1950.* New York: Columbia University Press, 1999.

Gallup, George H. *The Gallup Poll on Public Opinion, 1935–1971.* 3 vols. New York: Random House, 1972.

Groves, Leslie. *Now It Can Be Told: The Story of the Manhattan Project.* New York: Da Capo, 1962.

Huston, John, ed. *American Airpower Comes of Age: General Henry H. "Hap" Arnold's War Diaries.* Maxwell AFB, AL: Air University Press, 2005.

Kennan, George F. *The Kennan Diaries.* Edited by Frank Costigliola. New York: W. W. Norton, 2014.

———. *Memoirs, 1925–1950.* New York: Pantheon, 1967.

Khrushchev, Nikita. *Khrushchev Remembers.* Translated and edited by Strobe Talbott. Edited by Edward Crankshaw. Boston: Little, Brown, 1970.

Kohn, Richard, and Joseph Harahan, eds. *Strategic Air Warfare: An Interview with Generals Curtis E. LeMay, Leon W. Johnson, David A. Burchinal, and Jack J. Catton.* Washington, DC: Office of Air Force History, 1988.

Kunsman, David, and Douglas Lawson. *A Primer on U.S. Nuclear Policy.* Sandia Report SAND 2001-0053. Albuquerque: Sandia National Laboratories, 2001.

LeMay, Curtis, and MacKinlay Kantor. *Mission with LeMay.* Garden City, NY: Doubleday, 1965.

Levine, Isaac Don, ed. *Plain Talk: An Anthology from the Leading Anti-Communist Magazine of the 1940s.* New Rochelle, NY: Arlington House, 1976.

Lilienthal, David E. *The Journals of David E. Lilienthal.* Vol. 2, *The Atomic Energy Years, 1945–1950.* New York: Harper and Row, 1964.

Mao Tse-tung. *Selected Military Writings.* Praetorian, 2011.

McCarthy, Joseph R. *America's Retreat from Victory: The Story of George Catlett Marshall.* New York: Devin Adair, 1951.

Morse, Philip. *In at the Beginnings: A Physicist's Life.* Cambridge, MA: MIT Press, 1977.

Nitze, Paul H. *From Hiroshima to Glasnost: At the Center of Decision.* New York: Grove Weidenfeld, 1989.

The Public Papers of the Presidents of the United States: Harry S. Truman, . . . 1947. Washington, DC: U.S. Government Printing Office, 1962.

The Public Papers of the Presidents of the United States: Harry S. Truman, . . . 1949. Washington, DC: U.S. Government Printing Office, 1964.

Riehl, Nicolaus. *Stalin's Captive: Nicolaus Riehl and the Soviet Race for the Bomb.* Translated and edited by Fredrick Seitz.Washington, DC: American Chemical Society, 1996.

Ross, Steven T., and David Alan Rosenberg. *America's Plans for War against the Soviet Union, 1945–1950.* Vol. 13, *Evaluating the Air Offensive: The WSEG I Study.* New York: Garland, 1990.

Schrecker, Ellen. *The Age of McCarthyism: A Brief History with Documents.* 2nd ed. Boston: Bedford/St. Martin's, 2002.

Strauss, Lewis. *Men and Decisions.* New York: Doubleday, 1963.

Truman, Harry. *Memoirs.* Vol. 2. Garden City, NY: Doubleday, 1956.

———. *Years of Trial and Hope.* New York: Doubleday, 1956.

The United States Strategic Bombing Survey. 10 vols. Reprint. New York: Garland, 1976.

U.S. Congress, House. *Investigation of the B-36 Bomber Program: Report of the Committee on Armed Services, . . . Pursuant to H. Res. 234. . . .* Washington, DC: U.S. Government Printing Office, 1950.

———. *Unification and Strategy: A Report of Investigation by the Committee on Armed Services. . . .* Washington, DC: U.S. Government Printing Office, 1950.

U.S. Congress, Joint Committee on Atomic Energy. *The Hydrogen Bomb and International Control: Technical and Background Information.* Washington, DC: U.S. Government Printing Office, 1950.

U.S. Department of State. *The China White Paper: August 1949*. Reprint. Stanford, CA: Stanford University Press, 1967.

———. *Foreign Relations of the United States: Diplomatic Papers, 1945*. Vol. 7, *The Far East, China*. Washington, DC: U.S. Government Printing Office, 1968.

———. *United States Relations with China, with Special Reference to the Period 1944–1949*. Vol. 1. St. Clair Shores, MI: Scholarly Press, 1971.

U.S. Government, President's Air Policy Commission. *Survival in the Air Age: A Report*. Washington, DC: U.S. Government Printing Office, 1948.

U.S. Strategic Bombing Survey. *Summary Report (Pacific War)*. Reprint. Maxwell AFB, AL: Air University Press, 1987.

Wedemeyer, Albert C. *Wedemeyer Reports!* New York: Henry Holt, 1958.

Secondary Sources

Abrahamson, James, and Paul Carew. *Vanguard of American Deterrence: The Sandia Pioneers, 1946–1949*. Westport, CT: Praeger, 2002.

Allen, Robert S., and William V. Shannon. *The Truman Merry-Go-Round*. New York: Vanguard, 1950.

Bachrack, Stanley D. *The Committee of One Million: China Lobby Politics, 1953–1971*. New York: Columbia University Press, 1976.

Baggott, Jim. *The First War of Physics: The Secret History of the Atomic Bomb, 1939–1949*. New York: Pegasus, 2010.

Barlow, Jeffery. *From Hot War to Cold: The U.S. Navy and National Security Affairs, 1945–1955*. Stanford, CA: Stanford University Press, 2009.

———. *The Revolt of the Admirals: The Fight for Naval Aviation, 1945–1950*. Washington, DC: Brassey's, 1998.

Bernkopf-Tucker, Nancy. *China Confidential: American Diplomats and Sino-American Relations 1946–1996*. New York: Columbia University Press, 2001.

Bernstein, Jeremy. *Nuclear Weapons: What You Need to Know*. Cambridge: Cambridge University Press, 2008.

Bernstein, Richard. *China 1945: Mao's Revolution and America's Fateful Choice*. New York: Knopf, 2014.

Bjorge, Gary J. *Moving the Enemy: Operational Art in the Chinese PLA's Huai Hai Campaign*. Leavenworth Papers 22. Ft. Leavenworth, KS: Combat Studies Institute, 2003.

Bland, Larry, ed. *George C. Marshall's Mediation Mission to China, December 1945–January 1947*. Lexington, VA: George Marshall Foundation, 1998.

Blumberg, Stanley A., and Gwinn Owens. *Energy and Conflict: The Life and Times of Edward Teller*. New York: Putnam, 1976.

Brown, Kate. *Plutopia: Nuclear Families, Atomic Cities, and the Great Soviet Union and American Plutonium Disasters.* Oxford: Oxford University Press, 2013.

Brown, Michael E. *Flying Blind: The Politics of the US Strategic Bomber Program.* Ithaca, NY: Cornell University Press, 1992.

Coletta, Paolo E. *The United States Navy and Defense Unification, 1947–1952.* East Brunswick, NJ: Associated University Press, 1981.

Condit, Kenneth. *History of the Joint Chiefs of Staff: The Joint Chiefs of Staff and National Security Policy.* Vol. 2, *1947–1949.* Washington, DC: Office of the Secretary of Defense, 1996.

Converse, Elliot V., III. *Rearming for the Cold War, 1945–1960.* Washington, DC: Office of the Secretary of Defense, 2011.

Craig, Campbell, and Fredrik Logevall. *America's Cold War: The Politics of Insecurity.* Cambridge, MA: Harvard University Press, 2009.

Cray, Ed. *General of the Army: George C. Marshall, Soldier and Statesman.* New York: Cooper, 1990.

Curatola, John M. *Bigger Bombs for a Brighter Tomorrow: The Strategic Air Command and American War Plans at the Dawn of the Atomic Age.* Jefferson, NC: McFarland. 2015.

DeGroot, Gerard J. *The Bomb, a Life.* Cambridge, MA: Harvard University Press, 2004.

Diggins, John Patrick. *The Proud Decades: America in War and Peace, 1941–1960.* New York: W. W. Norton, 1988.

Dittmer, David Bruce. "The Firing of Admiral Denfeld: An Early Casualty of the Military Unification Process." Master's thesis, University of Nebraska–Omaha, 1995.

Donovan, Robert J. *Tumultuous Years: The Presidency of Harry S. Truman, 1949–1953.* New York: W. W. Norton, 1982.

Dunmore, Timothy. *Soviet Politics, 1945–1953.* New York: St Martin's, 1984.

Farquhar, John. *A Need to Know: The Role of Air Force Reconnaissance in War Planning, 1945–1953.* Maxwell AFB, AL: Air University Press, 2004.

Fredriksen, John C. *The B-45 Tornado: An Operational History of the First American Jet Bomber.* Jefferson, NC: McFarland, 2009.

Fuller, John F. *Thor's Legions: Weather Support to the U.S. Air Force and Army, 1937–1987.* Boston: American Metrological Society, 1990.

Furman, Necah S. "Sandia National Laboratories: A Product of Postwar Readiness, 1945–1950." Report, Sandia National Laboratories, Albuquerque, NM, 1988.

Futrell, Frank. *Ideas, Concepts, and Doctrine: Basic Thinking in the United States Air Force, 1907–1960.* Maxwell AFB, AL: Air University Press, 1989.

Gooden-Mulch, Barbara. "A Chinese Puzzle: Patrick Hurley and the Foreign Service Officer Controversy." PhD diss., University of Kansas, 1972.

Gordin, Michael. *Red Cloud at Dawn: Truman, Stalin, and the End of the American Atomic Monopoly*. New York: Picador, 2009.

Grauer, Ryan. *Commanding Military Power*. Cambridge: Cambridge University Press, 2016.

Halberstam, David. *The Fifties*. New York: Ballentine, 1993.

Hammond, Paul. *Super Carriers and B-36 Bombers: Appropriations, Strategy, and Politics*. Indianapolis: Bobbs-Merrill, 1963.

Haynes, Richard F. *The Awesome Power: Harry S. Truman as Commander in Chief*. Baton Rouge: Louisiana State University Press, 1971.

Herken, Gregg. *The Winning Weapon: The Atomic Bomb in the Cold War, 1945–1950*. Princeton, NJ: Princeton University Press, 2014.

Hewlett, Richard, and Francis Duncan. *Atomic Shield: A History of the United States Atomic Energy Commission*. Vol. 2. Berkeley: University of California Press, 1990.

Holley, Irving Brinton. *United States Army in World War II, Special Studies: Buying Aircraft Material Procurement for the Army Air Forces*. Washington, DC: Office of the Chief of Military History, 1964.

Holloway, David. *Stalin and the Bomb: The Soviet Union and Atomic Energy, 1939–1956*. New Haven, CT. Yale University Press, 1994.

Hopkins, J. C. *The Development of Strategic Air Command, 1946–1981: A Chronological History*. Omaha, NE: Office of the Historian, Headquarters Strategic Air Command, 1982.

Isaacson, Walter, and Evan Thomas. *The Wise Men: Six Friends and the World They Made*. New York: Simon and Schuster, 1986.

Jones, Vincent C. *United States Army in World War II, Special Studies, Manhattan: The Army and the Atomic Bomb*. Washington, DC: Center for Military History, 1988.

Keeley, Joseph C. *The China Lobby Man: The Story of Alfred Kohlberg*. New Rochelle, NY: Arlington, 1969.

Keeney, L. Douglas. *15 Minutes: General Curtis LeMay and the Countdown to Nuclear Annihilation*. New York: St. Martin's, 2011.

Kelly, Cynthia C., ed. *The Manhattan Project: The Birth of the Atomic Bomb in the Words of Its Creators, Eyewitnesses, and Historians*. New York: Black Dog and Leventhal, 2007.

Kitaruma Minoru and Lin Siyun. *The Reluctant Combatant: Japan and the Second Sino-Japanese War*. Translated by Connie Prener. Lanham, MD: University Press of America, 2014.

Knight, Amy. *Beria, Stalin's First Lieutenant*. Princeton, NJ: Princeton University Press, 1993.

Koen, Ross Y. *The China Lobby in American Politics*. New York: Harper and Row, 1974.

Kurtz-Phelan, Daniel. *The China Mission: George Marshall's Unfinished War, 1945–1947*. New York: W. W. Norton, 2018.

Leffler, Melvin. *A Preponderance of Power: National Security, the Truman Administration, and the Cold War*. Stanford, CA: Stanford University Press, 1992.

Loeber, Charles R. *Building the Bombs: A History of the Nuclear Weapons Complex*. Albuquerque: Sandia National Laboratories, 2002.

Mann, Robert A. *The B-29 Superfortress Chronology, 1934–1960*. Jefferson, NC: McFarland, 2009.

May, Elaine Tyler. *Homeward Bound—American Families in the Cold War Era*. New York: Basic Books, 1999.

McCullough, David. *Truman*. New York: Simon and Schuster, 1992.

McFarland, Keith D., and David L. Roll. *Louis Johnson and the Arming of America: The Roosevelt and Truman Years*. Bloomingdale: Indiana University Press, 2005.

McLellan, David S. *Dean Acheson, the State Department Years*. New York: Dodd, Mead, 1976.

Meilinger, Phillip S. *Bomber: The Formation and Early Years of Strategic Air Command*. Maxwell AFB, AL: Air University Press, 2012.

Miller, Jerry. *Stockpile and the Story behind 10,000 Strategic Nuclear Weapons*. Annapolis, MD: Naval Institute Press, 2010.

Mitter, Rana. *Forgotten Ally: China's World War II, 1937–1945*. Boston: Houghton, Mifflin, Harcourt, 2013.

Moody, Walter S. *Building a Strategic Air Force*. Washington, DC: Air Force History and Museum Program, 1996.

Naimark, Norman M. *The Russians in Germany: A History of the Soviet Zone of Occupation, 1945–1949*. London: Belknap, 1995.

Offner, Arnold. *Another Such Victory: President Truman and the Cold War, 1945–1953*. Stanford, CA: Stanford University Press, 2002.

Olson, James C. *Stuart Symington, a Life*. Columbia: University of Missouri Press, 2003.

Payne, S. C. M. *The Sino-Japanese War of 1894–1895: Perceptions, Power, and Primacy*. New York: Cambridge University Press, 2004.

Peraino, Kevin. *A Force So Swift: Mao, Truman, and the Birth of Modern China, 1949*. New York: Crown, 2017.

Pfau, Richard. *No Sacrifice Too Great: The Life of Lewis L. Strauss*. Charlottesville: University Press of Virginia, 1984.

Ponturo, John. *Analytical Support for the Joint Chiefs of Staff: The WSEG Experience, 1948–1976*. Arlington, VA: Institute for Defense Analysis International Studies Division, 1979.

Potter, E. B. *Admiral Arleigh Burke*. New York: Random House, 1990.

Pyeatt, Don, and Dennis Jenkins. *Cold War Peacemaker: The Story of Cowtown and the Convair B-36*. Manchester: Crecy, 2010.

Reardon, Steven L. *History of the Office of the Secretary of Defense: The Formative Years, 1947–1950*. Washington, DC: Historical Office of the Secretary of Defense, 1984.

Rhodes, Richard. *Dark Sun: The Making of the Hydrogen Bomb*. New York: Simon and Schuster, 1995.

Romanus, Charles F., and Riley Sunderland. *The United States Army in World War II: The China-Burma-India Theater*. Vol. 1, *Stillwell's Mission to China*. Reprint. Washington, DC: Center for Army History, 2002.

Rose, Lisle A. *The Cold War Comes to Main Street*. Lawrence: University Press of Kansas, 1999.

Sale, Sara L. *The Shaping of Containment: Harry S. Truman, the National Security Council, and the Cold War*. St. James, NY: Brandywine, 1998.

Selden, Mark. *China in Revolution: The Yenan Way Revisited*. Armonk, NY: M. E. Sharpe, 1995.

Shepley, James, and Clay Blair Jr. *The Hydrogen Bomb: The Men, the Menace, the Mechanism*. New York: David McKay, 1954.

Sheridan, James. *China in Disintegration: The Republican Era, 1912–1949*. New York: Free Press, 1975.

Shewmaker, Kenneth. *Americans and Chinese Communists, 1927–1945*. Ithaca, NY: Cornell University Press, 1971.

Spector, Ronald. *In the Ruins of Empire: The Japanese Surrender and the Battle for Postwar Asia*. New York: Random House, 2008.

Spence, Jonathan. *The Gate of Heavenly Peace: The Chinese and Their Revolution (1895–1980)*. New York: Penguin, 1981.

Stoler, Mark A. *George C. Marshall: Soldier Statesman of the American Century*. New York: Prentice Hall, 1989.

Stringer, David. "Roles, Missions, and Politics: The USAF and the B-36." Master's thesis, Air Command and Staff College, 1987.

Tang, Tsou. *America's Failure in China 1941–1950*. 2 vols. Chicago: University of Chicago Press, 1963.

Taylor, Jay. *The Generalissimo: Chiang Kai-shek and the Struggle for Modern China*. Cambridge, MA: Harvard University Press, 2009.

Thompson, Nicholas. *The Hawk and the Dove: Paul Nitze, George Kennan, and the History of the Cold War*. New York: Henry Holt, 2009.

Tuchman, Barbara. *Stillwell and the American Experience in China, 1911–1945*. New York: Macmillan, 1970.

Wilcox, William J. *K-25: A Brief History of the Manhattan Project's Biggest Secret.* Oak Ridge, TN, 2008.

Williams, Robert Chadwell. *Klaus Fuchs, Atom Spy.* Cambridge, MA: Harvard University Press, 1987.

Williamson, Samuel R., and Steven L. Reardon. *The Origins of US Nuclear Strategy, 1945–1953.* New York: St Martin's, 1993.

Wolk, Herman S. *Planning and Organizing for the Postwar Air Force, 1943–1947.* Washington, DC: Office of Air Force History, 1984.

Wu, Jiajing. "The Marshall Mission and KMT-CCP Negotiations after World War II." Master's thesis, Michigan State University, 1984. UMI Dissertation Information Services.

Periodicals

Air Force Magazine
American Heritage, Online Edition
Army-Navy Journal
Bulletin of American Meteorological Society
Bulletin of Atomic Scientists
Central European History Society of the American Historical Association
Collier's
Congressional Quarterly
Constructing the Past
Intelligence Review
International Security
Journal of American History
Naval History
Newsweek
Parameters
Reviews in American History
Saturday Evening Post
Tailhook Magazine
Time
Wings Magazine

Newspapers

Baltimore Sun
New York Herald Tribune
New York Times

Omaha World Herald
Pittsburgh Post-Gazette
Pittsburgh Sun-Telegraph
Washington Daily News
Washington Evening Star
Washington Post
Washington Times Herald

INDEX

About the Author

John Curatola is a professor of military history at the U.S. Army School of Advanced Military Studies at Fort Leavenworth, Kansas. A retired Marine Corps officer, he served for twenty-two years and participated in military operations around the globe. He received his doctorate from the University of Kansas, focusing on airpower and the early Cold War period.

The Naval Institute Press is the book-publishing arm of the U.S. Naval Institute, a private, nonprofit, membership society for sea service professionals and others who share an interest in naval and maritime affairs. Established in 1873 at the U.S. Naval Academy in Annapolis, Maryland, where its offices remain today, the Naval Institute has members worldwide.

Members of the Naval Institute support the education programs of the society and receive the influential monthly magazine *Proceedings* or the colorful bimonthly magazine *Naval History* and discounts on fine nautical prints and on ship and aircraft photos. They also have access to the transcripts of the Institute's Oral History Program and get discounted admission to any of the Institute-sponsored seminars offered around the country.

The Naval Institute's book-publishing program, begun in 1898 with basic guides to naval practices, has broadened its scope to include books of more general interest. Now the Naval Institute Press publishes about seventy titles each year, ranging from how-to books on boating and navigation to battle histories, biographies, ship and aircraft guides, and novels. Institute members receive significant discounts on the Press' more than eight hundred books in print.

Full-time students are eligible for special half-price membership rates. Life memberships are also available.

For a free catalog describing Naval Institute Press books currently available, and for further information about joining the U.S. Naval Institute, please write to:

Member Services
U.S. Naval Institute
291 Wood Road
Annapolis, MD 21402-5034
Telephone: (800) 233-8764
Fax: (410) 571-1703
Web address: www.usni.org